CITIZENS AND BELIEVERS

CITIZENS AND BELIEVERS

Religion and Politics in Revolutionary Jalisco, 1900–1930

Robert Curley

University of New Mexico Press — Albuquerque

© 2018 by the University of New Mexico Press
All rights reserved. Published 2018
Printed in the United States of America

First paperback printing, 2022

ISBN 978-0-8263-5537-9 (cloth)
ISBN 978-0-8263-6441-8 (paper)
ISBN 978-0-8263-5538-6 (e-book)

Library of Congress Cataloging-in-Publication Data is on file with the Library of Congress

Cover photograph courtesy of the Archivo Histórico de la Arquidiócesis de Guadalajara
Designed by Felicia Cedillos
Composed in Minion Pro 10/13.5

Contents

Illustrations

Maps

Tables

Acknowledgments

My first debt is to the University of Guadalajara, an outstanding public institution that offers basically free higher education to 120,000 students at any given time. The U de G hired me twenty years ago, gave me a great job teaching and doing research, and provided necessary infrastructure for me to do my work. I will always be grateful to my home institution, and I am privileged to share research interests, teaching, and friendship with Elisa Cárdenas Ayala, who nudged me along in this project for what seemed like eternity. Besides U de G, the University of Illinois at Chicago was a second home in 2010–2011, and I am grateful to Nora Bonnin, Chris Boyer, and Laurie Schaffner for their support during my sabbatical.

I have had great teachers, whose presence and guidance accompany me every day. I am particularly indebted to Friedrich Katz, who passed away in 2010 and is surely irreplaceable. Along with professor Katz, I have also benefited immeasurably from the lessons of Mary Kay Vaughan. I owe a debt of gratitude to Leora Auslander, John Coatsworth, Guillermo de la Peña, and Claudio Lomnitz as well. And several other scholars have taught me much along the way, including Manuel Ceballos Ramírez, Alan Knight, Jesus Gómez Fregoso, SJ, and Jean Meyer.

Many archivists and librarians provided much-needed support in Guadalajara, Mexico City, Chicago, College Park, and Oklahoma City. I cannot imagine this book without all the help, advice, and support they have given me. I am especially grateful to Enrique Lira Soria at the Biblioteca Nacional for his support at the outset of the project; to Juan Manuel Durán and Alejandro Solís, who facilitated work at the Biblioteca Pública del Estado de Jalisco; to Glafira Magaña Perales and Father Alberto Estévez Chávez at the Archivo Histórico de la Arquidiócesis de Guadalajara, who helped me find source material and acquire publishing rights for most of the photographs; to Father Tomás de Hijar Ornelas at Santa Teresa parish in Guadalajara, who has been a great interlocutor, as well as securing some of the photographs and aiding in the identification of historical figures who appear in many of them; and to Susana Urzua at the University of Guadalajara Geography Department, who plotted and drew the maps.

I am grateful for the friendship and intellect of my colleagues, including Carlos Barba, Celina Becerra, Isabel Blanco, Benjamín Chapa, Lorena Cortés, Fortino Domínguez, Elena de la Paz Hernández, Rosy López Taylor, Rosario Lugo, Rosa María Pineda, Jorge Regalado, Zeyda Rodríguez, Rosa Martha Romo, Enrique Valencia, Ofelia Woo, and my colleagues at the Departamento de Estudios Sociourbanos permanent seminar, who read many pieces of this book over the years. I have also benefited from my colleagues and students at University of Guadalajara's doctoral program in social sciences, master's program in Mexican history, and BA program in history. Lilia Bayardo, Luis Ángel Vargas, Karen Flores, and Omar Mora worked with me as research assistants during different stages of this book, and their support and enthusiasm were always welcome. Thanks also to Laura García, Lucía Lizarraga, Martha Ramírez, Ada Castro, Elba Villalpando, and Esther Gómez.

Many others read parts of the book, or commented on those arguments that I presented in public, and they include Stephen Andes, Sylvia Arrom, Ishita Banerjee, the late Adrian Bantjes, Roberto Blancarte, Matthew Butler, Roberto Di Stefano, Saurabh Dube, Ben Fallaw, Teresa Fernández, Servando Ortoll, Yolanda Padilla Rangel, Julia Preciado, Sol Serrano, Yves Solís, Eddie Wright-Rios, and Julia Young. Ben Smith read and commented on an early version of the entire manuscript.

Passages from chapters 5, 6, and 8 first appeared or were developed in the following publications: "The First Encounter: Catholic Politics in Revolutionary Jalisco, 1917–19," in *Faith and Impiety in Revolutionary Mexico*, edited by Matthew Butler (New York: Palgrave Macmillan, 2007), 131–48; "Anticlericalism and Public Space in Revolutionary Jalisco," *The Americas* 65, no. 4 (2009): 507–29; and "Transnational Subaltern Voices: Sexual Violence, Anticlericalism, and the Mexican Revolution," in *Local Church, Global Church: Catholic Activism in Latin America from* Rerum Novarum *to Vatican II*, edited by Stephen J. Andes and Julia G. Young (Washington DC: The Catholic University of America Press, 2016), 91–116. In each instance, I am grateful to the editors and presses for permission to use this material.

My wife, Wendy Olvera, listened patiently to me talk about this project for many years and gave me strength along the way. She and my children, Eduardo Xavier, Isabel, and Robert Joaquín, are my guiding light.

Abbreviations

AAOC	Archive of the Archdiocese of Oklahoma City
ABR	Archivo Bernardo Reyes, CONDUMEX
ACJM	Asociación Católica de la Juventud Mexicana
AFCS	American Federation of Catholic Societies
AHJ	Archivo Histórico de Jalisco, Guadalajara
AIP	Archivo de Instrumentos Públicos, Guadalajara
AMG	Archivo Municipal de Guadalajara, Guadalajara
APJ	Archivo de la Parroquia de Dulce Nombre de Jesús
BPE	Biblioteca Pública del Estado de Jalisco, Guadalajara
CAOLJ	Confederación de Agrupaciones Obreras Libertarias de Jalisco
CC	Caballeros de Colón
CCN	Círculo Católico Nacional
CCO	Confederación Católica Obrera (renamed CCT in 1920)
CCO	Confederación Católica de Obreras (1921 to 1922)
CCT	Confederación Católica del Trabajo
CGT	Confederación General de Trabajadores
CNCT	Confederación Nacional Católica del Trabajo
COC-Alcalde	Centro de Obreros Católicos "Fray Antonio Alcalde"
COC-XIII	Centro de Obreros Católicos "León XIII"
CRC	Cristero and Reguer Collection, Dr. Jorge Villalobos Padilla, S. J. Library, Instituto Tecnológico de Estudios Superiores de Occidente, Guadalajara
CROM	Confederación Regional Obrera Mexicana
FAOJ	Federación de Agrupaciones Obreras de Jalisco
FPyV	Fondo Palomar y Vizcarra, Biblioteca Nacional, Mexico City

INEHRM	Instituto Nacional de Estudios Históricos de la Revolución Mexicana, Secretaría de Gobernación
LNDLR	Liga Nacional Defensora de la Libertad Religiosa
OG	Operarios Guadalupanos
PCN	Partido Católico Nacional
PHO	Programa de Historia Oral, Archivo de la Palabra, Mexico City
PI / PDI	Partido Independiente / Partido Democrático Independiente
PLM	Partido Liberal Mexicano
PNC	Partido Nacional Cooperatista
PNP	Partido Nacional Porfirista
PNR	Partido Nacional Revolucionario
PRN	Partido Republicano Nacional
PRS	Partido Revolucionario Socialista
SCM	Seminario Conciliar Mexicano, Tlalpan
SD	State Department Records Relating to the Internal Affairs of Mexico, 1910–1929, United States Department of State
SMOAC	Sociedad Mutualista de Obreros y Artesanos Católicos "León XIII"
SMM	San Miguel de Mezquitán
SSM	Secretariado Social Mexicano
UCEC	Unión Católica de Empleadas del Comercio
UDC	Unión de Damas Católicas
UP	Unión Popular
UPEC	Unión Profesional de Empleados del Comercio
USOC	Unión de Sindicatos Obreros Católicos

1. The Ambivalence of the Sacred
An Introduction

EARLY AUGUST, 1926. The crowd moved about Sanctuary Garden as if attending a fair. The faithful entered and exited the temple. The constant incantation of the rosary spilled out into the street from within. A band of local boys patrolled the streets carrying banners, clubs, sticks, and the flag, shouting their protests and calls for reparations. "Long live Christ the King and the Virgin of Guadalupe," they clamored. "Death to the persecutors of the Church!"[1]

The excitement continued for days unabated. The sanctuary and other parish churches around the city of Guadalajara were full day and night; their doors open around the clock. Religious worship was formally suspended; the priests had turned the temples over to the faithful, and the prayer was constant. According to revolutionary law, government officials would need to visit each temple and appoint a ten-member committee from among the local faithful, who would be deputized to inventory the building's moveable assets, which were property of the state, according to the 1917 constitution. Given the level of agitation, however, it was unlikely any government representative would be willing to approach the crowd, much less broach the matter at hand.

A dozen blocks away, a few of the *JM* boys read mass to the neighborhood women at Jesus chapel in the heart of the Sweet Name of Jesus parish.[2] When the women exited the temple, a police inspector was passing by. Laughing at them, he shouted, "That's right, you old crows, spend all your time making a big thing out of your gossip." In retaliation, the women surrounded him while the JM boys grabbed him and took his pistol. Then the women pushed him to the ground on his back in the middle of the street. The inspector became enraged, but the women refused to let him up, instructing him to shout "*Viva Christ the King.*" The inspector refused, cursing his tormenters. The women beat him and, telling him his time was up, asked if he would like the solace of

1

a priest. The inspector cursed the idea. Having lost their patience with the blasphemous captive, the women lifted a large stone between them, and dropped it on his head.

The fire department arrived while the inspector lay in agony in the street, and the women took refuge in the chapel atrium. From the local market across the street, kids threw rocks at the firemen, striking their shiny helmets. The firemen countered, turning their hoses on the crowd and soaking everyone: the churchwomen, the JM boys, the market workers, and the sacrificial victim who lay dead on the street.

Some hours later, among the crowd at Sanctuary Garden, one of the Jesus chapel women chatted with a friend from the sanctuary parish. Relating the story, she offered that by the grace of God the firemen were armed only with water. Of the inspector, she quipped that nothing would have happened to him had he shown some manners. The way she saw it, he asked for it.[3]

———

The women who murdered the police inspector would have been members of the Popular Union, a lay-Catholic religious defense network. They were surely women who lived in the neighborhood and attended mass regularly. They would likely have been married; mothers who administered a household. Yet we know almost nothing about them. We do not know their names, ages, or stations in life. We can say that Sweet Name of Jesus parish was an artisan neighborhood and belonged to a prosperous working- and middle-class, *mestizo* demographic common to the established neighborhoods west of the city center. That day, they were moved by something akin to a mob mentality; they were moved to a kind of violence that they probably had never contemplated, an act forbidden by their faith. But although this was an act of riot, there was nothing spontaneous about their circumstance. They were highly mobilized, and had been for some time.

This episode recalls Scott Appleby's argument about the ambivalence of the sacred. Appleby writes of the religious experience as ambiguous, "containing *within itself* the authority to kill and to heal, to unleash savagery, or to bless humankind with healing and wholeness."[4] Here, *the sacred* evokes Rudolph Otto's thoughts on the numinous quality of the holy: "It may burst in sudden eruption, up from the depths of the soul with spasms or convulsions, or lead to the strangest excitements, to intoxicated frenzy, to transport, and to ecstasy. It has wild and demonic forms and can sink to an almost grisly horror and shuddering."[5] The basic mystery contained in the churchwomen's murder of the police inspector is not about consciousness, but motive and desire. We are limited in our ability to retrieve such sentiments, but I will argue that the violence was religiously motivated.

In addition to the sacred/holy, this episode brings to mind Emile Durkheim's idea of *collective effervescence*. Durkheim sought to explain the origins of religion in the shared feelings and experience that transported believers from the mundane daily activities of everyday life into the "extraordinary powers" of the sacred world.[6] William H. Sewell Jr. has worked through Durkheim's insight in a suggestive reading of the July 14, 1789, assault on the Paris Bastille. "Joy and rage blend into one another," he writes.[7] The scene he points to as an illustration is the lynching of the Marquis de Launay, the commander who was in charge of the garrison at the Bastille. Once captured, he was taken to city hall. There the crowd overwhelmed his captors, and he was trampled, bayoneted repeatedly, and his decapitated head was set on a pike. Whether reading the grand opera of the French Revolution, or the little theater of Catholic Guadalajara, the phenomenon of collective violence seems to point to the importance of emotion as a determinant in social behavior. Furthermore, in the case of post-revolutionary Mexico, I see such emotion as grounded in religious sentiment, channeled through the (ambivalent) experience of the sacred.

Catholic Politics and Revolution in Western Mexico

In the following chapters, I examine Catholic politics in Mexico during the revolutionary generation, stretching from the beginning of the twentieth century until the 1926 collapse of the political sphere, which triggered the religiously inspired Cristero Rebellion. I analyze the Mexican Revolution in the context of a generational span that captures the rise of opposition politics, the fall of the old regime, the years of civil war, and the overarching process of state formation. The issues and events are all part of a process through which competing actors struggled to influence the shape, modes, and ethos of the nation. By framing the revolutionary period in this manner, the book diverts attention from the causes of revolution. Instead it asks how the collapse of the Porfirian state and the years of civil war following 1910 changed the political arena in Mexico, as well as the actors who might compete in it. The focus of my answer to this question is fixed on those social movements that claimed a significant Catholic inspiration for their actions.

These movements marked the emergence of a distinctly modern political

Catholicism in Mexico. I see this phenomenon as modern due to its incorporation of and dependence on the tactics of mass politics, a basic characteristic that distinguishes these movements from nineteenth-century conservative parties. The term *political Catholicism* refers to political action that was Catholic in inspiration, rather than a simple recognition of Catholics involved in politics.[8] Moreover, these movements should not be seen as a product of Church authorities; in fact, although the bishops and other clergy are present throughout this book, the main thrust of the argument emphasizes the actions of lay Catholics. At times they act with clerical consent, other times without; but I never see them as mere vehicles of clerical will. Their agency is central to my argument, and does not derive naturally from clerical dictates.

Political Catholicism was most developed and successful in western Mexico, particularly in the state of Jalisco, with its capital at Guadalajara. The nation's second-largest city, Guadalajara was also the cathedral seat of a large archdiocese with a vast network of parishes. Since the eighteenth century, Guadalajara had been second in size only to the Mexico archdiocese,[9] and at the start of the twentieth century, it remained a prosperous archdiocese, with a large population, active seminaries, and important pilgrimage sites. In comparison with central Mexico, Jalisco was drier and hotter, lower in altitude—Guadalajara is at 5,000 feet—and population density. It was less mountainous than central Mexico, and easier to cross on horseback or by mule. Communications and transport improved over the nineteenth century, and facilitated a model of modest commercial agriculture organized through a rancher economy.

Guadalajara was at the center of several contiguous regions. To its north, Aguascalientes, Zacatecas, Colotlán, and Bolaños were semidesertic and scarcely populated. These towns abutted the Chichimeca frontier of northern Mexico. To the west, the coastal region had not been effectively subject to the Spanish crown during the eighteenth century; Manuel Lozada marshaled his troops there in the nineteenth century, currying favor through ties to the local parishes.[10] Yet the Guadalajara archdiocese maintained only a weak presence in the region at the dawn of the twentieth century. This area included such towns as Talpa and Guachinango and stretched northwest toward San Blas and Tepic.[11] To the northeast of Guadalajara, the Jalisco highland region presented sharp contrasts in terms of poverty (Tepatitlán) and wealth (Lagos de Moreno and San Juan de los Lagos). The area was densely populated, and well integrated in the archdiocesan parish network. Since the eighteenth century, the central region of western Mexican Catholicism stretched from the Jalisco

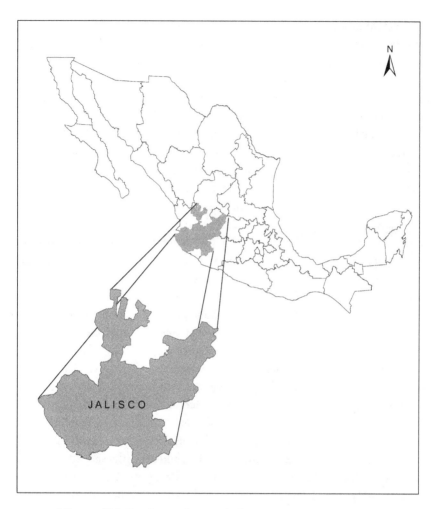

MAP 1. Jalisco and Mexico. Source: Susana Urzúa Soto.

highlands down through Guadalajara and south toward Ciudad Guzmán. It
was circumscribed by Lake Chapala to the east and Cocula to the west.

Indian villages in the Guadalajara region were distinct from those of
Mexico's central valley, having undergone a "more dynamic process of mis-
cegenation."[12] Seventeenth-century Spanish chroniclers wrote that the Indians of the Guadalajara diocese were quick to assimilate peninsular customs,
including consumption of meat and distilled alcohol, horses for transportation, farming and commercial practices, and "laughter and music of taverns

and neighborhood parties."[13] During the eighteenth century, according to William Taylor, these pueblos were more open and less autarchic with respect to the colonial system. Indian and mestizo populations alike were more mobile than those of Mexico's central valley. They emigrated in search of work or hacienda residence. They frequently owned their mule teams, and used them to access broader markets. Western Mexican society was more open, relied less on corn, had greater land distribution, but less fertile land.[14]

The main hypothesis guiding this book is that religiosity is central to the making of the Mexican Revolution. To take this abstraction and tease it out in terms of socially constructed human relationships, historians must be keen to the manifestations of devotion in diverse aspects of social life. A focus on devotion demands attention to believers in the many different, often contradictory, facets of their daily lives. It goes far beyond the conventional institutional logic of Church and state conflict. In particular, historians must be open to understanding the ways religiosity and politics mediate each other and thus condition the lifeworlds of women and men in concrete times and places. I tell the story of a popular Catholic political movement, centered in the Guadalajara archdiocese. The movement emerged after 1910, shaped the debates over citizenship and the revolutionary project, and constituted itself as an essential actor and interlocutor in post-revolutionary Mexico. In this manner, the movement was forged in conflict with anticlerical legislation and the widespread practice of revolutionary iconoclasm,[15] and emerged in the form of a combative, intransigent Catholicism that disputed revolutionary authority and fiat. As a system of beliefs and customs, Catholicism impacted the way Mexicans experienced the revolution, and generally shaped the political sphere during the twentieth century. Political Catholics saw anarchy in revolution, tyranny in reconstruction, and feared the emerging state would outlaw worship, thus destroying a pillar of local culture. Thus, religious identity became a fundamental aspect of citizenship during the twenty years following the start of the Mexican Revolution.

A Fortress Mentality

The long nineteenth century was a time of crisis for the Catholic Church across Europe and in America. The ideas of the Enlightenment challenged religious orthodoxy with new understandings of the secular and philosophical discussion of atheism. The French Revolution forged new paths in Church–state politics.[16] The pope and bishops countered with a reasoned rejection of liberalism, socialism, and the emerging phenomenon of the secular nation-state. By the 1830s, secularization became a central issue in the formation of independent states in Latin America, many of which developed anticlerical policies that sought to curb Church privilege, carve out spheres of institutional differentiation, or even limit religion to an imagined private sphere. State-building elites often saw politics and religion as antagonistic, two areas of life that should be legally separated. Across Western Europe, the revolutions of 1848 incited Vatican condemnation of the "perverse systems" of socialism and communism. As the Vatican became increasingly intransigent, liberal states responded in kind. In Mexico between 1854 and 1867, civil war and foreign military occupation violently altered the political terrain and destroyed the traditional conservative political elite; as a result, by the 1870s, liberals radically limited the wealth and power of the Church. At roughly the same time, Italian Republicans forged a nation at the expense of the Papal States, and anticlericalism became common across Western Europe.[17] This historical process is often understood in terms of secularization.[18]

The crisis was general. Initially, the Vatican opted to retreat from the public sphere and reject these changes in favor of a model of "perfect" autonomy.[19] The concept of a *societas perfecta* held that the Church did not rely on civil authority, but constituted a separate, autonomous authority in society, a Catholic "pillar," parallel to the state. The 1864 *Syllabus* of modern errors condemned liberalism and progress, while mapping out a separate sphere in which Catholics might be protected from the secularizing world. In this controversial text Pope Pius IX called for Catholics to reject all aspects of modern society: to retreat materially and spiritually from Western secularization. The Vatican policy sought to protect Catholics from liberalism and eventually to reconquer, or reevangelize society from below and beyond the liberal state. However, at the same time, another Catholic response emerged in the form of confessional political parties in many countries, including Belgium, the Netherlands, Austria, Germany, and Italy.[20] By the 1890s, Vatican policy would take a new turn. Pope Leo XIII was critical of liberalism and socialism as his predecessor had been. However, he favored a different strategy, one that would actively seek to confront the problems of the time, to shape the political arena in the new century, and with extraordinary zeal, to plot out a religiously inspired model for society.[21]

In 1891, Pope Leo XIII published *Rerum Novarum*, his encyclical on the condition of workers.[22] The letter's tone was provocative; it invited Catholics to play an active role in the solution of society's problems, and to reject liberalism and socialism as viable alternatives.[23] The philosophic inspiration of the Vatican policy dated from the thirteenth century, but the problems were novel. Thus, while the Church was faced with the separation of powers, the privatization of religion, the emergence of the individual, and the decline of corporate society, the pope sought answers in the theology of St. Thomas Aquinas. In *Rerum Novarum*, Pope Leo built on St. Thomas's concept of society as a *natural order*, using it to criticize modern economic, political, and social arrangements.[24] St. Thomas had written that the salvation of the spirit was tied to material life, and in particular, to community life. Derived from the work of Aristotle, his vision of community was defined in terms of political relations between thinking, reasoning actors.[25] But contrary to nineteenth-century liberalism, Thomist society did not progress with individual interest as its motor. In fact, the notion of "progress" would have been strange for St. Thomas and, in any case, his interest lay in the "harmony" of society, an idea that caught the attention of the late literary master, Umberto Eco.[26] This harmony should be the result of collaboration between individuals of different skills and rank, whose contribution was equally important for the common good. Rich and poor, employers and workers, statesmen and soldiers, men and women: all had a raison d'être and an ontologically stable identity in Thomist ideology. Their estates were as natural as their particular skills. For Pope Leo, "neither the talents, nor the skill, nor the health, nor the capacities of all are the same, and unequal fortune follows of itself upon necessary inequality in respect to these endowments."[27] The encyclical stopped clearly and consciously short of a call to organize politically. However, the issue was essentially moot, as Catholics in many countries were already doing so, without the bishops' blessing.

One of the great puzzles of Catholic politics is the process by which nineteenth-century confessional parties opened the way for and eventually gave way to a more secular vein of politics in the twentieth century. In Europe, Catholic political parties and other organizations were built around *Quanta Cura*—and its *Syllabus Errorum*—Pius's hallmark encyclical, a generation prior to *Rerum Novarum*. In these writings, Pius condemned the idea of popular sovereignty, the assertion of the right of civil society to interfere in religious matters, the separation of church and state, the doctrine of religious tolerance, and the idea of secular education. However, his writing did not call for the formation of confessional parties, or a lay-driven political arm to complement the power of the institutional Church. In fact, parties emerged in Belgium, the Netherlands, Austria, Germany, and Italy *in spite of* the Catholic Church.[28] France was exceptional, in that no lasting party emerged in response to anticlerical politics, although there was a potent movement-based Catholicism. In the absence of such politics, it is unremarkable that Irish Catholics saw no need to organize a confessional party. In more authoritarian circumstances, small parties did emerge in Spain,[29] Catalonia, Switzerland, Poland, Lithuania, Slovakia, Slovenia, and Croatia. But they ultimately had limited success.[30]

An important legacy of the nineteenth-century emergence of Catholic politics is the carryover of a "fortress mentality" into the period following the First World War. Martin Conway has described the "new mood of spiritual militancy" among European Catholics during the 1920s and 30s as an "enclosed world of distinctively and homogeneously Catholic spiritual, economic, social, and ultimately political organizations." Their politics varied from conservative, to philofascist, to democratic, but the defensive reflex forged in earlier conflicts provided an overarching unity, at least within national borders. A basic aspect of the fortress mentality of early twentieth-century Catholic politics was the formation of "pillarized" parallel societies. Other groups formed similar identity-based organizations as well, including socialists, liberals, and Protestants. Catholic parties belonged to this phenomenon: rather than acting as autonomous movements, they were seen as the extension into the political sphere of their pillar.[31]

In Mexico, there were some marked differences with the European experience. However, an important similarity was the emergence of lay associations in the social, economic, and cultural spheres of life, that only gradually ventured into the field of politics. Furthermore, in Mexico, once party politics was no longer an option, laity continued to organize outside the formal political sphere. Paradoxically, they continued to organize through "pillarized" confessional associations, despite the fact that there were no explicitly non-Catholic pillars from which to distinguish themselves.

Secularization as State Formation

José Casanova has written that the modernity of Christian cultures is the result of secularization, a long-term historical process. He has conceptualized secularization in terms of a fundamental rupture in the arrangements that ordered the Christian world. In *Public Religions in the Modern World*, Christian cultures are characterized by a double duality of medieval inspiration. It consists first of a division between the temporal world and the hereafter, which Casanova calls the City of God.[32] Second, it contains a duality within this world, between the religious sphere of the Church (the Papal Kingdom), and the secular sphere of the City of Man (the Holy Roman Empire and other Christian Kingdoms). The Church mediated both dualities in a system that functioned well as long as the doctrine of religious superiority over the secular prevailed.[33] This was the case in New Spain. To this point, Dino Bigongiari wrote that the Thomist concept of justice and government did not recognize an autonomous empire of the secular world. Put in Casanova's scheme, the City of Man was subordinate to the Papal Kingdom.[34] A sphere of authority proper to the exercise of political power did exist, but the Pope was included in it. As early as the thirteenth century, St. Thomas addressed this in his discussion of *justice*: "The secular power is subject to the spiritual, even as the body is subject to the soul. Consequently the judgment is not usurped if the spiritual authority interferes in those temporal matters that are subject to the spiritual authority or which have been committed to the spiritual by the temporal authority."[35]

Casanova characterized the process of secularization in terms of a gradual weakening and rupture in the order of spheres in this world, between the religious and the secular, and in the "sacramental structures of mediation" between this world and the City of God.[36] He has proposed a stylized model of an affair that was—no doubt—messy, partial, and slow. It would nevertheless be possible to demonstrate, at least for Europe, that such a process was already under way in the sixteenth century.[37] Reinhart Koselleck modeled it in terms of a shift in the "horizon of expectations," and argued that time has moved much faster in the centuries since than it had during the millennia prior. The change points to an emerging mode of reasoning, roughly as of the sixteenth century, which cannot be derivative of expectations regarding the Last Judgment. He conceptualized this foreshortening of time as *Neuzeit*, literally a new "plane of historicity" in which practically all of our concepts in the social sciences have their roots.[38] Alfonso Mendiola has explained this transformation by posing that reality no longer produces consensus, but dissent: "this dissent, proper to modernity, dictates that the only way that dialogue may be preserved is by asking why the other sees reality otherwise."[39]

Perhaps, for the purposes of this argument, we merely need to recognize the rupture inherent in the eighteenth-century Bourbon reforms.[40] A model similar to Casanova's, but focused on Mexican history, might characterize seventeenth-century New Spain in terms of the religious, extended far and wide, with the secular tolerated in the interstices and at the margins. Similarly, it might characterize nineteenth-century Mexico in terms of the secular, extended throughout society, with the marginal perseverance of the religious. In this conjectural history, society was constructed previously in terms of the religious, and subsequently in terms of the secular. This argument parallels Michel Foucault's interpretation of modernity as rooted in the fundamental shift from a society in which political power was articulated through control of the soul to one in which it became articulated through control of the body.[41] But above and beyond the questions of how and when exactly the change took place, questions that are beyond the scope of this book, I wonder just *how* complete the dominance of the religious in society was? And *how* profound the secular thereafter? It may well be the case that history was no longer organized around Christian eschatology—Koselleck's Last Judgment—but I argue here that citizenship was central to the Mexican Neuzeit, and that it was often constructed in concert with a Catholic "ritual constant."[42] One may readily find evidence of Casanova's rupture in the "sacramental structures of mediation," if one's gaze is set upon the institutions of state and Church; however, to understand secularity, one must look beyond them, to the practice of citizenship. There, modernity's dissent was plainly visible: the contentious relationship of politics to religiosity constructed citizenship in Reform-era and revolutionary Mexico.

By the late eighteenth century, the Spanish Crown was interested in limiting papal jurisdiction over subjects in New Spain, and this attempt at redefining the spheres of dominion between civil and ecclesiastic power generated conflict. The construction and delimitation of spheres of civil and ecclesiastic authority produced political conflict, with varying strains of anticlericalism. Broadly speaking, I think it is possible to discern a series of liberal policies of varied anticlerical accent that reflect particular moments unfolding between the decades of 1760 and 1940. In general, the events are widely known, but what I want to emphasize here is their diachronic logic. I do not wish to suggest there was only one possible path, nor do I believe this process simply reflects the unified work of generations toward a particular goal. We need to think more in terms of process than progress;[43] we must ask how and why change happened. Nonetheless, I think we can speak in retrospect of a Mexican script, a shared experience through the generations, a plausible history in which the process of secularization has forged a particular continuity in the Mexican state. With diverse objectives, the architects of the Mexican state constructed institutions that were both liberal and secular,[44] and in retrospect, the Mexican script offers points of comparison and contrast vis-à-vis other cases in Europe and America.[45]

Nineteenth-century liberal reformers generated divergent state policies and, in particular, varying grades of anticlericalism.[46] Social scientists have modeled political change and the construction of the *estado laico*—a state rooted in secular power—in terms of "stages of development"[47] as well as "thresholds of transition,"[48] with all the conceptual traps that such language may imply.[49] I will simply point out here that "stages" and "thresholds" would have to be analytically and methodologically distinct, the first dealing with different modes and moments of secularity, the second with the transitions that articulate them. In my opinion, both terms tend to push the discussion back in the direction of secularization as progress, an untenable position. One aspect of this discussion that may prove useful is the construction of a typology of anticlericalism. In Mexico, for example, I think there is a difference between the liberalism of 1830 and that of 1860, each with its attendant anticlerical ethic and repertoire of tactics—Annick Lempérière calls them *armas disolventes*—designed to undermine the remaining corporate structures of the ancien régime.[50] However, such consideration should not lead us to conclude that the events of the nineteenth century have led Mexico properly down a hypothetical path of secularization toward modernity. Secularization, like modernization, cannot be directional or all historicity is lost.

I want to consider three aspects of the secularization literature: differentiation, privatization, and decline. All merit discussion and shed light on the construction process of a Mexican estado laico. The most common and convincing argument regards institutional differentiation and the separation of church and state. This is an internal phenomenon proper to predominantly Christian nations and readily lends itself to a comparative historiography focused on the timing, form, and spaces of the secularization process.[51] On the basis of a discussion of similarities and differences, historians can compare the construction of modern states, the particular republicanisms that emerged in Latin America/Europe,[52] divergent configurations and uses of public space, and varying grades and forms of anticlericalism.

In Mexico, as I suggested above, institutional differentiation goes back as least as far as the eighteenth-century absolutist policies of the Bourbon crown. To this end, William Taylor has written:

The parental metaphor of the "Two Majesties" (Dos Magestades)—with the crown as father and the church as mother of the Hispanic family, or the two together as the collective head of the social body—gave way to a fully masculine conception of politics, with only one head and one parent, the king. Regalism—the subordination of church authority—became a hall-mark of the Bourbon reforms.[53]

With the institutional change that accompanied independence, this model would continue to inspire nineteenth-century state builders. The process of change was slow, however, due to the lag between the dissolution of juridical ties between Mexico and Spain, and the creation of a widely accepted legal framework for the new republic. This construction, Elías J. Palti has shown, was halting and slow, extending throughout much of the nineteenth century. "Circa 1843," Palti writes, "in Mexico there were, in fact, five constitutional projects in play, none of which seemed to have a greater claim to legitimacy than any of its contenders."[54] In this context, some degree of chaos was reasonable, as long as no accepted framework existed that might sort out disputes in society; and there was no certainty at all of a clean break with the colonial regime. After a century of struggles, and in spite of the many changes experienced, aspects of this regalist absolutism would reemerge, articulated through the 1917 constitution, *sin la corona*.

Here the idea of a colonial legacy is relevant to the study of continuity and change over the nineteenth century. How important has this legacy been? It is a commonplace that the Catholic Church is the most important institution to survive independence. However, Fernando Escalante Gonzalbo has argued that this affirmation is inexact. To the contrary, he wrote, the Church was fundamentally changed in the process. Not without irony, he has mused that

> the Church defended its separation from the state and refused to negotiate a concordat, while the state—faithful to colonial tradition—attempted to regulate devotion and intervene in the life of the Church. The ambitious secularization project promoted by liberal governments during the second half of the nineteenth century unfailingly bore this ambiguity, this trace of inconsequence.[55]

Escalante places the colonial legacy at the doorstep of the incipient Mexican state rather than with the Church.

Consonant with this line of reasoning, Annick Lempérière has demonstrated that the 1824 constitution founded a "corporatist republic," in which liberal doctrine coexisted uncomfortably with the presence, or perhaps perseverance, of the traditional "political bodies," constructed through the eighteenth century. Her argument throws into relief the inherent tension between liberalism and corporatism, and maps out the ways that the constitution's liberal underpinnings gradually eroded the residual esprit de corps of what Habermas called "representative publicness."[56] That corporatism, steeped in Catholic ritual, ceased to exist legally with the 1856 Lerdo Law, a key moment for liberal ascendancy and the construction of a bourgeois public sphere. In short, "liberal principles abrogated the need for religion as the sacred bond between citizens."[57]

The Liberal Reform may be seen as a historical moment bookended by the 1854 Ayutla revolution and the 1873 incorporation of the reform laws to the (1857) constitution. The reform institutionalized a series of binary oppositions that supposed the frank incompatibility of politics and religion.[58] Triumphant liberalism pitted citizen against believer, state against church, and modernity against obscurantism; and in the nationalist historiography that followed, reason, progress, and modernity appeared as the virtues of the new state, while Catholicism was banished to a subaltern invisibility. However, this discursive or rhetorical authority always only masked the polyphony of Catholic voices that persevered at the margins of the public sphere.[59] This book will argue that the binary opposition between citizen and believer is unstable and that religious identity shaped citizenship in the revolutionary period. In order to more clearly see the ways in which religiosity conditions politics, we must turn briefly to the concept of citizenship.

In Mexican historiography, modern citizenship is tied to the rise of Protestantism. Why is this? Basically, because citizenship is understood through the lens of liberalism, the doctrine of individual liberties, and Protestantism is cast in the role of protecting individual liberties against the communitarian tradition of Roman Catholicism. Jean-Pierre Bastian has argued that Protestantism fomented the "civic religion" of patriotism.[60] Here, faith is seen as civic, not religious; it is tied to the construction of a legitimate authority, that of the nation-state. Citizenship, then, becomes the practice of a nonreligious faith, one that Protestantism actively cultivated. Meanwhile, in this argument, Catholicism privileged the group over the individual, actively defending a traditional Mexican society.[61] This argument begs the question of what a Catholic citizenship might look like and whether it could be modern. More recently, Bastian has suggested that Catholicism was an impediment to religious modernity in countries like Mexico. A similar logic of laicization was found in Catholic societies on both sides of the Atlantic, he reasons. And yet the process was slower in countries like Mexico. The resistance of Catholics to laicization in Latin America was due to the strength of "communitarianism," as well as endemic poverty and illiteracy. Such conditions permitted popular religiosity to be mobilized against state-sponsored modernization policy.[62]

There are several problems in this line of analysis. First, historians should avoid reducing citizenship to a liberal imaginary. Liberalism was a project in nineteenth-century Mexico,[63] and even in the 1917 constitution, liberalism coexisted with other political philosophies. Bastian is correct to emphasize the civics of late nineteenth-century Protestants, but his findings should push historians to try and flesh out Catholic citizenship as well, rather than assume that the alternative was an anticivics. In particular, the communitarian logic of rural Mexico may well be understood as "traditional," but it was the backbone of a kind of civics, a practice of citizenship, that has persevered throughout the twentieth century.[64] Second, there is a basic flaw in the argument that Catholicism was an impediment or that liberal Protestantism facilitated religious modernity. It is the problem that much work in the area of postcolonial criticism has highlighted. For historians, religious modernity cannot be a set goal that all societies should work toward, and it makes little sense to suppose that Latin America should obviously follow the lead of Latin Europe, or that poverty and illiteracy permitted Catholics to resist laicization. This argument ultimately reduces religious modernity to a sort of mechanical modernization theory based on a Eurocentric idea of progress, just as it reduces Catholics to villainy. To this end, Dipesh Chakrabarty has critiqued Europe as the subject of all histories, and has argued that transition narratives are problematic precisely because they serve to characterize nonmetropolitan societies as not yet ready, not yet advanced enough.[65]

A more fruitful line of inquiry might try to understand how and why Latin America, or Mexico, took the path it did, and flesh out the ways it forged its own particular religious/political modernity.[66] To do this, it will be necessary to ultimately bracket terms such as "secularization," "laicization," and "modernization." They are simply overdetermined with Eurocentric historicism.[67]

Secularity and Public Religion

What then is the relation between "secularization" stories and the public sphere? Charles Taylor has warned of the traps that inhabit its theoretical formulations—what he calls secularization master narratives—and the need to distinguish empirically between *differentiation*, *privatization*, and *decline*. According to Taylor, one may understand secularity in more than one fashion, for example, in terms of public spaces allegedly emptied of God; in the falling off of religious belief and practice; or in the conditions of belief, that is, the move from a society in which belief in God is unchallenged or unproblematic to one in which it is understood to be one option among others.[68] In a similar vein, Casanova has pointed out that all three facets correspond to separate hypotheses regarding the social change of which secularization stories tell.[69] Both Taylor and Casanova are cautious in how they treat these conditions of faith. "Secularity in this sense is a matter of the whole context of understanding in which our moral, spiritual or religious experience and search take place."[70]

———

The phenomenon of privatization is more extreme than institutional differentiation. It is less common, characteristic of nations that have known radical anticlericalisms, cases characterized by greater Church and state conflict.[71] It entails, basically, the systematic reduction of legal space available to believers in society with the goal of confining worship to an imagined private sphere. In Europe, the French Third Republic offers an example,[72] and in America, Reform-era Mexico is characteristic. But social revolution in twentieth-century Mexico may offer more compelling evidence, a point to which I will return presently. In any case, Catholics' quests for new forms of publicity were as important as the (anticlerical) policies of state.

The intensity of anticlerical measures may not be decisive. Casanova found that religious practice simply does not privatize well and that churches tend to seek out—and find—new modes of expression. In Mexico and elsewhere, the Catholic Church responded to nineteenth-century liberal reform by retreating. But with time, Rome and the bishops developed a new strategy to underwrite Church presence in society. With the loss of traditional rights and privileges, clergy ceded or delegated important aspects of worship, education, and religious organization to laity. Pioneering work by Manuel Ceballos Ramírez laid out this argument by centering the phenomenon of "social Catholicism" as a major current in late nineteenth-century Mexican society for a large and populated area stretching from Puebla to Zacatecas.[73] Recent work by Edward Wright-Rios and José Alberto Moreno Chávez develop the ideas further. Wright Rios examines the tensions of Catholicism between Indian villages and the Oaxaca diocese. Moreno Chávez analyzes political and religious change in the Mexico Archdiocese as a problem of (anti)modernity. They both situate their work in the years between 1880 and the postrevolution.[74]

In effect, the Mexican case presents aspects of a conflictive secularization story, and a search for points of comparison in nineteenth-century Latin America reveals important differences. For example, Samuel Valenzuela and Erika Maza have argued that Chilean bishops favored a state-imposed concordat that essentially preserved the role of the Church in the public sphere. Sol Serrano demonstrated how Chilean women combined religious practice and civics in a liberal secular state.[75] And Roberto Di Stefano described a reciprocal process in which Church and state constructed each other in Argentina. In his argument, the emergence of the modern state, a process born of the independence movements after 1810, "invented" the Church.[76] The birth of the modern state was predicated on a redefinition of public space once considered religious. This aspect of secularization—separation of the religious sphere from secular life—not only gave rise to the state, but also to the Church, understood as a modern institution.[77] In this sense, according to Di Stefano, the state can be thought of as inventing the Church: it did not as such exist prior to independence. And yet, Stephen Andes has shown that, when the Chilean state legislated separation in 1925, it was so favorable to the Church that the Vatican decided not to pursue a concordat.[78] State power may be wielded in surprising ways.

Despite the problems inherent to the privatization of religious practice, it is crucial to recognize the importance of liberal reform in Mexico between the 1850s and 1870s. It is not only relevant in terms of an evolving anticlerical politics, or a shift from differentiation to privatization. Benito Juárez, Miguel Lerdo de Tejada, José María Iglesias, and their followers systematized and codified anticlerical policy in a manner reminiscent of the eighteenth-century Bourbon reform.[79] It was a major event in Mexican history and played a significant role in the order of anticlericalism that would characterize the revolution after 1913. Even still, a careful reading reveals that the liberal reform contained a mixture of moderate and radical measures, and that these measures changed the conditions of belief understood in terms of the whole context in which moral, spiritual, or religious experience take place. For example, abolition of the jurisdiction of religious courts for civil and criminal cases may be counted among the moderate measures, along with the creation of a civil registry and legislation that put an end to Church administration of cemeteries. These measures were consistent with the objective of institutional differentiation. But there was a special symbolic violence involved in the law that stripped priests of citizen rights, prohibiting them from voting in elections. This measure was not only antiliberal, but ironically reinforced the idea that Church loyalties should not be to the state. These believers could not be Mexican citizens. Other measures went further, in the interest of limiting the economic power—the basis of capitalism—of the Church. One example was the prohibition on parish collections, the source of a local priest's livelihood. Ultimately more important were strict limits placed on ecclesiastic property, which was reduced to those buildings used in the daily activities associated with worship—the temples. This forced the Church to relinquish a large number of properties through auction, and in practical terms forced the Church out of the credit market, where it had been the main lender since prior to independence.[80]

Whether measures were moderate or radical is ultimately academic; the Church, and often the faithful, perceived them as a frontal attack. In his classic *Historia de la Iglesia en México* [1928], the Jesuit Mariano Cuevas made a detailed representation of state hostility toward the nineteenth-century Church.[81] Yet it was not the anticlerical measures as such, but the years of war, the Conservative Party and Church debacle of 1867, and the emergence of a triumphant group of liberals that sealed the tenor of the reform. These liberal state builders found themselves, under Sebastián Lerdo de Tejada in 1873, in conditions to impose the reform laws and simultaneously strip the Catholic Church of legal institutional recognition, reducing it to the status of a private association.[82] But in the end, how successful was this attempt to limit faith and worship to the private sphere?

To focus clearly on privatization, we must distinguish it from religious decline, the falling off of religious belief and practice, typically associated with a more contemporary historical process. Arguments regarding decline usually look to explain phenomena characteristic of postwar Western Europe. According to Casanova, a major distinction may be drawn between nations that were home to a "caesaropapist embrace of throne and altar," such as France and Spain, and others in which the Church never had the privileges associated with an absolute monarchy, such as Poland and Ireland. In the first group, religious decline became palpable during the twentieth century; for the second group, decline seems to have been tempered.[83] For Latin American nations, historians must ask what role the history of colonialism played and whether it constitutes a third category, distinct from the two nominally European ones. In any case, Mexico seems to cut across the two European categories: it had, for a time, an official Church, and yet religion seems to have avoided decline during the twentieth century. In fact, a strong tradition of worship and popular Catholicism would seem to hint at similarities between Mexico and countries like

Poland and Ireland. This is certainly related to the considerable tension that often characterized Church–state relations. But again, it emphasizes the need to think critically about the models of Catholic Europe, and rethink the historiography of late nineteenth-century Mexico with a view toward diocesan scales of analysis and the determinants of local religious practice.[84]

During the 1920s, revolutionary chiefs like Tomás Garrido Canabal in Tabasco, Francisco Múgica in Michoacán, and José Guadalupe Zuno in Jalisco imposed anticlerical measures that were sufficiently radical so as to create the impression that they sought to destroy the Church. Adrian Bantjes recently characterized their policies as "irreligious."[85] Moreover, Catholic clergy and laity alike believed that the objective of these caudillos was precisely the elimination of religion. Such points may be debated, and President Calles, for one, made a 1926 policy pronouncement in the *New York Times*, in which he rejected any interest in the "descatolización" of Mexico.[86] Nevertheless, the anticlerical measures of Mexican radicals should be studied in terms of their impact on the privatization of religion, the reduction of space for worship to its minimum expression. They have no necessary link to decline in terms of the falling off of religious belief and practice. In fact, they may have the opposite effect.

Some pages up, I referred to the importance of bracketing secularization and remaining attentive to the ways it is constructed as a narrative of progress or modernization. It is easy enough to appreciate the dangers, and recognize in the historiography a heroic narrative of secularization as a triumph of the modern nation, forged through independence, liberal reform, and revolution. In contrast, there is a Catholic historiography that has interpreted secularization inversely, as *retroceso*, regress and setback. When writing the history of anticlerical conflict, sometimes acritically, sometimes with partisan zeal, historians on both sides have taken on the language of political struggle and the symbolism that emerged in the context of Church–state conflict, without distinguishing between historical time and their own time. In doing so, they have also often lost track of secularity, the conditions of faith as they were experienced by believers beyond the institutional strictures of state and Church.

The revisionist historiography of the past quarter century has often been able to moderate the heroic interpretation of the Mexican Revolution set forth by earlier generations. Yet it has generally shown little interest in treating the complex issue of religion and the Catholic (*lo católico*) as historical aspects of political actors, and has too often glossed over a central question, the relational nature of the state. As a result, one often encounters a reified state acting on an equally reified population of "fanatics" who are mobilized by the Church. In

FIGURE 1. Anacleto González Flores (right) with Archbishop Francisco Orozco y Jiménez (center), ca. 1921. Source: Archivo Histórico de la Arquidiócesis de Guadalajara.

part, this problem announces something bigger, and, I think, more important. In effect, we can interpret the conflict in Mexico during the decades of 1910 and 1920 as a cultural revolution with deep roots in the nineteenth century.[87] Both Jean Meyer and Manuel Ceballos Ramírez developed this argument.[88]

This cultural transformation emerged as a system of political participation and representation based on the premise that, *as a citizen*, one could not be Catholic.[89] Not only was public space emptied of God, as Taylor has put it, but modern citizenship was not permitted to situate itself in terms of God. Writing in the midtwenties, Anacleto González Flores recognized this problem: "The revolution has never permitted Catholics to vote."[90] In other words, beyond institutional differentiation, political speech was shackled. Except for a brief interlude between 1911 and 1914, political practice could not be expressed or manifested through religious belief.[91] This was a basic aspect of secularity in revolutionary Mexico, and twentieth-century Mexico would not be home to a party politics of Christian democracy.[92] In a longer view, nineteenth-century institutional differentiation may have defined—or even "invented"—state and Church,[93] and constructed a political tradition in which religion and politics were formally separated through the exclusion of religion. It is the case that privatization seems to follow almost naturally from differentiation in the historiography. But history did not follow a progressive lineal narrative and, beyond the limits of government, the tension between privatization and deprivatization of worship produced critical changes with the 1910 collapse of the Díaz regime. This topic is richly argued, with attention to Catholics, Protestants, Spiritists, and Anticlericals in Matthew Butler's important edited volume, *Faith and Impiety in Revolutionary Mexico*,[94] and in a recent topical issue of *The Americas*.[95]

There are important moments throughout the Mexican Revolution in which aspects of this exclusion appeared, forged even as Catholics pressured to redefine the political sphere in more inclusive terms. The initial offensive took place somewhat haphazardly in 1914, and included the execution of priests, the rape of religious women, the mass deportation of foreign religious, the exile of some Mexican clergy, and iconoclastic violence, such as the destruction of religious icons and Church property.[96] Antonio Villareal, the Constitutionalist army general, is famous for executing statues of saints by firing squad at Monterrey.[97] Such episodes are rich in imagery; they allow us to glimpse the terms of a cultural revolution in the making. They also provide a point of reference for better understanding the Catholic view of revolution as *ultraje*, or outrage. Luis González has referred to this as the memory of the *revolucionados*: those who were the object of revolutionary violence and change, those who were acted upon.[98]

During the waning days of 1916, the constitutional congress at Querétaro upheld and strengthened the nineteenth-century reform laws, adding important new restrictions, such as the general extension of the Lerdo Law to all Church property. As a result, the 1917 constitution made every chalice, monstrance, and tabernacle property of the nation and subject to inventory, with far-reaching consequences. Also in 1917, the congress outlawed confessional politics in order to avoid the resurgence of a Catholic or Christian Democratic party. A few years later, the same proscription was extended to the emerging mass organizations, such as labor unions. In Jalisco where the Catholic labor movement was centered, governor Zuno outlawed Catholic unions in 1923. With the wave of a fountain pen, tens of thousands of organized Catholics found themselves outside the law, offered the choice between disbanding and going clandestine. Many eventually took part in a religious rebellion that raged through central and western Mexico from 1926 until 1929.[99] But why did they rebel?

In a very real sense, the rebellion was a logical result of the collapse of the political sphere.[100] Deploying symbolism rooted in sacred scripture, Anacleto González Flores referred to this as the advance of the desert.[101] The desertion of civil society, the collapse of the political sphere, was the consequence of decisions made on both sides of the conflict. On one side, Jalisco governor Zuno and president Calles both pushed to limit the physical spaces where political Catholics might organize and project a public voice. On the other side, Catholic militants retreated from the spaces they had won, retrenching in religious defense leagues. As the tactics of religious defense played out through highly organized, but radically decentralized forms of association, the political importance of Guadalajara ceded to the local agency of parish-level groups throughout rural Jalisco, and spilling into Zacatecas, Colima, Michoacán, and Guanajuato. Drawing from the Catholic tradition of sacrifice,[102] González Flores saw the advancing desert as producing a plebiscite of martyrs and offered himself up in that vein, as can be seen in the final chapter of this book. But the rural militants of political Catholicism saw the world somewhat differently. They were not as interested in the spiritual redemption of the martyr, and preferred the worldly honor of the soldier. They opted to fight against the army of the revolution in defense of their customs, their temples, and their own particular language of politics.[103] This is the modernity of Mexican Catholicism: militant and proud of an idiosyncratic local worship organized around the parish. At the center of the parish was not necessarily the local priest, for they came and went. Rather, the center of worship was the temple itself and the saint within: they were eternal, and the idea of surrendering either to a godless government was anathema to local devotion.

———

The book is organized into eight chapters. The first two treat aspects of Catholic organization and politics during the final years of the Díaz regime. The middle three chapters are concerned with the ebb and flow of political Catholicism amidst the grand storm of the Mexican Revolution. The final three chapters, then, tease out the dual threads of Catholic and anticlerical politics in the context of the emerging post-revolutionary state. The arch of the book focuses the reader's attention on the complex series of events that gradually led militant Catholics to abandon politics and opt for rebellion in and after 1926. The consequences of this descent into rebellion are considered in the book's conclusion.

2. Religion and Society in Social Catholicism

Thomas Aquinas if he were alive today . . . would not rewrite
a *Summa Theologica*. He would take into account Marxism,
the Theory of Relativity, formal logic, Existentialism, phenomenology.
He would not comment on Aristotle, but on Marx and Freud.
He would change his methods of argumentation that would become a little
less harmonious and conciliatory. In sum, he would realize that it is
not possible or proper to develop a definitive system, finished as architecture,
but a sort of mobile system, a *summa* of replaceable pages,
because in his encyclopedia of sciences it would be necessary to
include the notion of the historical provisional.

—UMBERTO ECO, "IN PRAISE OF ST. THOMAS"

THIS CHAPTER EXAMINES the debates that formed social Catholicism in late
Porfirian Mexico, and gave it a plan of action, often referred to as *acción social*,
Catholic social action. The plan was openly debated and shaped at a 1906 meeting of Catholic activists, clergy, and laity, which convened in the city of Guadalajara. There, the most prominent intellectuals of social Catholicism attempted
to lay the foundation for a distinctly Catholic sociology, a scientific tool that
could be used to study society, analyze the "social question," and pose realistic
solutions that might serve as an alternative to socialism even as they explicitly
tried to reform the excesses of liberal society. In some ways the plans and the
sociology of the Third National Catholic and First Eucharistic Congress were

unrealistic and would prove impossible to apply. In other ways society was rapidly changing all around these religiously inspired sociologists, and their 1906 prescriptions would be modified. However, in a basic sense, the vision they laid out would continue to influence social action, and later Christian democracy movements, up until and beyond the 1926 religious rebellion known as *La cristiada* for its epic importance.

The construction of a Catholic sociology in Mexico occurred during the first decade of the twentieth century.[1] Catholic intellectuals, both clergy and laity, developed the basic topics and analysis. It brought together a description of contemporary social problems—alcoholism, penury, landlessness, and insufficient wages—and religiously inspired solutions. In this sociology they established the ideas and organizational forms that would articulate their struggle for a generation; in doing so, they began to construct a distinctive Catholic identity, religiously orthodox, often reformist, and potentially progressive, both socially and politically. With time, tempered by the struggles of the Mexican Revolution, this identity would also become increasingly combative.

The themes of Catholic sociology are evident in a series of congresses and seminars held during the first years of the twentieth century,[2] but in 1906 a group of Catholics from all over Mexico met in Guadalajara, with the objective of setting the intellectual foundations of the new science. Jean Meyer wrote that the 1906 congress was the most important forum in the formation of a Catholic criticism of the old regime.[3] Indeed, the papers delivered at the congress contributed to the development of a wide-ranging analysis of society's problems. They also formulated a critique of the regime, of the organization of liberal society, and of socialism as an alternative. Social Catholicism was constructed in reaction to the dominant liberal paradigm of the period, but also within the discursive fields generated by the great liberal thinkers of the eighteenth century.[4] I am not only referring here to the notions of "liberalism," "republic," and "sovereignty," but also "sexual division of labor," "social class," and "citizenship." Below I examine the collective work of the Guadalajara congress in order to demonstrate its breadth of focus, reveal the internal contradictions that characterized it, and demonstrate that the formation of social Catholic identity was necessarily entangled in, and mediated by, relations of class and gender.[5] I seek to analyze the writings of Catholic thinkers, their theological grounding and constructions of history, and their contradictions and paradoxes, with the goal of forming a more complex notion of Catholicity during the Porfirian *fin de régimen*.

I understand the fin de régimen as a historical moment characterized by the

TABLE 1. Catholic Congresses in Porfirian Mexico, 1903–1910

Date	Name and Place	Topics
1903	1st National Congress, Puebla	Organizational; mutualism; savings cooperatives; worker circles
1904	1st Agrarian Congress, Tulancingo	Charity and the responsibilities of landowners
1904	2nd National Congress, Morelia	Marian studies and "the social question"
1905	2nd Agrarian Congress, Tulancingo	Alcoholism; child labor; family; mechanization
1906	3rd National Congress, Guadalajara	Eucharist; family; class conflict; social justice; charity; agrarian reform
1906	3rd Agrarian Congress, Zamora	Family; marriage; child labor; rural education; nutrition
1908	1st Social Seminar, León	Social action applied to rural workers
1909	4th National Congress, Oaxaca	Indians and peasants; evangelization
1909	1st Annual Meeting, Operarios Guadalupanos, León	Election of leadership and platform
1910	2nd Social Seminar and Annual Meeting, Operarios Guadalupanos, Mexico City	Work and wages; Operarios Guadalupanos platform

Sources: *Primer Congreso Agrícola de Tulancingo* (México: Tip. Particular de la Sociedad Agrícola Mexicana, 1904); *Segundo Congreso Católico de México y Primero Mariano* (Morelia: Talleres Tipográficos de Agustín Martínez Mier, 1905); *Congreso tercero católico nacional y primero eucarístico*, 2 vols. (Guadalajara, Imprenta de El Regional, 1908); *Cuarto Congreso Católico Nacional Mexicano* (Oaxaca: Tipografía de la Casa de Gama, 1913). The papers of the 1903 Puebla congress were never published, but the handwritten memory exists in two large format volumes at the Mexico City offices of the Secretariado Social Mexicano, an independent organization once linked to the Catholic Church; the 1908 León meeting is documented through local and national press; the 1909 León meeting is documented through the reports and correspondence of the Operarios Guadalupanos, which are preserved in the Miguel Palomar y Vizcarra Papers at the National University in Mexico City; for the 1911 Mexico City social seminar, the papers were published in the biweekly magazine *Restauración Social*.

construction of new political expressions during the years prior to, and immediately following, the overthrow of Porfirio Díaz. Many events marked the
process. Demographic change was important, with the growth of urban areas
creating new social and economic realities. Historians have tended to place
particular emphasis on the emergence of the Partido Liberal Mexicano (PLM).
Camilo Arriaga, the heir to a wealthy provincial family with impeccable liberal
bona fides, published a manifesto calling for liberals to organize politically to
confront resurgent clericalism. His call struck a chord, and soon fifty clubs
sprang up in thirteen different states. The newspaper, *Regeneración*, provided
ideology and a language of struggle for workers, and a revolutionary appeal to
all who might sign up. Major strikes at Cananea Sonora (1906) and Río Blanco
Veracruz (1907) were violently crushed. There is no hydraulic mechanism in
play; the 1910 revolution was not caused by such change in Mexican society.
But still, by 1908, president Díaz saw fit to announce in an interview that he
would accept opposition candidates in the upcoming elections. The following
year, opposition formed around the candidacy of General Bernardo Reyes for
the office of vice president. Reyes declined candidacy, leaving his followers in
the lurch. But many gravitated toward the 1910 presidential candidacy of Francisco Madero, a wealthy landowner from Parras Coahuila who founded the
Anti-Reelectionist Party.[6]

The social Catholic movement initially belonged to this moment, and the
cycle of Catholic congresses marked the emergence of a new form of political
expression. This new language did not appear fully formed, but contradictory
and partial. In Guadalajara, the debates revealed tension between the sacred
and the profane. The motives of spiritual life coexisted, at times uncomfortably, with the imperatives of material life. The ideals of the delegates with
respect to domestic and civil society did not necessarily correspond to the
reality that they would later confront. Most notably, the participants had made
no attempt to reach out to the rural and urban poor who were the subject of
their discussions. The Guadalajara congress was, in the end, an elite affair.
Once the masses of believers opted in to a political Catholic movement, and
many thousands would, their presence would modify basic aspects of both
religion and politics. Nevertheless, at Guadalajara some of the basic ideas and
several of the protagonists that would shape Catholic policy during the revolutionary period first appeared. Basically, this policy aimed to reinscribe the
relations between state and citizenry within the general vision of social
Catholicism.

In this chapter I am interested in asking how those men formulated their demands, in whose name they did it, how they constructed the Catholic subject, and what differences existed among them. The chapter will treat three related themes with the objective of explaining how the participants imagined their world, what they saw as the main problems afflicting it, and how they thought that things might be properly resolved. In the first section, I examine the general ideas about society that congress participants presented, with particular emphasis on the intersection between society and religious belief. The second section focuses in on the central area of discussion at the congress, poverty and social class. In truth, the congress participants were unable to agree on a path of action for treating society's problems. So, in the third section of the chapter, I turn to a broader body of writing circulating among the participants at the time of the Guadalajara congress, to look for the beginnings of a proposal for public action. The final argument of the chapter posits that Catholics will come to modern politics through the pilgrimage tradition, a forum in which all Catholics will participate, the rich and poor, men and women, city and countryfolk.

Domestic Society and Civil Society

The Guadalajara congress was inaugurated on October 19, 1906. All the speakers were men. One by one they presented their work in whole or in summary, between the twentieth and the twenty-sixth; the night of the twenty-sixth, the delegates received the governor of Jalisco, Colonel Miguel Ahumada, at a literary-musical gathering that ended a little before two in the morning;[7] the closing ceremony was held on October 28. The congress brought together clergy and laymen from a large part of Mexico with the aim of reflecting on the problems of modern society, and the role of the Holy Eucharist as a factor of unity and remedy. The teacher's college for women (señoritas, or unmarried women, presumably), the seminary major, and the cathedral were the setting of sermons, speeches, music (sacred and profane), and poetry. The centerpiece of the congress was the presentation of more than sixty "working papers," divided into two groups: religious and sociological.[8] These papers were previously gathered, evaluated, and subjected to the censorship of an organizing committee months prior to the congress.[9]

The organizational bifurcation of the work sessions may reflect the internal struggles between liberal and social Catholics.[10] Manuel Ceballos Ramírez argued, in fact, that the mix of religious and social themes revealed the force that liberal Catholics still wielded.[11] In the inaugural sermon, Ignacio Montes de Oca, Bishop of San Luis Potosí and symbol of an almost aristocratic Catholic traditionalism, reflected autobiographically on the cycles that mark the lives of churchmen. Enigmatic, "the . . . speaker reminisced about the Congresses he had attended, noting that in the first ones he had gone unnoticed, because he was still young, while in others he was acclaimed, and perhaps in future congresses he [would] be cast aside."[12] Undoubtedly, Montes de Oca was from another era, and another Church. Born in 1840, he belonged to the generation of clerics that experienced the French Intervention and the liberal reform. Like Archbishop Gillow, of Oaxaca, he was a liberal, whose view of Catholicism matched the pragmatism of president Díaz.[13] He was not going to find his place among the social Catholics who began, in Guadalajara, to push Catholic politics in a new direction. In this palpable way, the congress highlighted a generational renovation, the end of one cycle and the beginning of another. Specifically, it marked the decline of the liberals and traditionalists, and the rise of the social Catholics and Democrats.[14]

It is likely that the struggles among groups had influenced the ideological composition of the Catholic congresses. Although it is difficult to trace these conflicts through the "proceedings" that were later published, at times they appear through the correspondence of the delegates. Some evidence supports Manuel Ceballos's hypothesis that there was a latent conflict between liberals and social Catholics. For example, there were disagreements between liberals who sought to limit Catholicism to religious observances, and social Catholics, who sought to project their religious practice further into the public sphere or even into politics. Ceballos has argued that this was especially the case at the 1904 and 1906 congresses. The first, celebrated at Morelia, mixed social themes with the Marian cult, while the second, the Guadalajara congress, mixed social themes with the study of the Holy Eucharist. In both cases there is evidence of conflicting views. Francisco Traslosheros, for example, was not convinced by the idea of mixing social themes with the Marian cult at the Morelia congress. Nor did he care for the structure of the congress; in his opinion it was too controlled, even authoritarian. He preferred more debate and fewer speeches.[15] During the 1906 congress, the Chihuahua newspaperman, Silvestre Terrazas, bristled at the idea of limiting the Catholic press by requiring that it extol the virtues of the Church. This was to reduce journalism to the realm of propaganda.[16] With great clarity he advocated for a journalism inspired by Christian ideals, but ultimately independent, so as to be able to work at the margin of all causes. For Terrazas, the religious press was marked by its rigidity.[17]

Such complaints, however, were not limited to the laity. There were also disagreements among some within the clergy. For example, referring to the theological and pedagogical orthodoxy practiced by his superiors, Father José María Soto lamented that the old, outmoded ways of thinking were resilient to destruction. He complained about being totally separated from the information network of the social movements. "Nothing is known in these parts," he wrote to Miguel Palomar y Vizcarra, referring to the Morelia seminary where he taught philosophy. "Or, rather, I am the one who knows nothing, because it may easily be the case that those of the upper spheres are informed, and I am as a stranger in my own house."[18] These comments date from early 1907, a few months after both participated actively in the Guadalajara congress.

In 1910 Soto would play an important role in defining the terms of one of the main issues of social action, the family wage. In a 1909 letter, he wrote with undisguised enthusiasm about the emerging social action movement, and advised Palomar y Vizcarra to throw down his books and take to the streets in pursuit of the cause. In a series of inspired letters, he outlined a proposal to reform the labor contract. Workers, he argued, ought to have an obligatory day off each week, preferably Sunday, in order to worship and rest. They ought to earn a wage sufficient to support their family, and the labor contract ought to protect them from the avarice of the wealthy; as it stood, they had almost no means of protection.[19] Though his approach was religiously inspired, Soto was clearly referring to social rights, of the kind the 1917 constitution would later articulate for working people. Wrapped up in an interest for new thinking, Soto's apprehension toward his superiors may well be part of the conflict between liberals and socials, but here it also reflects a difference attributable to generation, and expressed through new ideas and practices. Both generational and ideological differences were often intertwined at this conjuncture.

The reason such differences came to the fore is that there was a general conversation going on among Catholics regarding secularization, the proper place and limits of religious life and devotion in society. Refugio Galindo, the Tulancingo doctor, made a public name for himself by organizing Church-sponsored agrarian congresses that catered mostly to the interests of *hacendados*. In a series of 1907 letters, Galindo expressed his worries over the future of the congresses. There was pressure to make them more independent of the priests, a position he did not share. After suspending, and then resuming, preparation of the Fourth Agrarian Congress, he wrote to Palomar y Vizcarra that for Catholic social action to be viable, clergy should always guide it. The cooperation of laymen was necessary, but without the clergy absolutely nothing would be attained.[20] The Jesuit intellectual Arnulfo Castro was much less sanguine regarding the expansion of Church activities in society. Commenting on the 1911 foundation of the National Catholic Party, he wrote to Palomar y Vizcarra in no uncertain terms that he saw the party's openly Catholic identity as a limitation and a liability, for the Church, for the laity that would direct the party, and for the Catholic faithful in general. For Castro, the ideas expressed in the party platform were laudable and necessary, but the party should be a lay organization, without a self-consciously Catholic identity.[21] Such diversity of viewpoints is not easily reduced to issues of ideological affiliation, or generational difference, nor is it necessary that it be. The messiness of such divergent opinions was part of the process of forming a social Catholic movement in Mexico, and points to the basic weakness of explanations that look for a singular Catholic character, or rely on the assumed power of the bishops within a rigid hierarchy.

On the level of ideas, the tension between different viewpoints, factions, and ideological positions was also manifest in another way, through the working papers presented at the congress. It is often difficult to draw strict conclusions about the opinions of one or another activist in regard to concepts developed in the papers. However, when reconstructing the foundations of a Catholic sociology, their conceptual diversity is immediately striking. The papers on sociological themes considered "the social question" in a schematic fashion, shifting between two founding concepts, the domestic society and the civil society. The first corresponded to the relations of family, and the second corresponded to the relations of the larger community. The civil society, in this sense, was analogous to the domestic society. One section was dedicated to presenting the basic actors and relationships of domestic society, of which there were two: (1) marriage, with its prime subjects, the father and the mother/wife; and (2) family, with its prime subjects the parents, the children, and the servants. The other section focused on the basic actors and relations of civil society, of which there were three: (1) the priest; (2) the associations; and (3) the social classes, with their corresponding hierarchical oppositions: owner–worker and capital–labor.[22]

In the Guadalajara congress, the opposition between the domestic and the civil was built on the family, which was theorized as the radical foundation of the entire society. Domestic society, therefore, was constructed by actors and the relationships that were formed through marriage. In accord with the Thomist notion of "natural order," all society functioned because each had a place, and a particular and vital function. This notion articulated the domestic and the civil, because the domestic society reproduced a divine relationship that, in turn, should be the model for civil society.[23] The social question was conceived as the study of the reasons why society deviated from this model. In this sense, domestic society and civil society do not mark discrete or different spaces, as would be the notion of "separate spheres." Instead they suggest the form of society itself, conceived on a small scale, in the first case, and on a larger scale, in the second case. Civil society, then, reproduced the attributes of the domestic society: the state was to civil society as the father to domestic society.

In many of the papers delivered at the Guadalajara congress, sacred history determined the sociological relationships of contemporary society, creating a millenarian metanarrative.[24] In creation, God established marriage as a unique human relationship and as an indissoluble link between man and woman. This link or association was necessary for the construction of what Catholic thinkers would call domestic society. According to this history, in the fall, domestic society was dragged to the lowest depths of abjection. Pagan civilization was characterized as the perversion of what had been a divine creation. The pagan husband considered his wife a slave. Man lavished his degrading attentions on woman, who was little more than an object of pleasure, while her beauty lasted. Divorce, adultery, and sensuality predominated. It was Jesus Christ who remedied that state of things, raising marriage from wretchedness to the dignity of sacrament. In the opinion of the Guadalajara lawyer, Perfecto Méndez Padilla, "since marriage is the basis of the family, and the family is the basis of society, it was natural that the Divine Reformer would concern himself with that institution, placing it as the cornerstone of the social structure."[25] For him, Jesus Christ appeared as the historical reformer who saved the family and, by extension, society. Only through Christ, then, could that family maintain or reproduce its dignity and avoid its former infamy. This was the key to understanding the importance of the Eucharist in Holy Scripture and Catholic sociology. The bread and wine, Christ's sacramental flesh and blood, represented the ultimate sacrifice through which Christ secured the dignity of the Christian family. Family unity depended on Christ's sacrifice.

The Christian union of marriage was sustained by sacrifice. Through the Eucharist, the family must continually renew its pledge with good. Here the Holy Eucharist was seen as the most important of the sacraments. Through it, Jesus Christ manifested himself in domestic society to remind each member of their duties: the husband must be faithful; woman will in turn esteem her husband as the most important part of her being, while he must love his wife as the weaker part of his own self; parents will care for their children; and children must love and revere their parents as Jesus reveres the Heavenly Father.[26] Servants should feel themselves to be part of the family; they should participate in the Eucharist with the family. "With the family they kneel daily at home or in church, and address the same prayer to the Heavenly Father and to the blessed Mother. Seeing that the lowliness of their condition does not stand in the way of all this, gratitude will spring from their soul . . . toward their masters."[27] Through the Eucharist, the members of domestic society might reach reciprocity in the duties of the family, resulting in harmony.

Méndez Padilla's emphasis placed on woman's natural weakness was not casual, nor did it correspond only to a particular vision of the author. The contract theorists in general, and Jean-Jacques Rousseau in particular, promoted this characterization in the liberal tradition.[28] Ireneo Quintero understood this weakness in ontological terms, as "the natural inclination of gender." By way of example, he referred to the ritual of communion, the partaking of the Holy Eucharist. Women, Quintero noted, took communion with certain frequency, although he doubted that the practice reflected devotion: "Outside impulses, curiosity, and fashion have so much effect on them, [that] women run the risk of seeming devout without this devotion having in reality any great power over their souls."[29]

In Catholic tradition, this characterization of women was based on the story of the fall. Agustín Navarro also used the notions of original sin and the fall to explain contemporary sociological relationships. He argued that women embodied the perpetual battle between good and evil, symbolized in the lives of Eve and Mary. In this representation, woman's body was the site of a timeless battle on which the fate of domestic society was decided. On the one hand, he characterized Eve as "the black and endless waterfall from which flows evil over the damned surface of the earth; on its waves ride sin, diseases, and death; on its road we only find mourning, tears, misery, and desolation." In the original fall, Eve, the weaker of the two, succumbed to temptation and brought Adam with her. Eve was carnal licentiousness, the imminence of sexual disorder. She represented the natural threat of the female body: earthly and sensual. If Eve was supposed to be the weaker of the two, there was no doubt in Navarro's poetics that he placed formidable strengths in her body. Mary, in contrast, was "the diaphanous and pure fount of eternal life," she was the mother of God, the womb that gave life. In the battle between good and evil, the Christian mother was the apostle of the home; the moral order of domestic society depended on her. Mary represented the mother/wife: abnegated guardian of good customs and prudent living. She was heavenly, virginal even in conception, and above all, orderly and controlled. Following Michel Foucault, we may see hers as a disciplined body, yet more in the tradition of Christian rejection—"the body detested"—than a bourgeois political economy of sexuality. Even so, both ideas may well have inspired the author of these lines.[30]

Like the sacrament of marriage, work was also suspended in the creation myth. From the beginning of time, the lot of mankind was to work. In the book of Genesis, God said to Adam, "in the sweat of thy face shalt thou eat bread."[31] This circumstance was interpreted as the daily absence of the man who worked, and understood to condition woman's labors. To put it in another way, woman is understood in relation to a constructed man who is positioned as an ontological certainty.[32]

> If he leaves his house because work demands it, he will not be able to watch his family, and if he does not work, they will lack the necessary things to subsist. What can a man do in his conflict of imperative and incompatible necessities? The Lord, who in his wise providence makes order shine in all the things that spring from His hand, has resolved this conflict by means of the companion He gives to the honest and hard-working family father.[33]

In the father's absence, the woman was responsible for the house, the children, and the servant. She carried out the aim of Redemption. With Mary as an example, she must seek strength in the Eucharist, which "perfects and sanctifies the woman in all the states and conditions of her life: the child, with innocence, the virgin, with purity, the wife with abnegation, the widow with chastity."[34]

Domestic society, constructed as such, collected and ordered social difference, producing in the home what would have to be produced in civil society. It depended on a sexual hierarchy in which strength was masculine, weakness was feminine, and the two complemented each other reciprocally. The father was the head and the husband represented Jesus Christ himself. In this context, "women are subject to their husbands, as they are to the Lord."[35] But it also reproduced a class hierarchy, in which the bourgeois nuclear family was reified as the only legitimate family. Domestic society implicitly produced the relationship between those from above and those from below, *summorum e infirmorum*. As previously noted, husband and wife should include their servants in the sacrament of the Eucharist; and the servants should feel part of the family; they must accept their master with love, fidelity, and respect.[36] Finally, it rested on a generational hierarchy as well, explicit here in the case of woman, who is characterized by innocence, purity, abnegation, and chastity, according to the stages of the lifecycle.

In the Thomist intellectual tradition, civil society was analogous to domestic society, because civil society ("the body of the state"), was constituted through the medium of families.[37] It was the equivalent of the basic family relationship on a grand scale. Domestic society was a differentiated group in which harmony depended on the timely contribution of each of its members, according to their skills and responsibilities; according to the place they occupied in the division of labor. Both societies took the individual as a model, and the social body should function as a human body. In domestic society, father, mother, child, and servant had their place; in civil society, employer and worker had their place, as well as the soldier, statesman, and artisan; all had their place. The basic lesson of Thomist theology was that harmony in society depended on a common, collective effort, and the inevitable division of labor. Leo XIII explained it in terms of reciprocity and order, with its resulting aesthetic:

> Just as in the human body the different members harmonize with one another, whence arises that disposition of parts and proportion in the human figure rightly called symmetry, so likewise nature has commanded in the case of the State that the two classes mentioned should agree harmoniously and should properly form equally balanced counterparts to each other. Each needs the other completely: neither capital can do without labor, nor labor without capital. Concord begets beauty and order in things.[38]

In sum, through the filter of Christian morality, political economy revolved around the concepts of reciprocity and harmony of interests. This state of affairs was codified by Thomists as the "common good," the unifying concept of civil society.

However, Leo XIII's vision was more complex. He recognized the modern condition—class conflict—but not the socialist solution, since Christian morality condemned class struggle. He also recognized that class conflict was the direct result, the logical consequence of the liberal paradigm. The weak condition of artisan and proletarian alike, he believed, was due to the destruction of medieval corporations and the emergence of industrial society. The main dilemma for the pope was to outline a policy that addressed the conflict without resorting to means that would promote the tactics of the socialists. The way out of this dilemma would be to reprove socialism while recovering the guild tradition. With Leo XIII, the social Catholic theorists turned their gaze to the corporate tradition of medieval Europe. There they saw an ideal Christian fatherland, with a corporate society still valid as an ideal for their times.[39] Like Leo XIII, the delegates of the Guadalajara congress turned to this ideal for inspiration. With remarkable simplicity and almost ontological certainty, the Jesuit Luciano Achiaga summarized a basic Thomist syllogism, "because man lives in society, he has a natural tendency to form associations."[40] That is, Man lives in society; society is constructed like a grand association; ergo Man has a tendency to form associations. The association, in this logic, is a metaphor for the family, and functions in much the same way. By 1900, the estate society of ancien régime France and Spanish America no longer existed legally, but the corporatist tradition had not disappeared and the social Catholics claimed it as part of their strategy.

Although socialism too had its origins in the European guild, Leo XIII recognized it as the organizational form that had assured worker welfare before the advent of liberal society. Therefore, he prescribed forming associations in the guild tradition. For Mexico's social Catholics this notion was not illogical, because they lived in a society composed of estates (in practice, if not in law), made up of collective actors whose direct origin came from the old regime corporations and whose esprit d'corps partially survived nineteenth-century modernity.[41] This corporatist vision –in Achiaga's words, the natural tendency to form associations—provided a guideline by which Catholics would organize the many diverse actors and spaces of society, from mutualist societies and consumer cooperatives, to literary and scientific circles, confraternities, and prayer groups. But without a doubt, during the first quarter of the twentieth century, Catholic sociologists would focus most of their attention and efforts on professional associations, especially workers' societies.

Summorum/Infirmorum

A central lesson of *Rerum Novarum* was that of a particular hierarchy of oppressions. The theme itself, "the condition of workers," recognized class society, even if Leo XIII's reading of society's problems led him to reject class struggle as a political tactic. This hierarchy reveals one of the greatest paradoxes of social action: how to recognize the contingency (class conflict), without recommending the tactic (class struggle). *Rerum Novarum* suggested an answer, and the social Catholics, both in Europe and in Mexico, tried to adapt it to their circumstances. The answer it offered was the dream of a return to society built on the foundations of Christian morality. The project was utopian in its rejection of liberal and socialist paradigms, yet by constituting itself as a *tercero en discordia*, or third way, it revealed a realistic view of the prevailing political circumstance.[42] As a self-proclaimed mediator between liberalism and socialism, the Vatican could not hope to do away with these powerful social forces. But perhaps it could strike some sort of middle path between the two. Leo XIII recognized as much in a conversation that was paraphrased in the Mexico City press. "Socialism is a flood: there are three solutions at hand. Stand in its way, and expose oneself to be swept away by it. Stand calmly to one side, which is the role of the pious dreamer. Channel it: here we have the true solution, that which corresponds to the very essence of the Church."[43]

Pope Leo wrote about the problems of his time, the conflicts and contradictions of modernity. The goal that he outlined in *Rerum Novarum* was a "just" or family wage, and the means to obtain this was through association. Both aspects were remarked and contextualized in the encyclical, but Leo XIII stopped short of articulating a formula. The problems were particular to each place, and his recommendations could only serve as a general guide; they would have to be applied according to the needs and circumstances of each nation.

In the Guadalajara congress, following the initial discussions on the form of society, the delegates concentrated their efforts on the analysis of the main social problems of the day. Father Luis Macías began the discussion on workers' societies. He posed two basic matters that would have to be resolved: first, what form would a workers' organization assume, and second, what should be its objectives. In Macías's ideas, the influence of *Rerum Novarum* was obvious, although he worked them through in more detail than the papal encyclical. The organizational framework he proposed consisted of three different bodies that would guide worker societies (figure 2). First, and of highest authority, a council general should be formed, presided over by a bishop and a group of officials, "men of culture," who presumably would come from society's privileged classes.[44] The council would govern all the societies in a single diocese. Second, the council general would appoint an auxiliary board made up of artisans from each of the trades represented by worker societies. A workshop master (*jefe de taller*) and an "intelligent" artisan would represent each trade on the auxiliary board. Third, each worker society should form a local council, presided over by a priest and a group of dignitaries chosen by the priest from among the members of the society.[45]

```
┌─────────────────────────────────────────────────────────────┐
│     Bishop >>                                                 │
│                                                               │
│          Men of culture  >>                                   │
│                                                               │
│              Parish priest  >>                                │
│                                                               │
│                  Worker                                       │
└─────────────────────────────────────────────────────────────┘
```

FIGURE 2. Proposed hierarchy of intermediaries for worker societies. Source: *Congreso Tercero Católico Nacional y Primero Eucarístico*, vol. 2 (Guadalajara, Imprenta de El Regional, 1908): 500–504.

The form that Macías proposed for the worker societies reveals a power relationship. It recalls the 1903 project discussed by the delegates to the First National Catholic Congress, held in Puebla.[46] In Guadalajara, as in Puebla, the delegates considered models that imposed a desired social hierarchy. The Guadalajara model assumes the importance of social class woven into the ecclesiastic hierarchy that they hoped would order worker societies. Amidst the traditional channel, from bishop to parish priest to flock, Macías proposed that "men of culture" should form a further link in the chain, basically subordinate to the bishop, but above local parish priests. In other words, "cultured" lay activists should preside over these worker organizations as advisors, responsible only to the local bishop.

At least three other elements of the plan merit comment. First, the general council (bishop and men of culture) was accessible to workers and workshop masters through the auxiliary board. Supposing that the workshop heads were the workers' bosses, the auxiliary board would function as a mixed commission in which both groups negotiated their differences. It was here that harmony among social classes would be sought, and the general council would function as an enlightened mediator. Second, the local council included workers as a type of parish cabinet. This circumstance would assure, at least, that the priest was abreast of the material lives of his flock. He would be obliged to leave the sacristy and relate to his parishioners in an earthly context. Third, and most significantly, the model defined a discursive field and geography of power. The discursive field derived from Thomist epistemology, and defined a hierarchy descending from the sacred to the profane, from the Church representatives to the flock. I will have more to say about this epistemological model in the final section of the chapter. The particular geography of power described by Macías reaffirmed the diocese as the center of social life, articulated through the network of parishes. The objectives and form of the worker societies reflected this arrangement. Macías centered his proposal on the tasks of the general (diocesan) and local (parish) councils, such that all material matters would be considered at the diocesan level, while spiritual matters would be considered at the parish level. The result of this arrangement was to limit the people making decisions about local working conditions, and at the same time promote the importance of spiritual health through the relationship between pastor and worker. But the intellectual legacy of *Rerum Novarum* was not limited to this binary dyad opposing the material and the spiritual, and nor was Macías's proposal. Deploying the sociological language of the congress, he proposed three objectives for the worker society, all of them expressed in terms of "the worker's possessions." Worker associations should care for and foment the goods of the body (*bienes del cuerpo*), the goods of the soul (*bienes del alma*), and the goods of prosperity (*bienes de fortuna*), or worldly possessions, of their members.[47]

The goods of the soul should be the main priority of the worker association. Its chief objective was to moralize, to teach workers to be good Christians and Christian citizens. Moralization ought to form and discipline them in such a way as to make clear the absurdity of socialist doctrine. Practice was important, and Macías distinguished between spiritual exercises and licit distractions, both of which were necessary to promote Christian morality. Curiously, in regard to the spiritual exercises, Father Macías only recommended those of St. Ignatius, for fulfilling the demands of the holy days, confession, and annual communion, in addition to the general obligations of Christian life. He preferred to concentrate his interest (and perhaps his concern) on the aspect of leisure. Societies should offer an alternative to the taverns, since the vice of alcohol was considered a main cause of immoral behavior, material need, suffering, and even the loss of the family. The list of licit activities included excursions in the country, gymnastic exercise, listening to the gramophone, watching movies, participating in theater, building libraries, and gathering among members, especially with the goal of sharing moralizing stories that capture the attention.[48] As a concept, the goods of the soul encompassed a socializing practice that was more intellectual than mystical, based on exercises of memory and social gatherings.

The goods of the body—that is, material conditions in general—were the natural complement to the goods of the soul. In all cases they should be increased, but the formula depended in each case on the worker's circumstance. Macías proposed two different types. On the one hand, there were lazy workers, and it went without saying that they should work more. On the other hand, there were poorly paid workers. They should receive an adequate wage. In both cases, it was important to guide workers so that they did not consider taking usurious loans as a way out of poverty, or as an immediate response to en emerging problem. It was better to form mutual funds as a means of preparing for eventual sickness or death, although the topic of mutual funds formed part of another discussion, that of worldly possessions, the goods of prosperity.

The worldly possessions of the worker, which might also be understood as the worker's capital, refer to the thorny problem of property. Often, the fundamental conflict between Catholics and Socialists was articulated in terms of their stance regarding property. Manuel F. Chávez, an early proponent of Christian democracy and future president of the National Catholic Party's Jalisco chapter, expressed this conflict in terms of two paths. The revolutionary or socialist path sought universal wealth through the suppression of poverty, and led its followers to adopt violent procedures, propitiated by desperation. Most of those in attendance, unfamiliar as they were with socialism, most likely had a profound fear of such solutions. Chávez was careful to impress upon them the legitimacy of the problem. "All revolution," he warned, "is the corruption of a true principle, the exaggeration of a just desire, the deviation of a legitimate trend." If society were unwilling to attend to its very real problems, those problems would eventually force themselves on all. For this reason it was of paramount importance that the Catholic, "evolutionary," path seek the greatest possible distribution of capital; that it diminish the ravages of misery and improve the condition of the lower classes. Once people's needs were satisfied, they would seek their own individual and collective "perfection," or development.[49] However, he warned, "[if] the economic situation of the masses does not improve, neither will their intellectual and moral condition; in such circumstances the nation's progress will continue to be superficial and incomplete."[50]

To make the evolutionary way a real option, Macías stressed the need to save. If the key for the goods of the body was the wage, then savings was the key for the goods of prosperity. These two concepts, governed by an orthodox Christian ethics (goods of the soul), formed the basis of the Vatican recommendation, and over time they would become the favorite topic of Catholic sociologists. Beginning in 1903, Miguel Palomar y Vizcarra had advocated the Raiffeisen model of credit and savings cooperatives during the Puebla congress.[51] The role of money (wage and savings), as the means for productive relations, shaped Catholic attempts to reform work relations, construct a modern (Christian) citizenship, and moralize rural and urban "workers," including artisans. Although the vision was Christian and at least nominally antiliberal, the effort was similar to the "secular" policy that successive revolutionary governments would implement beginning in 1914.

The problem of the "evolutionary path" was how to convert workers into capitalists. The answer encompassed two different means: work and Christian charity. Regarding work, Manuel Chávez argued that the drops of sweat that soak the worker's forehead were more valuable than the capitalist's pesos. However, this paradox pointed out two dilemmas. On the one hand, how could work be made more fruitful without antagonizing capital? On the other hand, how, through work, could the worker assure economic and social security in the present, while saving for the future? In other words, how could workers be made into capitalists? Chávez thought that more agricultural, industrial, mining, and commercial businesses were needed. They should function in a healthy way, and this could be achieved if the workers were qualified, and if the workers and capitalists respected the work contract. The multiplication of agricultural businesses required, however, the moderate and prudent division of properties. This was not a proposal to expropriate private property, although in Chávez's opinion it was necessary to increase the number of landowners. Small-scale landowners ought to play an important role in the economic reform needed to generate harmony between work and capital.[52] In other words, Mexico needed a middle class, especially a rural middle class.

To increase the number of landowners, it was necessary to foment savings and protect the worker from unforeseen events that, frequently, propitiated the practice of usury. Leo XIII had written that the wage should not be less than what was needed to support a "thrifty and upright worker."[53] Faustino Rosales interpreted this to mean that Christian ethics allowed the play of supply and demand in the market, but its limit ought to be the welfare of a disciplined worker.[54] The notion of limits to the free market suggests a mixed economy, one in which the state plays the role of assuring social welfare. Nicolás Leaño extended the argument, insisting that the wage was the touchstone between capital and labor. For him it was indispensable that wages be paid in a timely fashion and in coin, that they cover the expenses required to support a family, and that they allow for savings.[55] Rosales, in turn, asserted:

> All the Catholic economists agree that a worker is perfectly entitled to form a family, and in such a way that he can support it by himself without demanding aid from his wife and children, other than that which is

compatible with the [wife's] household chores, and with the physical, intellectual, and moral education that the [children] demand.[56]

In fact, the notion of the family wage was not universally accepted among
the Catholic thinkers, and in Mexico as in Europe divergent stances were
defined.[57] However, opinions like those of Leaño or Rosales were not unusual,
either in their support of the family wage, or in their stubborn insistence that
the worker was a man. Women workers were common enough, but sociological analysis still tended to miss them, based as it was on the observations of
men who were educated and socialized to believe that women should not
work.[58] In the spring of 1909, José María Soto O.G., wrote to Miguel Palomar
y Vizcarra outlining a similar stance, formulating a sharp-edged critique of
the greed of society's "higher classes."[59] In October 1910, the Operarios Guadalupanos dedicated the Mexico City Social Seminar to the issue of wages, at
which time they further developed their analyses based on Christian ethics.[60]
However, in Guadalajara Chávez warned that only the market could generate
an increase in wages and the lowering of prices. He recognized the importance
of these two circumstances, but insisted that legislating them or decreeing
them would create an economic crisis. Although the market ought to set wages
and the price of food, labor relations were another story, and could indeed be
modified. In particular, rural workers were subject to numerous abuses in the
haciendas. The three principal abuses were the *tienda de raya*, or hacienda
store, that monopolized the distribution and cost of foods and other goods; the
practice of debt peonage, which tended to devaluate wages in real terms; and
payment through means other than coin money, a practice that prevented the
worker from participating in the modern economy, saving, or buying. All these
practices constituted abuses in his opinion, and could be vigorously combated.
Finally, the most common obstacles to saving were squandering, caused by
immoderate consumption of alcohol, and the existence of usurers who profited
from the unforeseen crises of workers.[61]

Along with economic policy considerations, entangled in a discursive field
fixed by liberal political economists, the other aspect of the "evolutionary
path" was charity, an orthodox Christian concept. The delegates expressed
their disagreement about whether to intervene in the "natural" rules of the
economy, and in regard to the wage, Chávez's stance would likely have been
applauded in the offices of Monsignor Limantour. But charity was a theme
apart. According to Catholic doctrine, it implied an act of love before God. It
could not be legislated because it was an act of conscience, and charity was a

widely recommended virtue. Manuel Chávez argued (from moralist doctrine), that the rich were not owners but administrators of the fruits of their wealth, and therefore were obliged to distribute "the surplus" among the poor.[62] In the writings of Chávez, Faustino Rosales, and Nicolás Leaño, the notion of charity was more complex, and all of them applied it in a particular context, that of justice.

In their writing, the link between charity and justice is complex. Justice evokes two different circumstances: in the first place, good relations among "men," and in the second place, between "man" and God. Charity, on the contrary, can have a bearing on the former, but belongs strictly to the latter. Let us consider first the question of justice.

When analyzing the social question, the congress members distinguished between two kinds of justice. There was natural justice, which preceded human laws, and commutative justice, which was characteristic of the exchange relations that occurred, for example, between employer and workers upon signing a labor contract. In this context, for example, Rosales insisted that the worker's labor should be worth what nature asked it to be worth—that it be enough to support the worker and his family.[63] His argument evokes commutative justice and refers to the ideal of the common good, but makes no direct reference to charity. It does, however, represent one school of thought, important to Catholic sociology, that held that the family wage was an issue of commutative justice. In this opinion Rosales was not alone, but found himself in the company of others such as Father José María Soto and Nicolás Leaño.

Manuel Chávez argued explicitly why charity could not be linked to justice. The reason, he wrote, was that to link the two would make charity a duty of commutative justice. In other words, to link charity to justice would be to subordinate it to contractual law. Thus, the deployment of charity, even in ordinary circumstances, as in the quest for welfare, would establish the grounds of a *perfect right*. According to Chávez, charity did not and could not constitute such a right, and to allow it would accommodate socialism.[64]

What did he mean by a "perfect right," and what relation did it have to socialism? By "perfect" he meant autonomous or independent, that is, a right that did not depend above all on God. In other words, if charity were a perfect right, then anyone who lived in need or aspired to welfare could, in effect, demand to receive charity as an act of justice. This was not possible, because charity was founded on the Creator–creature relationship, the relationship between God and he or she who offered charity. It could not be demanded, and therefore was not a perfect right. In the tradition of the *Summa Theologica*,

Chávez distinguished between the conscience before God and perfect right. Charity secured a sort of spiritual or moral justice, while perfect right could ensure certain aspects of the common good, such as wages paid in metallic currency, the prohibition of hacienda stores, or debt peonage. But if anyone might demand charity, this act would reach beyond contractual law to the realm of distributive justice; it would dictate that the wealthy appease the poor. Distributive justice, Chávez felt, opened the door to socialism. It was preferable to seek commutative justice through reformist legislation.[65]

Could the combination of reformist legislation and Christian charity assure the harmony invoked by Leo XIII in *Rerum Novarum*? Nicolás Leaño's rejoinder to Faustino Rosales questioned the feasibility of the enterprise.[66] At first glance the main difference between Leaño and Rosales seems more of temperament than the content of their arguments. Both, for example, subscribed to the notion of the family wage,[67] but unlike Rosales, Leaño pushed at his ideas regarding the just wage and concluded that they entered into stark contradiction with prevailing social conditions. Also unlike Rosales, he abandoned the fiction of imminent social harmony, and compelled his audience, including a contingent of bishops, to face the scandal of rural Mexico. The modern counterpart of the unjust wage, as Manuel Ceballos has pointed out, was the strike. But the strike was a political tactic belonging to the repertoire of class struggle, and was reproved by the Vatican. The way out of this predicament was not clear, and the congress would be unable to resolve the dilemma. It is important, however, to consider Leaño's contribution, since it defined the congress. The final part of his text is particularly convincing:

> Unfortunately, as the costs fall . . . production grows and manifests itself in the property-owner's luxury, but wages remain stagnant at the same level as years ago. What can be done by an unhappy laborer, a head of household with twenty-five centavos or a maximum of thirty-seven [per day] with which he must buy corn and beans at a price 550% greater than before? In what sort of dwelling does the hacienda owner have him? They seem more like pigsties than dwellings for rational people, as delicate and vulnerable as their masters, or more so, to lethal pneumonia! And what efforts do the majority of hacienda owners make for the moral and intellectual improvement of their servants? Oh! Whoever has had the opportunity to deal a little with these unhappy people can appreciate the responsibility that the owners have in this revolution that threatens us. The moral and religious formation of these poor people and their intellectual culture is so infinitely

small that, there is no doubt, they would embrace with fanaticism and hor-
rible fury any possibility of rebellion and revenge against their masters,
who treat them thus, keeping them like a tinderbox that would burn until
it consumes all or consumes itself.[68]

Nicolás Leaño began this rejoinder by praising thirty-three years of peace
in Mexico that had allowed—indeed begot—the economic boom of the Porfirian era. Capital, he said, showered blessings; mining, industry, and agriculture progressed. The good judgment of the government, the good sense of the
people, and Providence were to be thanked. This condition helped mining and
industrial workers to prosper; and although their wage was not the "just equivalent" of their "labor power," the population was scarce in these sectors and
the job supply exceeded the demand, increasing the wages. For Leaño, the
underlying dilemma was to be found in the difference between economic progress and the goods of the worker, those of body, soul, and fortune or prosperity.
Leaño chose to illustrate this circumstance by virtue of a comparison between
the industrial worker and the rural wage-laborer. As he saw it, the industrial
worker earned relatively well, while the situation of the rural proletarian was
deplorable, throwing into relief the fundamental injustice of the liberal system
in Mexico. Leaño explicitly blamed the hacienda owners: they paid an unfair
wage; they did not practice charity; they were responsible for a condition that
went against any hope of harmony. For Leaño, class conflict was not only a
European problem, but a Mexican problem as well. In the absence of both
commutative justice and Christian charity, the revolution was imminent and
the responsibility of the hacienda owners was obvious.[69]

The epitaph at the beginning of this chapter, words of Umberto Eco, suggests that had St. Thomas lived in the twentieth century, he would have
changed some of his ideas. One of them, Eco proposed, was the idea of harmony. Nicolás Leaño, a twentieth-century Thomist, would have understood
this. Leaño described a society that was starkly "less harmonious and conciliatory" than the Thomist utopia. In this sense, he demonstrated the possibility
of a Christian moral, neo-Thomist in the tradition of Leo XIII's powerful writing, yet incapable of evading the radical implications of class conflict.

Pilgrim and Soldier: The Paradox of Social Catholicism

The previous section has examined the forms of Catholic sociology as the delegates to the 1906 National Catholic Congress constructed them. Analysis of

the congress reveals a model of society, and a conflict over how to apply the model, as well as how to diagnose the fundamental aspects of the social question. In 1906, the social Catholics were unable to resolve the fundamental contradiction of their time: how to confront class injustice while avoiding class warfare. In this sense, Nicolás Leaño's rejoinder to Faustino Rosales was the most important moment of the congress. The congress had provided a model for studying the problems of the day, and Leaño argued convincingly that without concerted, active efforts, sociological contemplation was of little use. The only thing missing was a proposal for public action, a model of political practice. In fact, social Catholicism was already outfitted with a blueprint for political action. This model was the pilgrimage, and it would become central to the construction of a mobilized, intransigent, combative Catholic identity.

The pilgrimage is a trope that gives millenarian significance to the Catholic quest for a society united in harmony with Christ, or in opposition to liberalism. Many of the Guadalajara delegates had considered the role of pilgrims in modernity, which was a topic of discussion at the 1904 congress, held in Morelia. For social Catholics, the pilgrim embodied the attributes of a Christian citizen that belonged to an idealized society articulated in the terms laid out in 1906 at Guadalajara. First, as we shall see, the pilgrim was a man, the public figure or head of the Catholic family. The family, in fact, did not yet appear in this narrative of the pilgrimage. Although this view was changing, it still privileged the domestic over the social as women's and children's place. The pilgrimage was characteristic of civil society, a space restricted to men. Second, the pilgrim did not engage in class struggle, but in religious struggle. Through this lens social Catholics preserved the hope that the principal struggle of modernity would unite men across the barriers of social difference, against a common enemy, the liberal state with its supporters.

A future bishop of Zacatecas and San Luis Potosí, Canon Miguel M. de la Mora already understood this better than most. An early champion of Catholic sociology and social action, he attended the 1904 Morelia congress, the 1906 Guadalajara congress, and later belonged to the Guadalajara section of the Operarios Guadalupanos, where he collaborated with Nicolás Leaño and Miguel Palomar y Vizcarra.[70] His description of modern Christian pilgrimage is important on several accounts. First, he pays careful attention to local culture; second, he combines religious and martial symbolism; and third, he frames the description in the language of theological writing, such that there is no clear line between the religious and the social. Written on the eve of the Mexican Revolution, his thoughts on pilgrims and their place in society do not yet reveal themselves as political, but a modern reader cannot help but pick up on the political potential that inhabits this piece of writing:

> It is the first hour of the morn, the hour when jubilant life awakes amidst a teeming activity that translates into warbling and trills, into vague sounds and crystalline murmurs, into playful breezes and delicious aromas. The sorceress of twilight has turned over in the sky's Eastern region all the amphorae of her varied and brilliant colors, and has lit with a burning flame the tatters of cloud that float over the distant crests of the blue mountains, as if she wanted to prepare a splendid canopy and sumptuous Arch of Triumph for the King of Light who approaches.
>
> At that hour so fresh and so beautiful, an unusual army leaves the little town of X. . . . They are two hundred horsemen, who march two abreast, forming companies of ten each under the guidance and leadership of a corporal. At the forefront marches a Priest, radiant with jubilance, not without martial bearing; and to the right of the tonsured Chief advances the standard-bearer who carries in his callous laborer's hands, in the guise of a military pennant, an image of the Holiest Virgin Mary, Refuge of Sinners. . . .
>
> What does this so very unusual army mean? If you want to know, please accompany the novel soldiers along these pleasant and peaceful fields, of red dew-pearled sunflowers and simple Santa Maria flowers, of penetrant and agreeable perfume. Fear not, the peace will not be disturbed by men armed with rosaries and combatants whose war cry are the praises of the Mother of God, sung in hearty and resonant voice.
>
> Behold them: they arrive at the parish seat and enter by the modest streets, their lips keeping the deepest silence, more remarkable for the noise produced by their steeds' hooves, when treading the rough cobbles.
>
> On reaching the parish temple, all, in answer to a signal from the General, that is, the parish priest, dismount, and leaving the horses in the care of their companions, each company advances on its knees, first through the atrium, and then along the sacred pavement of the house of God, to the main altar, luminous as a glowing ember, by the multitude of long wax candles, and graciously crowned by the beloved Refuge of Mary.
>
> Beside the altar awaits the parish priest, attired with a white, crinkled surplice and with a golden-tasseled stole. The priest's bearing is grave and solemn, since he has to attend in the name of God himself, a serious and transcendental ceremony. Finally, the first company arrives, guided by its

corporal, at the foot of the holy altar, and there, those men of the countryside, accustomed to every kind of danger, with neither fear in their hearts,
nor respect for the enemy, bow their heads, and before heaven and earth,
escorted by an invisible cohort of angels that joyfully contemplates that
sublime picture, in the worshipful presence of God, whose minister represents him visibly, they promise to abstain for two or three years from alcohol that poisons the body and debases the soul, and they promise with the
aim of glorifying the Holiest Virgin Mary, their tender Mother, honoring
the name of Christians, to give good example to their families, and cooperate in the holy reform of social customs. All the companies follow suit.

If you were to remain in the temple a few more hours, you would see
these villagers return, after having left their horses in the house of some
neighbor or in one of the town's inns, to confess their sins and confirm
with a fervent communion their formal promises of men who know not
how to break their word.[71]

Thus Miguel de la Mora begins his reflection on the importance of sociology, offering a master narrative constructed with a utopian language and rhetorical technique that belong to the formation of a Catholic imaginary. This is
not—could not be—the anonymous reflection of a parishioner, although it
could belong to a sermon. But in this case it was a speech delivered to the participants of the 1910 social seminar, held in Mexico City at the end of Porfirio
Díaz's regime.[72] It is of interest because of its literary composition and because
it constructs a particular representation of the parish, of the flock, and of Catholic identity.

The opening paragraph uses a literary technique different from that of the
following paragraphs. This reflects the author's training as a theologian, in
particular within the neo-Thomist renovation. It has two notable aspects. First,
contrary to philosophy, the theological demonstration begins with God, from
the pinnacle, and proceeds downward toward nature, the human realm.[73]
Thus, De la Mora begins with divinity and proceeds toward humanity. Second,
the knowledge of God is achieved through reflection about created beings.
Therefore, the metaphysical point of departure is the sensual experience of
material objects. The colors, aromas, and breeze, the warm light of morning,
the warbling and trilling (*trino* in Spanish, a double entendre alluding to the
Holy Trinity) of the birds: the reader is supposed to feel the natural world and
inquire what this is all about. How is it that it exists? Who was its creator?
From here the reader is to wonder about the Being who is His own existence,

whose essence is to exist.[74] Thus, de la Mora takes the reader from the sensual to the providential: the sorceress of twilight prepares an arch of triumph for the King of Light.

De la Mora wrote with meticulous style, organization, and choice of content. His insistence on God as a point of departure for every social reflection is characteristic of neo-Thomism, and of social Catholicism in general. In the tradition of Pope Leo, De la Mora *instaura en Dios*, establishes in God, his representation of Catholic society and sociology. The King of Light illuminates an anonymous town that could well be metaphoric, even as De la Mora places it in the archdiocese of Guadalajara. Although there is little chance of clarifying the authenticity of the narrative, the ambiguity of this chronicle/allegory ought not to distract the reader. The narrative probably has greater historical transcendence by contributing to the construction of a utopian Catholic imaginary, than by recovering the extraordinary daily life of an anonymous village.

When the author shifts his attention from God to village, the narrative changes, from a providential to a martial language. The Holy War metaphor is common in the writings of this period of reconquest in opposition to the expansion of secular liberalism. Here the horsemen march in company; a corporal directs; the general is also the parish pastor.[75] Another priest forms the vanguard; his bearing is martial. A standard-bearer who is both soldier and peasant accompanies the corporal. His calloused hands identify him. He carries the banner of the Holiest Virgin, prefiguring Zapatistas, Villistas, and Cristeros. However, although only five months separate this narrative from the appearance of Zapata's armies on the historical stage, the Marian army of Canon De la Mora belongs to another era. This is because the social Catholic imaginary has yet to confront the dilemma of civil war. This army of peace makes war with rosary in hand to the shout of "Hail Mary, full of grace."

De la Mora's martial language acquires meaning through religious images. The site of struggle, the battleground, has a dual location articulated by the phrase "social customs." On one hand, it is external, belonging to society; on the other, it is internal, of the being-soul. The general barracks are situated at the parish church; there the battle plan is decided. The church, as a material and symbolic site, played a primary role in the formation of Catholic identity and union.[76] In this text the Marian soldiers are transformed into pilgrims by their arrival at the church-barracks, where they advance on their knees, humbled. Before the altar they bow their heads, and they humble themselves again. The pilgrimage conveys a special sense of sacrifice.

The pilgrim is a man. He is a soldier and laborer. His hands are callous; his voice is hearty; he is accustomed to danger and has no fears; he disdains his enemies. De la Mora uses common attributes in his construction of masculinity, and he deploys them in the formation of Catholic identity. His pilgrims, "escorted by angels," take the vows of a secular apostolate. In their abstinence from alcohol, we find another reference to sacrifice, and the first and only reference here to "the social question." After taking their vows, the soldiers confess their sins and take communion. Thus, the narrative ends with another reference to sacrifice, through the sacramental body of Jesus Christ, the Holy Eucharist.

In Canon De la Mora's narrative we find a particular construction of Catholic identity, characterized as masculine, disciplined, and committed to a cause: the reform of social customs. His soldier-pilgrims live in a society marked by social hierarchies, which they voluntarily accept when they humble themselves before the ecclesiastic authority. In the narrative there is no mention of another authority, and the relationship between the pilgrim-soldiers and the state is not clear; however, the existence of enemies who will be combated without quarter is clearly stated. Finally, the narrative alludes to Christ's sacrifice, and that of the Marian soldiers.

———

Catholic writings from the turn of the century reveal substantive change in the pilgrimage tradition. Although the tradition was ancient, millenarian, the context was novel. In Canon De la Mora's narrative, the humble suppliant is anonymous and mundane, the same as the church, the site of his supplication. Yet the martial demeanor of the pilgrims produces dissonance. José María Soto, a theology professor at the Morelia seminary, explained this attribute of modern pilgrimage in terms of changes registered in Christendom during the late nineteenth century. In antiquity, a pilgrim carried out a vow, or did penitence for particularly serious failings. By contrast, the contemporary context of pilgrimage was liberal ascendancy in the Christian world. For Soto, the critical moment was the 1870 dissolution of the Pontifical States, the loss of Rome, and the creation of a united Italy. He argued that these events formed the modern practice of pilgrimage. The difference, in terms of practice, lay in its *fin*, or purpose, and in its *significación social*, or social meaning. In modernity, the purpose of the pilgrimage was to protest, or offer public testimony. The pilgrims asked for pardon, not vengeance. "The modern pilgrim . . . will go to cry at sanctuaries for the guilty acts of others rather than for his, and invokes with his own prayers the effects of divine justice against his wayward or guilty brothers."[77] The social meaning, or context, was the emergence of "anti-Christian" governments that banished Jesus from civil society. In sum, Soto concluded, the Catholic peoples had atheist governments.[78]

The providential answer, in view of the "empire of anti-Christian governments," was the pilgrimage. Soto insisted on the public and collective character of these processions, and that they should fulfill two conditions: first, the multitude should assume a spirit of prayer, and second, it should assume a spirit of sacrifice. The prayer and sacrifice of the modern pilgrims ought to be directed towards Mary in Tepeyac, the Virgin of Guadalupe. In fact, pilgrimage, in the broadest sense of the word a collective public expression of religious conviction, worked hand in hand with the issues addressed by the 1906 Guadalajara congress. It could embrace and display the broad Catholic vision of civil society as a reflection of the family. It could also provide a mode of practice for the Catholic vision of harmony across the divisions of class. It did this by diverting attention from class conflict toward another source of oppression. Real or perceived, anticlerical government appeared as a shared enemy. But pilgrimage also generated a new state of affairs, one that would dovetail with the spirit of twentieth-century politics. And here, it departed from the basic form of the Guadalajara congress.

Pilgrimage would incorporate and mobilize masses of believers, across the boundaries of social class, gender, and ethnicity. It would provide a bridge for urban and rural—or Cathedral city and provincial parish—believers. The participants at Guadalajara had discussed the social question with little or no participation by the rural and urban poor. Their sentiments revealed an interest in social reform, but these reformers operated as an elite. The appearance of pilgrimage as a form of religious expression during the Mexican Revolution would bring a new set of voices to the table regarding the role of religion in modern life, the role of the state in regulating worship, and the practice of citizenship in the new century. Miguel de la Mora, José María Soto and others had imagined the novelty of popular piety in defense of the Church. However, it took the collapse of the Díaz dictatorship to generate a contingency in which political Catholicism emerged as a mobilizing discourse in Mexico. The next chapter asks how this happened.

3. Christian Democracy in Mexico

THE YEAR 1910 was a watershed in Mexican history. In September, the political class paraded through the streets of Mexico City, Guadalajara, and elsewhere, in celebration of the nation's first centennial. Monuments were unveiled and patriotic speech abounded. Then, on November 20, a call to revolution appeared in the Mexico City press, signed by Francisco I. Madero, the former Anti-Reelectionist Party candidate who had served time in a San Luis Potosí jail, and was by then living as a fugitive in San Antonio, Texas. His call to overthrow the government of president Porfirio Díaz did not make the watershed, but certainly it set in motion events that would change the country over the coming months and years. This is the context in which Catholics would form a political party in May the following year. Their effort should be understood as the first attempt at Christian democracy in Mexico. Although the attempt ultimately failed, it produced lasting consequences for the polity in twentieth-century Mexico. To understand it, Christian democracy must be conceptualized and understood historically.

Arguments regarding Christian democracy generally turn on a distinction between the social and the political, one that points out that the Catholic Church has always been involved in the social issues of the day, and stresses that politics are qualitatively distinct, proper to a formal—perhaps idealized—political sphere.[1] I have argued in favor of a move beyond the social action/political action cleavage, to a view that centered the transforming influence of the Mexican Revolution in collapsing this distinction so that *the social became political*.[2] More recently, my view has changed on at least two accounts. First, I had framed the argument to cover the period stretching from the Mexican Revolution until the Cristero Rebellion, roughly between 1911 and 1926. This periodization was too narrow. It failed to address the crucial years prior to the

Mexican Revolution, when Catholic laity and clergy debated the ideas set forth by Leo XIII and took the initial steps toward a practice of Christian democracy. Second, my initial conceptualization was limited by my choice of literature. I based my argument on the classic 1957 history of European Christian democracy written by Michael P. Fogarty.[3] This work had been quite influential, and continued to offer an excellent overview. Thus, I chose to model the concept of Christian democracy on Fogarty, a position I now see differently.

Fogarty cast his definition of Christian democracy in the present (the postwar twentieth century), and framed it in the language of US political history. In particular, Fogarty channeled Abraham Lincoln's 1863 Gettysburg Address, surely an inspiring moment, but not so clearly a formative moment in the history of Christian democracy. He wrote:

> It might be crudely defined as the movement of those laymen, engaged on their own responsibility in the solution of political, economic, and social problems in the light of Christian principles, who conclude from these principles and from practical experience that in the modern world democracy is normally best: that government, in the State, the firm, the local community, or the family, should be not merely of and for the people but also by them.[4]

This seems strange today, and perhaps unfairly depicts his work. To his credit, Fogarty recognized the deep historical roots of Christian democracy; pointed out its connection to the problems of the working class, as formulated in the writing of Leo XIII; and argued that the term referred to the activities of three, often distinguishable, actors: clergy, Christian Action associations, and lay movements. He also carefully grounded Christian democracy in a place, "from Flanders to Venice . . . a belt of high religious observance."[5] The link between Pope Leo and the plight of workers is important; the understanding that such practice may include a multiplicity of actors and theaters helps soften the rigid edges of the definition; and his spatial grounding gives Christian democracy a tangible, empirical space. A similar spatial grounding has been attempted for Mexico by Manuel Ceballos Ramírez, who describes a "geopolitical axis of Catholic restoration" running from Puebla northwest toward Zacatecas.[6] As with Fogarty, Ceballos Ramírez's spatial grounding is quite helpful in setting out the hypothetical parameters for empirical research.

However, Fogarty's presentist tone, coming as it did after the Allied victory in Western Europe, seems ill-suited for understanding the historical process of Christian democracy, in which democracy was a working concept rather than a given. Certainly for scholars of Mexico—I would argue the same for Europe—the idea of democracy begs to be historicized. In fact, an important point of departure is Leo XIII himself, who was uncomfortable with the term. It would be careless to assume that Mexican Christian democrats thought that democracy "is normally best," as Fogarty assumed of Europeans. Some may have speculated as much, but did so at their own risk, in uncertain circumstances. Porfirian Mexico was not a model of representative democracy, and Catholic activists were mapping out new ground as regards democracy in general and confessional politics in particular. The very notion of democracy is suggestive, demanding more careful interpretation of the forms and circumstances in which Catholics mobilized and participated politically; but it seems a stretch to speak of democracy "in the State, firm, community and family."

By linking the phenomenon of Christian democracy to a historical tradition of confessional politics, I have followed Stathis Kalyvas's recent work, which sees Christian democratic parties as the heirs to a long history dating back to nineteenth-century liberal reform movements and Catholic reaction to an emergent secular society.[7] He has been keenly interested in the confessional parties that were formed in the 1860s, always beholden to the institutional Church, and the ways they gradually became secular, rejecting clerical tutelage in favor of an autonomous Christian appeal that might more plausibly win elections. Like Kalyvas, I am interested in "the translation of religion, a supposedly premodern cleavage, into mass parties, the modern political weapon par excellence."[8] However, I am not ultimately interested in centering party politics, although they play a role in this history; I am more interested in arguing for a broader definition of confessional politics, one forged of a particular historical experience. Thus, while Mexico is surely distinct from France, Belgium, Italy, or Germany, there are important similarities as well. Foremost among them are the tensions wrought of nineteenth-century anticlericalisms, and the historical presence of papal opinion, a ubiquitous supranational interlocutor. At the turn of the century, both Leo XIII and Pius X addressed differences among catholic nationals in the many countries they shepherded, but they also sought to trace a general direction through their writings. Mexican Catholics applied those lessons to their particular historical contingency.

Like Fogarty, Kalyvas offers a working definition of Christian democracy. In this case, it is more succinctly focused on the phenomenon of party politics and identities. Kalyvas sees Christian democracy as more secular than religious, engaged in a secular political discourse and practice, and ultimately distinct from conservative parties. This distinction is, in turn, based on three elements constitutive of Christian democratic parties that are absent in traditional conservative parties: a mass organization; ties to trade unions; and concern with social welfare policies.[9] But he also sees a process of secularization, linking nineteenth-century confessional parties to twentieth-century Christian democracy.

From Fogarty, I wish to insist on understanding a series of actors that participate in confessional politics, including clergy, associations that are directly beholden to the institutional church, and laity, whose participation and forms of organization may differ in their degree of independence from the church. To this I would add Kalyvas's important insight into the differences between conservative parties and Christian democracy: mass organizations, trade unions, and social welfare policy. All of them are clearly present in Catholic politics during and after the Mexican Revolution. But I hasten to add that a historiographically grounded understanding of Christian democracy requires a definition focused on practice, rather than an abstract generalization. Like Talal Asad, I argue that Christian democracy is a modern crucible of religion and politics, and that, to be a viable analytical concept, it must be understood as a reflection of people's actions.[10] Therefore, this chapter describes and analyzes the emergence of a Catholic lay organization called the Operarios Guadalupanos, or Guadalupan Workers (OG). They were the first confessional group to grapple openly with the tension between Catholic identity and secular politics. They also clearly distinguished themselves from nineteenth-century conservative politics, by emphasizing social welfare policy and support for an incipient confessional labor movement. Finally, they may be seen as the first attempt at a Catholic mass politics, through their broad "social action" network and the role they played in the 1911 founding and local operations of the National Catholic Party (Partido Católico Nacional, or PCN).

Like other movements that emerged during the last years of the Díaz regime, the OG sought to define for themselves an independent political identity. In contrast to oppositions like Ricardo Flores Magón and the anarchist Mexican Liberal Party, the movement attempting to draw Bernardo Reyes[11] into national politics as President Díaz's vice-president, or Francisco Madero's presidential bid with the Anti-Reelectionist Party, the OG proved wary of direct participation in electoral politics. Instead, their members sat out the 1909–1910 election season, and worked instead to develop a broad network tied to local parishes. They discussed supporting the 1909 *Reyista* campaign, the 1910 *Maderista* campaign, as well as the reelection of President Díaz. And while the OG ultimately chose not to participate openly in politics until 1911, they were active in promoting what they called "social action" across much of the country.[12] A contemporary observer of these campaigns, Father Francisco Banegas Galván explained that the clergy was limited to "religious action," and as such, the laity must commit to "social action." This should consist in the application of Christian principles with the goal of attracting the masses to Catholicism through nonsacred means. In particular, he saw the importance of speaking to the needs and interests of men, as they were political subjects, and tended to be more easily influenced by the novelty of secularization.[13] In this definition, dating to 1915, one senses echoes of Fogarty's "engaged laymen" and Kalyvas's confessional organizations still beholden to the institutional church.

With the 1911 fall of Díaz, the OG and other Catholic organizations would finally opt for open political participation, and transform the locally rooted social action groups into a nationally focused Christian democracy movement articulated through the National Catholic Party. Their history is central to the definition of Christian democracy in Mexico.

Early Christian Democracy

The form, goals, and meaning of Christian democracy changed over time. As a result, one must distinguish between early twentieth-century experiences, in Mexico as well as Europe, and the mature, party-based version that came to dominate much European (and some Latin American) politics during the latter half of the century. It will also be important to clarify the concept here, in order to clarify how, when, and why it changed. Prior to 1910 Catholic activists organized locally and stayed clear of politicizing issues. Catechism was a common topic of discussion; so was the evil of alcohol; voting was only discreetly mentioned. Little in 1910 suggested further-reaching developments in Mexican politics. Therefore, I argue that the emergence of organized, confessional, party politics in 1911 was a significant departure from earlier social Catholicism as it had developed in response to Pope Leo's call to address "the social question." In short, the cycle of Mexican confessional party politics was a consequence of revolution, emerging in 1911 only to collapse by 1914, when the armies of Venustiano Carranza and Álvaro Obregón installed anticlerical military governors in the states they controlled. Nevertheless, ten years later central and western Mexico had become home to a mass movement based on religious identity and rooted in the same cities and towns where confessional party politics had been popular. But where did the term *Christian democracy* come from?

By the late 1880s, Leo XIII and other European Catholic thinkers were working with the concept of "Christian democracy,"[14] although the idea would become public currency only as of the 1901 encyclical *Graves de Communi*,[15] and then only with apparent reservation. An early formulation made by Pope Leo is found in a letter offering advice to Cardinal Manning[16] at the time of the 1889 London dock strike: "Oppose the socialists with popular Christian associations," he wrote. "It will depend on you that democracy be Christian; leave the sacristy, and go to the people."[17] This formulation seems circumstantial, yet it nicely frames the political position that would inspire postwar Christian democratic parties in Europe, whose main rivalry came from socialist parties. It also seems to foreshadow the 1891 encyclical *Rerum Novarum* in an interesting way.

There are really two recommendations present in the Manning letter fragment. The first, in order of importance, is to leave the sacristy and take to the streets; the second is to oppose socialism by Christian means. This duality belies a preoccupation that can be found in both *Rerum Novarum* and *Graves de Communi*. Leo XIII wanted to mobilize Catholicism, but he was wary of underwriting local political movements. In *Rerum Novarum*, he would develop his most famous writing on the topic of how to take Catholicism "to the streets," how priests should organize, how laity should participate, and what kind of goals were acceptable. Explicitly political goals clearly were not acceptable. Ten years later, shortly before his death, Leo XIII finally released his position on Christian democracy, in *Graves de Communi*. The text follows *Rerum Novarum* closely by tailoring its arguments toward the social, where the author asserts that no censorship may reasonably come in reaction to efforts that merely seek to make the lives of working people more tolerable, both spiritually and materially.[18] There is also, however, a warning:

> [It] would be a crime to distort this name of Christian Democracy to politics, for, although democracy, both in its philological and philosophical significations, implies popular government, yet in its present application it must be employed without any political significance, so as to mean nothing else than this beneficent Christian action in behalf of the people.[19]

The pope seemed to favor the term "social Christians," which was less likely to generate anticlerical backlash or a Catholic move toward the political sphere.[20] In fact, the whole discussion of naming is set in opposition to social democracy, which is characterized in the letter as the type of society sought by socialism. Therefore, in contrast to social democracy, the pope would have Catholics promote Christian democracy, the type of society sought by Christianity. However, it would be hasty to take from this reading that Pope Leo meant to say that movements should not be political. A more nuanced reading would be that, regardless of local government, Christian democracy might flourish as long as it was not reduced, a priori, to politics.[21]

Catholic activists in Mexico tried unsuccessfully to work such positions into their own organizing, at least until the fall of Porfirio Díaz. After President Díaz's 1908 interview with James Creelman, a journalist from the United States who wrote for *Pearson's Magazine*, there was discussion among Catholic activists and intellectuals regarding the founding of a confessional party. Francisco Traslosheros addressed the issue in writing, saying he saw President Díaz as a liar, but that in any case Catholics should take him at his word and organize politically.[22] Nevertheless, the prevailing attitude was to wait and see. Refugio Galindo wrote that, despite the admirable intentions of those who hoped for a Catholic electoral alternative, the only practical strategy was to limit themselves to encouraging like-minded men to run within the already established political channels.[23] Purportedly, there was even an elaborate plan—written by the Jesuit Bernard Bergöend and circulated among Catholic intellectuals like Miguel Palomar y Vizcarra—which laid out the foundation for a confessional political party.[24] But the Catholic conventional wisdom of late Porfirian Mexico was to bide time. The 1911 collapse of the Díaz presidency changed the political landscape, and afforded Catholic militants the opportunity to organize a confessional party and formally compete in electoral politics.

In summary, Christian democracy meant something particular to Catholic intellectuals and activists at the time, something that may be unclear and potentially confusing to modern readers. Its political genealogy stretches backward to include confessional parties formed in response to nineteenth-century anticlericalism in a host of European countries. It also stretches forward to include governing parties in many countries both in Europe and America. Stathis Kalyvas has argued convincingly that these two extremes are connected, and that Christian democracy, as a political ideology, was transformed over a long period of time. From a religious project beholden to the Catholic Church, it became secular, independent, and politically popular.[25] In Mexico, a similar phenomenon occurred on a smaller scale, in a shorter timeframe, reflecting the dynamic influence of the 1910 revolution. The role of clergy and the institutional Church was often prominent, and lay Catholic activists tended to work closely with their parish priests and a group of clerical activists from cities like Morelia and Guadalajara.

Confessional Politics

For a decade prior to the revolution of 1910, Catholic clergy and laity celebrated numerous regional and national meetings to debate what they called "the social question." These meetings set a strategy for Catholic expansion in civil society, but they also focused and coordinated trends born in the nineteenth century, like active campaigns to found new parishes, schools, and newspapers.[26] The congresses provided a forum for ideological and strategy debates, and an arena in which Catholic laity and clergy designed the groundwork for a political party. Crafting a new vision and agenda, this social catholic leadership gradually politicized the laity. From the 1903 Puebla conference, at which all "politics" were officially censored, to the 1911 launching of the National Catholic Party (PCN), these congresses pushed Mexico's social problems to the front of a Catholic political agenda. The meetings analyzed the situations faced by Indians, and by rural and urban workers; participants addressed issues of land ownership, agrarian reform, literacy, the right to strike, the family wage, and alcoholism; and they combined these social issues equally with more clearly doctrinal themes, such as the Eucharist, the rosary, and evangelization.[27] Overall, they plotted out a roadmap for social reform that touched on nearly every aspect of early twentieth-century society. As the Díaz regime dissolved in 1911, much of this itinerary grew into a political platform that was taken up—not without debate and dissent—by the PCN.

In 1909 two new lay organizations were formed, and both discussed how and when to form a Catholic political party. Each with its own leadership and territorial representation, the Operarios Guadalupanos (OG) and the National Catholic Circle (Círculo Católico Nacional, or CCN) would provide the institutional organization for the National Catholic Party (PCN). The CCN was formed by well-connected Mexico City Catholics. As early as August 1909, Francisco Traslosheros expressed fear that socially conservative Catholics of the Mexico City economic elite would dominate this group.[28] In contrast, the OG constituted a network of social Catholics organized mostly across the cities and towns of central and western Mexico, the region referred to by Manuel Ceballos Ramírez as the axis of Catholic restoration (Jalisco, Michoacán, Aguascalientes, Zacatecas, Colima, Guanajuato, Hidalgo, Puebla, and

Mexico).[29] Dissatisfied with the proceedings of the 1909 Oaxaca Catholic Congress, which was controlled by pro-Díaz bishops, six provincials met privately in Oaxaca to form a Marian study group with the idea that the social question ought to be treated through more active means— some argued openly for political participation—which they termed "Christian democracy."[30] They identified themselves with the Marian cult, used the initials OG (or OOGG to denote plurality) after their name in allusion to their secular order. Their founder, J. Refugio Galindo, was the Tulancingo doctor who organized the 1904 and 1905 agricultural congresses at the behest of Bishop José Mora y del Río. According to Manuel Ceballos Ramírez, the OG founded over 100 groups in twenty states and federal territories between January 1909 and the end of 1911, with hundreds of members, including individuals and group members such as Catholic worker circles.[31]

The backdrop for their writing, planning, and acting was the national political scene, and like other intellectuals of their day, the men who formed the Operarios Guadalupanos understood the 1908 Porfirio Díaz–James Creelman interview to be a portentous moment for national politics.[32] In fact, the OG were, in a way, as much a product of the Creelman interview as they were of social Catholicism. This deduction is possible because some future members of the OG were writing back and forth prior to the formation of the group, a circumstance that allows the historian to spy on their intentions even as they were working out their opinions, positions, and future plans. For example, Francisco Traslosheros and Miguel Palomar y Vizcarra maintained regular correspondence as of the 1903 Puebla congress. Following the Creelman interview, Traslosheros dismissed as insincere the president's indication that he would accept an opposition party in Mexican politics. Yet he suggested that Catholics take advantage of such an uncommon circumstance and form a party. A Catholic Party, he felt, could be prepared in time for the September 1910 centennial celebration of Mexican independence. It would need to line up with the official party, in support of Díaz, but perhaps as such Díaz would look favorably on it. In the meantime they could form a small and select group of social Catholics in preparation for the 1909 Oaxaca congress. There they could discretely analyze the specifics of a political party: how to promote it through the Catholic press; how to pose the issue of support for the National Porfirista Party (Partido Nacional Porfirista, or PNP); and whether to attempt to form a group of Porfirista Catholics in the federal congress, or *"ganar el sufragio haciéndolo efectivo,"* win elections by assuring a real vote.[33]

"Sufragio efectivo," a real vote: this is quite possibly the most famous phrase

of the Mexican Revolution.[34] It is not Traslosheros's, and although it is generally attributed to Francisco Madero, or even José Vasconcelos, it was also strategically deployed a generation earlier by General Porfirio Díaz, when he first
reached for the presidency.[35] Rather than look for some elusive authenticity, it
will suffice to note here that the phrase "effective suffrage," or alternately, "a
real vote," was on the lips of social Catholic activists prior to the publication of
Madero's formal attack on the Díaz regime.[36] It was a magical phrase that
signified different things to different people, and for social Catholics like
Traslosheros, it meant the possibility that one's candidate be able to openly
construct a party that faithfully reflected his ideology, in this case Christian
democracy. In short, it meant a practical transgression of the reform era laws.

Despite the official ban on Catholic political activism, the Operarios Guadalupanos openly discussed the issue in their written correspondence. By 1910,
they had developed a one-man-one-vote system for processing their ideas, and
they managed to execute this internally democratic process via letters sent
monthly from each of the dozens of groups, and funneled to a rotating, five-
man directorate that was in charge of collecting the news and data from
around the country and helping the OG president to put together the monthly
newsletter.[37] Considering the size and complexity of this task, the newsletters
are a remarkable source of information regarding the interests and operations
of this Catholic social organization. They reveal how the leadership was
elected, how new members joined or were sought and recruited, and how proposals were made, discussed, and voted on.

In a five-page, single-spaced, typewritten analysis of the papal encyclicals
written by Leo XIII, the Operarios Guadalupanos developed an explicit position regarding Church and state, and also what they called *la cosa pública*, or
political participation. In the document they embraced secularization, in the
sense of separate spheres for Church and state; they pledged obedience to constituted political authority; opposition within all licit means when faced with
state-policy encroachments on the rights of the institutional Church; and open
political participation within any and all licit means.[38] Among the debates leading up to, and the final conclusions of, their first annual meeting, held in León,
Guanajuato (1909), a proposal to field candidates for the 1910 elections was
defeated; but they pledged to work in favor of a *libertad práctica del sufragio*,
essentially universal male suffrage, and to participate in the election process by
promoting the campaigns for public office by social Catholic candidates, men
with ideas similar to their own, or preferably, men belonging to their immediate
circle of activists.[39]

The OG functioned as a vanguard association with an intense intellectual presence, manifest through their writing, and a highly decentralized structure. Activities focused on promoting social action in its different forms. Dr. Galindo, as president, preferred local cells to have no more than five or six members, and ideally less, although the OG did occasionally seek out "collective" members, particularly parish-based worker societies. As early as July 1909, cells as far afield as Oaxaca, Puebla, Hidalgo, and Chihuahua were cultivating collective memberships by incorporating mutualist societies, artisan and worker circles, some even with their own newspapers.[40] From this early point in time, two years prior to Francisco Madero's initial call for revolution in Mexico, there is a tension in Catholic lay organizing. The OG worked like a vanguard party and had already started to experiment with organizational forms that would open the movement more to the logic of mass politics. In these exercises, one can find the roots of National Catholic Party organization and success.

In 1909, the OG consciously remained on the margins of Mexican politics, although there is reason to believe that its leadership saw this arrangement as temporary. In order to securely send delicate information, the Tulancingo doctor, J. Refugio Galindo, proposed a secret code based on the number 1531, the year *Nfuz pk Wfqjbbd fsqffufe ghgpwh uij Loendo Kzdo Enhhp*. The code worked by displacing the letters of the original written statement, and replacing them with other letters according to a repeating sequence of numbers. Language to be presented in code would thus reflect the addition of one (1) letter, five (5) letters, three (3) letters, and again one (1) letter, based on the figure 1-5-3-1, or 1531. In the same way, by moving backward in the alphabet a precise number of spaces set by the key 1-5-3-1, the code became legible. So, Nfuz was read [(N-1=M) (f-5=a) (u-3=r) (z-1=y): Mary]. And *Nfuz pk Wfqjbbd fsqffufe ghgpwh uij Loendo Kzdo Enhhp* became Mary of Tepeyac appeared before the Indian Juan Diego. This event, a miracle in the eyes of Catholic believers, could be symbolized by the number 1531, the year in which it purportedly occurred. And the mystical significance of 1531 became the key to encoding secular speech, thus tying the religious with the political.[41]

Nearly 70 percent of the membership was laity, and the rest was clergy. Of the priests, a few were diocesan administrators, but most were parish priests, their assistants, or professors from seminaries and other educational institutions.[42] The OG were involved in, and promoted, social projects where they lived (or elsewhere when they were invited), but much energy was spent studying and planning. They circulated a monthly newsletter, and each member had a monthly obligation to report on his activities, generally to five of his com-rades in different parts of the country. Many wrote for local newspapers, and some were newspaper editors or owners, with circulation covering many cities, including Guadalajara, Puebla, Aguascalientes, Tulancingo, Zamora, Chihua-hua, León, Sahuayo, Ciudad Guzmán, Villanueva (Zac.), Orizaba, Cocula, and Ixtlan del Rio. Larger cities often had more than one Catholic newspaper affil-iated with the OG. Other members were involved in founding new schools, and common activity involved such issues as convincing couples living out of wedlock to marry, or protesting theater and press deemed immoral.[43] Schools, marriage, theater, and press were some of the many areas in which Catholic social teaching had clear positions. Such activities sought to strengthen the Church in modern society.

Within this broad network of activists, Guadalajara emerged as the center of the movement due to the successful organizational skills and intellectual contributions of a group of urban professionals. Miguel Palomar y Vizcarra was a lawyer and could claim family heritage; his grandfather had founded one of the first modern textile factories in the Guadalajara region in 1841. Luis B. de la Mora, Félix Araiza, and Nicolás Leaño were all engineers; Canon Miguel de la Mora was a rising social Catholic star.[44] A committed activist, Miguel de la Mora would soon become Bishop of Zacatecas; moreover, Palomar y Viz-carra was probably the most celebrated Mexican Catholic intellectual of his day. Following up on a suggestion made by Refugio Galindo, Archbishop José Mora y del Rio of Mexico City supported a proposal to have the Guadalajara group edit and publish a social Catholic magazine that was distributed across the country through the OG network. The magazine was called *Restauración Social* and was published between 1909 and 1913. In it, the Operarios Guadalu-panos and their guests debated everything from the importance of historical and religious figures like Agustín de Iturbide and the Virgin of Guadalupe, to emerging issues of social welfare, such as the family wage and just salary.[45] Within this context, the OG would be most numerous throughout Jalisco, with more than 100 members distributed across over twenty centers in as many cit-ies and towns.[46]

With the OG formally constituted, Luis B. de la Mora wrote to Palomar y Vizcarra about a chance meeting he had in Tampico with Francisco Madero, who had recently arrived from Mérida, on a tour to promote his Anti-Reelectionist Party. The theater was full, and people trailed out into the streets. There were many foreigners in the crowd, Spaniards and North Americans among them. De la Mora summarized:

His program boils down to "effective suffrage and no re-election." Although he isn't much of an orator, and he has trouble getting his ideas across, he seems as if he were an "Apostle of the Faith." I found no direct attacks against our religion, but I know his program to be firmly grounded in the Constitution.

In the eyes of this observer, only just becoming familiar with the novel presidential candidate, his charisma seemed to emanate from his commitment, his belief in a principle. Such candor was not lost on De la Mora. But his most detailed commentary was for Madero's secretary, Félix Palavicini, with whom he was even less familiar:

This gentleman has a romantic demeanor, a pale somewhat gaunt, but unwrinkled face, moist saddened eyes, his hair unnaturally long, and is of medium height. Don't picture him standing erect, no, he sort of hunches forward as if searching for something lost. This gentleman who you no doubt can imagine from the description I have given you, began talking to us of the blue beaches, of the ocean birds, of the waves that bathe the sand, of . . . who knows what more. Then he spoke of his program, always returning to the poetic form that seems most to inspire him. He attacked the government, as is accustomed of late, but I could not find a practical application for his ideas.[47]

The two come across as an eccentric couple, a far cry from the haughty statesmen a provincial intellectual might have expected. If not for Madero's "apostolic" aura, it seems likely that the chance meeting would have left De la Mora entirely uninterested. Later, De la Mora spoke privately with Madero, as both men took the same train to Monterrey, and on arrival, attended the anti-reelectionist event in the Nuevo León capital. To Palomar he later confided, "They're definitely not Reyistas; they think he will only bring about an autocracy more perfect than the one we already have. . . . Madero seems uninterested in attacking the Church; he won't touch the religious question." Madero's Monterrey hosts, however, used the occasion to speak out against "clerical tyranny," and assured the crowd that the new liberty would embrace the wealthy and the worker alike. As De la Mora took in the event, he overheard an exchange between two working-class men who were swayed by the anticlerical philippic. "You see," said one to the other, "now the friars are screwed, they'll no longer be able to limit everything to the sacristy where they used to arrange their political matters, you hear that?" De la Mora, the Guadalajaran OG, was tempted to strike up conversation with the two, but it was neither the time nor the place.[48]

Throughout 1909 and 1910, the OG studied, debated, and organized. In Jalisco, where Palomar y Vizcarra and his cohorts had several years of experience, the plans developed quickly. In Tapalpa and Arandas the first two rural credit and savings cooperatives were opened, the first toward the end of 1909, and the second in July of the following year. Known by the surname of its German inventor and propagator, the *caja Raiffeisen* was promoted by the OG as a means of combating rural usury by making cheap credit available to small holders.[49] In Mexico, its most zealous promoter was Palomar y Vizcarra. At the age of twenty-three, he was responsible for introducing the Raiffeisen cooperative to the 1903 Puebla Catholic congress; over the intervening years he had carried his message across the country and back. In 1909, the first Raiffeisen bank was founded and named for his grandfather, José Palomar, founder of Atemajac's *La Prosperidad Jalisciense* textile mill and noted nineteenth-century philanthropist.[50] The Tapalpa and Arandas initiatives were moderately successful, making loans that were used for planting, construction, and in one case to avoid foreclosure by a non-Catholic credit institution.[51]

Perhaps the key issue linking savings and credit to a broader policy of social reform was that of workers' wages. It is to that issue I will now turn.

On Work and Wages

In October 1910 the Second Catholic Social Week was celebrated in Mexico City and attended by many important intellectuals associated with social Catholicism nationally. The outstanding theme of the conference was worker salaries and the family wage. Certain common issues ran through the papers presented at the conference, among them criticism of socialism, class struggle, and the strike. Participants also tended to agree on the issue of harmony as the desired end to be sought by a policy of conciliating the different and often divergent interests in society through peaceful means. On some issues one senses, and on others one can clearly observe, tension among the Catholic intellectuals. What exactly was the family wage in early twentieth-century Mexico City? In what ways did the issue reveal divergent thinking among Catholics? What does the debate say about emerging political culture at the outset of the Mexican Revolution? These questions help to situate political Catholicism.

One of the main points of debate at the 1910 conference was the question of how to achieve a higher *real wage* for laborers. There was some ambiguity regarding the definition of the wage or salary, but a couple of examples will help define the idea that characterized Catholic thinking in the early twentieth century. Refugio Galindo, the Tulancingo doctor, hacendado, and founder of the Operarios Guadalupanos, defined a "decent real wage" as that which would permit "the acquisition of basic goods necessary for sustenance as well as moderate comfort, but not luxury." Galindo was predictably conservative in his positions and was not necessarily indicative of prevailing opinions. Another definition was posited by J. Félix Araiza, the civil engineer from Guadalajara who understood the "real wage" to cover "retribution for labor in goods and comforts to be obtained by workers in providing for their needs, striving for modest comfort, and achieving material and moral wellbeing."[52] There are similarities in the two definitions (basic necessities, moderate comfort), but Araiza goes further by appealing to the slippery goal of a wage that might assure material and moral well-being.

In any case, several distinct proposals were discussed and may be grouped in the following manner: first, social versus individual means of advancement; and second, state intervention versus market forces, with derivative arguments regarding what level of state or church intervention might be appropriate in the interest of improved salaries.

SOCIETY AND THE INDIVIDUAL

One of the most insistent proposals posed at the conference was the moral transformation of the individual through education. Some speakers, like the Guadalajara priest, Benigno Arregui, preferred to focus on the moral transformation of employers, who ought to be taught the importance of Christian charity and a healthy detachment from material luxury, so that they might improve the salaries of their laborers. For Arregui, "the wealthy [must] distance their hearts from wealth so that the poor might live free of poverty."[53] Juan Torres Septién insisted similarly, that employers ought to return to the Christian values of charity and justice in order to achieve harmony among the social classes. He also thought, however, that workers lacked "Christian resignation."[54] Others, like J. Ascención Reyes, argued that the moral degradation of the lower classes ought to be met with a concerted effort on behalf of government, the Church, and employers to campaign against the evils of alcohol.[55]

Another popular theme, inspired by *Rerum Novarum*, was the formation of lay associations. Many of the speakers present argued for the foundation of Catholic worker associations as a means toward raising real wages, although not everyone agreed on what the organizations ought to look like or how they ought to be led. Ascención Reyes[56] and Refugio Galindo[57] argued that priests, the government, and employers ought to organize worker associations, although others countered that workers needed to form their own organizations, with the support of the state. Dr. Tomás F. Iglesias saw the need for Catholic worker associations but refused to consider state intervention of any kind to assist in raising wages.[58]

Refugio Galindo saw the problem in terms of the relative difference between the nominal and real value of wages, and put the weight of advancement squarely on the shoulders of working people. Steeped in orthodox Christian social values, he echoed many of the ideas about family roles presented at the 1906 Guadalajara congress.[59] He argued that wages would stretch further if worker behavior could be altered. In his words, "the husband or head of family" must not squander money and ought to live honorably in "peace with God," while the woman or housewife should be a good administrator and instruct her daughters well so that in the future they too might grow up to be good housewives.[60] While many likely shared his sense of Catholic honor rooted in traditional family roles and values, not everybody agreed with him that such thinking would successfully avert impending social crisis. Ascención Reyes countered that workers were unable on their own to achieve the necessary improvements. He saw the working class as wallowing in vice and ignorance, and forcefully argued that both government and the Church ought to intervene on behalf of the poor.[61] Sounding a different note, Dr. Tomás F. Iglesias limited his analysis to the workplace, arguing that workers should procure wage increases first and foremost individually, by increasing their productivity and the quality of their work so as to become indispensable in their places of employment.[62]

STATE INTERVENTION OR THE MARKET?

The issue of state intervention was at the center of the debates regarding the minimum wage. Was it an appropriate way to procure wage increases? How nuanced were the different Catholic arguments? Should the state intervene directly or might it preferably play an indirect role? How could this be accomplished?

Ideas regarding the indirect intervention of the state were often vague, revealing little more than an implicit fear of state activism. Dr. Iglesias echoed conventional Church policy when he sought the just application of the law: "the law itself and State authority ought to be appropriately applied." However, he was wary of an expanded role for government, and concluded: "the State should avoid direct intervention on behalf of the increase of wages."[63] Refugio Galindo envisioned an even narrower role, in which government power ought to be indirect, limited to favoring "the abundance of basic goods."[64]

These were not the only Catholic positions on state intervention, however, and other speakers at the conference went much further in what they felt was the appropriate role of public power. Carlos A. Salas López laid out a series of proposals in which government ought to lower taxes on the sale of basic goods, limit what he called the "excesses of competition," and protect agricultural production so as to ensure lower prices for subsistence goods.[65] He also saw a role for new legislation

> to favor labor unions; to determine the proper mechanisms for establishing a minimum wage proper to each municipality as well as the maximum length of the workday; to mandate that employers establish and maintain worker insurance for accidents and retirement; to establish mandatory rest on Sundays; to deal with the problem of usury; to prohibit creditors from seizing the crops or salaries of rural laborers; to regulate sharecropping; to outlaw gambling; to all but exempt workers from taxes on basic goods and their homes; to mandate that employers build and provide decent housing for their laborers, or to the contrary provide a healthy stipend to those providing for their own housing.[66]

This position was clearly progressive, foreshadowing major social reforms that would eventually come with revolution, and generally speaking to many issues that would subsequently characterize the modern welfare state. In fact, one might go so far as to say that some of these proposals, such as mandatory housing for laborers or security for the crops and wages of laborers against what might be considered conventional market mechanisms, went even further.

Miguel M. de la Mora, a future bishop and outspoken advocate of Catholic sociology, requested time to rebut Salas López's position. He subscribed to the idea of limited state intervention, and reminded the audience that Pope Leo had established a general framework through *Rerum Novarum* and other encyclicals, arguing that state intervention should not be systematic, but should complement market forces.[67] However, Salas López was not the only speaker at the Mexico City conference pushing for greater government involvement in procuring the general well-being of working people.

Although more moderate than Salas López, J. Ascención Reyes also argued for state intervention. Any state role should be indirect, he argued. But he stressed the need to reform agricultural businesses to ensure the availability of food staples. He also called for labor legislation to protect workers and small-scale landowners and added that such policy reforms should be promoted through the creation of a labor ministry at the cabinet level that might serve as a presidential advisor.[68] In a similar vein, J. Félix Araiza called for indirect state intervention on behalf of workers through tax incentives for businesses involved in the production of food staples, higher taxes on goods deemed superfluous—perhaps along the lines of a sin tax—as well as legislation limiting the use of staple crops for the industrial production of harmful goods, such as alcohol. He also spoke to the importance of achieving greater yields on agricultural production, and improving communications infrastructure.[69]

Somewhat more marginal to the debate was the issue of Church intervention, and what role it might play in tandem with state policy. José Tomás Figueroa echoed contemporary ideas of Catholic reconquest when he criticized the slim margin in which Church intervention in society had been confined. The foundation of clergy-led lay associations, the construction of new places of worship, and the promotion of charitable institutions for the poor were a pale contrast to the type of role the Church ought to play in society. Figueroa lobbied for a new activism, defined by Church intervention in civil government in order to regulate questions like worker salaries and the relationship between labor and capital.[70] Juan Torres Septién perhaps agreed, lamenting the restriction of Church influence to the private sphere.[71]

These were big questions, ones that surely went beyond the limits of the 1910 Mexico City meeting. The privatization of religion, the institutional differentiation of Church and state, and the role of the market in determining poverty, wealth, and society's well-being: all were significant issues at the turn of the century, issues that would be reshaped by the changes wrought through revolution and civil war. But, in summary, it should be clear that Catholic activists held many different beliefs about what should be done, what was off-limits, and where change might be negotiated, legislated, or imposed. While some lamented the decline in Church power and prestige, others like Carlos A. Salas López, the Aguascalientes lawyer, saw Church activism as imprudent, and counseled a principled dialogue with state authorities in order to promote public means by which wage improvement might be implemented.[72] In a somewhat different take on the role of the Church, Refugio Galindo and J. Ascención Reyes preferred to adapt the long-standing doctrine on charity to the modern forms of poverty. Employers, they felt, should buy staple goods in bulk and sell them to workers at a discount, set a roof on corn prices, establish low-interest loan cooperatives on the Raiffeisen model, and establish everything from libraries to recreational centers and hygienic living conditions for workers. They should also provide moral guidance and actively distribute Catholic propaganda.[73] Historical evidence is scant on the role played by employers and large landowners in social reform. But while some evidently attempted to moralize and clean up workers they saw as living in degradation of their own making, mostly they seem to have shown little interest in participating in schemes promoting a corporatist utopia without class conflict.

Such exercises in social policy might have seemed abstract to some Catholic activists, living as they did outside the political sphere. But at the time they celebrated the Mexico City seminar, Francisco Madero was putting the finishing touches on his plan to challenge the Díaz dictatorship. In November he issued the San Luis Plan, calling for the president's ouster, and by the end of the year, local rebellions began to spring up across different areas of northern Mexico. Initially small in scale and local in composition, the Maderista rebels became a serious threat to political stability early in 1911. The last section in this chapter will follow Madero's revolution as it generated new possibilities for a confessional political party.

A Catholic Political Party

By March 1911, the rebellion had taken to the offensive through its myriad incarnations. In April, the border town of Agua Prieta, Sonora, fell to Maderista rebels. In Morelos, Zapata's peasant guerrilla grew. Meanwhile, Madero tried to engage government negotiator Francisco Carvajal at Ciudad Juárez, but to no avail. Carvajal simply was not authorized to negotiate the resignation of his boss, President Díaz. Then, on May 8, a breakthrough: Pascual Orozco and Francisco Villa, Chihuahuan rebels, disobeyed Madero's orders, and in an act of insubordination had their troops attack Ciudad Juárez. They fought through the night, and the following day defeated the Federal garrison that held the city. In great irony, Madero's hand was incalculably strengthened due to the insurrection of "his" army.[74]

At more or less the same time, the Mexico City Catholic lay leadership quickly drafted plans for a political party. On May 3, Gabriel Fernández

Somellera hosted a select group of Catholic lay leaders at his home with the objective of founding a political party of religious inspiration. The group decided that the organization would be explicitly confessional, the Partido Católico Nacional, or National Catholic Party (PCN). The founders belonged mainly to the Mexico City elite, though not necessarily to the Porfirian political class. Fernandez Somellera was an heir to the Martínez Negrete family, wealthy Guadalajara hacendados. Other founding members included Manuel F. de la Hoz (lawyer); Rafael Martínez del Campo; Alejandro Villaseñor y Villaseñor; Francisco Pascual García (born 1856, in an Indian village in Oaxaca, studied medicine and law); R. de la Barrera; Victoriano Agüeros; Fernando Segura; Carlos Díez de Sollano; Pedro G. de Arce; Rafael Santa Marina; Roberto Gayosso; Trinidad Sánchez Santos (born 1859, owner and publisher of the newspaper *El Tiempo*); Luis García Pimentel and Emanuel Amor (affluent Morelos sugar planters); Andrés Bermejillo; Miguel Cortina Rincón; and Manuel León. They also named an executive committee,[75] and a commission to write up the party program.[76] The initial meeting was attended exclusively by representatives of the CCN's Mexico City leadership and, according to the Aguascalientes newspaperman, Eduardo J. Correa, the entire PCN executive committee was recruited from the CCN.[77] It was a Mexico City network, and lacked representatives from the OG, the other, more clearly provincial, Catholic lay organization with national projection.

On May 5 a second meeting included several important leaders of the OG, as well as Francisco Elguero, a Morelia lawyer who was close to Sánchez Santos. Representing the OG were Palomar y Vizcarra and Luis B. de la Mora of Guadalajara, Carlos A. Salas López of Aguascalientes, and Dr. Refugio Galindo of Tulancingo. The entire group was composed of lawyers, doctors, and engineers. They put the finishing details on the party program, which was ostensibly modeled after a project drawn up by Bernard Bergöend, SJ, at the request of Palomar y Vizcarra.[78] The following day Galindo, Palomar, De la Mora and Salas, the four OG members, were charged with writing up party statutes. None of them was included in the executive committee, although two new positions were created for vice presidencies. As a result, the PCN commenced with a program formed in the image of European confessional parties, but relied on a political leadership schooled in the waning liberal Catholic tradition of Porfirian Mexico.[79] In nations as diverse as Italy, Germany, Austria, Belgium, and the Netherlands, confessional parties were already immersed in a process of secularization, and an effective split from Church tutelage. On this side of the Atlantic, activists attempted to build a "Christian social order" in revolutionary Mexico. Ultimately, however, their efforts had limited results, and were overshadowed by Vatican prudence and the construction of a revolutionary state.[80]

Composed of Porfirista, Reyista, and Maderista factions, the PCN struggled to define its political position and agree upon presidential and vice presidential candidates for the October elections. At the first PCN convention, delegates discussed three possible electoral strategies. They could either opt out of the electoral process in order to further organize the party structure, field their own candidates, or throw their support behind an external candidate such as Madero, on the logic that in exchange they would gain political favor. Madero was a realistic possibility for two basic reasons. First, because he was quite popular, and the PCN leadership was sure he would win. So, on grounds of pragmatism, the choice made sense. Second, he had made fairly explicit overtures to the Catholics. On receiving the PCN program, in Ciudad Juárez, he sent word by telegraph to the party leaders in the capital, that he considered the Mexican Catholic Party "the first accomplishment of our recently conquered liberties." He went on to point out that all points in the PCN program but one were also included in his own political platform.[81] So, on the grounds of principle, he was not antagonistic and might prove to be supportive of Catholic interests. The party convention decided not to field its own candidates, but left open the possibility of an alliance. Eduardo J. Correa put it this way: the PCN was strong enough to make a considerable contribution in the election of an external candidate like Madero, but not strong enough to field one of its own candidates and win. Thus, Madero was a pragmatic and opportunistic choice.

The voting was fairly even, but most delegates supported a ticket with Madero as the presidential candidate. The second place candidate, supported by the National Catholic Circle, was Francisco León de la Barra, the interim president. Going against its decision not to field its own candidates, the PCN decided to run De la Barra as the vice presidential candidate. De la Barra was conservative and openly Catholic, politically and ideologically close to the Mexico City–based Catholic lay leadership. However, he had also said that he was not interested in running. Nevertheless, the party leaders split their decision, adopting an external candidate, Madero, but fielding De la Barra, one of their own, for the vice presidency. Madero asked them to reconsider, and support his official running mate, José María Pino Suárez. Again, Correa's dispassionate commentary is helpful: Pino Suárez was seen as a radical liberal, whose ideas were frankly opposed to those of the PCN, and it was a stretch to suppose that the Catholic leadership could support him. In any case, the politically mature decision, Correa argued, would have been to negotiate their support for Madero's ticket in exchange for concessions that might soften Pino Suárez's influence on basic issues of interest to the Catholics.[82] After all, De la Barra had made clear that he would not be a candidate in the first place. However, Madero and the PCN both were convinced that Catholic voters would support the PCN candidates. This led the party leadership to a false sense of strength, just as it led Madero to put special emphasis on the need for a complete alliance.

———

Ultimately, anti-Madero elements among the PCN leadership made it clear to Madero that Pino Suárez was not an acceptable option and that party support for Madero's own candidacy would not be unconditional. Thus, even before the October elections, Madero and the PCN were becoming estranged. However, the elections would eventually correct these misconceptions. Madero won the presidency; Pino Suárez won the vice presidency; but the National Catholic Party also won important elections in some states. So, on one hand, Catholics did not unconditionally support the PCN, and on the other hand, the PCN ticket did win in some states. It turned out that their success was due less to Catholic unity and more to the strength of the party organization locally. This was particularly clear in Jalisco, where the Madero–De la Barra ticket prevailed, despite Madero's endorsement of Pino Suárez and despite De la Barra's stated rejection of his own candidacy.

Supporters of a confessional party were moved by the notion of social reform, by the possibility of constructing a Catholic politics, or by a combination of both ideas. Jalisco was the most successful state, but the OG and PCN were present throughout west-central Mexico. The nineteenth-century conservative debacle and the anticlerical legislation of the 1857 constitution conditioned the behavior of political Catholics, and as a result they were slow to participate openly, *as Catholics*. During 1909 to 1910 the OG diligently organized throughout the Mexico-Guadalajara corridor and beyond. But their efforts were directed outside the political sphere, and mostly self-contained within the recognized spaces of parochial life. As such they went undetected for the most part. Only in 1911 would the effects of their work begin to register publicly; and by 1912, the main areas of OG organizing would elect PCN activists, many of whom belonged to the Operarios Guadalupanos. Newspapers like *El Luchador Católico* would tap into the OG social network to drum up support for PCN candidates, get out the vote, and denounce interference or the uncivic behavior of anticlerical opponents when it threatened to obstruct Catholic politics. Such was the case in 1912 when several hundred women, *señoras* and *señoritas*, from Zapotiltic Jalisco published a letter of protest regarding several men who tried to impede the speech of a PCN candidate.[83] It is important to note here that Catholic politics became a pathway for women's participation in the public sphere, long before women became voting citizens. More generally, the call to action of *Rerum Novarum* inspired lay activists after 1900, and the issue of Christian democracy began to appear in their writing and civic practice, thus forging a political project in the emerging idiom of Christian democracy.

4.   The Limits of Catholic Party Rule in Jalisco

THIS CHAPTER EXAMINES the period of Catholic Party ascendancy and government in Jalisco.[1] It will focus on the electoral competition and party organization, the social reforms attempted by the Partido Católico Nacional (PCN) while it controlled the state legislature, and the political sphere at the margins of party politics. The national context for the chapter is the experience of the Madero administration, its eventual demise at the hands of Victoriano Huerta, and Catholic complicity with the Huerta dictatorship. Therefore, from the beginning, it is important to emphasize the heterogeneity of PCN leadership nationally. I will argue here that Mexico City leadership was distinct from that which could be found in Jalisco, and that these groups had different objectives. In Jalisco, the PCN organized a broad following that led the party to dozens of electoral victories in municipal, state, and federal elections, while in Mexico City it was not particularly successful. A prominent newspaperman argued at the time that the younger generation of Christian Democrats in Mexico City was simply ignored by the party leadership, which was restricted to an elite.[2] Similarly, the most prominent Catholics in the federal legislature disdained Madero, and worked systematically against the Maderista deputies.[3] In the judgment of one historian, the PCN fraction of the federal congress was "composed of novice politicians and directed by wealthy aficionados of public office."[4]

By contrast, the PCN-controlled Jalisco legislature worked with Madero to force the Porfirista interim governor, Alberto Robles Gil, to comply with electoral law and set a date for the gubernatorial elections in 1912. As a result, the local press, even the liberal press, was critical of Robles Gil for his foot-dragging, while recognizing that the PCN won elections due to better organization than the liberal parties.[5] In the federal legislature, where the Mexico City leadership held sway, most of the PCN deputies supported their Porfirista colleagues against Madero. By contrast, in Guadalajara the anti-Maderistas were grouped around Robles Gil, while the PCN used government to enact social reform.[6]

The success of the Jalisco PCN belongs to the Madero period, to the political opening that Madero created. His liberal policies favored political competition, and the local contingency of west central Mexico favored the PCN. Within this regionally defined context, the argument of this chapter is that Jalisco offers an example of what political reform looked like at the margins of social revolution.[7] In Morelos, peasant communities mobilized around basic survival issues like access to water and woods.[8] In Chihuahua, the former military colonies went to war to reclaim land and privileges that their ancestors had won and their parents had enjoyed; they saw recent encroachments on their liberties as a violation of their families' basic rights.[9] Jalisco neither offered such dire circumstances, nor such extraordinary popular insurgencies. To be sure, political strife in Jalisco could be intense, and it would grow in violence with time; but it was still basically political. The Jalisco PCN represented one possible formula for a transition from the Porfirian dictatorship to a form of liberal democracy. The party was not Porfirian; it was arguably more akin to a modern political party, perhaps the first in Mexico. It organized municipally, albeit through the parish organizations; it articulated its campaigns through local representatives; and it debated issues prior to the elections. This local experiment was eventually interrupted, swept away by much larger forces, and Jalisco became one of several arenas in which a civil war was fought by large armies that crossed the country. However, during 1912 and 1913, the Jalisco PCN organized, competed, and governed. There was also rebel activity in Jalisco, most notably Julián Medina's army, based in northwestern Jalisco, in the proximity of southern Zacatecas and the Tepic Territory. As in 1911, this region was rebellious in 1913. But most of the state was relatively quiet, save for banditry, and in Guadalajara a popularly elected government and state legislature provided stability.

The main historical legacy of the PCN is its collusion with the Huerta government following the military coup in which President Madero and Vice President Pino Suárez were assassinated. In Mexico City, the PCN leadership provided a veneer of legitimacy to the coup during the crucial months following the ascendancy of Victoriano Huerta as head of state. Gabriel Fernandez de Somellera, the PCN president, was a supporter of Felix Díaz, the nephew of the deposed dictator and a party to the coup. Eduardo Tamariz, the lawyer from Puebla who rose to prominence in the PCN leadership, was openly pro-Huerta. The catholic newspaper, *El Pais*, openly supported the coup; Tamariz and the Morelia lawyer, Francisco Elguero, financed the paper, and Elguero's son, José, was the editor. All three served as Catholic Party congressmen, and Tamariz eventually took a cabinet position in the Huerta administration. When the Huerta government fell, they abandoned Mexico for exile.[10]

In the words of historian José C. Valadés, Huerta had engaged in "political theater," mainly interested in buying time, and perhaps the added measure of legitimacy that the PCN all too willingly provided.[11] But an equally important legacy, one less well known,[12] is that of western Mexico, where a stretch of towns from Zamora in the south to Aguascalientes in the north, were the center of a reform-minded PCN movement that did not support the coup. Jalisco was at its center. These two forces coexisted uncomfortably and eventually split, destroying the party prior to the effective fall of the Huerta regime.[13] How did the PCN get there? How did an organization that started out looking a lot like the first modern political party in Mexico end up the unhappy prop to a dictatorship? Why did it disappear in 1914, almost as suddenly as it had appeared in 1911? What kind of popular support did it have? Were there anti-Huerta elements in the party? All of these questions are important, because the PCN was founded in one political moment, became successful in another, and was destroyed in yet a third moment, all within a three-year period.

The Electoral Success of the Jalisco PCN

In western Mexico, the National Catholic Party grew out of a network of local movements loosely characterized as *acción social*, or Catholic social action. The 1891 encyclical *Rerum Novarum* gave them inspiration, Guadalajara archbishop José de Jesús Ortiz promoted them, and as of 1909, the Operarios Guadalupanos gave them an efficient organizational structure. In this manner, acción social shaped the National Catholic Party in western Mexico.

A basic narrative of who, what, where, when, and why regarding the party only emerged in the 1990s, through the discovery and publication of Eduardo J. Correa's 1914 manuscript, *El Partido Católico Nacional y sus directores*. Correa was born in Aguascalientes in 1874, and studied in the local seminary before moving to Guadalajara to study law in the 1890s. He was old enough so that he worked briefly as a lawyer back in Aguascalientes prior to the fall of the Díaz regime.[14] But Correa was drawn to journalism, and worked in Aguascalientes, Guadalajara, and Mexico City, running several different newspapers, including the official Partido Católico Nacional press, *La Nación*. As a PCN militant, Correa wrote on the editorial page of the country's main Catholic newspaper. He was also elected to the lower house of congress, the Chamber of Deputies, in 1912 and 1913, each time representing the city of Aguascalientes. This is noteworthy because the first of these two elections belonged to the reform period of president Francisco I. Madero, but the second was held after president Madero had been deposed and assassinated in February 1913. The fact that Correa, the Catholic activist, was a friend of Madero, is one reason why his memoir is so interesting.

The book is a hybrid document that combines memoir with a chronicle of the many people and circumstances that accompanied the party's brief rise and fall from prominence. The chronicle is often punctuated by the inclusion of documents that Correa either had in his possession or had access to through *La Nación*. Correa wrote feverishly in the summer of 1914, as the country sank into civil war, hoping to explain the debacle and signal out for reproach those leaders he saw as responsible. The ending is portentous, a narrative of impending violence and doom. But Correa is quite clear in recognizing that Venustiano Carranza and José María Maytorena, the rebel leaders from Coahuila and Sonora, were acting within the law when they refused to recognize the Huerta government. In his opinion, the revolution had not started as an anticlerical affair, but had developed as such in response to the irresponsible acts of political jockeying that a few members of the Mexico City party leadership had committed. At the close of the book, Correa lapsed into the first person, as if dictating a letter to his future readers: "I write these lines even as alarming news arrives regarding terrible injustices committed against defenseless priests and laity in Zacatecas, Monterrey, Saltillo and Tepic." And yet, he unsparingly included a healthy list of clergy who had opposed the party and obstructed those who were committed to reform, cutting himself short by saying that he could name hundreds more.[15]

———

The PCN represented the first attempt in two generations to create a national political organization. Nevertheless, the PCN was built on a regionally specific movement, in which Guadalajara was at the center of one of the best organized, most active parish networks. In other words, its strength locally was not an effect of the PCN per se, but rather that the PCN-Jalisco was characteristic of a circumstance particular to the archdiocese. For this reason, any serious assessment of the PCN must take into consideration the contribution of its regionally based components. Moreover, if Correa was right in his observation that the PCN was the strongest and best organized in Jalisco, then it makes little sense to draw conclusions based only on the actions of the party leadership in Mexico City.[16]

Although the party leadership was often middle-class, urban professionals, and some even came from an economic elite, the PCN candidates did not emerge from the Porfirian political class.[17] The social composition of the group was more heterogeneous than has often been supposed, and there is also evidence of participation in local leadership by men of modest origins, from sharecroppers to brickmakers, as was the case in Mezquitán.[18] Party leaders and rank and file struggled against local caciques in rural Jalisco. In fact, contrary to Quirk's assertion that the "high Church" leadership dictated all, Eduardo Correa wrote in 1914 that important members of the Guadalajara Archdiocese had opposed the PCN from the very beginning. Among them, he named Fathers Antonio Gordillo, Ramón López, Luis Silva, and Faustino Rosales, all members of the Archdiocesan *cabildo*, or governing council.[19]

The elections of 1911 and 1912 constituted a unique political experiment in Mexican history, and in general, may be recognized as one of the few great contributions of the Madero period. In the case of Jalisco, the PCN records were preserved by Miguel Palomar y Vizcarra, and offer ample evidence that the party was building a network of support stretching across the state. To be sure, not all was a clean break from the patron-client practices of the Díaz regime: in Ciudad Guzmán, the party had ties to career politicians, while in Cocula, the local hacendado, Carlos L. Corcuera, rounded up the personnel on his estate and had them all go into town to vote for the Catholic Party. Such examples offer a glimpse into rural Mexico's traditional sociabilities; but they are but one aspect of a complex social phenomenon that requires a more nuanced explanation.[20]

Alongside the corporatist practices of rural power brokers, the seeds of a mass organization were sown throughout the state of Jalisco. In town after town, local PCN groups pleaded for printed copies of the party program and statutes, of speeches delivered by party leaders, and of Palomar's writings on rural credit institutions. Local activists from the villages wrote letters to the Guadalajara leadership asking its advice regarding innumerable matters, even as they debated how best to confront other candidates and local caciques. By June 1911, the party had established eighty-one local offices in county seats (*cabeceras de canton*), municipalities, factory towns (*colonias industriales*), and parishes across the state.[21] However, the party was not well organized everywhere, as its activists' letters sometimes indicated.[22] Laura O'Dogherty has argued for 1911 that the PCN had a harder time organizing in mining towns and Indian villages.[23] Moreover, organizing the party was often quite difficult, as is poignantly expressed in a letter sent by a PCN activist to Palomar y Vizcarra. The author had been recently jailed for his political activity. On release, he left the lakeside town of Cajititlán to develop support for the party in San Cristóbal de la Barranca, near the Zacatecas border. There, he found himself in precarious territory:

> I often cover long distances on foot in order to reach the ranches here, as traveling on horseback is difficult. I have found myself traversing the river on foot, my clothing all bundled up on top of my head so as not to get it wet. On more than a few occasions I have been at risk of falling from a cliff, you see, here the footpaths run through canyons and more canyons.[24]

The fact that the villages were mobilized for elections in the first place was noteworthy, because Porfirian elections had not only been fixed, but were often a complete fiction. François-Xavier Guerra has cautioned that the Porfirian electoral system followed a very different logic, and reflected a different power structure than that which was on display during the 1912 Maderista elections.[25] During the Díaz regime elections were not an exercise in popular sovereignty, but a ceremony celebrating the successful implantation of a politics of official candidates. In such circumstances, only the cities and larger towns might actually have ballot boxes. The inmates at the local prison might be in charge of filling out the electoral ballots. Voters might show up to find their votes already made for them. Such examples were fundamentally different than the 1912 elections, because they reflected a system in which there was not supposed to be political pluralism. The Maderista elections, to the contrary, revealed a diversity of actors. Even so, Guerra estimates that average voter turnout was about 12 percent nationally, and as high as 50 percent in the center-west, the region with Guadalajara at its center.[26] The variation between 12 and 50 percent is wide, and Guerra does not offer a more detailed explanation; but certainly this data suggests the importance of local factors. The most important of such factors in Jalisco may have been the breadth and success of local PCN organizing.

Between the summer of 1911 and the end of 1912, Jaliscans were called to vote on six separate occasions. During this fourteen-month period they voted for: (1) president and vice president; (2) mayor; (3) the reestablishment of the twenty-third state congress (partial term); (4) both houses of the federal congress; (5) governor; and finally (6) the twenty-fourth state congress (full term); as well as new municipal governments. This new public, civic competition was evidently popular, but no parties had any sort of statewide organizational infrastructure. Political parties, in a modern sense, were as new as the concept of electoral competition. Porfirian political campaigns had been carried out via a candidate around whom small support groups formed for a few months and then disappeared until the next elections. On occasion they might publish a newspaper briefly, before the elections. The newspaper that supported Manuel Ahumada during the 1906 gubernatorial campaign first appeared a few months prior to the elections, announcing itself as the official campaign newspaper. After the elections the newspaper disappeared.[27] All told, it was published for six months.

Although there were no established parties, the PCN organized very quickly across the state. Such organization was unheard of and was possible for two reasons. First, the Catholic Church had a statewide presence, maintained through the network of parishes. But the diocesan network could work as a double-edged sword. For example, when party activists from Guadalajara made the trip out to Mascota in western Jalisco, they were pleased to find a well-organized social base awaiting the arrival of PCN leadership. Here the local workers' society, a parish-based association, had existed prior to the call for elections, and accepted the PCN as a collaborator.[28] The town of Tototlán, near Guadalajara in central Jalisco, offered a similar situation. There the local priest, Donanciano Rubalcava, greeted the party delegate and called a meeting of the parish workers' circle. More than 120 attended and took on the commitment of organizing the PCN local there.[29] By early 1912, the party could circulate a printed questionnaire in order to better understand whether local sympathies would support an independent candidate such as José López Portillo y Rojas for governor.[30]

Nevertheless, a Catholic political campaign was a novel idea, and not all parishes, or priests, were ready for it or accepting of it. Located in the highland region northeast of Guadalajara, Tepatitlán was quite active on the many issues of social Catholicism, and would be a bulwark of the Cristero Rebellion after 1926. But during the PCN era, the lay leaders seemed to regularly come up against the opposition of local priests. In 1912 the Workers' Society decided to enlist the support of a "capitalist" who would be restricted to caring for the financial aspects of the association. They had first solicited the sponsorship of their pastor, who read the society statutes and responded, "You each will have a voice and a vote, but when I speak you all will obey."[31] The group, with 200 membership pledges, decided that it was preferable to seek moral authority among laity, rather than give up their just rights as members. The leaders, who belonged to the PCN, realized they would likely lose a part of their membership, but were unwilling to turn over autocratic control of the organization to the local priest. Two years later, one of the same party leaders sought the removal of the pastor after he tried to impose his own list of candidates for the upcoming municipal elections:

> We were studying the possible candidates for the city government, and a prominent member of the party appeared. Without explanation, he turned over a piece of paper with a list of names that he said would be our candidates. One of the committee members said that they would be subject to discussion, and if they prevailed, the committee would have no problem supporting them. At that, the prominent party member snapped back that he had not come to have his list discussed, but to have it accepted. This generated a commotion among the committee members. . . . [Then], the member who had brought the list revealed that the parish priest had summoned him, handed him the list, and told him that these were the candidates that he willed. The majority of the committee members, except for three, were opposed to proceeding in that manner, and . . . when the priest found out, he became so angry that he said he himself would contact the state party officials and ask them to authorize him to form a new committee, obedient and submissive before parochial authority. . . . Fortunately the national leadership decided to abstain from participating in the elections, and things calmed down. . . . No comment.[32]

Evidence of open conflict is rare in Catholic sources during the revolutionary period, and is overshadowed by the many cases of collaboration between clergy and laity. In the artisan village of Tonalá, the local pastor supported the PCN but, as in Mascota and Tototlán, this was an extension of social theology developed prior to 1911. In a letter written to state representative Miguel Palomar y Vizcarra, he shared his analysis of the problems facing workers, many of which were common to reformist thinking of the period. The litany included the dangers of socialism, usury, liquor, faulty parenting, and laxity of devotion; but also included problems in the areas of production, quality control, and basic social services. He was careful to point out that such ills were more often the effects of poverty rather than a lack of faith on the part of the artisans that lived in this potter village. And instead of simply pointing out the problems, he went on to offer a list of remedies, including local savings cooperatives and public workshops with collective storage facilities for pottery and materials, as well as family conferences on Christian sociology. He was adamant in linking the problems of the workplace with those of family life.[33] Such commentary is valuable in part because of the interlocutors, a local pastor writing to an elected politician serving in the state legislature. But it is also helpful because of the mixture of analysis and proposals offered, ideas that should push historians to think beyond the comfortable categories of left and right or progressive and conservative.

The second reason the PCN organized quickly was that social action campaigns had included the laity in parish-based organizations, and created new communication and contacts across the archdiocesan network where they had not existed before. Guadalajara archbishop José de Jesús Ortiz had had a favorable attitude toward social action as well as the parish reform mandated by the 1899 Latin American Council in Rome, in which he had participated.[34] So by 1911, the step from Marian Congregations, social study circles, worker circles, health care services, and moral theater, to a political campaign, was not an impossible leap. Such collaboration was facilitated by the Operarios Guadalupanos, who had founded local groups in 1909 and 1910 across the state, and who maintained constant communication through their newsletter as well as the monthly magazine, *Restauración Social*, both of which promoted social issues and the National Catholic Party. By 1911, members of the Jalisco OG traveled across the state as party delegates to bring their ideas and organizing expertise to the towns and villages. As a result, new recruits formed local party organizations alongside study circles, schools, savings cooperatives and newspapers, such as *El Luchador Católico*, a weekly founded in 1912 by the Ciudad Guzmán chapter.

Such efforts continued following Huerta's coup, suggesting that local conditions were the driving factor for the Jalisco PCN, rather than the vagaries of national politics. Following the fall of Madero, a Tenamaxtlan delegate reported on local struggles with outsiders "agitating" for agrarian reform.[35] In nearby Ayutla, another activist complained that the party's primary political enemies were also the town's most important citizens, supporters of Porfirian favorites like Félix Díaz and Alberto Robles Gil.[36] Further east, in the mountain town of Tapalpa, J. Encarnación Preciado wrote Palomar y Vizcarra in

1914 to suggest they develop an agrarian reform policy to include the parceling up of large haciendas, in exchange for long-term indemnification of the owners through a system of bonds paid by those who would receive land.[37] These issues and positions are to some extent contradictory, but they offer a complex mosaic of the different political views housed at the local level in Jalisco, and emphasize the gulf between accounts of PCN involvement in the Mexico City coup against Madero and the issue-driven local politics of provincial Jalisco.

Despite many problems, the Jalisco PCN was better organized than its opposition, and in Guadalajara this was most clear. The October 1911 presidential race offers a good example. Madero and Pino Suárez were not chosen in direct elections, but by an electoral college. In other words, votes were not cast for candidates, but for parties. And in each electoral district the parties had to have a representative to cast that district's vote. This was a complex system, which included 216 districts (or precincts) in Guadalajara alone. Prior to the election, the PCN published and circulated a list with the names of every elector in the city. In 211 districts (97.7 percent), the PCN was able to field electors. The names on the list are local, corresponding to people living in each and every neighborhood. A voter, hypothetically, would find his district on the list, recognize the name of his neighbor who was the party representative, and get the party line from him. The elector would be the party's official at the balloting place where the neighbor would have to vote.[38] The speed with which the party assured its presence across the city is surprising, but even more so is that the system actually worked. It is unthinkable that the PCN would have been able to create such a presence without the parish structure, because it provided a system of identifying traditional authority figures. This, for one, explains why de la Barra swept Jalisco: voters did not have to deliberate over candidates, but choose their party's elector. The electors would vote for them.[39]

Atemajac, for example, was a textile mill located to the north of the city. It was an industrial colony, and 1,500 "souls" lived within the factory walls according to the 1907 archdiocesan census.[40] It is highly unlikely that all adult men at the factory would have been PCN supporters, because the labor force included a group of liberals who competed with the Catholics for worker loyalty. However, the PCN did have a local group within the factory. This is evident due to a brief, formal letter written on a plain piece of paper without letterhead, and dated September 2, five weeks before the elections.[41] At the top of the page, the words "PCN Center in Atemajac" are written. In it Primitivo Salazar and Leonardo Cisneros, president and secretary of the local Center, referred to a rally held at the factory in which Palomar y Vizcarra made a speech. They wrote to ask him for a copy of the speech. As the election approached, Mr. Salazar's name appeared on the list of municipal electors, the Atemajac representative, a local authority figure with ties to the party structure and its leaders.

Even so, PCN organizing was not always successful, for a variety of reasons, including resistance from preexisting political groups often in the form of cacicazgos, patron-client networks underwriting the power of a local boss, or perhaps a hacienda owner. During the November 1911 mayoral elections, for example, Catholics lost most of the races. I have argued above that the party was not well organized in some towns, but there were also cases of voter intimidation by local caciques. In Tamazula, for example, PCN activists were jailed when they went to vote, and the liberal opposition spread the word that other Catholics that attempted to vote would be jailed as well. Another form of intimidation consisted in using the local tax office to fine PCN supporters arbitrarily.[42] In Tapalpa, the Catholic Party candidate won, but was promptly detained by a group of his opponent's supporters. In this case the parish priest, Jesús Hueso, was able to use his authority to negotiate the release of the detained candidate.[43] In correspondence, Catholic activists expressed frustration with the way the elections were manipulated, but dismissed it as their own lack of experience. Instead of protesting the outcome, the Guadalajara leadership decided to prepare for the January 1912 state congressional elections ten weeks later, in hopes of guaranteeing that the balloting would be unhindered. This time they won all twelve seats in the Jalisco legislature.

Although the Jalisco PCN became quickly successful in terms of electoral victory, voter intimidation continued to be common. During the June 1912 elections for the Federal Congress, many reported abuse at the hands of local bosses or political opponents. In Tamazula, which had previously reported problems, the local cacique organized roving bands of armed thugs, and announced that voters would be conscripted into the army. As a result voter turnout was under 10 percent. Still, the PCN only lost by a slim margin. In northwestern Jalisco, the June congressional elections were not held in Hostotipaquillo, because the municipal president, Julián Medina, refused to allow the balloting places to open. By contrast, in the highland town of Tepatitlán, where the PCN governed, the municipal president was suspended from office, and a group of supporters including his son was thrown in jail on the eve of the elections. Four months later, the Guadalajara leadership had successfully negotiated the liberty of the jailed activists, but the ex-municipal president had yet to be informed of the "crime" for which he had been thrown out of office.[44]

The cases I mention above all went against the Catholic Party, but surely voter intimidation could go both ways. In at least one case, such charges were leveled against the Catholics. In the highland town of Arandas, Dr. Marcelino Álvarez, the liberal candidate, demanded the elections be nullified after the PCN received 80 percent of the vote. His claim was that the Catholics had coerced voters by warning them that they would incur divine punishment were they to vote against religion. The PCN representative, Dr. José María Martínez, denied the charges, and as Alvarez offered no proof, no further action was taken.[45]

Catholic Social Reform in Jalisco

European movements, such as the *Volksverein* (People's Union for Catholic Germany) and the Belgian Catholic Party, greatly inspired the intellectuals who gave form to the party in Jalisco.[46] The Belgian experience with Christian democracy was of particular importance because they had governed their nation for a generation. One propaganda sheet that circulated in Guadalajara early in 1912 made a rational appeal to the moderation promised by the Catholic Party. Asking rhetorically whether the public worried about a PCN-inspired inquisition, it informed that when the Catholics rose to power in Belgium they had promised to surprise the world with their moderate policies, and for the past twenty-seven years, they had kept their promise. "This is what the Catholic Party proposes in the [Mexican] Fatherland!"[47] No doubt the PCN propagandists also found enticing the thought of governing for the next two or three decades.

But Catholic intellectuals like Arnulfo Castro, SJ, and Palomar y Vizcarra were not convinced that the party could achieve the desired social reform on its own, and sought means to promote a social Catholic alternative parallel to, but not necessarily controlled by, the party.[48] Palomar and others looked to the Volksverein, with over 700,000 members in 1912, as a potential model for constructing a national movement.[49] They expected the PCN to legislate in favor of working people, both rural and urban; but they did not believe that was enough, and emphasized the need for a broad nonpolitical movement to win the public over to supporting social reform. Although a social movement of national proportions did not accompany the expansion of the PCN, the foundation of a regional movement was laid as much through social Catholic organizations like the OG as through electoral party politics. "Catholic opinion was being mobilized," during the Madero regime, and "in certain quarters, Catholics displayed a lively social conscience and an eagerness to grapple with social questions in a constructive, 'progressive' fashion."[50] Herein lie the roots of Catholic mass politics.

Grappling with social questions took different forms, and to appreciate the breadth of the Catholic experiment, it is necessary to consider state government and its legislative initiatives as well as local interlocutors, their dilemmas, and responses. Formal or legal social reform started in the state legislature, where the Catholic Party swept the January 1912 elections, and proceeded to target the elections and education. First, legislators changed the electoral laws by adapting a measure of proportional representation. That is, while controlling every seat at the state legislature, the PCN passed a law to ensure that they would never again do so. As a result, in the elections for the twenty-fourth state congress, although the PCN again won all the races, it could only control ten of twelve seats. The other two went to liberal opposition candidates.[51]

Second, the education reform created an official channel for the state government to recognize studies completed at private schools. This was a delicate matter, as it affected a basic aspect of Mexico's nineteenth-century liberal reform, the doctrine of educational freedom. In Mexico, education was understood as *laica*, or laicized, to the extent that it disregarded or dispensed with religious instruction. This notion was central to nineteenth-century secularization that aimed to separate Church and state. It was developed through the writing and legislation of liberal statesmen like Valentín Gómez Farías, José María Luis Mora, Ignacio Ramírez, Melchor Ocampo, Benito Juárez, Justo Sierra, and Gabino Barreda, men whose contributions spanned the century. In the 1857 constitution, the concept of educational freedom dictated a break with the Church monopoly in education and teaching, and an opening for private schools as well as a public education system, neither of which existed up till that point.[52] The way the law operated in the early twentieth century was through state sanction of diplomas. In this context, diplomas issuing from Catholic schools were not recognized.

This Jalisco reform has been described in the historiography as cynical or opportunistic, because it ostensibly permitted PCN activists to obtain recognition for their Catholic school studies.[53] But this assessment is unduly harsh. Evidently Catholics were the primary beneficiaries; most private schools continued to be Catholic, and seminary-based education was common across the nation. However, in a long interview given shortly before his death, Miguel Palomar y Vizcarra recalled that the congress recognized the diplomas issued by "protestant" schools as well.[54] In all, the state congress recorded 171 individual cases in which privately issued diplomas were validated between August

1912 and June 1914.[55] Those receiving validation in Guadalajara for their studies came not only from around the state of Jalisco, but also from Aguascalientes, Colima, Michoacán, Tepic Territory, and as far away as Puebla and Morelos. Women made up seven cases, while the rest were men, a telling reflection on the extent to which the formal political sphere was at once a boys club, but also finally fair game for pioneering women.[56] Their efforts may be understood as a clear rejection of the doctrine of separate spheres. Among the wide-ranging list of Catholic institutions, there were also individuals who had studied at the Colegio Internacional and Escuela López Cotilla, evidently not Catholic schools.[57] Finally, among many individuals whose names ring no bells, such liberal notables as Enrique Díaz de León, future dean of the Universidad de Guadalajara, and Silvano Barba, future governor, also took advantage of the reform, further suggesting that it was not simply an inside favor among a new political elite.[58]

In any case, the language of the law was meant to limit the role of the state in education, by relegating government authority to the task of setting minimum academic standards that ought to be followed by schools, and to authorizing diplomas to be issued. Without doubt, the main practical change was that the anticlerical content of public schools would be weakened to the extent that parents could enroll their children at Catholic schools without worrying whether their studies would be recognized. Uniformly, the PCN legislators voted to approve petitions made by those who had studied at Catholic schools, and the two opposition legislators voted against such petitions.[59]

But the signature legislation of 1912, submitted in early April, referred to the *bien de familia*, or homestead. The bill was written by Miguel Palomar y Vizcarra, the Guadalajara lawyer who had tirelessly promoted the establishment of savings and loan cooperatives for the poor. At that time, even *La Gaceta de Guadalajara*, no fan of confessional politics, remarked on the importance of the bill.[60] A sub-committee chaired by Manuel F. Chávez made some changes, and presented a legal opinion along with the revised version that became law in September. Palomar and Chávez studied the Homestead Act of the United States of America, and a similar law adopted in France. In addition, they studied and compared the application of the US legislation in nine different states.[61] Based on these wide and varying experiences, they wrote the Jalisco legislation to fit local exigencies and idiosyncrasies.

Basically, the bien de familia was a legal status open to anybody of limited resources, and its objective was to protect and insure the family home. The homestead was inalienable, indivisible, and could not be lost through foreclosure. By extension, it was also antiliberal, as it interfered with the so-called free play of the market. It was exempt of all property taxes for a ten-year period, an attractive incentive that was added to encourage families to save, to accumulate capital. Any head of household could establish one; a married woman could, for example, without the consent of her husband. Once established, it could not be terminated by the same individual, or by any other without the consent of all those who had gained rights through the homestead. For example, a farmer who established a homestead to protect his piece of land could not then opt out on his own, or against the opinion of his family. This included the children, who were family members. Contrary to the orthodox definition of family that was developed at the 1906 Guadalajara Congress,[62] Chávez and Palomar argued for a more flexible definition: "any group of people linked by kinship ties, regardless of the origin or grade of these ties, that live in the same home or under the guardianship of one them, who is in charge of feeding and caring for the collective needs of the others. Mexican nationality was not requisite to establishing a bien de familia, and the authors hoped it might attract immigration from countries in America and Europe. Nor was it tied to a husband, or even a mother, but to a theoretical head of household. Chávez argued in the legal opinion that wherever there is a family, there ought to be the possibility of a bien de familia. In this spirit, an aunt or uncle that had taken in relatives, a brother or sister who acted as the primary caregiver to younger siblings, were also eligible. A parent who had two families could have two homesteads.[63]

The only real condition was a nominal situation of poverty; nominal in the sense that many impoverished Mexicans were not going to be eligible due to the extent of their poverty. For those who could not establish a homestead, this law offered no solution.[64] But it was aimed at a sector of the population that did exist, and its goal was to help them avoid catastrophic circumstances that could ruin their possibilities of survival as property owners. The more people who owned property, the authors reasoned, the more Mexico would prosper. In this sense, the aim of the bien de familia was to create or foment a class of small-scale property owners who might eventually strengthen a middle class. Towards this end, the homestead was not limited to rural property, but recognized that an urban factory worker or artisan ought to be able to assure his o her family's home.[65]

There were limits placed on the value of the homestead, and they varied according to whether it was rural (a house with land for cultivation), or urban (simply a house). Agricultural laborers of any sort could establish a homestead worth up to nearly 4,000 pesos, including the value of the house, land, tools, and animals, while the urban homestead could have a value of 1,500 pesos. On this issue Chávez wrote that he was not convinced that such arbitrary limits were satisfactory, but that he did not see a more sophisticated way of proceeding. It would be preferable to take into consideration the extension, the value and quality of the land, the population, the number of family members, local economic conditions, the capital of the founder. Unfortunately, he noted, that would mean having statistical data that simply did not exist at that time.[66]

One problem in particular inspired this legislation, and that was the widespread existence of usury. In particular, rural families faced recurring financial situations that made access to credit necessary. Whether due to the weak "moral" character of the male head of household fond of drinking or gambling, a work-related injury, an illness, or a bad harvest, rural life was precarious. There were no rural banks, and the cost of credit was prohibitively high. Often such tribulations pushed the rural poor to borrow money at extremely high interest rates, a last resort that was in itself all too often disastrous. This was the context for the bien de familia, and for the one basic innovation that Palomar introduced to the general guidelines used in the US and French legislation: the rural savings and loan cooperative, or caja Raiffeisen.

In Palomar's mind the two should work together to do away with usury and promote the prosperity of a class of petty landowners. The homestead could not be mortgaged or foreclosed on, so in effect it created a dilemma: those who claimed such status for their capital could not borrow, because they had nothing to mortgage, nothing to offer as collateral. The Raiffeisen credit cooperative was the answer to the dilemma. These small-scale lending institutions could only lend to their shareholders. If the loans were circulated only among the members, there was no incentive for usurious interest rates. The loans were modest, as were the interest rates, and the equally modest profits were fed back into the cooperative. In 1912, there were still few such cooperatives in Mexico, and the homestead law was designed to give them a legal framework in which to expand.

Since 1910 three such cooperatives existed, one in Hidalgo, and two more in Jalisco, located in Tapalpa and Arandas. Following the homestead legislation, three more were opened, one in December 1912, at the highland village of El Refugio; a second in February 1914 at the southern town of Ciudad Guzmán; and a third in March 1914 near El Refugio, in the municipality of Tepatitlán.[67] All of the cooperatives were founded under the guidance and authority of the local priest, who was seen as a moral guide who would assure the integrity of the institution.[68] Of the five, three cooperatives were opened in Los Altos, the highland region northeast of Guadalajara, and the other two in southern Jalisco. However, Tapalpa is the only case in which reference is made to the founding of homesteads in addition to the credit cooperatives. There, a local catholic activist named José Encarnación Preciado actively promoted the bien de familia reform, referring to himself in correspondence as a "Maderista utopian," in memory of the president, who had been recently assassinated.[69]

None of the five Jalisco cooperatives remained in business after the summer of 1914, victims of the violence and general insecurity that swept the state with the arrival of Obregón's army and the civil war waged between Carrancistas and Villistas. For three years following the arrival of the Carrancista army, no such activity was attempted. Generally speaking, social Catholic initiatives would not begin to flourish again until after the adoption of the 1917 constitution. Then, eleven cooperatives were founded between 1920 and 1925, the first case consisting of the reopening of the one at El Refugio. By 1922 four cooperatives had formed a confederation.[70] Although data is generally scarce, most were founded using José Encarnación Preciado's Tapalpa model, and they all disappeared during the Cristero Rebellion. After 1930, a new institution would appear, the "caja popular," inspired like its predecessors, by the notion of Christian credit, and organized in association with the parish priest as the authority figure capable of ensuring the integrity of the institution.

In retrospect, social Catholicism to 1914 was both strong and weak because of its utopian, perhaps millenarian, pretensions. There can be no doubt but that the movement mobilized many, and made a lasting impression. But it also seems that some of the most interesting, most progressive policies and projects of the movement were unrealistic, and ultimately failed. This is the case with the homestead. Perhaps had the PCN governed during the span of a generation, like the Belgian Catholics, government legislation and Catholic social policy would have developed more evenly, and initiatives such as the homestead would have been successful. As it was, these reforms were out of step with the enormous social commotion of the times. Nevertheless, they drove PCN organizing for two years, following the election of Francisco Madero.

The political philosophy of the National Catholic Party was summed up most simply, perhaps, by a satirical handbill written by Guadalajara attorney Agustín Navarro Flores under the pen name T. Tumbo, which when spoken means something like "I knock you down," te tumbo. The propaganda sheet appeared around the city in early 1912 amidst the political wrangling between liberal supporters of Governor Robles Gil and the Catholic Party–controlled state congress. Offended by the raucous politicking of the liberals, whom he referred to as a jacobin mob, T. Tumbo responded, "El Partido Católico evoluciona, pero no revoluciona," the Catholic Party is for evolution, not revolution.[71] Robles Gil, a liberal, had been dragging his feet to avoid scheduling the gubernatorial election, despite the fact that Madero had placed a sixty-day limit.[72] The time was up, and the Catholics, who had recently swept the state congressional contest, had little faith in the governor's intentions. While Palomar y Vizcarra lobbied the Federal Congress at Mexico City with Winstano Luis Orozco, the liberal newspapers branded him as a traitor to Jalisco for having carried the conflict beyond local jurisdiction. The Robles Gil faction organized a public protest against the Catholics at the state legislature, which nearly dissolved into a riot. Wary of anarchy, the Catholic state legislature confirmed deeply rooted fears as they confronted *la porra*, the crowd.

This formula, evolution as orderly progress, was commonplace among the PCN leadership, and revealing of the party's conservatism. Miguel Palomar evoked these ideas in support of his homestead act, *el bien de familia*, concluding that it would have better results than the revolutionary program of handing out expropriated lands.[73] It was not simply a reaction to the times, but rather a political ideology born of Catholic social theology and its practice in Mexico. The same caution was written into every page of *Rerum Novarum* (1891), where Leo XIII spelled out eloquently his reservations regarding liberal society and socialist opposition movements. Rather than condemning socialism outright, *Rerum Novarum* reflected on what caused workers to seek out radical solutions, and recognized the deep injustice of their lives. Although Leo XIII was clearly against such radical alternatives, he recognized that the socialists were responding to a very real and painful circumstance, and he proposed an alternative. Fifteen years hence, Guadalajara attorney Manuel F. Chávez had addressed the 1906 National Catholic Congress in much the same tone. The revolutionary path was born of desperation, and therefore ultimately destructive, even though it was born of real unsolved problems and people's just desires. In response, the Catholic path must be evolutionary: edifying and ultimately constructive.[74]

The Huerta Coup, 1913

The decisive event of the Maderista revolution was the military coup in February 1913 that led to the assassination of Francisco Madero and José María Pino Suárez. Victoriano Huerta orchestrated the coup, following a barracks uprising on February 18 near Mexico City, in which Bernardo Reyes and Félix Díaz were freed from prison and attempted to oust the president. During the uprising, Bernardo Reyes was shot and killed outside the presidential palace on the Mexico City zócalo. That evening Huerta and Díaz conspired with the US ambassador, Henry Lane Wilson, as their witness.[75] The president and his cabinet were arrested, along with General Felipe Ángeles, and the president's younger brother, Gustavo. Later that night Gustavo Madero was murdered, and on the twenty-second, Huerta had the president and vice president shot.[76] This series of events signals the close of the Madero period, but it also sets into relief the aspirations of his reformist presidency, the modest changes that were achieved, and the brutal backlash ultimately provoked by the 1910 revolution.

After the coup, general Huerta formed a government that received diplomatic recognition from twenty-eight states, including Great Britain, France, Italy, Germany, Norway, and China.[77] United States foreign policy precedent called for recognition, and out-going US president William H. Taft (1909–1913), who was no supporter of Madero, might plausibly have granted it. But following the coup, and the swearing-in of Woodrow Wilson two weeks later, the new foreign policy broke with tradition and pressured Huerta to schedule elections in which he would not be a candidate.[78] Huerta initially tried to negotiate, bribe, or buy support from conservatives in order to shore up his government. His army controlled as much as 80 percent of the country and was strengthened by the addition of Pascual Orozco, who joined the coup in February, even as Venustiano Carranza, Francisco Villa, Álvaro Obregón, and Emiliano Zapata came out against Huerta. During the spring, the Federal Army fanned out across northern and southern Mexico in response to a growing state of rebellion in Sonora, Chihuahua, Coahuila, and Morelos. Meanwhile, the United States pressured and postured from Washington as well as from warships in the Gulf of Mexico. Rebel victories along with US diplomacy combined to pressure Huerta. In response he deployed large armies against the Constitutionalist north and forced Morelos villagers into concentration camps or shipped them off in cattle cars under the guise of military conscription.[79]

In Mexico City, where there was no rebellion to tend to, Huerta sought and received the support of the *Porfiristas* as well as some Catholic Party leaders. But from the beginning, he had to cope with the stature and popularity of Félix Díaz.[80] In Jalisco, Huerta had the support of accomplished politicians such as José María Lozano, Alberto Robles Gil, and José Lopez Portillo y Rojas.[81] Yet Guadalajara was further removed from the traditional center of national politics, and his efforts at recruiting support for his government garnered only some of the potential endorsements that might have been available. In this western capital, barely a month after the murders of Madero and Pino Suárez, local notables formed under the banner of the Independent Liberal Party in order to promote a ticket with Félix Díaz for president and Francisco León de la Barra for vice president. The initiative was not hatched by the Catholic Party, but by a regional elite that had prospered during the administration of Porfirio Díaz and had received the Madero presidency with generally ill will. Yet they did not flock to Huerta's side. Thus, when the group printed its manifesto calling for political stability, the list of signers read like the directory of the Casino Jalisciense,[82] including members of the Ahumada, Álvarez del Castillo, Corcuera, Cuesta Gallardo, Pérez Verdía, and Campos Kunhardt clans, among hundreds of other signers.[83] Amado Aguirre, an early supporter of Coahuila governor Venustiano Carranza, and a future general in the Constitutionalist army, commented on the situation in his memoir. Regarding the manifesto, he wrote:

> Among the signers one finds every element of the highest professional intellectual caste, high commerce, [and] industry . . . ancestral conservatives some, known moderates others, and many who may be considered not only liberal, but even radical . . . [as well as] some notable masons.[84]

But he added that in Jalisco, following the assassination of the president, virtually nobody knew who Carranza was; and the press, regardless of political tendencies, tended not to take him seriously. In these rare circumstances, conservatives, moderates, and liberals rallied around the candidacies of Félix Díaz and Francisco León de la Barra.[85]

By summer, dogged by political and military opponents, Huerta exiled potential rivals such as Félix Díaz and Felipe Ángeles. The break with the Felicistas was no surprise, as Huerta had begun to purge his cabinet of Díaz supporters as early as April. One by one, Alberto García Granados (interior secretary), Manuel Mondragón (war secretary), Jorge Vera Estañol (education secretary), Toribio Esquivel Obregón (finance secretary), and Rodolfo Reyes (justice secretary) were all forced to resign, leaving Huerta to surround himself with loyalists. By September, Huerta had entirely replaced his cabinet. Meanwhile, he skirmished with the Congress, where there was a heterogeneous opposition comprising Maderistas, Felicistas, and other anti-Huerta congressmen. On September 17, Huerta and the Congress sparred over the nomination of Catholic Party leader, Eduardo Tamariz, after Huerta swore him in as education minister without constitutionally mandated congressional approval. In this instance, the Congress forced Huerta to backtrack, voting more than five to one against the nomination, which was dropped.[86]

After this incident, congressional attacks on President Huerta grew more frequent and more direct. Belisario Domínguez, the senator from Chiapas, was a particularly vehement critic, publicly referring to Huerta as a traitor and accusing him of the Madero and Pino Suarez assassinations. When Domínguez disappeared on October 8, Congress demanded the president assure the safety of its members and threatened to move its sessions outside of Mexico City. Domínguez was shot on the tenth, while Huerta dissolved Congress, arresting eighty-four of its members initially, and another twenty-six the following day. The Catholic Party congressmen were conspicuously absent among those arrested, with the exception of José Martínez Rojas (Chiapas) and Carlos Vargas Galeana (Guanajuato). Thus, by mid-October 1913, Huerta had distinguished himself as a military dictator, and the political party least affected was the PCN.[87] However, PCN relations with the Huerta government were uneven, and there was a clear and growing rift within the party.

Following plainly fraudulent elections marked by widespread abstention, Huerta reinstated the Congress.[88] He chose the congressmen who would participate, and generally assigned them to electoral districts. Although most Catholic Party congressmen were not reseated, some were, including José Elguero, editor of the pro-Catholic daily *El País*, Francisco Pascual García and Eduardo Tamariz. Perhaps the most important example of Catholic Party collusion with Huerta was, in retrospect, that of Tamariz, who had already shown his willingness to play by the new rules. A member of the PCN executive committee, he accepted Huerta's offer of a seat in the reinstated legislature, as well as the honor of inaugurating the new Congress.[89] This decision was not broadly popular among the PCN, as the comments of Correa and Francisco Traslosheros make clear. Correa referred to the inauguration of an "illegitimate" Congress by Tamariz as a disgrace, and wrote that as a result common people would reasonably assume that the Catholic Party had committed itself to Huerta, a position Correa rejected.[90] When Tamariz left the Congress to serve Huerta as agriculture secretary in early 1914, Traslosheros wrote Miguel Palomar y Vizcarra from Mexico City to complain, saying that Tamariz neither asked for nor was given PCN central committee permission to take a cabinet post. In his opinion, the situation was not all bad, because, on the one hand, the PCN was avoided the task of denying permission, and on the other, Tamariz's behavior ought to come as a timely wake-up call to several in the PCN leadership.[91] In retrospect, one would have to consider the "wake-up" too little too late, but it is important to point out the dissent that existed openly in the PCN at the time of the Huerta administration.

Beyond the Congress, Huerta clamped down on the press as well. *La Nación*, in Correa's mind, grew in circulation with respect to other newspapers like *El Pais*, *El Independiente*, or *El Imparcial*, because it was independent, and avoided the pro-government line of the others. After *La Nación* published critical editorials, Huerta arrested its editor, Enrique M. Zepeda, along with the president of the National Catholic Party, Gabriel Fernandez Somellera. Both men were locked up in the military prison at San Juan de Ulua Island, off the port of Veracruz. Weeks later, Fernandez Somellera was released and exiled to Spain. Traslosheros reported that prior to his exile, he received death threats.[92] Subsequently, Zepeda was also released, *La Nación* was enjoined to resume publication without its former editor, and cautioned to avoid stories critical of the regime. This too, Correa wrote, was a serious error of judgment on behalf of the Catholic political elite. It was unjustifiable that the paper publish under the threat of censorship exemplified by the exile of the PCN president.[93]

Huerta's *golpe de estado*, the assassination of the president and vice president, and the establishment of a military dictatorship in Mexico City were a watershed. In that moment of crisis, however, three responses emerged: armed resistance; alliance with the Huerta regime; or a course of political opposition within the preexisting order. In the Plan de Guadalupe, Venustiano Carranza argued that constitutional order had been destroyed by the coup, and therefore, the only possible opposition was armed resistance. Chihuahua was a good example of this logic. There, Madero's governor was brutally assassinated and the hacendados went on the offensive against the Maderistas: there was little or no room for a political solution. Moises González Navarro saw the contrast with typical common sense:

> Jalisco had one third the land mass of Chihuahua and five or six times the population; across the state one found towns with telephones, telegraph and police, moderate fortunes were numerous and the property was well-divided, a "soft feudalism"; there were relatively few Yankees to injure middle class pride, and few enslaving overseers like the Spaniards of southern Mexico. Jalisco, therefore, produced neither a Pascual Orozco, nor Zapatas, nor the flags of nationalism.[94]

Contrary to the situation in many regions of the country, in Jalisco things were less polarized, while at the same time they functioned with a degree of independence from Mexico City. The Carrancistas eventually prevailed militarily, and they set the terms of the earliest historiographical interpretation of what transpired. With an enduring policy of anticlericalism, historical actors as well as historians generally adopted their position: political opposition was tantamount to support for Huerta. But at the time, in 1913, Carranza's victory was far less obvious. Political opposition by way of upholding the institutions that were established during the Madero administration did not automatically mean capitulation to Huerta.

One must ask what Huertismo meant, in practical terms, in a state like Jalisco, with a tradition of political conflict vis à vis Mexico City. The Jalisco Maderistas did not suffer the fate of their comrades in Chihuahua. Huerta was from Jalisco, but he did not have a strong following there. Nor was there a clear-cut hacendado class that opposed the Maderista reforms, as was the case in Morelos or Chihuahua. In Jalisco, unlike Morelos, there were proportionately few autonomous Indian communities.[95] Instead, there was a fairly solid urban middle class, made up of professionals and merchants. It filled the gap left by the ousted Porfirian political elite, and while Madero did not universally satisfy it, neither did it feel bound by Huerta. There was also an agrarian middle sector, basically a rancher society oftentimes of plebian origins, and there were few large estates comparable to those of the north, and few Indian communities comparable to those in the south.[96] Haciendas and pueblos existed, but they were not nearly so polarized in Jalisco as in other parts of the country.[97]

The emerging political class was not familiar with Carranza, and Obregón, who would eventually occupy the state militarily, was unknown. There was some support for Félix Díaz, and more perhaps for Francisco León de la Barra; there were enclaves of armed support that followed the cue of the northern rebels, and there was the Catholic Party, which controlled many municipal governments and the state congress. It had also hoped to control its civilian candidate to the governor's office, with limited results.[98] Only in 1914, when Governor López Portillo y Rojas was called to Mexico City to take a ministerial position in Huerta's cabinet, did the military dictatorship become an unavoidable, daily reality in Guadalajara. It was then that General José María Mier was sent by Huerta to take charge of the governor's office and the Western Division of the Federal Army, in preparation for the probable advance of Obregón's rebel army.

The Jalisco PCN was convinced that a political solution was possible, and that it was preferable to a renewed civil war. In the end the armed rebellion prevailed and, in Correa's words, the National Catholic Party was consumed by the revolution. But this was not yet clear in 1912 or even in 1913, and Jalisco was a staging ground in which the political transition seemed convincing and successful in the short run. Nevertheless, it is important to note that the PCN participated as a modern political actor. Its limited experience with legislative reform did not suggest theocratic radicalism, but democratic republicanism. They were democratic in their attempts to mobilize society in support of their political movement, and republican in their use of state power to guarantee a minimum plurality in Congress and a minimum wealth for society's less fortunate. It is also true that a priority of the national leadership was to repeal the anticlerical articles of the 1857 constitution. The only step taken in that direction by the Jalisco PCN was the education reform, which permitted those who had studied in private schools to have their studies recognized by the state. Ironically, Protestants as well as Catholics benefited from the reform; so did liberals like Enrique Díaz de León, not just Catholic Party cronies. Moreover, and perhaps more significant, there was no organized effort to do away with the political separation of Church and state.

So ultimately, how conservative was the PCN project? Robert Quirk thought that the PCN reforms were radically conservative: "If successful, [they] would have completely destroyed the liberal system and substituted it for a polity based on the teachings of Leo XIII."[99] This is overstated and ahistorical. PCN leaders were obviously in disagreement with the anticlerical reforms of the Juárez period, and in parts of the country they found solid popular support. But there was also a traditional liberal component to Mexican politics, and it was visible even in Jalisco, the PCN bastion, during the Madero period. It is more realistic to suppose that, were the PCN to have lasted for more than three years, it would have negotiated its policies with liberal parties and constituencies as well. For the same reasons, it is instructive to recall, the revolutionary state would not unilaterally impose its project. As recent historiography has shown, it would be obliged to negotiate.[100]

Any Catholic political project was attempted in a radically different context in 1912 than prior to the nineteenth-century liberal reforms. In Jalisco, the PCN represented a gradual, or controlled transition, which took advantage of an unexpected democratic *apertura*, and combined it with a moderate program of social reforms. The Catholic movement of 1911–1914 did not depend on a foreign army, but upon the organization and votes of a highly mobilized, if ultimately regional, Mexican citizenry. It was neither illegitimate, nor treasonous in origin. Its illegitimacy emerged largely from the political tactics, imposed by its Mexico City leadership, of attempting to endure the constitutional crisis caused by the assassinations of Madero and Pino Suárez, instead of repudiating the coup directed by Victoriano Huerta.[101] This view was shared by Maderistas within the PCN, such as Eduardo J. Correa, who wrote time and again to Palomar y Vizcarra lamenting the unprincipled pragmatism of the PCN faction in Mexico City that supported Huerta. In a letter written soon after the Huertista coup, a disheartened Correa wrote, "Will our party sanction something unjustifiable?"[102]

The Mexico City PCN leadership was ultimately unwilling to maintain a middle path between the Constitutionalist armies of the north, whose revolution it feared, and Huerta, who seemed to promise order. In its path toward political self-immolation, it dragged along those who had built the party in other parts of the country. Correa felt that this flaw led the party leadership to set aside its principles, ignore the reasons for the Constitutionalist insurrection, deny the legality with which Carranza refused to recognize an illegitimate regime, and finally, confer a veneer of legitimacy on the regime by participating in the Federal Legislature. Citing the Plan de Guadalupe, Correa wrote that the Constitutionalist rebellion was not born antireligious, rather it became that way in response to the PCN. The PCN leadership thought Huerta would quell the rebellion in the north, and this made it easier to abandon its principles. Due to the shortsighted political decisions of the party leadership (Gabriel Fernández Somellera, Eduardo Tamariz, Francisco Elguero and his son José, Francisco Pascual García, José Villela, and a few others), Correa sensed that all of Mexico's Catholics would suffer: "The revolution is going to triumph, the Party is condemned to death, and an unheard of persecution is let loose against the Church and its faithful."[103]

The Christ the King Pilgrimage, 1914

This chapter has been focused on the National Catholic Party, but the underlying discussion is about the limits of political space and discourse in the early years of the Mexican Revolution. The variables were many, from the difficult transition under President Madero, to the tensions within the party, to Huerta's coup. Given this context, it makes sense to ask what the margins of the political sphere looked like in 1913. Another way to put it is to ask what happened to Catholic politics with the demise of the Catholic Party. What did political practice look like beyond the formal space of party politics?

The fall of the National Catholic Party has recently been set into relief against the January 1914 consecration of Mexico to the Sacred Heart of Christ. This event, conceived a year earlier through a formal petition to Pope Pius X, culminated with a series of public marches on January 11. They were not explicitly linked to the Catholic Party, nor were they necessarily controversial or overtly religious.[104] But the difference between the way these public displays of popular sentiment were executed and received in Mexico City, Guadalajara, and elsewhere, helps explain the varying levels of tension that existed between political Catholics, government, and anti-Huerta rebels. General Huerta's reaction to the proposed marches also provides a telling counterpoint to the way they were understood by Jalisco governor López Portillo y Rojas.

Laura O'Dogherty has explained the 1914 Christ the King marches as a logical move toward an alternative form of political action characteristic of an environment in which formal institutional politics is no longer reliable. The marches, treated at the close of a chapter on the fall of the Catholic Party, appear as a tactical, perhaps even desperate, move in a context of narrowing opportunities.[105] This view supposes that political action beyond the party was secondary, derivative of practice in the formal political sphere. It makes sense in the framework of O'Dogherty's work, which is specifically on the rise and fall of the National Catholic Party. But it looks somewhat different when placed in the broader context of Catholic politics during the revolutionary period, because the Catholic social movement existed prior to the advent of party politics. Political action beyond the party is the very logic of social movements, but moreover, in this case, the party grew out of the social movement. This pattern is true for Mexico City, and much more clearly so for Jalisco. O'Dogherty concludes, correctly in my opinion, by stressing that the PCN failed the way Madero did, unable to function as a civil political alternative amidst revolution. She emphasizes that the rebel armies of Álvaro Obregón and Manuel M. Diéguez did not find the Catholic Party on arrival at Guadalajara in July 1914, only the intransigent opposition of the parish associations. In the last part of this chapter, I want to build on this general historiography, with special reference to the contributions of O'Dogherty.

The January Christ the King marches gave new form and meaning to the ancient custom of Catholic pilgrimage. As I argued in chapter 1, new thinking about pilgrimage followed the nineteenth-century dissolution of the Pontifical States, and surfaced in debates among Catholics prior to the Madero revolution or the birth of the National Catholic Party. But only after the 1911 fall of president Díaz did the faithful begin to mobilize around themes that were at once religious and political. As political theater, these marches were scripted in the idiom of the Mexican Revolution and marked the emergence of a contentious new Catholic identity with a more combative tactical repertoire. In Mexico, mass politics was born of revolution, and became the privileged form of twentieth-century politics. Thus, much has been written on how revolutionary state-builders organized masses in order to create new political actors.[106] More recently, historians have also demonstrated how state agents and masses negotiated the political. This change of significance, to paraphrase Jesús Martín-Barbero, should prompt us to avoid the notion that mass politics is external to the masses, subverting or acting on the popular *from without*. Mass culture and its countless political expressions manifest potential always already *within the popular*.[107] In the context of the 1914 marches, we can take Martín-Barbero's comment on mass culture as a suggestion that we think not only about the archbishop's motives, but those of the pilgrims who marched. What were they doing? How would the march fit into a broader series of events in which they would eagerly participate? The 1914 marches may have served some conservatives as a desperate gambit when the possibilities of party politics slipped away; however, the marches were made significant by those men, women, and children who were involved. In this sense, they symbolized the beginning of a new practice of militant Catholicism, the practice of pilgrimage as public witness.

Political Catholics adapted the idea of a formal politics through the 1911 foundation of the National Catholic Party, but by 1914, militants had pushed the practice of mass public witness beyond party politics.[108] In this sense, the 1914 marches offer robust empirical evidence for the argument that politics and religion may not be analyzed in a vacuum, but were intertwined and significant precisely because they were inseparable. It is worth mentioning here that the initial idea for the march seems not to have been confrontational, and for the most part the marches were celebrated without incident. The fallout subsequent to the marches was a result of the conflict that occurred in Guadalajara; it was local in origin, but would have national repercussions in more ways than one.

Prior to the marches, and formally beyond the political sphere, the Mexican bishops had requested that Pope Pius X consecrate the Americas in the name of the Sacred Heart of Christ. On November 12, 1913, Pope Pius X accepted the request, and in Mexico, masses of thanksgiving were scheduled for January 6.[109] In Guadalajara, Orozco y Jiménez published his second pastoral letter on December 18, with the exclusive objective of addressing the coming celebration.[110] All of this transpired within the conventional channels of institutional

Catholicism, beyond the corridors of the state, and within the expected modes of institutional behavior that had been established and rehearsed during the late nineteenth century.

In addition to the consecration, a conventionally religious event, groups of Catholic laity in the capital and elsewhere planned silent marches in order to draw attention to the escalating civil strife in Mexico and as a call for peace. The Mexico City march was launched from Manuel Tolsa's famous equestrian statue to King Charles IV. The marchers walked, evidently in complete silence, to the cathedral, where a mass was offered in the name of peace. Similar events were carried off without a hitch in Puebla and Oaxaca. In some accounts, there is confusion over whether such an event contravened the nineteenth-century reform laws prohibiting the public celebration of religious worship. The Catholic historian Antonio Rius Facius privileged events in Mexico City and its Episcopal hierarchy in his history of the ACJM[111] As a result, he focused on the care taken in avoiding confrontation with local authorities. In the Mexico City march, the silence of the participants and the restriction of the mass to the Mexico City cathedral both suggested an effort was made to avoid a confrontational or clearly religious use of public space. In Puebla and Oaxaca the marches were similarly prudent. Guadalajara was distinct, though; in the western Mexican capital the march was overtly religious and confrontational.

Francisco Traslosheros, longtime friend and pen pal to Miguel Palomar y Vizcarra noted the difference between Guadalajara and other cities. Writing from Mexico City, Traslosheros felt no need to disguise his anxious enthusiasm. In an edgy letter on the worsening political situation, he recalled the intensity of daily emergency meetings due to the imprisonment of PCN president Gabriel Fernández Somellera, and La Nación editor, Enrique Zepeda. Still, he added, paraphrasing Tacitus with self-conscious irony, "such activity is always preferable to the silence of the sepulcher." In the face of general pessimism, the Cristo Rey celebrations were meant to unify Catholics through religious devotion.[112] However, devotion became political when it challenged the separation of public and private that was supposed to define the space of worship in modern Mexico. A public march did not necessarily issue such a challenge, and the one carried out in Mexico City seems to have generated little tension. But Traslosheros readily discerned. Comparing the experiences of the major cities, he wrote that Guadalajara would take the prize without a doubt. Nowhere had there been a larger and more combative public march.[113]

———

According to Vicente Camberos Vizcaíno, the bishops decided to celebrate with "civic-social" marches and to formally request permission of local authorities prior to scheduling. With this agreement, Orozco y Jiménez sought and received permission from Governor López Portillo y Rojas on January 8, under the condition that the participants abstain from religious acts. This begs the question: What exactly might be considered *religious*? And the short answer is that the religious is variable. The position of the archdiocese was understandably that the nineteenth-century reform laws prohibited formal worship in public spaces. Accordingly, none was scheduled. But anticlericals interpreted any allusion to religious figures or beliefs as an illegal act of worship. It was illegal for clergy to wear the cassock or Roman collar in public; but could an individual legally wear a religious symbol or insigne, such as a crucifix, on her lapel or necklace? Did government have the right to enter the home and dress the citizenry? Was it formally distinct if thousands did this, rather than an individual? It was illegal to celebrate mass in public. But what about a silent march in which participants were ostensibly motivated by religious belief? Was it distinct if a group of marchers shouted religiously motivated slogans? Did government have the authority to limit what people might say in the public sphere? These were issues of legal interest, but political authority was ultimately discretional to some extent, the realm of government or governance. This apparent ambiguity explains—at least in part—why the January marches were not everywhere perceived as provocative, and offers insight into the weight of local events in national history.

Any ambiguity was less legal than political. A brief look at reform era legislation is in order here, as the answers to some of the questions I have posed are pretty clear. President Juárez's decree on freedom of worship (December 4, 1860) stipulated that solemn religious acts in public were prohibited unless local political authority granted written permission, and that public order was mandatory (Article 11).[114] President Lerdo de Tejada later amended this law on several occasions. The decree on religious gatherings, *manifestaciones*, flatly prohibited religious acts outside of church buildings (May 13, 1873). A clarification to this decree authorized religious funerals in cemeteries, comparing them to large buildings in which each room may accommodate the particular customs of its inhabitants (November 27, 1874). Finally, the law on religious liberty formalized these prohibitions (December 14, 1874). One of its contributions was to subordinate many issues of worship to federal jurisdiction, centralizing interpretation and making punishment more severe. For example, the "State" exercised authority over questions of public order

(Article 1), implicitly overriding local officials. Any public worship must be confined to the interior of a church building; violations incurred fines as well as prison; neither clergy nor laity were permitted to use religious clothing or other articles—*distintivos*—in public (Article 5). Discourse by ministers of the faith calling on individuals to disobey established laws was illegal, and violations committed in such circumstances would be prosecuted in the understanding that the minister involved was the principal author of the crime committed (Article 11). Religious associations had the right to organize hierarchically, designate a superior who might petition on behalf of the association; however, the State did not recognize any minister of the faith, *qua minister*, as an official interlocutor; they could address authority only invested with the rights granted to any other citizen (Articles 13 and 15).[115]

Guadalajara's first minister of the faith was archbishop Francisco Orozco y Jiménez. Born at Zamora Michoacán in 1864, he was sent to Rome at the age of twelve to study for the priesthood at the Colegio Pio Latino Americano. He later returned to Zamora, where he celebrated his first mass in 1888 when he was twenty-four years old. Pope Leo XIII made him bishop of Chiapas in 1902, and he went on to garner a reputation as a defender of the Indian pueblos of that southeastern diocese. Referred to mockingly as bishop "Chamula" by his detractors, he was forty-eight when he took over the Guadalajara archdiocese in December 1912.[116] In this western Mexican city he would make a lasting contribution during the final twenty years of his life, through his example as a religious leader who maintained close ties to his flock during periods of unrest and violence. The 1914 consecration of Mexico to the Sacred Heart of Christ was his first test.[117]

After receiving permission for the event, the archbishop issued an open invitation to the faithful for January 11, named commissions to handle press and public order, and established the parade route. On the afternoon of the eleventh, the participants assembled along Alcalde Avenue between the metropolitan cathedral and Our Lady of Guadalupe Church, nine blocks to the north. Following a corporate logic, they formed groups according to social, religious, or trade activities. This corridor, the path from Our Lady of Guadalupe—popularly known as the Sanctuary—to the Cathedral, would be central to future struggles over public space, inscribed by the Christ the King pilgrimage. Time passed and the march did not begin; impatience set in, and turned to frustration with the rumor that the governor had issued an order rescinding the parade permit.

The Catholic leadership saw the revocation as a sign that the governor was

FIGURE 3. Seminary students in Rome at the Colegio Pio Latino Americano, ca. 1876. As numbered in the photograph: 1. Pbro. J. Antonio Plancarte y Labastida; 2. Nicanor Mora; 3. Mauro Navarro; 4. Luis G. Orozco, Cngo. Tit. de León; 5. Francisco Orozco y Jiménez, Arz. de Guadalajara; 6. Vicente Vaca; 7. Juan Herrera, Arz. de Monterrey; 8. Luis Betancourt; 9. Enrique Villaseñor; 10. Adrián Plancarte; 11. Miguel Plancarte, Cngo. de Guadalupe; 12. Francisco Plancarte, Arz. de Monterrey; 13. José Mora, Arz. de México; 14. José Ma. Méndez, Cngo. de México; 15. Tiburcio Cárdenas; 16. Francisco Navarro. Source: Archivo Histórico de la Arquidiócesis de Guadalajara.

unstable or unprincipled. With the crowd already assembled along central Guadalajara's main thoroughfare, the archbishop sent envoys to speak with the governor at home. Accompanied by his state's attorney, López Portillo y Rojas received a group of four women from prestigious local families. Two married and two single, they represented several of the groups assembled downtown. On making their case, the state's attorney pointed out that one of the women bore a religious medal around her neck, and charged that it constituted an act of public worship, and was therefore illegal. However, the governor wavered, giving in partially to the request by permitting women and children to march, but not men.

This solution generated even greater irritation, and influenced public reaction out on the street. The archbishop reasoned that there were two possible interpretations. The first was that the march was illegal and, out of condescension, the governor had permitted the Catholic women and children to break the law. The second was that there was in fact nothing illegal about the march, and that the governor was impinging on the citizens' right of assembly. Archbishop Orozco y Jiménez opted to announce the governor's decision and call for the march to be carried out exclusively by women and children. But the reaction of the crowd was adverse, and when it was clear that the march would not be curtailed, the archbishop decided to lead it, accompanied by the archdiocesan cabildo, or governing council, Archbishop Mendoza of Durango, Bishop Uranga of Culiacan, and Antonio Correa, the parish head at the Sanctuary.

The march began without incident, but when it reached the San Francisco Gardens, on confronting a group of Liberal Party activists, many of the marchers began to shout political slogans such as *mueran los liberales*, "death to the liberals"; others sang *Corazón Santo*, which eventually was taken up by all the marchers. In the plaza in front of the cathedral a seminarian dressed in *sotana*, probably Miguel Gómez Loza,[118] challenged some liberals who, according to *El Diario de Occidente*, "innocently watched the event," and "shouted down the liberal spectators who observed politely."[119]

What had been planned and advertised as a silent march turned into a parade: a referendum on the governor and the liberal reform in general. The authorities tried to close off the streets in order to limit the march, but to no avail. The crowd covered the originally established route through downtown and back to the cathedral. When the march concluded around nine o'clock that evening, the archbishop dressed in pontifical white and gold, and intoned the *Hymnus Ambrosianus*, or Te-Deum, in thanksgiving before blessing the crowd. Thus, the celebration ended with an act of worship, confined to the cathedral, attended by a crowd many times too large to fit within the walls of the ancient building. The irony of the events is that the archbishop scrupulously adhered to the reform laws with respect to the celebration of formal acts of worship, but led a major protest through the streets of the city. The march, no less political than religious, can be seen as a watershed in terms of political identity among Guadalajara Catholics, but also with respect to worship, the *culto público*. And Orozco y Jiménez, nearing his first anniversary as head of the archdiocese, emerged as a civic leader of considerable authority at a time when the state was on the verge of collapse.

There is a further subtext to the Christ the King pilgrimage which emerges under the scrutiny of a gendered reading. Newspaper analysis appearing after

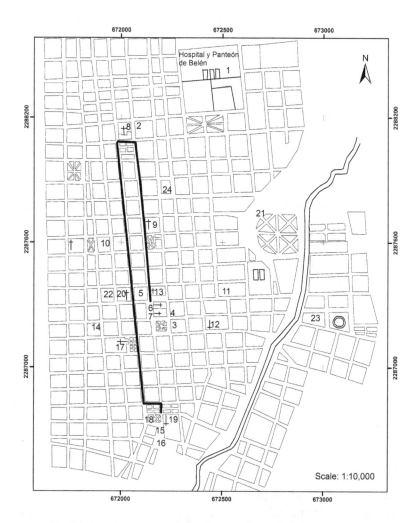

MAP 2. Guadalajara city center and parade route for Catholic protest, 1914–1926.
Key: 1. Belén Hospital and Cemetery; 2. Military hospital; 3. Seat of State Govern-
ment; 4. Seat of City Government; 5. Archbishop's palace; 6. Catedral; 7. Sagrario; 8.
Santuario de Nuestra Señora de Guadalupe; 9. San José de Gracia; 10. Santa Mónica;
11. Santa María de Gracia; 12. San Agustín; 13. La Soledad; 14. Santa Teresa; 15. San
Francisco Gardens; 16. Train station; 17. University of Guadalajara; 18. San Francisco;
19. Aranzazú; 20. La Merced; 21. Alameda Park; 22. Corona Market; 23. Libertad
Market; 24. Alcalde Market. Source: Susana Urzúa Soto.

the event offered a range of ideal Catholic types, including the curious; the ignorant; the ardent faithful; and the rebellious. This analysis argued that all of these types were present on the eleventh, but that only the last one, the rebellious, presented a clear and present danger to the legal foundations of society. The Catholic Party members who marched belonged to this category, and ought to be treated accordingly. But the most interesting aspect of the argument was that it only sought to explain male participation, the typology is male. Women are not included; they are beyond sociological analysis. The only woman referred to in the article is the reified *dama* represented by the Church itself.[120]

Orozco y Jiménez understood this. In effect, the governor had permitted women and children to march because he too considered them to be outside the political sphere. They were Mexican, but not citizens. They did not vote; they did not count politically. The archbishop's decision to call for the crowd to follow the governor's instructions was a tactical decision to measure the political strength of the Church. An editorial, signed with the penname "Gavroche" and published the day after the march, accused Catholic men of hiding behind the ruse of a women's march in an act of cowardice.[121] History, the author wrote, has recorded a march of skirts, and the PCN has ceased to be a party of men. The editorial challenged the manhood of the men who marched, and equated women with children. They were not accountable, and the men who "hid" behind their skirts were not worthy of citizenship. They could not be trusted.[122]

———

This narrative of a separate public sphere, in which male citizens engaged in politics according to the rules of nineteenth-century liberalism, depended on an unwritten pact in which the institutions of modern society upheld a secularized bourgeois hegemony. Catholic protest in 1914 challenged it on several different levels: first, to the extent that men did not uphold the liberal pact regarding religion and politics; and second, to the extent that women invaded the public spaces of modern politics and used their presence, their very bodies, to impose a new configuration of the political. Both forms of Catholic politics were counterhegemonic.

The fallout from the Christ the King marches was multiple. In Guadalajara, arrest warrants were issued for the archbishop, Francisco Orozco y Jiménez, as well as for other leaders of the January 11 pilgrimage. Father Correa voluntarily walked into the offices of the Jefe Politico, Carlos Cortés Ortigosa, and was arrested. Liberal anger was especially directed at Catholic Party congressmen who participated in the event. In Mexico City, Huerta had initially favored the marches, but changed course after the fact, essentially abandoning the tactic of trying to cultivate Catholic political support for his government. Instead, he took action against the PCN by exiling its president, Gabriel Fernández Somellera. Within a month of the march, Governor López Portillo y Rojas had been called to Mexico City to take a cabinet post as Minister of Foreign Affairs, while Jalisco was entrusted to the federal army, under the command of General José María Mier.[123]

The fallout could be felt across the state. In March, a bemused Luis Álvarez wrote Miguel Palomar y Vizcarra from Puebla: "So, your good friend Lopez Portillo finally fell? I'll bet [the Jalisco PCN leaders] are treading with great care, as the let-down you experienced with the new minister was considerable."[124] The depiction is accurate, in the sense that the Jalisco leadership continued to network, despite the gloomy outlook. The Jalostotlan representative requested help founding rural savings institutions;[125] the Juanacatlán representative attempted to establish a Catholic store;[126] in Tapalpa, plans were underway for the application of homesteads;[127] and following the US occupation of Veracruz in April, military training became popular in many towns.[128] But the Jalisco Catholics were isolated, no longer hitched to the national party apparatus. Soon, all activity would be overshadowed by the arrival of the great revolutionary armies of the north. In the end, the party was as much a victim of the Huerta regime as it was a casualty of its own misguided politics.

5. The Battles for Jalisco

IN LATE JUNE 1914, Álvaro Obregón's army made its way amid the heavy summer rains from Tepic along the Sierra Volcánica Transversal down into Jalisco.[1] On July 1, in the western town of Ahualulco, Obregón was promoted to Division General. There he planned the attack on Guadalajara, using three different columns. The first, consisting of Lucio Blanco's cavalry division, circumvented the area to the south, and cut the train line to Manzanillo on July 6. At the same time, Diéguez's troops, with the incorporation of Julián Medina and his local rebels, went around the Federal army garrison at Orendáin, and attacked their rearguard at La Venta, cutting off their retreat to Guadalajara. At midnight, Obregón led the third column against the Orendáin garrison from the west. By dawn on July 7, the Federal soldiers were embattled from either side and by ten o'clock that morning, they were dispersed. Obregón then took his troops on to Zapopan leaving his camp behind along with the captured trains, soldiers, and arms. On July 8, General Mier, commander of the Federal Army's Western Division, fled Guadalajara, only to be attacked and defeated by Blanco's cavalry at El Castillo hacienda southeast of the city.

Obregón's final rout of the Federal army was achieved in less than a week, between Orendáin and La Venta in the Tequila region, and El Castillo hacienda southeast of Guadalajara. If we are to believe Obregón's memoir, the offensive killed approximately 2,000 Federal troops, including General Mier, and 170 officers. It took nearly 5,000 prisoners, collected 16 cannons, 18 artillery trains, 40 locomotives, 5,000 rifles with ammunition, as well as mule teams for moving artillery, horses, uniforms, marching bands, and half a million pesos that had been demanded of the local banks by Mier prior to fleeing. Obregón reported 300 casualties including dead and wounded.[2]

The defeat Obregón's Constitutionalist forces inflicted on the Federal Army at Guadalajara made for a sharp contrast with the conservative reformist politics of the PCN. Militarily, the end of the old regime was decisive. But politically, it had begun several years earlier. For this reason the arrival of the Constitutionalist army at Guadalajara was seen more as an occupation than a liberation. Simply stated, the local government was popular. By the summer of 1914, the PCN no longer existed, but popular sentiment in Jalisco had been profoundly shaped by the experiment in Catholic politics. This view was quite different than the Carrancista view, which saw the PCN government as part of the Huertista dictatorship. Whatever the Jaliscans felt about Huerta's policies, he did not directly govern them the way he did Mexico City, for instance. In Jalisco, the governments of the Madero era were by and large popular, and were not repressed in 1913 following the execution of Madero and Pino Suarez. So the arrival of the Carrancistas was not popular, and the imposition of radical anticlerical and anti-Catholic measures caused locals a great deal of animosity.

This chapter will consider what I refer to as the battles for Jalisco, in local, national, and international terms. On all three levels Catholic politics and culture are important. The main argument is that one cannot isolate Jalisco and Guadalajara from the revolutionary process, but must ultimately tie local history into the broader issues and events of the Mexican Revolution. The reverse will also be true; the Mexican revolution cannot be subtly interpreted without factoring in the enormous importance of Jalisco, "that most un-revolutionary state."[3]

Symbolic Violence and Ideological Battle

By the time the Huerta regime fell, the PCN had disappeared, the lay organizations were disarticulated—in many cases even at the parish level—and for the Church the general situation was worsening. Huerta's interest in the Catholics had only been as deep as his immediate needs, whether the need for political support, or emergency financing. Although neither Zapata nor Villa were systematically anticlerical, nor opposed to the Catholic movements, Venustiano Carranza's Constitutionalist army adopted an openly anticlerical stance, blaming the Catholic Church for having facilitated the Huerta coup. Manuel Aguirre Berlanga, interim governor of Jalisco (and subsequently secretary of the interior under President Carranza), wrote that the clergy had strayed from its "mystical functions" when it became involved in politics by coming to the aid of traitors. For Aguirre Berlanga, as for Carranza, in 1913 this was tantamount to treason.[4]

FIGURE 4. Guadalajara
Archbishop Francisco
Orozco y Jiménez, Rome,
1914. Source: Archivo
Histórico de la Arqui-
diócesis de Guadalajara.

During the summer of 1914, the Mexican bishops were exiled,[5] with the
exception of the Bishop of Cuernavaca, who lived in Zapatista territory.[6] Most
went to San Antonio, Texas, or Havana, Cuba. One exception was Guadalajara
archbishop Francisco Orozco y Jiménez, who was dispatched to Rome by the
Mexico City archbishop, José Mora y del Río, in order to advise Pius X regarding the Mexican Church. Orozco y Jiménez would spend two years in Rome,
where he became friends with Francis Clement Kelley, the Canadian born
priest who ran the US-based Catholic Extension Society out of an office located
at the Archdiocese of Chicago.

Meanwhile in Mexico, Catholic intellectuals and lower clergy had either
disappeared from public life or went undercover: PCN president Gabriel
Fernández Somellera was jailed by Huerta, and subsequently exiled in

mid-February. That August he wrote to Miguel Palomar of his torment for having left the country, in his opinion the mark of a coward.[7] In Guadalajara, Father Antonio Correa had recently been jailed. Identified as a leader of the January Christ the King marches, he closed down the popular Catholic Workers' Society at Our Lady of Guadalupe Parish, and went into hiding prior to the arrival of Obregón's army in July.[8] Similarly, Father José Cornejo gave up his razor, cultivated a bushy beard, let his hair grow, and abandoned the use of religious clothing. Then he donned a carpenter's clothing and went to work under an alias.[9] The locals knew him, but they weren't talking. With the arrival of Obregón's rebel army, PCN Congressman Miguel Palomar y Vizcarra was forced to flee for his life, and went into hiding at a Zapopan ranch. A year later, with the possibility of a Villista victory quickly fading, Ignacio Ramos Praslow signed an order banishing Palomar y Vizcarra from the state of Jalisco, at which time he left Zapopan for Mexico City. The order identified Palomar as a "reactionary politician," and made clear that, were he caught in Jalisco, he would be dealt with summarily.[10]

However, such was not always the case, and some among the Catholic leadership were well connected even among the revolutionaries. Manuel F. Chávez, the Guadalajara lawyer who had presided over the Jalisco PCN, neither hid out nor went into exile. He died of natural causes a decade later, rather than at the hands of the Constitutionalist hardliners; and an elaborate funeral procession carried his coffin through the city's streets followed by a large crowd of mourners. This most public display of Christian devotion made its way from the Metropolitan Cathedral across town to the Municipal Cemetery at Mezquitán on the eve of the Cristero Rebellion, and did so with the consent of the anticlerical governor, José Guadalupe Zuno.

US Consul Davis reported in November 1914 that the Carrancistas had discovered that mass was being celebrated in a private home, and in response detained twenty-five men who had attended. They were subsequently charged with conspiring against the government and fined 1,000 pesos each in exchange for their freedom.[11] Extortion was surely a common form of taxing a begrudging citizenry. And semiprivate religious ceremonies would continue to be widespread for the foreseeable future. In 1918 Luis B. de la Mora wrote to his old friend Miguel Palomar, to inform him of the ongoing resistance in Guadalajara:

Regarding the private celebration of mass, it is actually semi-public;
the people have free entry; anyone can enter the homes where mass is

celebrated, and there are homes where several masses are celebrated on Sundays. In my house at San Pedro (Tlaquepaque) all may attend. It can't be said that only the wealthy have such privileges.[12]

Beginning in July 1914, the Sonoran revolutionaries and the leadership of the Guadalajara Archdiocese became entrenched in what might be considered a war of position. The Carrancista press told of a revolutionary crusade against clerical privileges and abuse; the archdiocese saw it as a campaign to wipe out the Catholic Church as a viable institution in Mexican society. Both claims were exaggerated, but such was the expediency of propaganda. Confronted by an army, the archdiocese discovered it possessed a method of defense, or resistance, that would become quite important for its survival in the coming years: the indignation of laity, of different social strata, sexes, and generations, civilians who were less interested in the details of constitutional restoration than in the attacks against their customs. For them, *"los revolucionados"* in Luis González's colloquialism, the arrival of the Sonoran revolutionaries meant "savage crimes, robbery, kidnappings, hanging corpses, ravished women, and religious images stripped of their *milagros*."[13]

The initial Carrancista assault on the Catholic Church was broad and sweeping: Guadalajara, Tepic, Durango, Monterrey, Ciudad Victoria, Tampico, Veracruz, and Mexico City to name some of the major cities. The Carrancista generals jailed the priests, occupied churches, seminaries, and schools, and shut down the Catholic press.[14] In Guadalajara, General Manuel M. Diéguez removed the saints from plazas and markets; with comparable insistence but greater imagination, in Monterrey General Antonio Villareal had the sacred effigies marched out of the cathedral, lined up in the public plaza and executed by firing squad.[15] The vicar general and governor of the Guadalajara archdiocese, Manuel Alvarado sent President Carranza a list of the religious sites that the army occupied as barracks beginning July 8, 1914: the buildings that housed the Seminary Major and Minor, the Sacred Heart College for boys and girls, the Holy Spirit Vocational School, the Exercise Houses at Saint Sebastian of Analco, Our Lady of Guadalupe and Our Lady of Afflictions. Later the archbishop's residence, the printing press of the Catholic daily, *El Regional*, and all Catholic schools affiliated with the ecclesiastic administration were seized. According to Alvarado's estimates, the education of 20,000 children was interrupted, many of whom had previously received free food and clothing, and almost all of whom had received free instruction.[16]

On July 22 the *Boletín Militar*, official publication of the Carrancistas in

Jalisco, reported a supposed conspiracy organized by the clergy to lead an armed insurrection against the military government. On July 21 the soldiers had detained every priest they could find, jailing 135, including the Bishop of Tehuantepec. The military authorities closed the churches in the city, alleging that they had stockpiled arms and ammunition.[17] Following the initial siege, on July 29, the priests were freed without charge, but in exchange for a 200,000 peso "fine." The *Boletín Militar* continued reporting on the so-called "Sanctuary plot," but nobody was prosecuted.[18] Francis Kelley, the Oklahoma bishop and a friend to Mexican Catholics, wrote that the arms at the center of the scandal were "thirty or forty old guns which had been bought for 25 cents each by the Marist Brothers for the military drills of their students."[19] The release of the priests was accompanied—perhaps motivated—by public expressions of loyalty and support for the Church on the part of civilian groups, including teachers and public servants, mostly composed of women.[20]

The veracity of the conspiracy has never been convincingly demonstrated.[21] Although the Carrancista army's newspaper continuously denounced the so-called Sanctuary plot, the available evidence suggests to the contrary, that it was more likely an invention of Diéguez's propagandists. First of all, no additional evidence has been discovered to corroborate the charges made in the *Boletín Militar.* Second, Vicar General Manuel Alvarado was able to write to Carranza four years later, in 1918, and totally dismiss the charges as a pretext to sack the churches.[22] Third, during the armed phase of the revolution, there were no other such cases reported in which the Catholic clergy planned an armed rebellion. To the contrary, even during the Cristero Rebellion, the Catholic Church systematically opposed an armed alternative. Fourth, Amado Aguirre wrote extensively on the occupation of Guadalajara, and during those first days, Obregón ordered him to head up the search for money in the metropolitan cathedral. Although Aguirre wrote in great detail of his findings, regarding the cathedral he mentioned nothing that could even remotely be understood as subversive. Nor did he ever mention the Our Lady of Guadalupe conspiracy in his memoirs. One would suppose that an anti-Carrancista clerical plot involving more than 100 priests would warrant some sort of mention in a relation of the occupation of Guadalajara.[23] Fifth, and most importantly, Diéguez's troops never executed anybody.[24] Not a single priest went before a firing squad, even as the Carrancistas did not hesitate to shoot or hang priests in other less offensive circumstances during their campaign against Huerta's Federal troops, or for that matter during the war against Villa.[25] *Pelotón y paredón,* the firing squad and the pock-marked adobe wall used for staging executions, these were an integral part of the cultural idiom of the era, especially 1914 to 1915, the middle years of the revolution. An armed clerical plot would surely have been foiled with exemplary violence. Contrary to the official line, the way the so-called conspiracy played out is reminiscent of another aspect of the idiom of violence that characterized the period. More likely it was a case of extortion, also part of the politico-military modus operandi, not exclusive to Carrancismo, but rather general during the revolution.

With the fall of Huerta, and the disbanding of the PCN, the Carrancistas began to prepare their government, exchanging their military strategy for a political strategy in the cities and towns they controlled. But the atmosphere of occupation continued. After the priests' release, Manuel M. Diéguez decreed that foreign priests would be deported in reprisal for their role in the supposed conspiracy.[26] Vicar General Alvarado described the deportation as a sarcastic affair, a forced exodus in which the military sent a band down to the train station to play festive marches as the faithful bade farewell to their pastors.[27]

Important aspects of the tactics adopted by Carrancista military governor Diéguez during the fall of 1914 were meant to weaken or destroy common religious symbols. The military government removed the *"Ave María"* customarily inscribed above the doorways of houses, stores, tenements, middle and grade schools; and the saints disappeared from streets, plazas, markets, and towns.[28] In a vivid example of symbolic, if pragmatic, violence, the 13th Battalion of Sonora supplied its drum corps with 300-year-old parchment from the Cathedral choral books to repair its drums.[29] But the main focus, as suggested by the initial occupation of Guadalajara, was on the *templos*, or church buildings, and their pastors. For the Carrancista leadership, establishing government and forging a new society belonged to a process of cultural, as much as political, revolution. For men like Diéguez, the "battlefield of ideas" was as important as the military battlefield, and they understood that in order to win in such difficult terrain, they must control the forums as well as the voices of dissent. As a result, the churches and their pastors became a site of struggle, one that Catholic Guadalajara would not easily abandon.[30]

Guadalajara as Battlefield

For the Carrancista army, the construction of a new order in Jalisco began with a long battle on two fronts. Militarily, it controlled little more than the state capital and the railroads to Colima and Irapuato. The Jalisco countryside was "Villista," whether due to ideological motivations or simple pragmatism.

Politically, neither did the Carrancistas control Guadalajara. The capital was Catholic—not only in terms of religion, but politically as well—and the Catholics were acutely aware of the approaching confrontation. These two oppositions, one rural and the other urban, resisted for years, and the Carrancista triumph would only be partial. However, it is not so much an issue of whether the opposition was annihilated. It was not.

While the military government tried to impose its authority in Guadalajara, the rest of the state offered a different panorama, one in which banditry, revolt, and rebellion prevailed. Julián del Real continued to be active in the Ameca region, and reports of Rubén Zamora's pillaging came from Autlán to Ciudad Guzmán and all the way to the outskirts of Guadalajara. By October 1914, both had declared themselves in rebellion against Manuel M. Diéguez.[31]

In northern Jalisco Julián Medina had a solid base of support, combat experience, and two new elements: American arms and authority conferred by his incorporation into the Constitutionalist army.[32] Although the Constitutionalist army lacked cohesion, and was fast splitting into two hostile camps, the arms were certainly real, as was his good standing with the Villista faction. Around Teocaltiche and Lagos de Moreno in the Altos region, Tomás Urbina fought against Orozquista troops.[33] Like Medina, Urbina would side with Villa against Carranza and the Constitutionalists.

Following the Aguascalientes Convention in October 1914, and the Villa-Carranza break, Jalisco was transformed into one of the principal theaters of the 1915 civil war. The Conventionist forces of Julián Medina, with crucial support from Villa, then Calixto Contreras and Rodolfo Fierro, sought to take control of Guadalajara from Constitutionalist forces loyal to Carranza. The Constitutionalist forces were led by Manuel M. Diéguez, who later received support from Francisco Murguía. In this context, Jalisco was a major prize, seemingly up for grabs following the Convention at Aguascalientes.[34] Between December 1914 and April 1915 the two factions fought to control Guadalajara, and the city changed hands four times as each army tried repeatedly to defeat the other. The fighting ranged mostly between the center of the city and Ciudad Guzmán in southern Jalisco, along the railroad line to Manzanillo.

Military forces governed Jalisco during these months, and comparable challenges and obstacles confronted governors Medina and Diéguez. First, each governed harassed by the other's troops. Second, each was forced to use the government to raise money for their respective armies, and because Guadalajara did not generate taxes in the way that Tampico (oil) or Veracruz (customs) did, the methods of choice were to tax the Catholic Church and the wealthy.

Both attempted this, which argues against the notion that Medina and the Jalisco Villistas were little more than a bunch of reactionaries.[35] Third, each acted against foreigners, generating fear and anger in the local diplomatic corps. Diéguez attempted to confiscate the legally held firearms of foreign nationals and their consulates, while Medina attempted to collect emergency taxes from foreign citizens, most of whom ran businesses in Guadalajara.[36] Fourth, each was confronted with the riddle of how to generate, mobilize, and maintain popular support. But most importantly, during the first four months of 1915, each was faced with the real possibility of military annihilation at the hands of the other's army. In this rarified atmosphere, the most important challenge for both was to control the capital city of Guadalajara and the railroad junction located south of the city at La Junta. From there, a campaign could be directed toward Irapuato, Celaya, Querétaro, and Mexico City to the east, or toward Ciudad Guzmán, Colima, and Manzanillo to the south. It would also prove to be an escape route for Medina toward Ameca to the northwest.

During 1914, Diéguez did little to ingratiate himself with the locals in Guadalajara. His anticlerical policy was poorly received. By closing most of the city's churches, he created reminders all over the city, at once symbols of his unpopular policies and of local resistance to an outsider and an occupying army. If his anticlerical policies were generally unpopular, his Decree 28 establishing a six-day workweek drew protests from different quarters. Employees' unions, often more middle class in their composition, saw it as an arbitrary obstacle that hindered their workweek; but so did independent petty merchants, such as those who worked at the *Libertad* market downtown. Butchers and candlemakers protested, as did the *fonderas*, women who ran the tiny restaurant stalls at the market, and earned their income cooking meals for those who shopped and worked there. With Diéguez absent on military duty in October, interim governor Manuel Aguirre Berlanga signed Decree 39 establishing a minimum wage. This also backfired because the government was unable to enforce it. As a result rural and urban workers, whose expectations had been falsely raised by the decree, were subsequently threatened by their bosses, shop or hacienda foremen, and with some frequency were fired.[37] Moreover, hacienda peons and textile mill workers were not the only ones complaining that the minimum wage decree was not being honored. An October letter of protest sent by city workers from the Guadalajara Public Works Department suggests that even local government had balked at the measure.[38]

During the final months of 1914, the city became increasingly isolated from the outside world. Banditry made travel difficult beyond the city limits; by

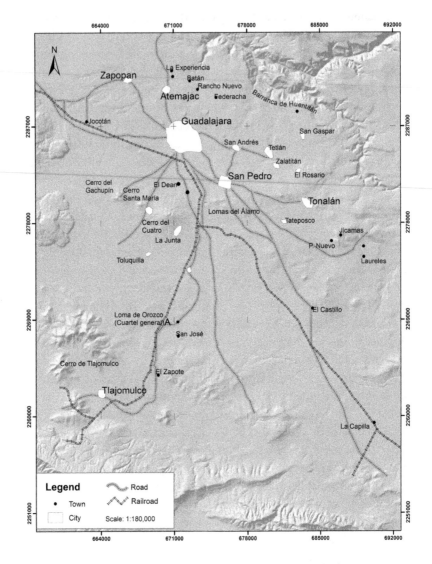

MAP 3. Guadalajara and surrounding area, 1914. Source: Susana Urzúa Soto.

November trains ran only sporadically and then stopped completely. Telegraph service generally followed the patterns along the railway. When the trains did not run, wire service often went down, too. Villista troops controlled the railway to Irapuato by November 25, which meant that evacuating Guadalajara was an option limited to the Manzanillo line southbound. Meanwhile, Admiral T. B. Howard tried to arrange for a US vessel near Manzanillo to secure communication—as well, no doubt, as to remind the warring parties of the latent threat of invasion. Vice Consul Davis, feeling abandoned in Guadalajara, had taken to sending his dispatches along with travelers headed toward El Paso, one railroad line that seemed to function regularly.[39]

As of December 8, the Carrancistas began to evacuate the city. First, Diéguez sent soldiers out to Ocotlán to burn the bridge on the Irapuato railroad line near Lake Chapala. That would impede the arrival of Villista troops from the east. They also, it seems, fixed the telegraph lines, to the jubilation of the US vice consul. Having executed several political prisoners before dawn on the twelfth, and emptied both state and municipal treasuries, Diéguez decreed that the new emergency capital of the state of Jalisco would be Ciudad Guzmán, and beat a hasty retreat south. Diéguez deputized a civilian, Luis Castellanos y Tapia, to take charge of the city until the arrival of the Villista army. Vice Consul Davis found Castellanos at City Hall, and was duly informed that there were no police on hand to protect the peace, that there was no money to pay a police force, and that he, Castellanos, would call a meeting that afternoon of representative citizens and the diplomatic corps, in order to make arrangements for safeguarding the city until the arrival of Villa. That afternoon Castellanos formed a five-member citizens committee, secured money to pay for a citizens' police force, and proceeded to organize it section by section throughout the city. All who could offer their services for police duty were to report to their local police stations, with arms, to receive written authority to act according to their new, temporary status as keepers of the peace. This arrangement lasted for nearly three days, from the fourteenth until the seventeenth, during which time all businesses were closed, few ventured out into the street, and "not the least disturbance of any nature whatever occurred."[40]

Meanwhile, Villa had taken the town of Lagos de Moreno, the gateway to Jalisco from the north. His administrators proceeded to implement a land reform policy premised on confiscating land belonging to local enemies. As in the north, the lands were not parceled out to the poor. Instead, the locals who worked the land were invited to continue doing so, and were paid their habitual wages, while Villista partisans managed the enterprise. Villa's army ran the farms, marketed steers, sheep, goats, horses, milk, beans, corn, chilies, and more. They hired locals to retool their army, including fittings for the horses, and other such products. They also left detailed information on who they paid to govern, and how much. Their Lagos de Moreno mayor, for example, earned $68 pesos per month, a comfortable but modest salary.[41]

Before arriving at Guadalajara, Francisco Villa appointed Julián Medina, the Maderista rebel and former mayor of Hostotipaquillo (1912), to be governor of Jalisco. Together they freed the jailed priests and reopened the churches that Diéguez had kept shut since July.[42] On the afternoon of December 17, Villa made his entrance at Guadalajara amidst the cheers and relief of the general public. A few days later, Villa was off to Mexico City for his historic meeting with Emiliano Zapata. Medina's first period as Villa's governor in Jalisco lasted for less than one month and was interrupted by a Christmas lull when neither much fighting nor governing got done.

While Diéguez and his general staff planned to retake Guadalajara, Medina held the city for the first half of January. Shortly after New Year 1915, his troops arrested a group of erstwhile Villistas accused of crossing over to the Felicista camp, and had them shot in the cemetery at Poncitlán near Lake Chapala. The victims included Antonio Delgadillo (former general of the Federal army and governor of Colima), Colonel Tomás Bravo (whom Medina had engaged in combat on several occasions in 1913), Father Miguel Pérez Rubio, and his brother (a lieutenant), the telegraph operator, and perhaps ten others. According to M. Cuzin, the French vice consul, Colonel Bravo had previously executed Medina's brother.[43] Although US consul Davis was outraged by the brutality of the executions, they did not seem to affect Medina's general popularity, perhaps because they were focused on particular enemies, rather than generalized, arbitrary acts.[44] Anacleto González Flores, a Catholic law student from Guadalajara, had volunteered with the group several weeks earlier in the southern Jalisco town of Concepción de Buenos Aires. Since then he had been Delgadillo's spokesman, secretary, and scribe.[45] The executed priest, Pérez Rubio, was González Flores's godfather, the pastor who baptized him in 1888. His biographer, Antonio Gómez Robledo, wrote that the execution of father Pérez Rubio caused in González Flores a "total disillusion" with violent struggle, after which point he turned his energies toward nonviolent forms of protest.[46] Still in his twenties, González Flores was not yet well known in Jalisco, but the events of 1914 and 1915 seem to have set him on a new path, one that would make him the preeminent voice of political Catholicism during the following decade.

On January 5, Medina announced that all property would be re-evaluated in preparation for a raise in taxes. Owners would have to declare the value of their property, and some properties would be expropriated for "public utility," not without compensation to their owners. They would be partitioned as part of the Villista agrarian reform in Jalisco. For landowners, this presented a dilemma: If they under-reported the value of their land, they risked having it expropriated with little compensation in exchange. If they reported the real value of the property, then they would be charged much higher taxes than they were accustomed to paying. On January 10, Medina's administration began preparations for a land reform like the one in place at Lagos de Moreno, announcing plans to expropriate the haciendas at Atequiza and Zapotlanejo.[47] Medina did not have enough time to seize the haciendas, because Diéguez forced him to retreat from Guadalajara a week later. However, that such measures were under consideration was no surprise, even though it was unsettling for Jalisco Carrancistas and large landowners. The Lagos de Moreno experience, as well as Medina's Guadalajara tenure, serve as an indication of the sort of policy a Villista government would pursue. It is impossible to know how successful Medina might have been in applying a policy of land reform; however, he was in his home state, and he had made public his interest in land distribution as early as 1912, while mayor of Hostotipaquillo.[48] Jalisco was not Chihuahua, but there was surely room for a land reform.[49]

Medina's government was fatally weakened by three serious problems that he was never able to solve: a shortage of the arms, ammunition, and troops needed to hold off the advance of Diéguez and Murguía; a shortage of money in the state treasury; and a shortage of food to cover the needs of the capital city. Despite these serious shortcomings, Medina was genuinely popular, no doubt in part due to a local chauvinism that valued the illustrious sons of Jalisco over outsiders. This was clearly something that US consul Davis was ill prepared to grasp. In a letter to his daughter, he revealed an unbridled racism, bitterly complaining about Medina, whom he characterized as looking and acting like an untutored Indian. Yet Amado Aguirre, the mining engineer turned Constitutionalist general, left a contrasting opinion, characterizing Medina as an accomplished warrior, an outstanding mechanic, and an honest individual. Ángel Moreno Ochoa wrote similarly of Medina, an honest man of humble origins, of strong character, brave and well intentioned. And Mssr. Cuzin, a French merchant and consular employee, despite his misgivings about Medina's tax and land expropriation policy, wrote that he made a better governor than Diéguez, "more serious, more orderly, even though he has tightened the screws on us."[50]

Whatever his personal strengths or shortcomings, Medina found himself entrenched in Guadalajara on January 15, trying to hold back the combined armies of Diéguez and Francisco Murguía as they waged an aggressive campaign to the south of the city. The fighting went on for three days before General Diéguez's troops routed the Villistas, and sent Medina in retreat toward the northwestern Jalisco town of Ameca.

That evening the US vice consul was at dinner, when General Murguía appeared with his staff, leaving two sentries posted at the door. Some minutes later, a man walked by the hotel. As he passed, a sentry called to him, "¿Quién vive?" ("Who lives?") The man responded, "Villa," and he was shot dead. Davis finished his dinner, and then went out to see. At that point the man, Davis identified him as a "soldier," had already been stripped of his hat, shoes, and all else that was not soaked in blood. It is difficult to determine whether he was a soldier, as Davis reported, or a civilian. However, it is hard to imagine that an enemy soldier would have been wandering around the city that night, following the battle. The man was partially stripped of his clothing, but was he uniformed? The reader is not told. However, in his memoir Aguirre wrote reprovingly on the soldiers' practice of shooting civilians who did not answer correctly to the question "Who lives?" out of confusion or ignorance as to which forces were before them. It is impossible to know whether the victim was a soldier or a civilian.[51]

The following day groups of civilians walked through the streets observing the dead; two by the Governor's palace; two more in front of the New World shop; two in front of Mr. Celouso's shop; five near the Degollado theater; two behind the cathedral; four at the station; hundreds in all, lying where they had been shot, stripped of all that was salvageable. At nine-thirty in the morning, soldiers began to collect the cadavers, carrying them away on stretchers. Around three in the afternoon, they made it over to the Fénix and removed the body of the man who was shot in front of the hotel.[52]

At eight o'clock the next morning, Obregón's Yaqui regiment entered the city, marching slowly, "to an eerie, lugubrious drumbeat." The sound and sight was otherworldly in the eyes of a European observer who was impressed by the feathers the Yaqui's wore in their sombreros. The city was totally calm.[53] Three hours later Diéguez made his entrance, unexpectedly, without fanfare, without cheering. From the palace balcony he addressed those who were assembled below in the plaza. The French vice consul Cuzin wrote that one of his officers gave a long speech, railing against the traitors who had been defeated. Diéguez in turn said little, as he had trouble giving speeches. Years later, an old farmer from Ajijic, on Lake Chapala, would recall Diéguez's anger as he reminded the assembled that Villa had marched into the city on a carpet of flowers, while he had arrived stepping over corpses: "The people asked for my head, I have been told; well here is my head. Who wants it? Raise your hand."[54]

On January 20, a long train carried the families of Diéguez's troops from the southern Jalisco town of Tuxpan to Guadalajara. Crossing the sierra at Sayula, it lost its brakes and went speeding down the mountainside, until it jumped the tracks and crashed into the basin below. Twenty-three soldiers rode on the train, and hundreds of women and children. The cars were full and many rode on the roof. Two days later, 382 survivors arrived at Guadalajara, their bodies maimed, many missing limbs. Estimates ranged from 500 to 700 dead in the accident.[55] This tragedy insurmountably shaped Diéguez's second stay in Guadalajara, which would be short and violent, lasting just three weeks.

General Diéguez had barely enough time to improvise hospital space for the hundreds of wounded civilians, when Medina's troops made a renewed assault on the city. On January 30, the much-reduced Jalisco Villistas planned an early morning surprise attack. No longer accompanied by northern Villistas such as Fierro and Contreras, the raid had the feel of guerrilla war such as Medina had fought prior to the Aguascalientes Convention. The objective, it seems clear, was to strike a blow at the military leadership with the hope of killing the generals. The strike seems to have had two stages. During the first stage, Julián and Jesús Medina, Manuel Caloca, and Leocadio Parra[56] struck at five military barracks in the different sections of the city, as well as the home of Diéguez, although the general was not there. During the second stage, they converged on the palace downtown, approaching on twelve different streets, three on each side of the plaza.

The early morning attack went on for several hours within the city, and seems to have left a sizeable number of casualties strewn throughout the streets of downtown Guadalajara.[57] By morning, the Villista guerrilla had withdrawn to the northwest of the city, and Diéguez's troops commenced to clean up. It was after the battle had ended and the troops had withdrawn, that the most historically significant consequence of the attack was registered: the execution of Father David Galván.

Certain aspects of the story remain vague, although he was clearly executed, and the paredón was on the east side of the Belen Hospital, along Coronel Calderón Street. A recent vignette written by Felipe Cobián and Rodrigo

FIGURE 5. Altar to Father David Galván, ca. 1915. Source: Archivo Histórico de la Arquidiócesis de Guadalajara.

Vera places Father Galván at the site of the January 18 La Junta battle, but mistakenly places the battle on the thirtieth. According to the authors, Galván helped dozens of wounded on the battlefield, including Villistas and Carrancistas, and was detained, along with Father José María Araiza, by a Carrancista officer named Enrique Vera. Captain Vera obtained permission to execute the two priests behind a hospital, and had Galván shot, although Araiza was given a reprieve after a wealthy benefactor paid to save his life.[58] Given the enormous distance between La Junta and the civil hospital, this story seems unlikely.

However, Anacleto González Flores wrote that Galván rode his bicycle out to the La Junta and other battle sites near the city, to administer the sacrament of extreme unction to wounded soldiers.[59] In other words, Galván was a privileged witness to the La Junta battle twelve days before his death. Camarena wrote that he was shot while confessing wounded soldiers in the shallow river-bed east of the hospital. Luis Páez Brotchie wrote a similar account, omitting the shallow riverbed, and specifying that the wounded soldier being confessed was a Villista. Cuzin also noted this version in his diary, which suggests that it circulated around the city at the time of the execution. A Catholic version by Vicente Camberos Vizcaíno is quite similar, but adds that the neighbors took away his body, buried it, and brought stones from the riverbed to mark the place where he was shot.⁶⁰ The Catholics of Guadalajara appropriated the paredón, and made of it a site of popular devotion. Today a chapel stands near the site; the remains of St. David Galván, martyr, are kept there, and the devotion continues.

The story is now part of an official Vatican narrative, because Father Galván was canonized in May 2000. It contains elements of all of the above stories. According to a recent biographical sketch that received ecclesiastic imprimatur, and which has become popular in Guadalajara since the canonization, Galván was staying at a house near Our Lady of Guadalupe Church north of downtown on Pedro Loza Street. This was one of the routes of attack on the palace taken by Medina's troops, according to Camarena. Galván took a small bottle of Holy Oil, and set out to help the wounded, stopping first at Solitude Church downtown to ask Father José María Araiza to join him. The two set out on the way to the botanical garden, located near the civil hospital where prisoners would be shot. As they walked past a military barracks (probably the Cuartel Colorado grande, on Belén Street), they were apprehended by a soldier, and held prisoner for two hours. During that time, Father Araiza lamented not having had breakfast, to which Galván responded, "Soon we will eat at the table of the Lord."⁶¹ They confessed each other and, absolved of their sins, were marched out to the eastern wall of the civil hospital. Enrique Vera gave the order with the consent of General Diéguez. Knowing that his death was imminent, Galván distributed his earthly possessions, a few coins and the bottle of Holy Oil, among the soldiers in emulation of Jesus Christ. He asked not to be blindfolded, and when they took aim, he told them to aim at his chest.⁶² This action is reminiscent of a common male code of honor during the revolution: the valiant look death in the eye. In this story, so do the holy, and Galván "awaited death his face to the sun without batting an eye."⁶³ Thus the story of Saint David Galván offers parallels to scripture and contemporary constructions of masculinity at the same time.

The execution of Father Galván is only the most well known among many.

In fact, Diéguez's second period as governor has been characterized as a reign of terror, during which he ordered or permitted many assassinations and extra-judicial executions. His first order of business on returning to Guadalajara was to execute Luis Martínez Gracida and Manuel Santoscoy. Both had been civil servants during Diéguez's first administration, employed by the secretary of government; and both had declined to abandon the city with Diéguez's troops and administration in December 1914 when Villa took Guadalajara.[64] Both were from well-connected, liberal families, though in the case of Martínez Gracida, it probably did not help that his father and Porfirio Díaz were related through kinship ties of *compadrazgo*. Vice Consul Davis reported that Mr. Martínez's six small children pled with Diéguez—unsuccessfully—for their father's life. Davis also reported the execution of Father Galván, and mentioned four other priests that he knew to have been murdered by the soldiers.[65] But many others, mostly anonymous, were marched before a firing squad during the three weeks that Diéguez held the city, or simply hung from a tree by the cover of night. The cases often permit little detail, only the corpses left behind to be counted by the first light of day: "six, well-dressed, on Liceo Street"; "three more in Alameda Park, two of whom, shot, were peons, while a third, well-dressed, was found hung." On their way through San Pedro Tlaquepaque on January 20, Carrancista troops shot sixteen. During that time it was common to march the condemned out to the municipal cemetery at Mezquitán, north of the city, and shoot them there.[66]

However, not all violence was perpetrated under the cover of night, and that which was committed openly and in the presence of witnesses begs explanation. I have argued that the paredón belonged to an idiom of violence particular to a society in social upheaval and civil war. Yet I have not offered an explanation of how this idiom of violence is constructed, what it means, or how it might work. By turning to the acts of violence committed by the Carrancista army in Guadalajara, to the specific circumstances surrounding the February occupation of the city, perhaps the logic of violence may be rendered more clearly. It is a truism that unchecked military might is given to acts of violence. Yet I believe we can say a word or two about the conscious use of terror as a tool of government. For one thing, it was likely a political and military tactic to deter further rebel activity through terror in the form of violence arbitrarily imposed on a civilian population. And furthermore, especially following the *albazo*, terror was used as a form of retribution, or vengeance, against a population perceived as hostile. In the following examples, these motives, deterrence and retribution, become confused in the exemplary acts of violence meted out on the civilian population.

Following Medina's albazo, for example, Carrancista troops acted on a tip that two Villistas were hiding in a house by demolishing the house; in the act, twenty-two men, women, and children perished inside. Nearby two workers exiting the Guadalajara Packing House were fired on by the same troops. One was killed instantly, while the other lay wounded on the ground. A group of coworkers rushed out to explain to the soldiers that the two were not rebels but packers. When they asked permission to take the wounded man to a doctor, the commanding officer ordered a soldier to put his gun to the wounded man's forehead and blow his brains out. In another case, along one of the main city streets, a man carrying a load of lumber was shot dead by a Carrancista soldier, "because he looked like a Villista." In a final example, a Carrancista official who had been rejected by a young woman had the woman's boyfriend detained, dragged to a military barracks, and shot.[67] Such explanations demystify the violence of civil war, rendering it at once mundane and terrifying. What emerges is a portrait of armed occupation in which the Carrancista soldiers acted as if there was no clear line dividing Villa's soldiers and the civilian population. This, of course, is the grand dilemma of prosecuting a war against guerrilla fighters. Although the Villista army may not be characterized as such in February 1915, civilian partisanship and the official use of terror in west-central Mexico would mark the processes of state-building and popular resistance into the thirties.

The second Diéguez administration lasted from January 19 until February 12. During that time civilian Guadalajara lived in a fairly constant state of terror, and probably of great resentment. To complicate things, Diéguez and his troops were forced to deal not only with the casualties from ongoing battles with Medina and the Jalisco Villistas, but also with personal tragedy in the form of the hundreds of wounded and dead wives and children, the victims of January's train wreck. On the heels of tragedy, a substantial enemy guerrilla force under Medina had been able to surround the city from within, attack all of the barracks simultaneously, assault the palace, wage a running war with Diéguez's troops on horseback and from rooftop, and retreat without undue trouble. Although Diéguez reported fewer than thirty deaths on his side, the Carrancista body count on the street may have been much higher. These were clearly extreme circumstances for the Carrancista troops, and more than likely morale was low as they left the city for the second time in under two months, fleeing before the troops of Pancho Villa. In any case, Diéguez decided to withdraw from Guadalajara on the grounds that the city was a strategically poor location to mount a defense. He moved his troops south toward Colima and set up his defense in a mountain pass near the town of Sayula. Villa arrived at Guadalajara the afternoon of February 13, and the population received him "with even more enthusiasm—if that were possible—than the first time."[68]

Troop movement was very slow. By the night of the fifteenth, General Murguía traveled from Michoacán to Jalisco and joined General Diéguez in Ciudad Guzmán. While the two generals bickered among themselves, all of the Carrancista trains sat north of Sayula, at the foot of a steep mountain pass, precisely where the train had crashed carrying the families of Diéguez's troops in January. For two days Diéguez's officers worked at getting trains, troops, and equipment up over the pass, while Villa assembled a very large force in the valley below. On February 17 the battle of Sayula began, and by the afternoon of the eighteenth, Villa's troops had routed the Carrancistas, who retreated willy-nilly toward Michoacán and Colima, leaving behind their trains, equipment, and many dead. On receiving the order from General Diéguez to retreat, his chief of staff would comment, "Villa already issued this order, but in a less courteous manner."[69]

At this most crucial moment in the campaign, Villa decided to return to the north in order to provide backup for General Ángeles in Monterrey. As a result, he left the Carrancista forces virtually devastated, but protected by the canyons of southern Jalisco and Colima. There they regrouped, and in late March Diéguez emerged from the Colima nether land, fought his way back to Guadalajara, and then marshaled his troops triumphantly against Villa in the decisive battles of León, alongside Álvaro Obregón.

The Weight of International Events

This chapter has thus far been concerned fundamentally with events unfolding domestically in one region, particularly in one city, but always within the context of the revolutionary upheaval during the bloodiest months of a civil war that engulfed the nation. Thus, I have tried to situate a regional experience as part of a national process. I have also tried to clarify how these events affected Catholic Guadalajara. However, there is an international dimension to the events I have examined, and although it was by no means the crucial or deciding factor in the civil war, it was an important element within the process. In fact, three issues of international dimension frame the period I have considered in this chapter, and influenced the attitudes and decisions of the actors. The first was the US occupation of Veracruz on the Gulf of Mexico; the second was Roman Catholic internationalism and the supranational character of the Church; and the third was Woodrow Wilson's decision to formally recognize the Carranza faction as the legitimate government. Veracruz (April 1914) and recognition (October 1915) must both be considered within the context of the European war, and happened at a time when Great Britain, France, and Germany were otherwise committed, and limited in their ability to influence the outcome of the Mexican Revolution. These countries all had interests in Mexico, and their agents all participated in the intrigues of the day. But the United States had a decisive presence in Mexico, above and beyond that of any other nation, and acted in Mexico as if it were the only great power.[70] The issue of Roman Catholic internationalism is somewhat distinct, and although it had its own special parameter, it was important in terms of Mexican national identity and Catholic identity. It was also thoroughly linked to the question of recognition.

The April 1914 occupation of Veracruz received the most press coverage of any international aspect of the Mexican Revolution. In a sense, it was quite important in mobilizing nationalist sentiment. However, nationalism had many manifestations, and certainly, many uses. When the US troops arrived, it was entirely possible to frame the event as an invasion, the consequences of which were as far-reaching as the imagination might permit. Quickly, however, it became clear that the objectives of the Wilson government were limited. But this says little about the way the event was received and used in Mexico. In terms of national politics, much has been written, and it is clear that the major actors (Huerta, Carranza, Villa, and Zapata) had different reactions and different objectives.[71] It is also evident that the occupation meant something entirely different in the city of Veracruz than in Guadalajara. In the first instance, the violation of national sovereignty was intimately, physically real; in the second instance, it was by and large imagined. Perhaps it was no less real, but it was fundamentally distinct, over-determined by the press, government propagandists, and the popular imaginary.

In Guadalajara, as in much of the country, patriotic rage was blustery, but not often violent.[72] For example, a well-known lawyer from the Porfirian political class, Antonio Pérez Verdía, climbed on top of the table where he had been seated at the Hotel Fénix restaurant, and railed against the Yankee invasion. The press invoked a national mythology in defense of sovereignty by tracing a line of virile founding fathers. These included Benito Juárez, Pedro Moreno, José María Morelos, and Miguel Hidalgo—but reached all the way back to Cuitlahuac and Cuauhtémoc—in an effort to evoke a patriotic, conquest-era imaginary that lionized the Aztec *tlatoanis* who had resisted the Spanish conquerors. In the name of this imagined pantheon, Antonio Ortíz y Gordoa rallied the young men of Guadalajara, that they might offer their lives for the nation:

> The hour has come in which we will know whether or not we deserve to have had as fathers the men our history judges heroes. It is time to prove that they should feel no shame for having willed us a Free Fatherland! . . . The beautiful country of Anahuac needs the efforts of all its sons; all of them; all of them! History must write, should it be necessary, these words: MEXICO LOST HER LIBERTY; BUT ONLY AFTER THE LAST OF HER SONS HAD DISAPPEARED.[73]

Will Davis, the US consular officer, was forced to make his way to the train station, his octogenarian mother on his arm, flanked by an angry mob that heckled and humiliated him. They smashed the US coat of arms at the consulate and trampled upon the flag. They did not, however, lynch a single Yankee. This distinction is important, because Guadalajara had been the site of much more violent anti-Yankee rioting in 1910, just prior to Madero's call to arms. In that instance, mobs had attacked the properties of American residents in the city. The crowd did not manage to catch any Yankees, but many feared it would have ultimately lynched those whom it might have apprehended.[74] The precedent was very much in the minds of the fleeing US citizens. However, when Davis returned to Guadalajara five months later, he was well received by his own account.[75]

Popular reaction and the expression of national identity are often difficult to gauge. "Data" are impressionistic, relying on individual cases that offer anecdotal evidence: The heckling mob that bid Davis farewell was similar to those that congregated in other cities.[76] Pérez Verdía improvised a podium atop a table in one of the city's more exclusive restaurants. His sense of national identity was common among the liberal professions of Mexico's rapidly growing cities. The Jalostotitlan Catholics formed a volunteer corps and received military instruction with the goal of joining Huerta's national front.[77] Their small-town Catholic patriotism was no doubt distinct from the metropolitan, liberal nationalism of Pérez Verdía. Nevertheless, they would also likely recognize themselves, reflected in the call to duty of *El Correo de Jalisco*, which identified the Catholic undercurrent of Mexican national identity, in the legacy of Fathers Hidalgo and Morelos.

At Tepatitlán, a local member of the Catholic Party, Sabás G. Gutiérrez described the swearing-in of the new authorities days after the US occupation, in what can be described as a civic-religious event:

> A formal mass with a sermon was celebrated in which the new authorities were reminded of their duties so that they might better serve their mission. That afternoon, an act of devotion was dedicated in the presence of his Divine Majesty, imploring his protection, and then we marched, in correct formation, through the streets celebrating the Sacred Heart, the holy Virgin of Guadalupe, as well as the Deputies of the state Congress, the Mexican Nation, President Huerta and the entire Mexican army, followed by shouts of death to the Yankee invaders! The women joined in too, such was the enthusiasm, and we finished with a rendition of our beautiful National Anthem, accompanied by the town marching band. Before and after the march there were many fireworks, and groups of people following the music through the streets.[78]

Gutiérrez ended this letter by noting that the following day he would commence giving military training to volunteers who had enlisted to defend Mexico from the invasion. In towns like Jalostotitlan and Tepatitlán, patriotism was imbued with religious fervor, and the Catholicism expressed was strikingly Mexican. Thus, nationalistic fervor aroused by the US occupation of Veracruz was both civic and religious at the same time, transgressing the boundaries of secular society, as laid out by the Juárista reform. No doubt it would have been unacceptable to the middle-class urban nationalists of Carranza's office corps, but it was evidently popular in Jalisco's highland region.

Another incident further complicates this composite. Of the few remaining documents of the administration of General José María Mier, a letter written to the military governor sheds some light on popular sentiment. The author tells of the anti-Huerta sentiments of several drinkers at a local pub:

> By way of this letter I inform you that Florentino Parra, Patricio Ornelas, Cecilio Sotomayor, Manuel Ermosillo, speak very badly about the Government during their frequent drunken meetings at the *Limoncito* tavern, they have said several times that those who call themselves patriots are nothing more than ridiculous and stupid, and that the bandit and assassin Huerta's so-called intervention is nothing more than a strategic measure to confuse so many idiots and take them off to fight the revolutionaries so that he can remain longer in power and continue robbing the nation and that the

real american [*sic*] intervention is to topple this government of bandit and
assassin dogs . . . (*El Limonsito* is on the block of the 4th [Military] Zone).[79]

The author asks no favors and likely was driven by a combination of civic pride,
nationalist fervor, and perhaps a personal distaste for his fellow drinkers.
What is more interesting and telling is the conversation. In Guadalajara civilians were recruited and sent off as soldiers under the pretense of resisting the
Yankee invasion; quite possibly they ended up in Torreón, facing the Villista
cavalry charge. It is significant that the word on the street—in Guadalajara—
reflected this soon after the initial occupation of the port. Information regarding the occupation was surely limited. Yet, in Guadalajara, sentiments of
national identity were mediated by knowledge that the regime was using Veracruz as a means to apply the "leva," or draft soldiers, as a prop for the failing
campaign against the northern revolutionaries.

Meanwhile, back in the port city, the Yankees had struck up a surprising
and not altogether comfortable relationship with an unexpected visitor.
According to Francis P. Joyce, the Catholic chaplain to the US troops, refugee
priests and nuns had arrived at Veracruz from points north and west, fleeing
anticlerical violence. By October 1914, dozens of Mexican clergymen and
women found themselves in the ironic circumstance of seeking asylum from
the invading army of a protestant nation. Father Joyce had heard the stories of
atrocities committed by Carranza's army against the Catholic faith. So he
sought out president Wilson's envoy, John Lind, and John R. Silliman, the
American vice counsel, in an attempt to secure passage for Mexican clergy on
cargo ships returning from Veracruz to Galveston Texas. But ultimately, his
efforts were frustrated when neither of the two diplomats proved sympathetic.
In fact, Joyce took great offense to Silliman, who informed him that the Catholic Church was Mexico's second bane after prostitution, and that, like the
whores the Church must go.[80] Frustrated in his attempt to harness American
noblesse oblige, Joyce would eventually help broker passage for the fleeing religious to Cuba.[81]

If Veracruz was most important in the press, by contrast, the most important concern in the liberal discourse of nationalist leaders like Obregón and
Diéguez was the Roman Catholic Church. This liberal suspicion of Catholicism was not dissimilar to that which moved the Spanish Crown to decree the
1767 expulsion of the Jesuits. They were seen as loyal first to papal authority,
and second to the Crown. In the same way, the liberal revolutionaries of 1915—
and later—were obsessed with the foreign loyalties of the clergy. Catholicism

was anathema to their nationalism, quite in spite of the fact that Mexican Catholic nationalism was deeply rooted. It is not surprising, then, that liberal attacks on the symbols, sites, and authorities of Catholicism could incite protest, resistance, and violence in the twentieth century as it had in the eighteenth century.[82] This circumstance leads to the question: How exactly might the Roman Catholic Church act politically from without, to influence the conflict within the nation?

There are many answers to this question, as there are many actors. One obvious response is through official writing. Pope Benedict XV wrote letters of encouragement to the Mexican bishops, and Pope Pius XI issued *Iniquis Afflictisque*, the 1926 encyclical on religious persecution during the Cristero Rebellion. Closer to Mexico, the exiled bishops issued a 1914 pastoral letter condemning the anticlerical violence of the Constitutionalist insurrection, and a 1917 pastoral letter condemning the new constitution.[83] Such activity did not convince the anticlerical liberals, but probably strengthened the resolve of those faithful who identified with episcopal policy. Letters like the 1914 pastoral could work to rally the Catholic laity, because it had a literate leadership and an organizational infrastructure capable of spreading the word. Perhaps the best example of Catholicism taking on an international dimension was linked to the question of recognition.

Veracruz offered widespread press coverage, and the proclamations of the anticlerical liberals demonstrate their obsession with the foreign influence of Catholic loyalties, but US recognition of Carranza was probably of greater historical significance than the other two. Following the Villista collapse, the Carrancista army consolidated its control over most strategic points across the country. During September and October 1915, Catholics mobilized in the United States to sway President Wilson against recognition of Carranza. Many letters written by Catholics from across the United States argued, sometimes passionately, that Carranza would not uphold the basic freedom of religious expression, and should not receive US recognition. There were also letters to the opposite effect, arguing in favor of the Carrancistas, but they were the minority. As for the practical importance of recognition, the experience of the Huerta regime was a recent example of the difficulties a government might face without US approval. The main threat was not another invasion, but the possibility of being unable to borrow loans internationally.

The letter-writing campaign was waged mostly during the first three weeks of October.[84] In Robert Quirk's interpretation, the campaign was obviously organized by American clergy, a conclusion based on the observation that the letters were similarly worded.[85] There is an inferred logic here: the Church is a strict hierarchy; thus the campaign is organized by the bishops; who in turn require it be carried out by their flocks; therefore, it is of little impact and import. I disagree. First, there is no doubt that the campaign was organized, and that the "American clergy" were involved. However, the laity sent most of the letters, and the variety is much richer than one might expect, based on Quirk's cavalier dismissal. Most importantly, however, the fact that the campaign was organized, by clergy or anyone else, is no reason to treat it dismissively. To the contrary, because it was organized, it was explicitly political, and should be considered as such. There is no scientific way to estimate the number of votes that the Catholic Church and its organizations could sway, nor can it be argued that people would necessarily vote based exclusively on the Mexican question. But it would be shortsighted to underestimate the extent to which Catholic identity was a unifying factor for many such groups in the United States. Catholics were a religious minority, and generally an ethnic minority too, as is reflected in the names of several of the organizations.[86]

I examined sixty-one letters included among the State Department consular dispatches, of which fifty-two were against recognition, and nine were in favor. Those in favor were often written after recognition, and were of a congratulatory nature. They were generally written by people who identified themselves with Protestant churches. One came from a Los Angeles–based solidarity group called the Unión Constitucionalista de Obreros Mexicanos; in English they called themselves the Union Mexico Colony.[87] Some expressed explicit anti-Catholic sentiments, like the Rochester man who reassured President Wilson that anti-Catholic voters outnumbered Catholics five to one, and sent in press clippings declaring that the "Romish prelates," despite their oaths of celibacy, were responsible for the vast numbers of illegitimate children in Rome and Brussels, and for the Philippine "old maids" with their large families.[88] Another letter argued that 60 percent of Americans have no church at all. E. W. Dodge, of *Riches* magazine offered the following read on the Mexico question:

> [The] trouble was commenced in Mexico at the instigation of the catholic hierarchy in return for a fund of $20,000,000, furnished by Standard Oil in order to gain a foot-hold in the Tampico Oil fields and that the Christian Fathers knocked down the money, were unable to deliver the goods and have finally been reduced to a point where they have had to murder

American soldiers and citizens and organize raids into American territory for the purpose of causing intervention to be followed by annexation and a subsequent looting of the United States Treasury along the fruitful lines followed in the Philippines, Cuba, and Porta Rica [sic].[89]

The pact with Standard Oil seems unlikely, as does a conspiracy in which Christian Fathers murdered American citizens; on the issue of border raids, the author might be thinking of Villa's attack on Columbus, New Mexico, except that it was still about five months in the future. However, it was not the first time rumors surfaced of a "Villista clerical party."[90] The final reference illustrates how race imbued US imperialism: in this author's view, poor brown peoples take advantage of the white man's burden to leech the benefits of the affluent society. This is the underlying message of the letter. Recognize Carranza; don't get the United States involved in Mexico.

No Catholic wrote to endorse or congratulate the recognition of Carranza, and all fifty-two letters against recognition were sent by Catholics. They were sent from all regions of the United States. Many were telegrams, and because of the nature of that particular mode of correspondence, they were similarly phrased. But many others were letters, and their form often unique. Among the similarities, most of the correspondence was written on letterhead from Catholic lay organizations, although bishops did send eleven letters. The secretary or president of the organization would begin by saying that he or she wrote on behalf of so many thousands of Catholic citizens. For example, the Archbishop of Brooklyn represented 750,000 faithful; the Catholic Ladies of Columbia in Kenton, Ohio, represented 4,500 women; the Central Verein National Federation of German-American Catholics in New York represented 50,000 citizens; the Lithuanian Roman Catholic Alliance of America, located in Baltimore, represented 10,000 citizens; and the Ancient Order of Hibernians in America, located in Philadelphia, represented 175,000 citizens.[91] The Chicago-based Catholic Church Extension Society, Bishop Francis Kelley's organization, simply warned that recognition would bring sorrow to sixteen million Catholics in the United States:

The Catholic Church Extension Society . . . has more knowledge of [Mexico's] condition; has done more to alleviate its horrors than any single factor in America. In all its works it kept well within the spirit of true Americanism; it forestalled criticism against you, Mr. President, in well-founded conviction that you, as the champion of an ideal Democracy, would meet the tremendous obligation that has come to you in solving the problem of Mexico. It is our profound conviction that what you have done for the unfortunate people of Mexico would collapse entirely by the recognition of a man who is poles asunder in all that goes to make up the representative of a people who are striving to get to some plane of peace and security.[92]

Another letter, written by a priest from Jackson, Missouri, includes a composite of the press he had received on the chautauqua circuit across Nebraska, Iowa, Illinois, Indiana, and Ohio. Father Michael Collins had lived for years in Mexico, and in 1915 had spent his time going from town to town and speaking on the problems of Catholic Mexico. One newspaper wrote, impressed, "Father Collins gave proof of his broad-mindedness, by saying that if he were not a Catholic and a Catholic priest, he would not mind being a Mason." No doubt such heterodoxy would not have been appreciated in Mexico, where the Masons were generally blamed for Catholic ills. Collins for his part, made his opinion abundantly clear to President Wilson:

No priest can officiate at the graves of their deserted flocks, either at the time of sepulture or after; no priest is allowed to wear his clerical garb as the clergy of all denominations do here, when traveling or otherwise; no nun can wear the garb of her profession; were I to send a chalice, or other vessel or utensil, needed in the Church of a brother clergyman in Mexico, they would automatically and simultaneously become property of the State as soon as was brought into the church edifice [sic]; no donations or legacy can be willed to the Church; if attempted they become property of the State; the Church cannot and does not own so much as a splinter of wood, a grain of sand, or a piece of rock . . . [and] in the future, priests will not be allowed to hear confessions of their people, in health or dying . . . [R]ecognition of Carranza, at best, would be calamity to the Mexicans and the beginning of worse troubles. . . . [93]

The campaign was ultimately unsuccessful, and recognition was extended on October 18. However, Catholic public opinion was mobilized. The State Department was concerned to send out something more than a mere acknowledgment in response to all the letters it received, and assured those who wrote that Carranza had promised to abide by his country's law.[94] No doubt this was of little comfort to the Catholic activists. Surely, despite anticlerical paranoia, the Catholic Church was far less powerful in the arena of the great powers than was Washington. And whether or not the five-to-one ratio of anti-Catholic to Catholic voters could be counted on domestically, Wilson went ahead and extended diplomatic recognition. What the Church could do, however, that Washington could not, was unify people under a faith across national borders. The campaigns certainly educated Catholics, and contributed in the formation of public opinion. And while neither the Pope nor the US Catholics were of much help once the political sphere had collapsed and negotiation had ceded to rebellion, such outside influence would eventually play a role in the political resolution that achieved the 1929 cease-fire. Within Mexico, however, the experience of political mobilization, protest, and resistance forged a lasting collective identity.

———

The argument developed in this chapter began with a strict focus on events developing in Guadalajara surrounding the arrival of the Constitutionalist army and the final fall of the old regime. In that context, I argued that the task facing Generals Obregón and Diéguez included elements of both military and political struggle. Because the main opposition in Guadalajara was political, constituted through Catholic traditions, organizations, and government, the objective of Manuel Diéguez and his subordinates was to control the voices and venues of dissent. As the war shifted from military actions to the political sphere in Guadalajara, an important aspect of revolutionary government would be its campaign of symbolic violence, in other words, a politics designed to repress, silence, or at least contain, the symbols of Catholic identity. This campaign was begun during the summer of 1914, but it soon became difficult for Governor Diéguez to implement his policies due to the increasing military threat posed by the Villista army. After a short five months, Diéguez was forced to abandon the city in December, leaving the politics of government in favor of a renewed military campaign.

The second part of the argument was accompanied by a broader focus, which took into consideration events in the greater Guadalajara region. Still primarily concerned with Guadalajara, the military battles fought in and around the city link local history to a national narrative, one in which large armies fought in Jalisco with the goal of controlling the country. In this respect, the battles for Jalisco reveal two important points. First, the history of Jalisco during the Mexican Revolution is quite important for achieving a nuanced understanding of the larger revolutionary process; and second, the different military and political tactics practiced by the subordinates of Carranza and Villa were differentially experienced by Guadalajara's population. To be sure, both groups used violence toward political, as well as military, ends. And certainly, they did so not only in Jalisco, but back and forth across the country. Yet Guadalajarans commonly sensed that Diéguez and his soldiers meted out an extraordinary measure of violence against the general population, and the Catholic Church in particular. They also looked to Villa—however naively—as the one who could deliver them from their tribulations. But the argument here is that the local perception of events counts because it contributed in shaping political and religious identity with consequences over the long term.

Compare, for example, the afterlives of Diéguez, Medina, and Galván. Diéguez won, and has a statue in his honor at the capital city's *Rotonda de los Hombres Ilustres*, a memorial in the center of town, as well as a place in the official-history books.[95] On special occasions, floral wreaths are laid at his bronze feet. Medina lost, and although he has a small residential street named after him in a working-class neighborhood, he is mostly known through state-sanctioned history books, where he has often been painted as a reactionary. Galván, who was not even a combatant, has inspired a robust popular devotion. He was recently immortalized in Catholic tradition, when Pope John Paul II canonized him as a Christian martyr.

The third section of the chapter proposed a much broader focus, one in which international events are considered and tied into more particular historical processes. All three examples (the occupation of Veracruz, Roman Catholic internationalism, and US recognition of Carranza) had local impact in terms of popular sentiment, the formation of both state and nation, and the political realities that would characterize Jalisco during the process of reconstruction.

In the next chapter, once again it will be important to focus alternately on Guadalajara and small-town Jalisco with its political dependence on government established in the state capital. And once again, the issues of state-building and popular sentiment will guide the chapter, forcing the reader to consider the process of nation formation, the struggles of citizens and believers to influence the form and modes of revolutionary Mexico.

6. Local Politics and the Mexican Revolution in Jalisco

A CARBON COPY retained by the Jalisco state government in mid-1916, corresponding to a letter sent by Manuel M. Diéguez to First Chief Carranza and War Secretary Obregón, preserves for historians a semblance of the conflicting forces that shaped the political arena only months prior to the Constitutional Congress of Querétaro. The text reads as follows:

> I have recently come across a flyer in which the reactionaries, engaging in
> a superficial comparison between our liberation movement and the French
> revolution of the XVIII century, vigorously censure the actions of the Con-
> stitutionalist Government in such a manner as to leave no doubt that our
> enemies will make every effort and stoop as low as is necessary to interrupt
> the work for which we have so struggled and continue to struggle not only
> militarily, but on the battle field of ideas. . . . I believe it my duty, and am
> certain you will approve in such case my actions, to persecute tenaciously
> those who veil themselves in anonymity such as the case to which I refer
> . . . and who merit nothing more than the greatest punishment in recom-
> pense for their reprehensible actions.[1]

Unfortunately, a copy of the flyer has not survived in accompaniment with the letter. Nevertheless, several aspects of the text cited by General Diéguez in his letter merit discussion, because they offer a context for understanding the tensions that characterized the first years of Constitutionalist government in Jalisco. Two are of interest here. First, who are the "reactionaries"? They are likely militant Catholics, and their reference to the French Revolution probably is concerned with the period of the terror, and the persecution of Church privilege in general, or freedom of worship in particular. There is a clue at the end of the letter, in which Diéguez assures Obregón and Carranza that such schemes by "clerical trash and other despicable reactionaries" will not destroy their efforts. Second, what is the significance of Diéguez's response, and why did he formulate it as such? The response suggests the Constitutionalist shift in strategy, from military to political battles. The Villistas were no longer a threat, and the remaining opposition was not armed, but civilian. Nevertheless, this shift was not perceived as irreversible. After all, Diéguez felt obliged to send the letter to the war secretary. While a contemporary reader might simply note the comparison drawn with the French Revolution, Diéguez saw reactionaries who would resort to anything. This is a clear example of how political renovation was couched in Manichean terms, and there is an unmistakable clarity in the resolve with which the author suggests combating this revolutionary heresy.[2]

The letter also helps, in the words of Jeffrey Rubin, to "decenter the regime,"[3] to demonstrate how national history is not forged only from events transpiring in Mexico City, but through major conflicts occurring elsewhere, events that emerge from regional historical contingencies to shape the nation. The passage quoted above makes clear the national importance of the conflict. Rather than a discussion between locals regarding a provincial idiosyncrasy, we have General Diéguez, Carranza's man in western Mexico, reporting directly to the first chief and Obregón, the revolution's second in command. In this way, the national importance of regional phenomena emerges from within the official sources of the Mexican Revolution. This chapter will analyze a regional phenomenon—a social movement that developed in opposition to the anticlerical content of the 1917 constitution—and argue that the conflict that unfolded in Jalisco during 1918 shaped the course of post-revolutionary Mexico for years hence.

Local Politics and the 1917 Constitution

In 1918, Jalisco's lay Catholic associations organized a lockout of their churches to protest legislation designed to limit the Church's role in society.[4] With clerical support, students, workers, employees, mothers, and domestic servants used their churches to focus Catholic anger against the state government. These confessional organizations successfully established a radical discursive and political polarity between Catholics and revolutionaries, couched in terms of *pueblo* and tyrant, good and evil. The views held by Catholic political activists, both clerical and lay, were repeated by many different groups, who demanded the repeal of laws they considered offensive. Through such polarization, these groups succeeded in associating a particular practice of Catholic worship with the liberal concept of individual liberty, despite the fact that the Church was neither "liberal," nor had a strong tradition of defending individual liberties in Mexico.

In another respect too, the events of 1918 were unlike earlier Church-state conflicts. The revolution had destroyed the old regime, and the post-revolutionary state was only just being constructed. In the absence of effective central government, power dispersed to the regions and did not necessarily emanate from Mexico City. In Jalisco, the most aggressive anticlerical legislation derived not from the 1917 constitution but from its local application. Likewise, Jalisco's Church-state conflict was resolved in the local Congress with the encouragement of Manuel M. Diéguez, then at the tail end of his tenure as governor of Jalisco (1914–1917, 1917–1919). Probably Carranza convinced Diéguez that Jalisco's religious problem was likely to have repercussions elsewhere; nevertheless, the dynamic remained locally rooted up to this point. The fundamental conflict concerned the politically charged question of religious liberty, on the one hand, and the revolutionary program for constructing a secular society on the other.[5] This clash was one aspect of the revolutionary process that rapidly affected—and mobilized—large sectors of society, crossing differences of class, sex, ethnicity, and generation, and forging a distinctly religious political identity. Although conflictual, the process was interactive; as Jalisco's Catholics resisted the revolution, they articulated a discourse of "sacred" rights and a mass-based political practice reflecting wider social developments.

Church-state tensions were refocused in Mexico by the 1917 constitution. Disagreement centered on the following areas: Article 3, which prohibited religious schools; Article 5, which equated religious vows with servitude and established that the state would not recognize them; Article 13, which denied legal status to religious organizations; Article 27, which prohibited religious associations from owning property and established that churches were property of the nation; and Article 130, which established that the state would exercise final authority above and beyond any other institution regarding religious worship.[6] The episcopate responded in a pastoral letter of February 1917, signed by fourteen exiled bishops in Texas and published that April. The episcopate protested against the restriction of religious liberty, but ended on a conciliatory note, arguing that the Church was not interested in power and would cooperate with government if an air of tolerance and mutual respect were restored in Church-state relations: "We are persuaded," the prelates concluded, "of the benefits of a healthy exercise in democracy, as the only way to bring to our nation a firm and stable government that balances and moderates, respecting the rights of all and giving to each that which belongs to him."[7]

The archbishop of Guadalajara, Francisco Orozco y Jiménez, did not sign the 1917 collective pastoral because he had already returned from exile.[8] Back in Rome, he had informed Pope Pius X of his desire to return home to Mexico despite the fact that hundreds of clergy members were living in exile, including almost all of the bishops. The pope agreed, but told him he must see the Mexico City archbishop, José Mora y del Río, and ask for his blessing as well. Orozco y Jiménez left Rome in the fall of 1916, sailed to New York, and proceeded by train to Chicago. There he discussed his plans with Father Francis C. Kelley, his buddy from Rome, and a small contingent of exiled Mexican clergy. From Chicago he made his way to San Antonio, where he met with the Mexico City archbishop. Once he had convinced José Mora y del Río, the fifty-two-year-old Orozco y Jiménez crossed the border on foot and headed incognito for Jalisco. His return is chronicled in a ten-page journal written at the time.[9]

Orozco did not arrive at Guadalajara, and there were no welcoming processions. Rather, he arrived privately, disguised by a long beard and traveler's clothes, from the north: via Aguascalientes and the sparsely populated south Zacatecas sierra, until reaching Totatiche. Like the bishop of Zapatista Cuernavaca, Orozco could move around with some security, confident that the region's countryfolk did not share the anticlericalism of urban revolutionaries.[10] He began his pastoral visit under cover in Totatiche, using at least two aliases, and continued town-to-town, following the Sierra southward before moving into the highland region of northeast Jalisco known as *Los Altos*.[11] Two aspects of his trip that foreshadow subsequent historical events bear mention. First, Orozco writes with fraternal affection of a young priest who accompanies him along his dangerous journey. This priest turns out to be father José Garibi Rivera who, twenty years later, succeeded Orozco as archbishop of Guadalajara.[12] Second, Orozco wrote to the Totatiche parish priest in order to safeguard his arrival. He then describes the local priest with marked admiration, this in 1916. The priest in question was subsequently martyred in 1927, and canonized in 2000, Saint Cristóbal Magallanes.

Orozco almost certainly learned of the collective pastoral weeks after publication. At about the same time—May 1917—he received a supportive letter from the Vatican's secretary of state, Cardinal Gaspari, relating a greeting of

FIGURE 6. Guadalajara
Archbishop Francisco
Orozco y Jiménez,
San Antonio, Texas,
1916. Source: Archivo
Histórico de la Arqui-
diócesis de Guadalajara.

Benedict XIV.[13] Shortly after, on June 4, Orozco seconded the April letter in a
pastoral written from an unidentified parish in the archdiocese. Orozco's short
letter protested against the 1917 constitution but instructed his faithful to
abstain from seditious acts that would play into the hands of the Church's
enemies. At the same time he advised his supporters that circumstances did
not warrant a retreat into idle lamentations; rather, Catholics should take
advantage of their suffering in order to build religious unity.[14]

On June 1, 1917, Manuel M. Diéguez assumed office as Jalisco's constitutional
governor, initially to general indifference.[15] Diéguez immediately adopted a
hard-line position in religious affairs, however, and embodied a Constitutionalist intransigence bred partially of uncertainty. Both he and his interim governor,

Manuel Aguirre Berlanga (part of 1914, most of 1915–1916), were outsiders: Diéguez, a former employee of the Cananea copper mines, was a Sonoran, while Aguirre belonged to Coahuila's coterie of Carrancistas.[16] In certain other respects, too, Diéguez resembled Carranza's proconsuls to the Mexican south.[17] Like Salvador Alvarado, Jesus Castro, or Francisco Múgica, he came from "plebeian" origins and saw privilege, hierarchy, and entrenched officialdom—both secular and clerical—as enemies; he also lacked local connections and popular support, but was driven by a "powerful blend of idealism and ambition," rooted in *Magonismo*,[18] nationalism, and anticlericalism. As Jalisco's governor and military commander, Diéguez operated in accordance with a binary vision pitting liberal against conservative, reform against reaction.

Political Catholics received Diéguez's attacks on entrenched—particularly Church—privilege as open hostility. Anacleto González Flores, for example, viewed the Constitutionalists as descendants of the French Jacobins who treated Jalisco as "conquered" territory. In his 1920 essay on Jalisco's religious persecution, González Flores wrote: "The revolution . . . has neither understood nor recognized the *pueblo* . . . [but] reduced it to a meaningless word, and tortured it with the guillotine of the Terror."[19] Diéguez's "reactionaries" also comprised intellectuals, therefore, who produced written propaganda and availed themselves of a comparative historical vision reaching back to the French Revolution. This distinguished them from most Catholics who often saw revolutionary hostility toward their customs in more immediate terms.[20] All this points to a basic paradox of the Mexican Revolution: while Carrancistas saw themselves in a struggle to rid the country of the old regime, political Catholics saw a people persecuted by alien revolutionaries for their religious customs. Although divergent in their goals, both sides labored to forge a "new" citizen from the mire of revolution.

Three days after Diéguez took office, on June 4, Archbishop Orozco's pastoral was read out in mass at several Guadalajara churches, where it could most easily be distributed. In response, Diéguez ordered the state attorney to close these churches and arrest their priests on charges of rebellion. In all, eight churches were closed, including the Cathedral and Our Lady of Guadalupe, which, as previously stated, was popularly known as the Sanctuary (*El Santuario*). Charges of sedition were filed against Orozco and priests who read the letter at mass, resulting in several arrests.[21] On July 12, the recently founded Association of Mexican Catholic Youth (ACJM) organized its first public protest, inviting Catholics to march from *El Santuario* to the governor's palace in exercise of their constitutional right (Article 9) to protest. The marchers were composed of men and women of varied ages and classes, carrying banners that read, "We Protest Energetically Against the Apprehension of Priests," and "We Protest Against Criminal Searches of Church Buildings." In González Flores's account, the march progressed southward through the artisan neighborhood near *El Santuario* to the city center. Passersby watched with surprise, and people came to doors and windows to observe the march.[22] As the marchers passed University Gardens, four blocks from the governor's palace, they were cut off by police reservists with pistols drawn: many marchers were beaten up and two dozen men—including the organizers—and a group of women were arrested. The US consul reported that some women had fought with police.[23]

González Flores, among those arrested, referred to the clash as "the first encounter." The women were eventually scolded and told to go home, suggesting officials considered them less threatening than the men, and perhaps misled. The male detainees—law, medicine, and engineering students, high-schoolers, and a *cargador*, or carrier (the only working-class detainee mentioned)—were jailed. González Flores mused on the irony of their imprisonment: the mayor's office, as well as the local jail, was installed in the former archbishop's palace, confiscated by revolutionaries in 1914. Locked up in the palace basement, the twenty-four detainees continued their protest, praying the rosary aloud, singing songs, and reciting a poem—"*Los Pueblos Tristes*"— by nineteenth-century Cuban poet and independence champion Bonifacio Byrne. The poem exhorts the God of pity to take the side of the persecuted:

> Lord of mercy: because you exist
> On the side put yourself of the downtrodden
> and they will vanquish their oppressor.
> Allow them that, breaking their chains
> they might root out from their spirit the pain.
> That they may stand tall like heroes
> and to You they will lift their prayers.
> And there will be in this land more lions,
> but there will also be fewer serpents.[24]

Next day, the detainees were marched before the mayor, Luis Castellanos y Tapia, who censured their protest. Particularly reprehensible, in his eyes, was the fact that young women had been involved in public protest; here was an indicator that gender relations, and a particular construction of Woman as being "outside" the political, were changing.[25] Fines were set at 200 pesos per head, at which point the carrier asked that his fine be set in accordance with the law: no more than a week's wages. When this petition was denied, all of the detainees refused to pay, and thus served fifteen-day sentences.[26]

Alarmist newspapers reported an imposing protest, a clear indication of Catholic discontent.[27] Two days later, archdiocesan secretary Miguel Cano was arrested and charged with rebellion.[28] For several months afterward, Guadalajara's liberal press—*El Gato, El Occidental, El Independiente,* and *El Radical* in particular—ran stories of the alleged criminality, rebelliousness, and lawlessness of priests and lay Catholics in Guadalajara and rural Jalisco, in what seemed to be an orchestrated media campaign.[29] For his part, González Flores wrote in 1920 that "the first encounter" gave Jalisco Catholics an important lesson in the limitations of legal protest: Article 9 *did not* guarantee Catholics the right to peaceful protest, and the constitution was a lie.[30]

Following the July 12 march, Catholic attention in Guadalajara focused on reopening the churches. Organized across and within parish structures, two mass petitions circulated in the diverse neighborhoods affected by the closures. The petitions comprised some 3,000 signatures in all. One third corresponded to neighborhoods north and west of the city center, which demanded the reopening of the churches of Dolores, Mezquitán, San Diego, Santa María, San José, and Our Lady of Guadalupe; the remaining two thirds of petitioners focused solely on the parish church in Mexicaltzingo. The first petition included churches from two different parishes—Our Lady of Guadalupe and Sweet Name of Jesus—which covered the city's entire north and northwest; Mexicaltzingo was the parish seat of a broad artisan and Indian neighborhood south of the city center.[31]

The petitions' most significant aspect, other than their broad appeal, is perhaps their independently constructed identity. These are not the standard, community-based petitions one might find in many rural towns. Indeed, the signatories' only commonality was their rejection of a government policy affecting their local customs; otherwise, they did not necessarily have much in common with one another. It is difficult to unpack the signatories' social demographics except in rudimentary terms, but two-thirds were women, and—judging from the churches cited—most were probably artisans, *mestizos,* and Indians. This does offer a tentative hypothesis: that Guadalajara's lower-middle and lower sectors did act politically, and in ways that a social scientist might consider "modern," even though their objective was the preservation of customs that might be considered "traditional," conservative, or reactive. If the petitions are further considered in light of the ACJM's July march, the threads binding this incipient social movement were parish-based and organized through lay associations. The local press certainly compared this new Catholic social movement to the National Catholic Party (PCN) success of 1911–1914; the 1917 protests were organized in the same way, and with similar success, as an early exercise in a Catholicized mass politics.[32]

Church Property and the National Interest

The 1917 constitution dominated Church-state relations and the strategies of political Catholics for the next ten years. Initially, however, religious conflicts were played out regionally between state and diocesan governments. This was partly because Carranza, as president, was inclined to play down Church-state antagonisms through nonenforcement of the constitution's anticlerical articles. Similarly, the episcopate sought conciliation and cooperation. Among Carrancista governors as well as bishops, though, there were widely divergent positions. In this regionally defined context, the first important confrontation occurred in Jalisco in 1918 between Governor Manuel Bouquet Jr. (Diéguez's interim replacement from February 1918 to January 1919) and Archbishop Orozco.[33] The episode's historical significance was to involve the same issue (indeed many of the same actors) that later triggered the Cristero Rebellion, with the difference that Church and state came to a political solution in the first case, after months of coordinated Catholic protest. In 1926, this would no longer be possible. The resolution in 1918–1919 likely inflated Catholic expectations of a later settlement and encouraged dangerous brinkmanship.

The 1918 conflict began with the state government's decision to survey churches for expropriation and pass enabling legislation to regulate religious worship under constitutional Article 130. According to the constitution, regulation ought to reflect local circumstances; and in Jalisco, government wanted to license clergy and limit their numbers. In February, public works department director Rafael Sálazar surveyed Guadalajara's churches in order to decide which should be closed and expropriated under Article 27. Sálazar targeted thirty-two of the city's fifty-four churches for expropriation: twenty-one were projected for use as elementary schools, five as museums, four as artisan workshops, and two as drawing academies; sixteen churches would be preserved as places of worship, while three still under construction were not evaluated, and two more, characterized as ruins, would disappear.[34] The larger churches serving Guadalajara's popular artisan and Indian neighborhoods were singled out as centers of "propaganda and fanaticism," in particular

Mexicaltzingo and *El Santuario*: both were parish seats and at the center of large, deeply religious neighborhoods. The churches of La Merced in the city center and San Martín to the northeast were also singled out. All were active promoters of Catholic politics.

Sálazar's report offers a fascinating glimpse into a mind convinced of the existence of scientific utopias. An engineer, he seems to have had little empathy with religion, which he described as completely superfluous to progress. Sálazar's vision was evolutionist, with primacy placed on material and intellectual progress. Like many revolutionaries, Sálazar was driven by a view of progress rooted in education. As far as religion was concerned, his mentality was curatorial: churches and their possessions were objects belonging to the fine arts department, and ought to be inventoried as part of the nation's natural history.[35] For Sálazar, expropriated Church property should serve

> a higher order than the simple devotion that enervates the individual with illusory expectations of imagined miracles, which have never contributed anything to humanity's intellectual, moral, or material progress; for none of the knowledge to which we owe the inventions and discoveries that have allowed our societies to enjoy well-being [is] in any sense . . . due to religious devotion. Clearly, religious dogma has not guided men towards the discovery of a single truth useful to humanity; it is not religious dogma to which we owe the many inventions of machines and methods for producing artifacts, which in their different applications to industry and human activity have facilitated life and increased wealth; nor is it religious dogma to which we owe the discovery of Laws, either in the moral or physical order. . . . These inventions and discoveries . . . and all that has enabled mankind to prosper and flourish, are due to science.[36]

After surveying Church property, Jalisco's state legislature prepared a legal framework for expropriation based on a bill introduced by Jorge Villaseñor.[37] The legislation, eventually known as Decree 1913, would restrict all religious denominations to one priest and church per 5,000 faithful, while requiring all religious "professionals" (that is, priests and ministers) to be licensed by the state. For the licensing, photographs of practicing priests would be collected in an official registry along with a description of each priest's physical appearance, place of work, residence, earnings, and so on.[38] Similar registries had been used previously, as far back as the French Intervention, to keep track of prostitutes and prisoners. Porfirian bureaucrats had also used such measures to track domestic servants and unskilled laborers. But priests had never been considered for such demeaning treatment, and the law was met with widespread anger and rejection.[39]

On May 31, 1918, the state legislature approved a law limiting the number of churches and priests;[40] on July 3 the governor published Decree 1913, permitting one church for every 5,000 citizens or fraction thereof, based on the 1910 census.[41] With approximately 110,000 inhabitants in 1910, the law might conceivably allow twenty-two churches, each with a priest, a vast reduction in the material and human resources of the Catholic Church. However, according to Salazar's own estimates, the local population was about 176,000 in 1918, and the sixteen churches he designated for religious use in Guadalajara would fall woefully short of the city's needs. According to the plan, each place of worship would be staffed by only one priest, and according to the 1917 constitution, only Mexicans by birth would be permitted to work as priests.[42] To put this into perspective, there were 3,232 priests in Mexico in 1851, and the number grew to 4,461 by the outset of the revolution. In 1910, 569 priests lived in Jalisco (or 12.75 percent), 457 in Michoacán, and 431 in Mexico City. Precise data is not available for 1918, but it is reasonable to assume that the plan sought to radically curtail religious practice in Jalisco, and particularly in the capital city.[43]

The Church-state problem was not simply legal, but political, as Diéguez seems to have recognized. Two days after the publication of Decree 1913, Archbishop Orozco y Jiménez was arrested in Lagos de Moreno by soldiers acting on orders from Diéguez. The following day, General César López de Lara arrived at Lagos by train from Michoacán, and escorted the archbishop to Tampico.[44] At several stops along the way, the archbishop's defenders presented *amparos*, legal restraining orders against his detention and forced exile; but each time the military refused to abide by the injunctions. In Tampico, Orozco was charged with treason and strongly advised to leave the country, which he did.[45] In Chicago for the next year, Orozco was the distinguished guest of Monsignor Francis Kelley, author of the 1915 diatribe against Mexico's revolutionaries, *The Book of Red and Yellow: Being a Story of Blood and a Yellow Streak*.[46]

Petition, Politics, and the Public Sphere

If the old regime's disintegration and the PCN disappearance in 1914 disarticulated Catholic politics, then the Constitutional Congress and establishment of a new regime in 1917 reenergized the movement, mobilizing large

TABLE 2. Evaluation and Projected Use of Guadalajara Catholic Churches, 1918

Name	Seating	Observations	Projected use
Catedral	3,000	Provides a necessary service	Religious worship
El Sagrario	1,500	Unnecessary	Elementary school
La Soledad	500	Unnecessary	Elementary school
La Merced	1,200	Propaganda and fanaticism	Industrial museum
San José	1,000	Provides a necessary service	Religious worship
Santa Monica	800	Unnecessary	Knitting workshop
San Felipe	1,000	Unnecessary	Elementary school
San Diego	600	Unnecessary	Carpentry workshop
El Refugio	600	Unnecessary	Drawing academy
Capilla de Jesús	800	Provides a necessary service	Religious worship
La Luz	300	Unnecessary	Elementary school
Beata Margarita	300	Unnecessary	Elementary school
Santuario de Guadalupe	1,200	Propaganda and fanaticism	Elementary school
Los Dolores	400	Provides a necessary service	Religious worship
Belén	600	Provides a necessary service	Religious worship
Preciosa Sangre	400	Unnecessary	Elementary school
Capuchinas	1,200	Unnecessary	Elementary school
Jesús María	1,200	Unnecessary	Raw materials museum
Santiago	900	Under construction	No recommendation
Inmaculada	600	Unnecessary	Elementary school
Asociación de Hijas de María	250	Under construction	Elementary school
Siervas de María	250	Unnecessary	Elementary school
Hospital de San Antonio	200	Provides a necessary service	Religious worship
Mezquitán	800	Provides a necessary service	Religious worship
Capilla del Padre Leal	300	Unnecessary	Elementary school
Santa María de Gracia	1,000	Unnecessary	Museum
Herederos del Padre Plascencia	500	Under construction; unnecessary	No recommendation
Santa Teresa	800	Unnecessary	Arts museum
El Carmen	1,000	Provides a necessary service	Religious worship

Name	Seating	Observations	Projected use
Parroquia del Pilar	800	Unnecessary	Elementary school
Adoratrices del Santísimo	250	Unnecessary	Elementary school
Hospital de la Trinidad	300	Unnecessary	Elementary school
La Trinidad	800	Unnecessary	Sewing workshop
San Antonio	800	Provides a necessary service	Religious worship
Templo de Expiación	1,500	Under construction	No recommendation
Patronato	300	Unnecessary	Elementary school
Los Angeles	500	Provides a necessary service	Religious worship
San Francisco	2,000	Provides a necessary service	Religious worship
Santo Cenáculo	500	Ruins	Disappeared
Aranzazú	800	Unnecessary	Elementary school
Mexicaltzingo	2,000	Propaganda and fanaticism	Weaving workshop
Capilla del Sagrado Corazón	300	Provides a necessary service	Religious worship
San Agustín	2,000	Unnecessary	Agricultural museum
San Juan de Dios	1,000	Provides a necessary service	Religious worship
Capilla de la Milagrosa	500	Unnecessary	Elementary school
Nuestra Señora del Sagrado Corazón	800	Unnecessary	Drawing academy
La Concepción	1,200	Provides a necessary service	Religious worship
Verbo Encarnado	300	Provides a necessary service	Religious worship
San Martín	800	Propaganda and fanaticism	Elementary school
Hospital del Sagrado Corazón	400	Provides a necessary service	Elementary school
San José de Analco	1,000	Provides a necessary service	Religious worship
San Sebastián de Analco	1,300	Limits width of adjacent street	Elementary school
Santo Domingo	400	Ruins	Disappeared

Source: Archivo Municipal de Guadalajara, Guadalajara, exp. 139, 1918.

numbers of Catholics in opposition to the restrictions placed on the practice of religious worship. The 1918 movements voiced opposition to Decree 1913, and support for Jalisco's exiled archbishop. They took on diverse organizational forms. Some were parish-based, others were community-based; but all were articulated through lay Catholic organizations such as the ACJM and the Mexican Union of Catholic Ladies (UDCM). All engaged with civil government at different levels, from the town council to the state congress, from the governor's office to President Carranza. The campaign was waged through petitions, public demonstrations, mass pilgrimages, economic boycotts, and civil disobedience. This diversity of protest forms is of considerable importance because it underscores the broad appeal of the demands and the formation of a Catholic political identity. These were the strategies of a "public Catholicism" that was highly politicized and willing to challenge the regime in spheres that the state considered proper to the revolution.[47]

Guadalajara Catholics first petitioned President Carranza in June 1918, prior to the archbishop's exile. Their petition was devised as an expression of popular support for an April *memorial* sent to Carranza by the archdiocesan vicar general, Manuel Alvarado. The April document recounted the aggressions committed by the military government against Catholics prior to the reestablishment of constitutional rule (1914–1917). While the memorial was detailed and lengthy, the June petition was brief and alluded to the principal complaints of those affected: church closures; the authorities' refusal to comply with court orders that churches reopen; the confiscation of corn under the pretext that it was tithe; the arrest of newspaper vendors who sold Catholic dailies; the detention and fining of faithful for publicly wearing Ash Wednesday crosses on their foreheads; the confiscation without due process of private property allegedly belonging to the Church.[48]

Significantly, the petition focused less on Catholic *complaints* regarding the constitution than on constitutional articles protecting religious worship and Catholics' rights of assembly and protest. In particular, Catholics pointed to Article 130's prescription concerning the regulation of religious practice, which stipulated that priests and churches should be licensed in numbers according with local needs. Finally, the signatories argued that, as Mexicans, they had a fundamental right to protection under the new laws. Speaking in their own names, for Guadalajara's lay Catholic organizations, and for the Catholics of all Jalisco, they demanded that the laws reflect the desires of "public opinion."[49] Rather than a negative litany of complaints, therefore, Catholics here asserted a positive discourse of politico-religious rights. As the petition circulated, however, Decree 1913 was published, further straining an already tense situation. The petition was sent to Carranza with the signatures of more than 4,500 Guadalajara Catholics—both men and women—just as Orozco y Jiménez was driven into exile by state authorities.

Following the June petition, considerable numbers of lay Catholic organizations in Guadalajara began circulating signed protests in the form of pamphlets, flyers, and open letters to the "authorities." These constructed a Catholic identity on the basis of group affiliation, through the various lenses of youth (catechists, students, minors), gender (middle- to upper-class women, unmarried women, nonmothers), occupation (workers, servants, teachers, employees), and church congregation. The role of young women catechists is relevant, as catechism teachers likely formulated worker and servant petitions. For example, the protest sent by the catechists, servants, and workers of the Santa Zita Association started with the surnames of some of Guadalajara's elite families, and concluded with 100 surnames belonging to servants and workers (this should not be interpreted as bourgeois manipulation of the lower classes).[50] Many protesters simply decried their circumstances, demanding respect for their customs, religion, and archbishop. Energetic legal protest was generally signified as virile or manly for young Catholic men. In contrast, for women in the UDCM, protest was articulated in terms of female suffering and selflessness:[51] one women's protest stated that

> there are moments when a woman, naturally resigned to suffering, cannot but make herself heard. Such is the case when she is aggrieved with respect to that which she most loves and which is most deserving of her love. She will remain silent confronted with offenses made toward her person; but confronted with assaults on her Faith, her life's force and vigor, woman must always respond with the sublime cry of protest.[52]

In general, this image of unselfish suffering recurs across the social hierarchies, providing a common or unifying construction of Catholic feminine identity. Catholic victimhood also pervades Alvarado's 1918 memorial, which in this sense provides the millenarian master-narrative for a Catholic reading of the Mexican Revolution as a reliving of ancient Rome, with martyrdom and sacrifice as the fruits of the faith:

> The Church was born on the Cross, grew up in the Catacombs, and has always lived combated and persecuted: its true children have never lifted a

hand against their persecutors, nor committed offense against their executioners, nor caused aggression, but rather [have lived] suffering, [granted] pardon and [accepted] martyrdom . . . [S]till, when a law has favored them or their Church, they have not missed the chance to defend themselves by it.[53]

Unlike the June petition, the July petitions carried the signatures of organization members, ranging from a few who signed on behalf of the group to a few hundred. In all I am aware of twenty-four protests circulating in Guadalajara, mostly in July 1918. These were generated by specific groups, often tied to parishes; between them carried some 1,300 signatures (roughly 25 percent of the June signatures); and were more often signed by women than men (the ratio was about 8:1). This bias may reflect official intimidation. In mid-July, 120 signatories—mostly young men—were arrested and sentenced by the criminal court.[54]

Meanwhile, the UDCM called for action. In a meeting with members of the ACJM and the Cervantes Academy (a Catholic school), Catholic women agreed to print signs denouncing Decree 1913 and the archbishop's enforced exile, and to place them in all homes in the city.[55] Black bows also appeared over doors and in windows of Catholic homes as a sign of mourning. The ACJM distributed thousands of fliers inviting city Catholics to congregate peacefully on the afternoon of July 22 at Diéguez's house. The text of the invitation, attributed to González Flores, is telling:

> To the Catholics of Guadalajara: You are invited, without distinction of class or sex, to gather on Monday the 22nd at 5 p.m., in the plaza of the train station, in order to demonstrate to General Manuel M Diéguez, in response to indications that he made to a commission of Catholic women, that the majority of Guadalajara is Catholic and does not agree with Decree 1913.—Order is requested, and employers are asked to give leave to their employees.[56]

Crowd estimates ranged from 10,000 to 60,000, and a Catholic publication cited one eyewitness who offered a breakdown made by a man named Ángel Corsi: 35,000 in the plaza and gardens, 15,000 along Calle Ferrocarril, and 10,000 along the plaza's side streets.[57]

From his balcony, Diéguez addressed the crowd; after a resounding "yes" to his inquiry as to whether the demonstrators were Catholic, he told them that he was well aware of their religious affiliation and never questioned it. Diéguez

FIGURE 7.   Massive protest at San Francisco Gardens, July 22, 1918. Source: Archivo
Histórico de la Arquidiócesis de Guadalajara.

told the crowd that their priests had misled them, for which he received loud
cries of "no" and catcalls; and he continued by telling demonstrators that their
priests were unwilling to abide by the law. Diéguez finished by warning the
crowd that if they were Mexicans they had but two choices: abide by Decree
1913, or leave the state as pariahs.[58] Interestingly, this challenge parallels the
conversation between Calles and the bishops of Morelia and Tabasco on the
eve of the Cristero Rebellion in 1926. Then, Calles told prelates Díaz and Ruíz
y Flores that the Church had only two choices, to petition Congress to amend
the constitution or rise up in arms. In 1918 and 1926, thousands of Catholics
opted not to abide by the law, but with very different results.[59] In Jalisco in 1918,
the response was legal protest and peaceful noncooperation. This experience
was surely in Church leaders' minds in 1926 when they once again decided to
close the churches, this time nationally.

    Following his encounter with the crowd, Diéguez withdrew from his bal-
cony. Shortly afterward, mounted police attacked, creating space in the plaza
for a larger police contingent on foot. In the ensuing chaos, many Catholics
were beaten. An eyewitness reported seeing Police Commissar Borrayo
severely wound two women, both of whom died subsequently. Another pro-
tester ran from Borrayo and took shelter in the nearby Bolivian consulate. A

woman named Herrera was reportedly killed by a saber blow to the neck, while petty merchants lining the train station's entrance were arrested on charges of concealing weapons for the crowd. Writing to his old friend Miguel Palomar, Marcelino Álvarez Tostado ended with the following irony: "We have two more martyrs to add to the many victims of the most glorious [revolution]."[60]

In Antonio Gómez Robledo's interpretation, this was the moment the government lost any moral authority it might hitherto have held over Jaliscan society.[61] For his part, González Flores wrote that

the ire of Caesar was felt, when police on foot and horseback threw themselves against the unarmed crowd, as if they were attacking an army at war. Women, children, elderly, and young, all who had the misfortune of finding themselves within the reach of those cossacks, were beaten, trampled under charging horses, and struck with machetes.[62]

Despite the repression, the protest generated a feeling of Catholic victory. Newspapers were warned not to report the incident; in protest, *La Epoca* left its front page blank, except for the caption: "Silence is, after speech, the world's second power."[63] In Guadalajara, mused Gómez Robledo, there was no need to put the story in writing because the locals could read not only between the lines, but without them.[64]

After the violent dispersal of the July 22 protest, Jalisco's legislature published an amended version of Decree 1913, called Decree 1927, which repealed the first. Decree 1927 retained its predecessor's basic content, but specified fines of 10 to 200 pesos and one to eleven months' imprisonment for priests who did not comply.[65] Compliance meant that priests must be licensed by the state in order to minister. The archdiocese's response was to end priest-led worship in the churches. If priests did not exercise their vocation, they would not need state licenses. And, while much worship went underground during the following months, as of August 1, mass would not be given in any Guadalajara churches.[66] These actions were extended to the rest of the state as of September 1.[67]

In Guadalajara in the final days of July, church attendance swelled under the pressure of those who wished to confess, marry, receive baptism, or receive the Eucharist, an important, if impressionistic, indicator of popular interest in the orthodox aspects of Catholic worship.[68] The same pattern was repeated outside the capital in the days before September 1. From August, a state of mourning which entailed two distinct forms of protest was rigorously observed. The first was inward, recalling the practices of abstention observed during Advent and Lent: black ribbons appeared in windows and over doors in homes across the city; Catholics refrained from recreation; made purchases of basic necessity only; abstained from music and celebration; and boycotted the use of carriages, cars, and the city's trams.[69] The symbolism of mourning was widespread in the city, in addition to the discontinuation of all church-based activity or religious practice. From September, the mourning protest was extended throughout the state. Empty church buildings were converted into symbols of resistance across the archdiocesan landscape; at the same time, Catholic homes became clandestine churches, a move consciously modeled on the catacombs of antiquity. The self-imposed distance between worshippers and their formal places of worship, and the relocation of the cult to primitive Church settings, served to strengthen Catholic resolve.

On August 14, the archdiocese published a circular for the faithful declaring two days of obligatory mass for all clergy and laity, respectively falling on August 22 and 23 in the Zapopan Basilica and *parroquia* of San Pedro Tlaquepaque.[70] As customary pilgrimage sites just outside Guadalajara's city limits, these two churches temporarily became the material and symbolic focus of Catholic identity. The faithful created en masse a modern-day pilgrimage for religious liberty, which served as a point of union and a reaffirmation of Catholic identity in the struggle against civil authority.

The Catholic newspaper, *El Futuro*, published the following note:

Things continue without change in the city; the Government sustains its campaign of persecution and the Catholics [continue their] passive resistance, protesting with extreme piety, during these final days of worship in the towns near Guadalajara; more than three quarters of the population has been to San Pedro and Zapopan; of course, the majority make the trip on foot, there and back.[71]

The article went on to comment, with a certain irony, that Decree 1927 was a blessing in disguise and had sown a "miraculous crop" that the Church would harvest.

The second part of the mourning protest was directed as much outwardly as inwardly. Its principal target was the pro-government daily, *El Occidental*, which was held by Catholic laity systematically to misreport the news pertaining to government repression of their movements. González Flores referred to the protest as an assertion of "economic sovereignty," a term echoing the language used by Gandhi in his struggle against the British in India. The campaign consisted of a boycott of the newspaper, not only in terms of consumption but also pressuring those who used the newspaper for advertising purposes. The pro-Catholic newspaper, *La Epoca*, published a list of city businesses that advertised in the newspaper. According to Camberos Vizcaíno, *La Lucha* did likewise, including a list of prominent Masons in the city, whose businesses were then boycotted by the faithful.[72] The boycott was effective: in a matter of weeks, *El Occidental* was forced to discontinue circulation, and never again reappeared.

Concurrently with the August boycott, the state governor and legislature were bombarded with protests from Jalisco's rural towns and secondary cities. Between mid-August and mid-September, I have counted forty-five protest letters representing thirty-two different towns. Although a few were sent directly to Carranza, most went to the state legislature or governor. In at least one-third of towns, the ACJM was directly involved in the petition campaign. In all, these protests carried approximately 35,000 signatures. Unlike the July petitions, men now signed more often than women. Protests signed exclusively by men generated nearly 19,000 signatures; over 9,000 accompanied protests sent exclusively by women; and another 6,000 accompanied petitions signed by men and women. Most petitions came from towns that were also parish seats. For example, 600 *vecinos*—"Mexican citizens of Ciudad Guzmán in full exercise of their Constitutional rights" (read men)— petitioned the governor; three days later, over 200 Damas Católicas of Ciudad Guzmán protested in a separate petition to the state congress.[73]

What do the petitions reveal about Jalisco's towns? As might be expected, there is a loose correlation between town size and the numbers signing the petitions. Many towns sent separate petitions for men and women, a reflection of the sexual division observed by lay organizations. In two cases—Arandas and San Miguel el Alto, important highland parishes that became vital centers of Cristero resistance—three petitions were sent. In the case of San Miguel, women and men circulated separate petitions, the latter signed by more than 1,100 vecinos and sent to the governor, who answered. On receiving the governor's reply, the men of San Miguel formulated a response, which was again signed by over 1,000 Catholics. Similarly, in Arandas, separate men's and women's petitions were sent to Carranza, the first with over 900 signatures, the second with over 3,000; at roughly the same time, a third petition circulated among the men of Arandas, which was also signed by over 3,000 vecinos. Hence the 1918 petitions were in some cases good religious predictors of future Cristero militancy.

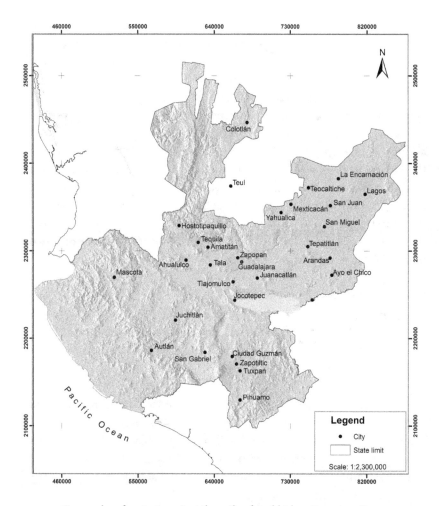

MAP 4. Geography of protests against the exile of Archbishop Francisco Orozco y Jiménez, 1918. Source: Susana Urzúa Soto.

Elsewhere in Los Altos, for example, Encarnación de Díaz and Mexticacán pledged civil disobedience and refused to obey Decree 1913/1927.[74] In Mexticacán on August 21, 1918, over 800 men and almost 1,000 women exercised their constitutional right to petition the authorities (Article 8) by signing a joint protest. Instead of petitioning the president, the governor, or state Congress, however, they directed their demands to the municipality. Specifically, they asked that Decrees 1913 and 1927 be repealed; that no other decrees of similar nature be substituted for them; and that their local representatives make use of the constitutional right of municipal governments to send bills to Congress. The Mexticacán *ayuntamiento* supported the petition by sending a written version of its position to Congress. In a four-point agreement, the ayuntamiento unanimously applauded the townspeople's pacific attitude; approved the protest, as Catholic citizens pledging to "honor the favor of God before that of the State"; formally petitioned Congress on the town's behalf, asking it to take up the issue of repeal; and requested a formal response from the authorities in Guadalajara. The ayuntamiento's president, vice president, legal counsel, and secretary signed the petition. Following their signatures, the document read: "These are the actions of those who are, and know how to be, true representatives of the people!"[75] Some 10,000 copies of Mexticacán's petition were printed and distributed en masse in Guadalajara and each of Jalisco's more than 100 municipal governments.[76]

Politics and Religion at the Río Grande Textile Mill

In September 1918, just outside Guadalajara in the company town of El Salto, almost 400 Catholic women workers of the Río Grande textile factory petitioned the governor:

> Neither schooling nor science is necessary in order to measure exactly the profound injustice of Decrees 1913 and 1927 . . . One needs only natural reason to comprehend that there are sacred rights that can be violated by nobody . . . [particularly not when] those violators proclaim themselves representatives of the people knowing full well that they are making martyrs of us with their tyrannical dispositions.[77]

In many cases the petitions sent in protest of Decree 1913/1927, or in repudiation of the archbishop's forced exile, there were likely local issues involved that aren't easily understood at a distance of eighty years. The petitions, for their part, are textually rich but rather brief. In the case of Río Grande, however, the Jalisco Historical Archive offers a glimpse behind the petition. At least as early as January of 1918 a conflict pitted two groups of workers against each other within the factory. Although some of the details are sketchy, thirteen documents outline the course of the conflict over the next year, coinciding with the crisis over Decree 1927 and the petition drive organized by the Catholics of the Archdiocese.[78]

In January, a group of "liberal" workers, led by Benito Gómez, sent a letter of protest to governor Bouquet, complaining that a small group of women (they call them *mujeres*, rather than *obreras*), led by J. Refugio Carrillo and a group of agitators within the factory labor force, were attempting to divide worker unity. They explained that the priest who gave religious services at the factory had solicited 300 pesos from the worker mutualist fund in order to prepare the religious feast honoring the Virgin of Guadalupe, December 12. According to the aggrieved, a majority of the workers opposed the idea, which led a minority faction within the labor force, mostly women, insisted Gómez, to retaliate, withdrawing from an ongoing agreement that every worker would contribute 10 cents per pay period to the mutual fund.[79]

Angered at this show of dissent, Gómez and the "liberal" group effectively blocked the mutualist expenditure (3 percent of worker earnings) that sustained the priest, the health service, and pharmacy. They argued that the presence of the friar was unconstitutional, and that the constitution of 1917 dictated that the owners of the factory should provide workers with health services. The male workers, they explained, had decided that the friar's salary would be better spent on adult education, while the women workers, "guided by the bad comrades," demanded that the friar's salary be reinstated. When notified of the decision, the priest read the notice from the pulpit, pitting workers against workers.[80]

In addition, they charged the group led by Carrillo and the priest with distributing seditious material in favor of "Ex-Archbishop Orozco y Jiménez" and calling for people not to accept the 1917 constitution. They also attempted to pull the factory labor force into a strike over the issue of the priest's salary. The strike, Gómez alleged, was only avoided by the superior numbers of "liberal" workers, who were unwilling to go along.[81]

Initially, Gómez and the "liberals" asked that the governor pressure the president of the Juanacatlán Ayuntamiento to pull the Catholic workers into line. But as the conflict developed, they solicited the governor's intervention to prohibit the mutualist fund's use for the friar's salary. The material is unfortunately vague on each group's popular support, and there is no indication that governor Bouquet intervened on behalf of the "liberals." However, Gómez's petition to the governor suggests that the Catholic group may not have been such a small minority. If the "liberals" were a clear majority of the workers, why petition the governor? Gómez's group, subsequently reconstituted as the Union of Río Grande, consisted of 179 men and 25 women in January 1919, a year later.[82]

Although there is no mention of the size of the pro-Catholic group, there is correspondence between the group and the governor, in which the group formally constituted itself as the Union of Free Workers of Río Grande, under the leadership of José M. Vizcarra. The secretary of government of the state of Jalisco formally acknowledged the group, and in later correspondence, Vizcarra informed the governor that among the Union's legal representatives were three Guadalajara lawyers, including Pedro Vázquez Cisneros, head of the ACJM for the Western Mexico. Vizcarra also mentioned that the union would shortly have legal representation in Mexico City.[83]

Over the next several years the Catholic Union of Free Workers was consolidated. By June 1919 it had a worker center and a cooperative. By July, the Catholics won the board election for the factory mutualist society, crowning a two-year struggle with the liberal union. In August, the worker center formed a religious and social study circle. In November the moral theater troop put on a play attended by over 1,000 people. By 1921, the Catholic union had negotiated lower rents for part-time workers, and the suspension of certain common penalties imposed by management. At the same time, 200 Catholic workers formed a development society to buy land for a new worker colony. Meanwhile, the study circle expanded to formally offer religion, sociology, grammar, and history. Two groups, one with thirty-five men, and another with thirty-eight women formed it. By early 1922, the Catholic union would also establish a band and an English language academy, to further promote worker education.[84]

It is possible that a minority of workers at Río Grande founded the Catholic union. But it is also clear that the union had sustained, popular support, composed of men and women. That support seems to have grown by 1919, when the Catholics defeated the liberals in an election for the mutualist fund board. It is also clear that the Catholic workers were involved in a wide variety of activities, from adult education to recreation, cooperative investments, and of course, religion.

Whatever the local dynamics that pushed the organization of Catholic unions and other lay organizations, the crisis of 1918 over religious worship and the forced exile of the archbishop proved a catalyst. This portrait of the incipient union movement at the Río Grande textile mill will be considered in much greater detail in the next chapter, which will focus exclusively on the Catholic union movement that grew out of the 1918 crisis.

———

In December 1918, the US consul in Guadalajara, John Silliman, called on Carranza in Mexico City. Carranza received him cordially, asking if Mrs. Silliman had made the trip and suggesting they have dinner soon at the president's home. Regarding the religious question in Jalisco, Carranza remarked that he saw no reason for the ongoing conflict, and that he trusted it would soon be resolved. He was pushing legislation in the Federal Congress—he confided— that would put an end to the troubles in Guadalajara. He also hoped to abolish the 1917 constitution's provision that prohibited foreign-born priests and ministers in Mexico. Silliman filed a positive report on this occasion, and although he was somewhat vague on the measures to be taken, the conflict was indeed soon resolved.[85]

Concurrently, in late 1918, a new state legislature and governor were elected in Jalisco, clearing the way for a repeal of Decree 1913/1927. Following his sixteen-month leave of military absence, Governor Diéguez returned to office on January 31, 1919, in order to give his final State-of-the-State address prior to handing government over to his successor. In a 1920 history of the Catholic struggle, the firebrand Anacleto González Flores went out of his way to credit Diéguez with recognizing the need to repeal Jalisco's anticlerical legislation, and with taking the proper action before handing over power.[86] On February 4, 1919, the state's legislature rescinded Decree 1927 in a vote of 15 in favor to 5 against.[87]

Following the repeal of Decree 1927, Archbishop Orozco y Jiménez wrote from exile to Interior Secretary Manuel Aguirre Berlanga, in Mexico City, to request a passport along with guarantees for his return to Guadalajara. Prior to responding, Aguirre Berlanga consulted with Luis Tapia Castellanos, the recently elected Jalisco governor. Tapia responded that if and when the opportunity presented itself, he would arrest Orozco y Jiménez on an outstanding warrant dating back to 1914. Notwithstanding the eventual threat of a new arrest, Aguirre Berlanga notified the Guadalajara archbishop granting permission for travel to Mexico, providing he first go to Mexico City in order to consult with federal government officials. Thus, Orozco y Jiménez set out for Mexico City in August. Meanwhile, his legal counsel in Guadalajara, the former Jalisco PCN head Manuel F. Chávez, won an important battle, when a district judge threw out the remaining warrant for the archbishop's arrest.[88] On arrival at Mexico City, Orozco y Jiménez wrote President Carranza and Governor Tapia. The letters are self-consciously diplomatic, informing of his arrival, saying he will be in Mexico City for a time, declaring himself a servant of both, and promising to communicate his travel plans prior to departing for

Guadalajara.[89] When finally the Archbishop arrived at Guadalajara in October, the celebrations were noisy and public. Men, women, and children of all classes lined the streets to greet him and shouted victory slogans; for days thereafter, Orozco y Jiménez received countless commissions from every corner of the archdiocese.[90]

There is a marked contrast embedded in this conflict that ought to be clarified. On the one hand, Church representatives like the archbishop of Guadalajara, as well as state agents like the interior secretary and even General/Governor Diéguez, sought out a delicate status quo in which both institutions might back away from conflict. In 1919, on the other hand, highly mobilized and antagonistic social bases supported both Church and state. The repeal of Decree 1927 and Orozco y Jiménez's return were celebrated loudly and publicly, signaling a new Church offensive. Anticlerical violence would soon follow, initially through informal channels and eventually through a newly articulated state policy. Neither Church nor state leaders could then be counted on to control their social bases; furthermore, it is not always clear whether they wanted to.

This story raises a significant question of general interest to historians: To what extent did conflicts between groups of revolutionaries and Catholics forge a new politico-religious Catholic identity, shape revolutionary practice, or construct the political sphere of post-revolutionary Mexico? The conflicts analyzed in this episode suggest all of the above. First, the events of 1917–1919 proved to be a catalyst for a nationally based movement, sustained by a coalition of lay organizations including the ACJM, the Mexican Union of Catholic Ladies (UDCM), and the various Catholic labor unions, both rural and urban, that formed the Confederación Católica Obrera (CCO).[91] These organizations assumed that Catholicism was a basic component of identity and compatible within the framework of other special interest constituencies (women, workers, youth). Second, as I have attempted to demonstrate, people of different backgrounds and localities—and surely with different expectations—were able to band together in a clear, militant expression of confessional identity politics for a limited period of time. In so doing, they reached two basic goals: on the one hand, they forced a political retreat from their civil authorities, and on the other, they created a situation in which all of their ecclesiastical authorities could return from exile—the archbishop from his forced expatriation, and the parish priests from a self-imposed separation from their Church.

The role of lay Catholic organizations in the political battle was central, and their victory was significant. During the following six years, groups of Catholic men and women, youth and workers would grow, constituting themselves as parallel organizations in competition with the state for its constituencies and exercising a major influence in the public sphere. This final point is particularly relevant. Although weak and internally divided, the Mexican state did claim for itself legitimacy and authority conferred by revolution. In practice, however, Mexico's religiously inspired political movement questioned both this authority and its fundamental legitimacy.

7. Work and Religion in Post-Revolutionary Mexico

THE LAST GREAT period of political expansion and experimentation among lay Catholics was forged in the absence of the archbishop. As I have explained, Francisco Orozco y Jiménez was carted off to exile in early July 1918, an event that galvanized Catholics across the archdiocese in opposition to the revolutionary regime.[1] He was absent for fifteen months, during which time his flock undertook a crusade on his behalf using novel tactics. The clerical strike shut the churches and sharpened Catholic anger; the boycott of specific businesses focused political tactics; a statewide campaign of written petition broadened the political echo and put government officials on notice; massive sustained mourning through rigorous use of black clothing incorporated Catholic bodies as signs of protest in the public plaza; the use of the press coordinated actions. These activities signaled a new kind of tactics, a mass politics. They were as new for Catholics and the Church as they were for the post-revolutionary state. But that is not all that happened. Somewhat surreptitiously, the focus of organizing shifted toward Catholics as working people, as workers who might organize through unions.

The legal and political context of the shift toward union organization was determined by the 1917 constitution, which formally prohibited confessional political organizations like the defunct National Catholic Party. Political Catholicism could not be channeled through a party structure and the prospects for a successful electoral strategy were dim. However, Articles 8 and 9 did encourage organization, petition, and civic engagement over the definition and uses of public space. Since Porfirian times, Catholics had been grappling with issues like the family wage, the right of association, and the more contentious issue of strikes. But the new constitution provided a catalyst for organizing beyond the narrow corridors of local parish and village politics. Outwardly, union organization would forego explicit political goals and tactics: "Politics is paralysis" was the slogan.[2] But contrary to Catholic discourse, the emergence of a mass confessional movement organized around workers, their local churches, and an urban vanguard leadership could not help but alter the political sphere in revolutionary Mexico.

The Catholic union movement that swept western Mexico in the 1920s was rooted in Guadalajara's lay associations and their clerical advocates. Archbishop Orozco y Jiménez was an enthusiastic supporter, and he had interlocutors of national importance, such as the Jesuit Alfredo Méndez Medina. But locally, too, he counted on a group of Guadalajara priests, such as Manuel Yerena, José Toral Moreno, Antonio Correa, Librado Tovar, Eduardo Huerta, and the Jesuit Arnulfo Castro. These men were trusted advisors to the archbishop, but they were also tireless organizers and propagandists who traveled throughout the region speaking to local gatherings on a parish-by-parish basis. However, they did not act solely at the behest of the archdiocese. In fact, they were part of a broader organizing effort that incorporated the skills and knowledge of laity, some of which had been involved in Catholic social movements going back over a decade. Miguel Palomar y Vizcarra, for example, had lived in Mexico City since 1914, but continued to participate in the Guadalajara movement through his writing and as a special advisor. His buddy Luis de la Mora ran a consumer cooperative where activist Catholics shopped. Nicolás Leaño, an engineer by trade, played a major role in the worker newspaper, *El Obrero*, published weekly between 1919 and 1925. All three were urban professionals from established families, and all had participated in political Catholic movements prior to the 1910 fall of President Díaz. Like them, Maximiano Reyes had been active since the days of the National Catholic Party. Unlike them, Reyes came from humble roots in the Mezquitán Indian community. Reyes was a central figure in the Catholic union movement and became both secretary and president of the National Federation of Catholic Labor. Other leaders of humble origins, like Anacleto González Flores, Ignacio S. Orozco,[3] J. Jesús Flores, and Miguel Gómez Loza, were young men who cut their teeth politically in opposition to the 1917 constitution.

Collectively, this leadership was responsible for the network of Guadalajara associations that gave form, consistence, objectives, and a sense of broad scope to the local parish groups. These men and others formed the editorial boards of *La Palabra*, *El Obrero*, and *El Archivo Social*;[4] they ran the Centro de Obreros Católicos "Fray Antonio Alcalde" and "Leon XIII"; Union of Catholic Worker Syndicates (USOC); and the evolving labor confederation;[5] they participated in the Catholic Association of Mexican Youth (ACJM) and the Knights of Columbus (CC); and they founded the Popular Union (UP). These men—clergy and laity—were involved in all the parish-level efforts at union organizing, and they are named time and again by the rural worker circles, cooperatives, mutualist societies, unions, and other related organizations, as the Guadalajara visitors that supplied propaganda, knowledge, and material resources at the village level.

The major source of material on Catholic unions is *El Obrero*, the official weekly of the Catholic Labor Federation (CCT).[6] This newspaper carried several different kinds of information: official business of the federation; editorials addressing issues of interest to the newspaper's writers and editors; general interest articles on specific themes pertaining to religion, women, or literature (prose as well as poetry), all meant to teach social or moral lessons or reflect on basic truths; miscellanea including ex-votos and other expressions of thanksgiving, kitchen recipes, convocations, letters of protest, and international wire service news; and local news sent to the paper from towns, factories, unions, and other associations from across Mexico, but predominantly from Jalisco. These thematic areas are present in practically every edition of *El Obrero*. And while collectively they provide a rich source of information regarding the Catholic union movement, perhaps the most interesting of all the sections is the local news, because it represents data and description sent directly from the associations.[7]

Though news was sent from as far away as Europe and South America, most communiqués came from towns and villages of rural Jalisco or from neighboring states. The state of Jalisco is relatively large, composed of several distinct regions. Historians have characterized these regions based on economic production, language, climate, and other phenomena. Such characterizations commonly identify the following areas: Center/Guadalajara, Highland, Lake Chapala, South, West, Coast, and North.[8] Such distinctions are helpful for certain kinds of comparison, for example, language or commercial agriculture. Furthermore, it is clear that the Catholic union movement was stronger in some areas and weaker in others. For example, the towns of northern Jalisco, in particular the Huichol sierra, show little evidence of unions.[9] The same may be said of the Pacific Coast. Western Jalisco, particularly the Autlán-Mascota corridor, had modest activity. Closer to Guadalajara, there was an important presence in the mining town of Etzatlán.[10] The richest abundance of material came from Jalisco's highlands in the northeast, the lake district, and toward points farther south. This corridor stretched from Lagos de Moreno, the highland city commercially and culturally linked to Aguascalientes and León. As it ran south, it included the Guadalajara hinterland and the lakeside villages running from Chapala east to Ocotlán. Beyond the lake, it stretched to Ciudad Guzmán, with its ties to Colima. Finally, of all the areas covered, Guadalajara and its hinterland were the best represented; this is where most of the lay associations were located. Guadalajara was home to scores of groups, and a ring of factories circled the capital—mostly textile producers—that were well represented in the movement.

Nevertheless, regional difference seems to explain little in terms of the kind of news sent by Catholic lay associations from different parts of the state or beyond. This was largely a function of the type of correspondence sent. Each village, union, or affiliate association reported on its activities, members, or finances. The posts talk about members who received support, speakers who visited, the opening of a new savings cooperative or recreation hall, the establishment of a religious studies circle or a local band, theater troupe, or choir. Occasionally they speak of attacks made by their detractors. There is more discussion of wages in the reports sent from textile factories than other manufacturers. Similarly, there is some talk of working conditions by unions representing rural sharecroppers or wage laborers. But most associations represented groups of artisans, and talked less about wages than issues of mutual aid. However, none of this comprised a set of rules regarding Catholic unions. In the end, what follows is a bricolage constructed from the many bits and pieces of testimony that were transformed into historical data through the forum of the periodical press. The mosaic of information regarding the lives and jobs of political Catholics says more about the union experience than the possible regional differences between them. Therefore, the object of this chapter will not rely on regional analysis, but on a sort of indiciary building of data with the goal of creating a composite picture of the Catholic unions.

A Confessional Union Movement

Between 1919 and 1926 a Catholic union movement flourished in west central Mexico, built on the existing foundations of mutualism, based on the parish structure, and conceived in the late nineteenth century.[11] For example, a turn of the century Catholic worker circle listed as its objectives the spread of Catholic, apostolic, and Roman beliefs; good customs; religious, moral, scientific, literary, and artistic knowledge; mutual aid societies; honest recreation; and efficiency at work. The society was opposed to strikes and prohibited political discussion. Dues were six cents per week in 1895.[12]

FIGURE 8. Directorate of the First Regional Congress of Catholic Workers, April 24, 1919. Seated from left: Ignacio S. Orozco, Nicolás Leaño, Rosendo Vizcaíno; Standing from left: Maximiano Reyes, Librado Tovar, Luis Chávez Hayhoe, and F. González. Source: Archivo Histórico de la Arquidiócesis de Guadalajara.

Since the early twentieth century, social Catholics inspired by *Rerum Novarum* had given these local institutions a new language, and a new sense of belonging to a growing, vibrant network. For members, the community was national and Catholic. They shared in it through a periodical press as well as the institutional network of a confederation of unions, mutualist societies, cooperatives, and other associations.[13] The main organizations were located in Guadalajara and its small town hinterland, where they were pulled together in the form of a federation in 1919 and subsequently renamed as the Catholic Labor Confederation (CCT).[14] For the next two years, the organization grew, strengthening its base in Jalisco and expanding into the states of Michoacán, Guanajuato, Mexico, and the Federal District. By 1921, when the leadership met during the festivities planned for the Virgin of Zapopan coronation, a central topic of discussion was how to achieve national prominence.[15] Over the following year a plan was discussed and implemented.

In April 1922 delegates representing over 1,300 Catholic worker organizations from twelve states and Mexico City met in Guadalajara to form a national confederation, set up an operating framework, and discuss the elements of a common ideology.[16] About 60 percent of the delegates came from Jalisco, where organizations had been forged under fire during the 1918 campaigns against Decree 1913 and the forced exile of the archbishop. Another 20 percent of delegates came from Michoacán and Guanajuato. Despite its expansion, the organization was still more regional than national in scope. Although it never achieved a national presence, over the next four years, the National Catholic Confederation of Labor (CNCT) grew prodigiously.

There is some speculation over the size of the organization, and historians have offered divergent estimates. Manuel Ceballos Ramírez has suggested cautiously that the CNCT had 22,000 members, basing his estimate on an open letter published by the organization's leadership in 1926 and addressed to CROM leader Luis Morones.[17] Jean Meyer cited a much larger figure of 80,000 members in 353 different organizations.[18] Barry Carr has observed that estimates ranged from 2,000 to 100,000.[19] Although both extremes are likely exaggerated, the larger figure is more accurate. For one thing, a 1926 letter cited by Ceballos captured the movement in decline after a two-year period during which the Calles government and the CROM carried out a sustained attack on Catholic unions.[20] But how reasonable is Meyer's claim of a movement 80,000 strong? One indication emerges in a little known report published in 1922 by Alfredo Méndez Medina, the Jesuit labor organizer who coordinated the activities surrounding the 1922 Guadalajara congress. Méndez Medina wrote of "eight hundred workers . . . from all points of the Republic in representation of eighty thousand like-minded brothers." The data are perhaps soft, but do lend credence to the figure of 80,000 members mentioned by Márquez Montiel and later cited by Meyer.[21] In the absence of hard data, the real question is whether or not the figure is plausible, and to what extent Catholic unions successfully competed for worker loyalties.[22]

Further inspection of CNCT documentation strengthens the plausibility of Meyer's larger estimate. Maximiano Reyes, president of the Catholic labor federation, reported 600 worker delegates at the April 1922 Guadalajara congress, a figure that suggests somewhere near 60,000 members.[23] But the official congress papers are more specific, reporting 683 official delegates, and a system that suggests a rounded number that might easily have reached 80,000.[24] Ultimately, the difference in data might be a function of how carefully the delegates were counted. Only subsequently did the CNCT set itself the task of processing the delegates with respect to the members they reported to represent; and the work of officially admitting members, and keeping union records on them, was evidently slow. Still, the CNCT was expanding quickly and, by Reyes's own account, official reports lagged behind the numbers of members.[25]

Such speculation is impressionistic, but it raises an important question regarding the historical process of Catholic unionizing. How should historians interpret divergent data on membership that range from 7,000 to 80,000? There are clearly different kinds of data present in the sources, some reporting individual memberships, others referring to delegate estimates.[26] Although some of the pieces here are missing, one phenomenon in particular, the ever-growing backlog of membership applications, may help historians with a more sure-footed interpretation. It offers a glimpse into the institutional life of the confederation, and strongly suggests that reported data on individual members fell short of overall membership. There can be no doubt that unions were popular in 1922–1923: there was consistently a waiting list to join even though the application protocol was not simple. The model they used required that unions legalize their statutes with notaries, an activity that could only be achieved by hiring a lawyer.[27] This aspect of union organizing was of central importance, not least because, as early as 1923, Catholic unions were outlawed by revolutionary decree. The union leadership seems to have expected this, and they were meticulous about establishing unions on the basis of profession, not creed. Therefore, the locals were ideologically confessional, but legally they followed the protocol of trade unions.[28] However, this tactic of legal positioning was ultimately unsuccessful, trumped by the political imperative of an anticlerical state. As a result, Catholic unions fell victim to pressures brought to bear by President Calles, Governor Zuno, and the official labor movements.

———

At the 1922 Guadalajara congress, several important ideological and programmatic issues were debated that help explain the tactics of the unions and the CNCT. The congress decided against the concept of a single obligatory union, as this would be an unnecessary limitation of the natural right to association. Although the delegates rejected the concept of class struggle and any commitment to participate in formal politics, they did embrace the right to strike. They favored the expansion of small-scale private property, the creation of Catholic schools for working-class children, and their own savings and loan institutions, and they voted to adopt the Guadalajara journal, *El Obrero*, as the official newspaper of the CNCT. They also agreed to establish institutional relationships with other unions not part of their confederation, with the goal of forming alliances. Although they did not foresee allying with the socialists, the Catholic leadership did decide to send its publications to the socialist unions; and despite the obvious differences between Catholic, socialist, and government unions, there would be at least one case of a CNCT-CGT-CROM alliance.[29]

The issue that occasioned most debate, and which was most transcendent historically, was "confessionalism," the openly religious identity of the confederation.[30] The debate over confessionalism was neither new nor restricted to Mexico.[31] Italian Catholics began to organize confessional unions in the 1880s, taking advantage of the parish structure in order to compete with socialist unions.[32] In Germany, social Catholics founded interconfessional parties and unions, and in Spain, there were Catholic intellectuals on both sides of the debate. While some argued for a general Christian moral orientation, others responded that Catholic unions would only be effective if they were militantly Catholic. With the publication of *Singulari Quadam* (1912), Pope Pius X called for Catholic associations to be confessional, although he pragmatically decided not to enforce this model in Germany.[33] In France during the Third Republic, the secular-confessional division had been a central issue of public policy,[34] and at the turn of the century, French liberals legislated a reform similar to that which shaped the 1857 constitution in Mexico. Yet social Catholicism grew, and Catholics founded unions in many of the trades.[35] In France, as in the rest of Europe, lay organizations abandoned confessionalism in the 1950s, and yet, Christian democracy has been considered the most important western European political movement of the last half of the twentieth century.[36] Within Mexico, too, the idea of confessionalism had generated criticism. A good example may be found in a letter that the Jesuit, Arnulfo Castro, wrote to Palomar y Vizcarra in 1911 expressing his reserve regarding the name given to the newly founded Catholic political party.

> The problem with the name, as I see it, is that not only its enemies but people in general will identify the Catholic Party with the Catholics and with the Catholic Church. Those who for one reason or another do not belong to the party will be non-Catholic. In short, "Catholic" on one hand will be reduced to the political party, and on the other the mistakes and errors that the party may eventually commit (after all it is only human), will be extended to the whole of Catholics. This is without a doubt a serious shortcoming.[37]

As in France, the confessional-secular divide defined the formation of the Mexican state, although in Mexico the binary was generally situated in terms of Revolutionary-Catholic, or more commonly, revolution-reaction. In social Catholic circles, the issue of confessionalism was discussed, from the formation of the PCN down to the CCT union movement, and it clearly was an issue in the 1922 Guadalajara congress.[38]

Alfredo Méndez Medina was a central figure in the debate over confessionalism in Mexico. Born in Villanueva Zacatecas in 1877, he joined the Jesuits in 1899, and spent the waning years of the Díaz era in Europe. There he was ordained as a priest in 1910, in Oña, Spain, and in 1912 completed his doctoral studies at the famous Catholic University of Louvain in Belgium. Méndez Medina was a keen observer of continental social Catholicism, especially the strategies of the modern union movements. In 1920 he was commissioned by Archbishop Mora y del Rio of Mexico City to organize the Secretariado Social Mexicano (SSM), a formal office charged with disseminating the social teaching of the Church. Méndez Medina immediately oriented the office toward the incipient confessional union movement, deploying its resources with the objective of organizing the Catholic lay associations in support of workers. His tenure at the Secretariado Social lasted until 1925, when he was removed by the Jesuit Superior General, Wlodimir Ledóchowski, ostensibly due to his excessive independence.[39]

Although the Catholic worker congress was organized by Guadalajara activists, Méndez Medina was one of the main speakers.[40] He was an advocate for confessionalism, but also understood that local contingencies imposed limitations on a strictly confessional movement, and thus supported a more flexible strategy. In particular, this meant courting the so-called free workers, or *obreros libres*, in places like México, Toluca, Puebla, Orizaba, Saltillo, Monterrey and Querétaro.[41]

The congress was in session from April 23 until April 30. Soon after, Méndez Medina reviewed the confessionalism dilemma in a piece he wrote for the Mexico City magazine *Acción y Fe*. Stylistically, he represented the congress through a combination of vignettes and commentary. The vignettes are quite detailed, and suggest that someone involved with the congress organization made a transcript of the proceedings. It is alternately possible that Méndez Medina wrote from memory consciously in the idiom of "worker voices," essentially recreating their contribution to the congress. In any case, the article is rich in passages that are presented as the direct voices and thoughts of the participants. The main ideas and discussion of the article are represented in the form of worker debate.

This poses a dilemma: How authentic or believable is the material presented? In the absence of a clear answer to this question, I will describe and analyze the most important material presented by Méndez Medina.

The review situates the worker congress in the direct aftermath of the San Francisco Gardens massacre of March 26, 1922, in which Catholic worshipers were gunned down by a group of "anarchists" who were ostensibly marching in support of a renters strike. In all, six Catholics died in the central Guadalajara plaza.[42] Méndez Medina describes a solemn gathering around a large ash tree at the massacre site, in which 800 worker delegates participated in remembrance of their comrades, gunned down a month earlier. He also mentions that there was Catholic resistance to the congress from some quarters in which it was seen as an unnecessary provocation. According to Méndez Medina, Archbishop Orozco y Jiménez played a spiritual role, dedicating a mass at the beginning of the congress and a *Te Deum* at the closing. But he attributes the idea for the congress to local workers, whom he refers to as the initiators.

The main idea of the article focuses primarily on the participation of the workers as delegates and speakers. Méndez Medina's vision of the congress is best understood by considering the three main interventions represented and the broader message that is conveyed by the author through these passages. In other words, the importance of these vignettes is not to be found in the ideas of the speakers, per se, but in the ideas offered by the author, who chose three interventions, ordered them, and presented them as if they were unfiltered. They are more representative of what Méndez Medina wanted to convey, than of the Catholic workers themselves. And so, they shed light on the way he understood the congress.

The discussion revolved around Méndez Medina's keynote address to the group on the importance of religion as the foundation of the union movement. Canon José Mercedes Esparza then summarized the main points of the keynote address in order to facilitate the discussion. The discussion that followed was notable for the active participation of the Veracruz contingent. It is evidence of the possibility—in 1922—that a Catholic worker movement might seriously compete with pro-government unions.[43]

The first voice was that of a worker from the Río Blanco textile mill in Orizaba, Veracruz. He argued for a loose confessionalism as the best way to include free workers who otherwise would be under direct attack from the left. Manuel Ceballos Ramírez noted the importance of his contribution to the debate in a path-breaking article on Catholic unionism written over twenty years ago.[44]

I was a Bolshevik, as red as they come, and I got out because they're a bunch of charlatans. All they do is exploit the workers and use them for their political wheeling and dealing; but I am Catholic, apostolic and Roman; for the love of Christ I tell you I am not ashamed of my Religion; but I'm asking you to think about what you're doing with regards to religion, because if you insist, the poor free laborers who have only just split with the Bolsheviks won't be strong enough to resist. I won't stand down and I won't go back, but I can only speak for myself, not for all our brothers out there on the firing line . . . They are Catholic too, but they aren't ready for what you have here; may they be spared the fate of the man whose legs healed badly because he was obliged to stand on them too soon. I ask you not to demand that the free workers associations carry the name of the Catholics, so that they may truly be Catholic . . . Comrades, if you could only see how different it is to speak of things Catholic here in Guadalajara, and there in Río Blanco.[45]

In response, a worker from Santa Rosa, Veracruz, argued for a strict confessionalism as the best way to assure that Catholic unions would be off-limits to those who might wish to cultivate members there for the Communist and pro-government unions:

I too come from the firing line . . . in the name of three hundred Catholic workers who, living in a veritable soviet, do not boast, not for lack of faith, but when there is a reason they proclaim it loudly, and are that much more respected for showing no cowardice. I propose . . . not only that the Confederation be denominated Catholic, but that each and every affiliated group be as well. With vacillation and luke-warm efforts we will get nowhere. Neutral unions are a breeding ground for socialism and yellow unions, because they have no moral bearing, no character, no direction nor courage.

A third speaker, *pachorrudo*, or sluggish in appearance and speech, offered the opposite opinion. A minimum of religion would be preferable:

I certainly like Religion, but it makes me anxious to see it forced into everything. It'd be better to leave it to each individual, after all here in Mexico we are all Catholics.

At this point the order broke down, and the *pachorrudo* was interrupted:

Right, Catholics. And what about the gunmen the other day at San Francisco?

This prompted Esparza to restate the issue and put more emphasis on the need for flexibility:

I insist that the point I was trying to make is not that the different groups make a public display of Catholicism. That would be ideal, but a minimum of religion would demand far less, as has been said.

The discussion continued, with the participants hashing out the different ideas, debating until they were hoarse, *hasta que caiga la campanilla*, in the words of the former Bolshevik.[46] Finally, the *pachorrudo* concluded:

I am very grateful for the speaker's advice and the explanations of my comrades. Now I get it. True Catholics, neither hypocrites nor detractors, neither shameful nor cowardly. If the Confederation becomes triumphant, the triumph must not be attributed to a secular morality, as they say, which is neither here nor there. That's right comrades, the triumph should belong to Catholic morality, sound merchandise, neither spurious nor contraband and, for that reason, it ought to present itself honestly and openly, like this delightful sun that illuminates us.

In his commentary on the dialogue, Mendéz Medina wrote that the obreros worked out the principles that would guide their organization, such as an insistence on an exclusively worker leadership, but ceded to the "professional sociologists" most discussion of the practical aspects. Regarding the nuts and bolts of organization, they participated mostly by requesting clarification of arcane points, or asking how particular arrangements have worked in other places. Among the resolutions adopted, the organization opted for cultivating cordial relations with management, and to call on capitalists to discuss labor relations formally. This point is interesting, because it may be seen as an instance of worker organizations taking a proactive stand in trying to set the agenda for future labor relations. The reality was that capital generally did not participate as a willing interlocutor, although there were exceptions. They also opted not to enter into formal organizational relationships with socialist unions, but to remain open to possible alliances based on mutually beneficial objectives, as future experience would corroborate.

In a brief final section, Mendéz Medina foregrounded the decision adopted at the congress to avoid politics. "Politics is paralysis," the participants chanted.[47] This position, clearly stated here and elsewhere in Catholic writing from the early twentieth century, obliges historians to consider the proper context, the form and limits of the political. The congress participants noted that each and every citizen had grave civic duties, but that the confederation, as well as each of its constitutive member associations, must remain outside the political arena. On tactical grounds as well as on principal, the delegates decided to avoid "that which today is called politics."

The alliance was apparently less successful in practice, and there is little evidence that the two movements continued to work together. The most likely reason is that 1923 and 1924 brought a concerted effort by Calles and Morones to shut down the options of Catholic unions and aggressively recruit free workers for the CROM. It is also the case that in western Mexico where confessional unions were strongest the free labor movement had very little presence. Likewise in the Gulf region, free workers and Catholics faced frequent hostility from both the CGT and CROM unions.[48] The most common line of attack against Catholic unions by secular competitors was that they did not defend class interests.

This charge is exaggerated and simplistic, forcing Catholic unions into the binary scale of progressive versus conservative, revolutionary versus reactionary, and capital versus labor. Martin Conway has written that

the dominant interpretation of European history since the First World War has portrayed Europe as a battlefield between conflicting secular ideologies of left and right, each of which offered an alternative model of political, social, and economic organization. Catholic movements, both by virtue of their religious inspiration and their reluctance to identify with the conventional categories of left and right, fit uncomfortably into this schema.[49]

In Mexican historiography the 1910 revolution, rather than the First World War, is the temporal measuring stick. *Rerum Novarum* was important to the thinking of Catholic workers in both Europe and America, but in the case of Mexico, social revolution was a tremendous contingent force. Religious practice was transformed during the first quarter of the twentieth century in ways that were unprecedented, and can only be understood within that particular historical context. And yet, in some ways a similar circumstance prevails.

In Mexico as in Europe, the logic of the Catholic unions was different than that of nonconfessional unions, most explicitly because it assumed that they had a social value for both material and spiritual reasons. Rank and file did not organize, speak, or act through the idiom of liberal secular politics, and often constructed a shared consciousness through the defense of religion. Their inspiration was sought in the Sacred Heart, Christ the King, and the Virgin of Guadalupe, but a special place of prominence was reserved for the carpenter, Joseph, patron saint of workers in Roman Catholicism.[50] Instead of celebrating May 1 as Labor Day as the communist unions did, they observed Saint Joseph's feast day, the nineteenth of March. Perhaps not coincidentally, in 1870 Pope Pius IX had declared Saint Joseph the protector of the Roman Catholic Church as well.[51] In any case, in 1920 Catholic union locals celebrated the fiftieth anniversary of the proclamation of Saint Joseph's protection.[52] This is a good example of how the spiritual and the material were intertwined for Catholic workers.

A principal commitment of social Catholicism was to reinsert religious influence into public life, *instaurare omnia in Christo*. In this tradition, confessional unions established schools, cooperatives, and mutualist societies, all basic institutions of social welfare. Thus, unions would pressure to create Catholic schools recognized by the state, as the PCN had done. Robert Quirk wrote that, were social Catholicism successful, it would have destroyed the liberal system and replaced it with government based on the teachings of Pope Leo XIII.[53] This seems unlikely, and it makes sense to seek analogies elsewhere; for example, Belgian Catholics governed for years, designing reforms based on the teachings of Pope Leo, all within the accepted parameters of a liberal, democratic regime.[54] Representative democracy was perhaps new in Mexico, but liberalism was well consolidated, and no government acted without checks and balances of both the institutional and the popular kind.

Some Catholic writers called for unions to be mixed, meaning that "capitalists" and "workers" should be integrated into the union structure.[55] This idea was common to the period, appearing in discussions over social legislation in countries as diverse as Spain and the United States. For the Spanish case, José Andrés-Gallego has written that there was no "oligarchization" of confessional worker societies.[56] In the United States, the populist Catholic intellectual, John A. Ryan, reached back to English Quaker tradition to propose that workers should share in industrial management. Essentially, he took the notion of mixed unions and extrapolated that worker pressure on the productive process would keep capitalists honest and workers dignified.[57] By the 1920s, however, the Mexican Catholic movement was no longer interested in mixed unions. The 1922 congress that established the National Federation of Catholic

Workers set union policy. Toward owners, their position was to avoid acts of violence, respect the rights demanded by law, attempt negotiation, and reserve use of the strike for last resorts.[58]

Not surprisingly, class-based unions fiercely attacked the conciliatory language of Catholic discourse, as they competed for clients with the confessional unions. In their interpretation, bourgeois and proletarian interests were irreconcilable, tantamount to a zero-sum game in which the capitalist could only succeed at the expense of the worker. Any cooperation undermined class interests, and Catholic unions were "scab" unions, firmly in the pocket of the bourgeoisie and clergy.[59] In the final analysis, the mixed character of these unions in Mexico was limited. For Spain, Andrés-Gallego has written that the main obstacle to such cooperation was lack of interest on behalf of capitalists themselves. Even in Monterrey, where business successfully channeled the terms of unionization and paternalism prevailed, worker relations with management were fraught with tension and workers were not docile.[60] So how close were the confessional unions to business?

The issue of capitalist or bourgeois sanction of the Catholic unions is potentially thorny. It is reasonable that capitalists might have preferred them to the class-based unions, due to their ideology of respect for private property and their preference to avoid class struggle as a political tactic. Furthermore, Catholic unions competed with the CROM and CGT for worker loyalties. But what evidence is there that the confessional unions were financed by *gran capital*, big business, and therefore were committed to combating all class-based labor movements? Is there evidence of ideological deceit on behalf of the clergy, in order to trick humble workers into taking up the cause?[61] During the 1980s, Manuel Ceballos Ramírez conducted the pioneering research on Catholic workers and their organizations, a body of work that is still relevant today. Yet he does not mention either of these issues.[62] There may have been such collusion in specific cases, although I found no evidence to support this claim. A methodological problem with this interpretation is that it renders the worker passive, alienated in a narrative space where capitalists and clergy make history. It also rests on the assumption that the primary interest and very identity of any historical actor may be reduced to his or her place in the mode of production. To the contrary, the evidence here suggests that worker identities were formed by and subject to a series of social hierarchies, including but not limited to class and gender difference. They were also deeply influenced by religious identity in a time of anticlericalism. Perhaps William H. Sewell put it best in his critique of E. P. Thompson:

It is also very important to recognize that class discourse is only one of several discourses available to workers to conceptualize and act out their place in society and the State. Even workers involved in class institutions are interpellated . . . by various other discourses: unreconstructed Radical democracy, reformist meliorism, self-help, Toryism, nationalism, various religious ideologies, consumerism, and so on. These rival discourses may coexist, not only in the same class, but in the same mind.[63]

As with the English and their nineteenth-century religious ideologies, workers across western Mexico were interpellated by the discourse of social Catholicism at the start of the twentieth century. There is no reason to suppose that workers, men and women, industrial laborers, artisans, sharecroppers and rural day-laborers, would have the same loyalties, interests, or identities. Nor is there reason to believe they would understand the world through an identity forged by work alone.

The Catholic labor federation built during the 1920s networked through lay associations across class lines. Covered by the organizing umbrella of the Mexican Social Secretariat, Catholic workers received institutional support from the Mexican Association of Catholic Youth (ACJM) and the Union of Catholic Ladies (UDC), two associations with markedly bourgeois identities. A 1920 report illustrates well the way these associations were articulated through a broader network during the preparation of the 1919 regional worker's congress.[64] At the request of the ACJM, the UDC fund-raised in support of the congress, an activity that may accurately be thought of as bourgeois financing, but that is ultimately less sinister than the idea of gran capital. The Catholic Ladies visited the owners of local businesses to solicit donations in merchandise, such as clothing and workshop tools. These goods were offered as prizes to workers who competed during the congress by exhibiting their crafts. One union member, Jesús Flores recalled the incident:

The idea [was] to show off the skills of Catholic workers and artisans: painters: landscape painting, theatrical decoration; carpenters: carved work, incrustations; mason workers: graphic art, printing; blacksmiths, mechanics, braziers, founders: art and industrial locksmithing; cobblers, scaffold-makers, weavers, upholsterers, tailors, potters, hatters . . . pretty much everyone exhibited because the convocation said: To the authors of the best work, as decided by a special jury made up of experts in each field, will by awarded many prizes and diplomas.[65]

FIGURE 9. Central Committee of the National Catholic Labor Confederation, dedicated to Msgr. Francisco Orozco y Jiménez, ca. 1923. The back is signed by Arnulfo
Castro, SJ (seated middle), Elpidio Yañez (seated right), Maximiano Reyes (second
from left standing), Ignacio S. Orozco (third from left standing), J. Jesús Flores López
(fourth from left standing), Faustino Rivera, Rodolfo Cortés, E. Gómez Vázquez, and
Father José Toral Moreno (not pictured). Source: Archivo Histórico de la Arquidiócesis
de Guadalajara.

One might argue that this is bourgeois financing, backing, or even co-opting
of the congress. But to dismiss it as such is to miss the point, and to misinterpret
the cultural framework in which it occurred. The activities of the Catholic Ladies
were acts of charity, understood as such. Historians may bring different ideological views to interpretation, but they should analyze such activities within the
tradition of Christian charity. More importantly than the redistribution of
(minor amounts of) bourgeois capital among proletarians, these acts of charity
involved the deployment of class-based knowledge and connections through a
social network that reaffirmed the status of the Catholic Ladies. Furthermore,
gender relations constructed this particular status as much as class hierarchies.
Ultimately, one needed not be bourgeois to belong to the Damas Católicas—not
all members were from well-to-do families—but one did need to be a woman.
The point here is that class was mediated by gender, and vice versa.[66]

Unions, Affiliates, and Local Practice

The confessional unions and their affiliate associations were guided by an ideology that celebrated the common good, or *bien común*, and pursued the goal of harmony among the different classes of society.[67] On principle, they rejected class struggle as a legitimate form of redress and deployed a discourse that emphasized the goal of balance in society through negotiation of the interests of capital and labor; still, in practice they reserved the right to strike. There is ample evidence that they were successful in achieving material improvement in working conditions and remuneration. To be sure, this was not the radical transformation of society sought by socialism. But regardless of the discourse on harmony, Catholic workers also expressed class-specific interests.

As early as 1912, the Jesuit Alfredo Méndez Medina theorized an articulation of the public and private so as to implicitly abandon commitment to hostile government. He did this by joining family and labor union in a fashion that recalls Catholic thinking on civil society and domestic society.[68] Catholic teaching modeled civil society on the family, recognizing government as the head, an authority analogous to the father. But in the midst of the Mexican Revolution, he seems to have taken the idea of society with government as its head, and substituted union for government, with the parish as its head, at least as reflects the working-class family:

> The union is the grand working-class family . . . an extension of the domestic family . . . [this] institution defends the salary and workplace conditions, procures jobs, acts as spokesperson and leader of the working class, is a means of technical formation, of social elevation and moral education, of support in bad times, of shelter in times of disaster, of relief and solace in old age.[69]

This idea was rooted in the corporatist vision of social Catholicism, that did not separate work from family and society, and considered poor working conditions in general, and insufficient salaries in particular, to be intimately linked to both moral and material deterioration of the family.[70] To put it into perspective, one must examine the breadth of the Catholic union movement. Following the writing of Pope Leo and his Mexican interpreters, such as Jose Toral Moreno,[71] the Catholic union was really a network of organizations, from mutual aid society to consumer cooperative, night school to catechism circle, and health clinic to philharmonic. Thus, it is fair to say that it's realm of influence spanned the horizon from material considerations like salary and workplace conditions, to training and education, and spiritual concerns like the sacraments and devotional practice. These different aspects of social life were often intertwined in the local practice of the unions and their members.

What kind of material grievances did the unions address? In 1922, for example, workers at the Hercules textile factory in Querétaro struck for higher wages. Catholic labor federation delegates negotiated a settlement that included a 65 percent raise over 1912 salaries, although workers had been willing to accept a 50 percent increase. In Guadalajara, the CNCT leadership sat down with representatives of the Guadalajara Industrial Company, CIJARA, and negotiated a similar deal to be extended to workers of the Atemajac, Experiencia, and Río Blanco textile mills.[72] In this case, workers won a 65 percent increase as well as 12,000 pesos to be invested in a consumer cooperative. At Río Grande, the other large textile mill, built near Guadalajara at the Juanacatlán falls, the CNCT union won a 50 percent salary increase and 12,000 pesos to establish a worker-run consumer cooperative in a strike settlement a year later in June 1923.[73] Such achievements were not solely the dominion of Catholic unions. CROM and CGT workers also scored important victories during the 1920s.[74] What is important about the achievements of Catholic unions, however, is that through such victories they did compete with pro-government and anarcho-syndicalist federations.

Beyond the factory belt that ran along Guadalajara's perimeter to the north and east, the unions of rural, small-town Jalisco were further removed from the logic of the strike, and more oriented toward mutualism. However, the absence of strikes should not be confused with a lack of attention to material interests. What grabs the attention, however, is how the unions provided a space in which material and spiritual aspects of life coexisted. For example, in Lagos de Moreno, the local peasant league had 20 sections and over 600 paying members, drawn from nearby villages. In December 1921, 500 participated in a daylong spiritual retreat on the eve of the Guadalupe feast, after which they reported conflicts with landowners over the working conditions of sharecroppers employed to harvest the properties of the wealthy. Specifically, *El Obrero* reported that some landowners were collecting peasant debts by withholding seeds for planting. The union took up the defense of those denied seeds and announced a campaign to publicly pressure landowners in hopes that the bad publicity would push them to abandon such abuses.[75]

The unions frequently maintained consumer, credit, or insurance cooperatives. In an era prior to the advent of the welfare state, these institutions were of primary importance. Some common examples illustrate the issues covered by union correspondence published by *El Obrero*. In San Miguel el Alto, where the mutualist society had 100 members, it was able to provide medical attention for 28, who were victims of a 1920 typhoid fever epidemic.[76] In Encarnación de Díaz, also in the highland region, the women's seamstress union, Sindicato de Obreras de la Industria del Vestido, created a producer's cooperative, which allowed them to expand into the larger market at Aguascalientes, the nearest city. As a result, between 1919 and 1921, they were able to provide work for 60 members during sixteen months, and double their salaries. In the same town the men's mutual fund maintained 1,000 paying members.[77] At Chapala, two workers organized the local union while laying the railroad line that would connect Guadalajara with the lakeside town. In this case, both had worked previously as masons in Guadalajara, where they belonged to the Leo XIII Catholic Worker Center (COC-XIII). When they left the capital to work on the Chapala railroad project, they took with them organizing knowledge and activist experience. In 1919, after its foundation, the union had a men's mutualist society with over 100 paying members, and a women's chapter with over 150 paying members, in addition to a consumer co-op, a workers' social studies circle, a night school, and a theater company.[78]

Further west in the mining region, generally considered more friendly to communist unions, the Fray Antonio Margil de Jesús Catholic Worker Center at Etzatlán played an important role in the social life of the town. An example of this was the center's response to the 1920 earthquakes that left many homeless across the country in Puebla and Veracruz. Through a variety of means, including a festival of "moral theater" in which they staged two plays, the center collected 200 pesos in support of the victims.[79] By projecting their activities in such a way as to make them accessible to the society at large, members positioned the worker center as a legitimate institution. By 1921, the union had doubled its membership, with 130 paying members of the mutualist society, and a recently established savings and loan cooperative with 36 members. The center established a recreation center with a gymnasium and training rings for physical fitness, as well as a game room with tables for chess, Parcheesi, and domino. The local priest was building a union library, for which he donated his own books and bought union specific literature by mail order from Guadalajara.[80]

The Lagos de Moreno union reported the financial status of its cooperative through the newspaper in early 1921. At the time of the report, the end of February, it had over 1,000 pesos in goods, cash, and other belongings. About half that amount had been collected through membership dues, while the other half was profit. As dictated by the cooperative statutes, the profit was distributed three ways: 20 percent went into a reserve emergency fund; another 20 percent went to benefit the local workers' center; and the other 60 percent was distributed among the consumer membership, distributed to reflect each member as a consumer, so that those who spent more also receive a greater proportion of the utilities.[81] Such news would have been inspiring for other unions that had invested in consumer cooperatives. And in fact, the word seems to have gotten around: four months later the Lagos union was in the paper again after the consumer cooperative and a school were looted. Fortunately for the members, savings were not kept on the premises, and the loss was small.[82]

On the other end of the state, reports from the southern Jalisco town of Zapotlan el Grande—called Ciudad Guzmán by state government—indicated that workers had banded together prior to the emergence of the union movement, and that, without a formal leadership or institutional infrastructure they had founded two cooperatives, one called La Union, and the other called La Popular.[83] By early August they had been consolidated into one Cooperative Society called La Union Popular and moved into a permanent location, which was christened by the parish priest, Antonio Ochoa Mendoza.[84] Over the next two years La Union Popular was quite successful, generating profits that were channeled into new projects, such as the building of a school, a workers' center, and a recreation hall.[85]

Another indicator of the relative success of the local union, Zapotlan el Grande held the honor of being the largest single market for El Obrero at the end of its first semester of publication.[86] One reason for this is that the workers' center formed an office for the propagation of "good press," with over a dozen agents dedicated to the distribution of a variety of titles. They sold 140 copies of El Obrero each week, in addition to 110 copies of La Epoca, 356 copies of El Amigo de la Niñez, 17 copies of El Amigo de la Verdad, 70 copies of Ecos Guadalupanos, 60 copies of Mensajeros del Sagrado Corazón de Jesús, and 5 copies of La Revista Social.[87] By the end of the year, Father Ochoa Mendoza had blessed the print workshop that produced a new local paper to add to the others, with the auspicious title La Modernista. And barely a month later, on New Year's Day 1921, El Orden also made its debut.[88]

Catholic syndicalism placed strong emphasis on education, organizational skills, and additional training. The breadth of training included arithmetic, history, metallurgy, chemistry, sociology, drawing and painting, reading, agriculture/farming, ethics, European social Catholicism, singing, orchestra, sewing and needlework, English, French, telegraphy, accounting, typing, shorthand, acting, public speaking, religious studies, and catechism.[89] Courses were free for members, and they reflected the vocational interests of workers. In fact, the additional training courses offered in Guadalajara by the Catholic Union of Commercial Employees were so popular that the union had to find a larger space.[90] New skills were necessary for political activity, for job placement and advancement, and improved pay. Some were more social, like singing, orchestra, and theater, while others, like religion and catechism, were strictly devotional. All may be seen, on one level at least, as propaganda, that is, they actively promoted the movement and the faith. Study circles, whether focused on sociology or religious studies, catered to men as well as women. Courses were sex specific, reflecting the sexual division of social space and the organization of society in general. They also extended the social to include family, work, recreation, and education. Similarly, unions founded primary and secondary schools for boys and girls, and night schools for men and women, sometimes in collaboration with the Damas Católicas. The Catholic worker federation organized study circles, and a statewide speakers circuit that offered seminars in practically any little town where there was an affiliated union, a Catholic Association of Mexico Youth local, or Union of Catholic Ladies chapter. In this manner, the more experienced members could share their expertise with those who were more isolated from the dynamic center of the union movement.

Speakers tended to be men, and certainly some came from the clergy or liberal professions. But the speaker profile is more complex, including activists that rose up from the movement's social base over the years. This was the case of Anacleto González Flores, a man of very modest origins who rose to become the undisputed leader of political Catholics in the 1920s. Another example would be Maximiano Reyes, a man of humble origins from Mezquitán who joined the PCN in the summer of 1911, served as party delegate in that community, and went on to become president of the National Federation of Catholic Labor.[91] In this position, he traveled around the archdiocese with other Catholic intellectuals and militants advising on union organizing.

Most speakers were men, but not all, and women speakers gave conferences, too. Such was the case of Rosa González Garibay, of the Guadalajara-based Confederación Católica de Obreras (CCO), a network of women's labor associations that formed in May 1924 in response to a convocation issued by the Liga Protectora de las Obreras.[92] The first item of business for the CCO was to form competing slates of candidates and vote on a governing council. González Garibay participated on the winning slate and took up the position of interior

FIGURE 10. Portrait of Maximiano Reyes, flag bearer of the National Catholic Labor Confederation, dedicated by the Central Committee to Francisco Orozco y Jiménez, Archbishop of Guadalajara, ca. 1923. The back is signed by Arnulfo Castro, SJ, Father José Toral Moreno, Maximiano Reyes (pictured), J. Jesús Flores López, Ignacio S. Orozco, Faustino Rivera, Elpidio Yañez, Rodolfo Cortés, and E. Gómez Vásquez. Source: Archivo Histórico de la Arquidiócesis de Guadalajara.

secretary to the CCO. The women on the governing council were all unmarried according to *El Obrero*.[93] By the summer of 1921, González Garibay also played an active role as a public speaker tied to the Feminine Social Action propaganda group. In this role, she addressed women's unions on the founding and administering of mutualist societies.[94] Over subsequent months, she and the other CCO leaders organized pilgrimages, religious fiestas, benefits in favor of other women's associations, mutualist societies, sewing workshops, a movie house, fund-raising events, and elections to renew the governing council the following year.[95] After a new election, the CCO rank and file organized a fiesta to mark its first anniversary. There they swore in a new governing council.[96]

Work and Worship

These examples serve to illustrate a basic argument: the Catholic unions were formed by working people across the state, who lived in generally precarious circumstances, and who had few luxuries in their lives. Jean Meyer wrote of these organizations as part of a Catholic socialism. His characterization is meant to reveal a paradox, set as it is in a time of struggle between Catholics and socialists. But it also raises an intriguing point of comparison between utopian socialism in the tradition of Robert Owens or Charles Fournier, for example, and the subject of this history. The term is problematic, but it points to an aspect of local solidarities that is on display here: these communities endeavored to create their own safety nets; and in times of civil war, frequent poor harvests, and epidemics, such local cooperation was of vital importance. Furthermore, Meyer is not alone in this appreciation: the German Volksverein was also occasionally characterized as "Christian socialist," particularly the writing of the Jesuit Heinrich Pesch.[97]

Such local solidarities were wrapped up in a combination of material and spiritual relations. This is most simply and articulately stated through the ex-voto tradition, the votive offering to a saint, that was also popular in many of these towns. The form of this devotional practice was simple: an individual was injured, fell ill, or was somehow unable to work. Traditionally, once recovered, they might paint a small representation of their tribulation and the divine intercession that saved them. Such paintings would be offered in a chapel at the feet of a saint. In this refiguring of the ex-voto tradition, a worker's savings and loan cooperative or mutual-aid society—perhaps with the help of a saint—provided the necessary support until the individual recovered; on returning to work, he or she then sent notice of their gratitude and devotion to the newspaper.[98] Or, sometimes, they died and a family member might send an acknowledgment of support received.[99]

This practice appeared occasionally in *La Palabra*, the newspaper that Anacleto González Flores edited and published from 1917 until 1919. They followed a basic formula: an individual gave thanks to a saint for a miracle.[100] For example:

I give thanks to the Sacred Heart of Jesus and to Our Lady Mary of Guadalupe for having conceded me the recovery from illness of my wife
—Feliciano González, Juanacatlan, Nov. 1918.[101]

I offer thanks to the Child of Prague for having conceded me a great miracle.
—D. G.[102]

With the emergence of a union movement and a worker newspaper, the practice evolved. In *El Obrero*, the descriptions are generally more detailed, but most importantly, the unions became as central to the *voto de gracias* as the saints, and the grateful regularly recorded the amount of monetary support they received while they were ill or injured. Often, the amount was relatively small—though it should be taken seriously regardless but if a worker died, the amount given to the family might be substantial, more than 100 pesos. In a moment of financial as well as emotional crisis, this support could be vital:

> I offer the most heartfelt thanks to the Men's Conference of the Holy Trinity and to Our Lady of Refuge for the many benefits I received from them during my illness, including $13.20, and visits by Manuel Hernandez, Mariano Gomez, J. Dolores Lorenzano, J. Guadalupe Jiménez, and other members . . . For this, I will never cease to share with my workmates these benefits in order to convince them to join.
> —Rio Grande Factory, 19 March 1922, Andres Davila

Such expressions of thanksgiving were common, sent from factories, rural towns, small villages, ranches, and the capital city of Guadalajara.[103]

When a Catholic worker died in Chapala in June 1919, the union made sure he received a Christian burial. Then, some 200 union members published a note manifesting their condolences for the lost comrade. According to the resulting chronicle, they accompanied the comrade through his wake, funeral, and burial ceremony.[104] The benefits offered by the Catholic unions were material indeed; but they were also spiritual. Members could live their precarious lives in the security that they would die a Christian death; as sheep in the fold, they would not die alone.

Worker publication of ex-votos reconstructed this tradition, and simultaneously transformed it, converting the newspaper into an ephemeral altar at which the faithful address the Divine. However, this display and deployment of faith generated a manifestation of massive consumption, even as it played a role as propaganda, that is, in the mission of the Catholic union movement and the Faith. A good example of an emerging devotion with transcendent consequences was faith in the divine intercession of a recently martyred local priest:

> I offer infinite thanks to God for having conceded me a grace that I requested by intercession of Father Galvan.
> —Atotonilco el Alto, 18 Nov. 1921, Micaela Gutierrez[105]

I make public my gratitude to Father David Galvan for having obtained by
the Infinite Mercy of God the remedy for a need through his intercession.
—Ignacio S. Orozco, Guadalajara, 20 June 1921[106]

Such examples allude to a particular aspect of the ex-voto tradition that was in
play during and after the decade of 1920. As stated, David Galván's execution
in 1915 generated a kind of religious sentiment that quickly had political consequences, and in the long term transformed him from a local Guadalajara
priest to a symbol and a saint. It is significant that in 1920 he was already perceived as a figure that might intercede on behalf of the ill.[107]

In all these ways, the ex-voto tradition was transformed through its incorporation into newsprint as a form of mass communication. It was no longer
shared merely with the faithful at a local chapel, but by thousands affiliated
with a political-religious movement of regional extension and national ambition. In fact, this change turned the act of devotion on its head. Prior to the
advent of newspaper distribution, the ex-voto was placed in a single spot, and
became part of an altar at which the faithful might assemble to pray. Through
the newspaper, the act of assembling, or visiting an altar, is transformed. Here
the altar is mobile, it goes to the faithful. The faithful consume altars and
prayer from far and wide through membership in their local union. Whether
or not we find convincing Benedict Anderson's argument that the press unites
strangers in a political community through a shared imaginary, this case demonstrates that it is not merely, or even necessarily, the nation that is constructed
in the act of popular consumption, or imagination. Here it is the faith—a
political Catholicism—as well, perhaps, as the Catholic nation.[108]

A Coronation

In the last part of the chapter, I will look at one more example in which Catholic workers are constructed through a multilayered social hierarchy that was at
the same time shot through with gender and class relations.

In January 1921, the Guadalajara archdiocese celebrated the coronation of
the Virgin of Zapopan. The event and the spectacle were large and very public.
The Virgin of Zapopan coronation was reminiscent of earlier celebrations,
such as the 1905 coronation of Our Lady of the Pillar at Zaragoza, Spain's
greatest Marian shrine,[109] or the 1909 coronation of the Virgin of Solitude in
Oaxaca.[110] Edward Wright-Ríos has identified three basic elements, all of
which were present in the 1921 coronation: first, a period of preparatory

FIGURE 11. Seminarians
and laity at Zapopan
Convent Orchard, Curso
Social Zapopano, 1921.
Jorge Padilla (top left),
Manuel B. Gómez (third
from left, standing). Source:
Luis Padilla Family Col-
lection.

devotion in which masses were offered and diverse groups of pilgrims visited
the miraculous statue; second, the coronation proper, with its regal overtones
linking the material and spiritual in a metaphor of authority and obedience;
and third, a social gathering linked to the coronation in order to take advantage of the distinguished visitors from points beyond the diocese. All of these
elements were part of the Virgin of Zapopan coronation. In both cases, the
social gathering that followed the coronation was significant. In the Oaxaca
case, Wright-Rios documents the Fourth National Catholic Congress, which
was inaugurated directly following the Virgin of Solitude coronation. It was
the last major Catholic congress of the Porfirian era.[111] In Guadalajara, the
Curso Social Agricola Zapopano followed the coronation. It was there that
Alfredo Méndez Medina and others discussed how to transform the Catholic
worker movement into a national phenomenon.[112]

———

In preparation, the faithful decorated the streets in blue-and-white banners from the Guadalajara center all the way to Zapopan, ten kilometers away. Elaborate strings of flowers made their way across the facade of the metropolitan cathedral. By night, multicolored lanterns illuminated the windows of countless homes and fireworks boomed over Solitude Plaza. In the center of town, street vendors sold sweets to the passersby. For nights on end, the young and old, men, women, and children all invaded the city center; all came out for the fiesta.[113]

The Guadalajara celebration began with a period of preparatory devotion characterized by large pilgrimages that arrived daily from the many rural and small-town parishes across the archdiocese and further afield. Beginning on January 8, for ten days pilgrims were received at the Guadalajara cathedral around six-thirty in the morning, often organized through lay associations and accompanied by their pastor. The pilgrims were welcomed at the main doors of the cathedral by a member of the diocesan *cabildo*, or council, and ushered in. The rural priests who arrived with their flocks proceeded to occupy the many altars of the cathedral and offer impromptu masses and communion simultaneously for the faithful, generating a coordinated confusion in which prayer and devotion seemed to mix with the chaos of a local *tianguis*, or street market.

Later, at 9:00 a.m., the archdiocese offered a pontifical mass each morning, in which the bishops shared responsibilities with local clergy or rural priests who had arrived with the pilgrims.[114] In a typical case, the bishop of León offered the mass, his deacon was Father Orozco of Chapala, the subdeacon was Father Vega of Juchitlán, and the presbyter was Father Tovar of Ahualulco.[115] The mass reveals a hierarchical division of labor, but more importantly, expresses a meticulous coordination that allowed priests from different cities and towns to work together in the service of a common goal. Another priest, in this case canon Miguel Cano y Rodríguez of Guadalajara, offered the sermon. This distribution of labor reflected an interest in accentuating the collective nature of the endeavor, but also allowed the organizers the privilege of including noted orators in the delivery of the sermons. Thus, important speakers such as Francisco Banegas Galván (bishop of Querétaro), and Emeterio Valverde Téllez (bishop of León) offered sermons at the pilgrimage masses. Following mass, pilgrims were photographed with Archbishop Orozco y Jiménez and other bishops who had come to Guadalajara to take part in the festivities from León, Tulancingo, Sonora, Puebla, Cuernavaca, Aguascalientes, Querétaro, Saltillo, Michoacán, Zacatecas, Colima, Tepic, and Zamora. Every afternoon a second round of pilgrimages arrived from nearby parishes, led by local pastors and their lay associations of workers, women, youth, and an array of religious devotions.[116]

On the eighteenth, the crowd gathered in the early hours of the morning. The faithful represented parishes located in towns and villages from across the state of Jalisco and beyond. Behind the main altar, the miraculous statue was on display. Across her chest hung a blue sash that conveyed her superior hierarchy, *la banda de Generala*. Her crown was fashioned in three shades of gold. In this manner the coronation revealed a tension, inherent in the figure and dressing of the Virgin, between two competing metaphors of power, one regal and the other martial.[117] Miguel de la Mora, the Guadalajara-raised bishop of Zacatecas, referenced this military metaphor in the coronation sermon:

> In the year of 1821, following Independence one hundred years ago, She was proclaimed the undefeated *caudillo* of the Mexican troops, and dressed with a General's sword in order that she might lead to victory the defending armies of the cause of Christ.[118]

Steeped in patriotism, the military metaphor gave way to one that was more properly regal as the ceremony progressed: Archbishop Orozco y Jiménez stepped down from his throne and approached the Virgin, hands trembling, the official chronicle tells us. Placing the crown upon her head, he decreed, "As by our hands you are crowned on earth, may we be worthy in heaven to have the honor to be crowned by you."[119]

At that point, the solemnity of the occasion was lost in an explosion of shouts and applause, while a marching band slipped back to the military idiom, serenading Jalisco's new Queen as a triumphant general. The Sayula poet, Father Rodrigo Águilar Alemán, commemorated the moment with a lengthy poem called "*Canción Guerrera*," a warrior's song, which lionizes the martial demeanor of the celebration:

> Were it my fortune to offer my blood
> For the faith of your Purity, your love and your Cause
> Falling beneath the folds of the mystical flag,
> Cry out I would—Long Live! Long Live!—my valiant GENERAL!![120]

Across the city every church bell rang, while those who witnessed the coronation wept with enthusiasm. The crowd was well in excess of the Cathedral's capacity, and those who could not enter spilled out across the plaza. All kneeled as the bells tolled, and rejoiced in unison.[121]

Following the mass, between 20,000 to 30,000 faithful gathered in San Francisco gardens for a parade in honor of Our Lady of Zapopan.[122] At six o'clock in the evening, the crowd began an orderly march through the city center. In the lead paraded the women's associations, organized by the Union of Catholic Ladies (UDC). Each member carried a green crepe paper lantern with a candle in it. They were followed by a male vanguard carrying white lanterns, including the Knights of Columbus, the Catholic Association of Mexican Youth (ACJM), and the San Luis Gonzaga Congregation. Finally, workers' associations affiliated with the Catholic Confederation of Labor (CCT), brought up the rear carrying red lanterns. Together they represented the colors of the Mexican flag, symbolizing patriotism and commitment to the nation. However, it is equally important to note the organizational logic that went into the parade. The corporatist identities of social Catholicism were on display here, including the main constituent groups of confessional politics. The Damas, the Knights, the Catholic Youth, and particularly the workers' associations were central to the organizing strategy of the Mexican Social Secretariat under the leadership of Alfredo Méndez Medina. At the same time, it is important to explore the ways that the tactics of alliance, which channeled worker identity along with those of other groups through the lens of religious practice, shaped the union experience of workers. In this case, workers formed the red band of a gigantic, flickering, human flag that extended for twelve city blocks, an offering to the Virgin and the Republic at one and the same time. Along the way the crowd shouted *vivas* to Christ the King, the Virgin of Zapopan, the Catholic Church, Pope Benedict XV, the Mexican episcopate, Mexico, Jalisco, and to religious freedom.

When the parade arrived at its destination along San Francisco Street, Luis Beltrán y Mendoza, Anacleto González Flores and Gabriel Ortiz Garcia climbed onto the monument located there in honor of Ramón Corona.[123] General Corona had been Jalisco's most important liberal hero of the previous generation, a military leader on a par with Bernardo Reyes or Porfirio Díaz.[124] The three transgressors were local ACJM leaders, and perched upon the great bronze statue they offered combative speeches in defense of their *patria*, a Mexico in which national identity was Catholic. For this group of emerging lay leaders, the rich irony of the situation was obvious: the Catholic crowd had taken over the city streets—to the revolutionaries they were a new breed of savages—and had figuratively laid siege to the public space dedicated to the hero of a prior generation of liberal reformers. This Catholic movement fashioned itself as the aspiration and possibility of a counter-reform.

The following day, Wednesday the nineteenth, 15,000 accompanied the Virgin along the route from Guadalajara's Cathedral to the Basilica in Zapopan. She was carried along in a regal carriage covered in silk with a gold-embroidered canopy and a crown of precious stones. Its interior was perfumed with bouquets of white flowers. Impeccably dressed lackeys led the carriage with a team of black horses adorned in white *gualdrapas*, hand-knitted covers extending almost to the ground, and harnesses decorated with blue silk. After some blocks the crowd unhitched the team of horses, and in alternating groups, pulled the carriage the entire distance of the parade route by hand, a two-and-a-half-hour march. The parade wound its way northwest past the Municipal Cemetery in the old Indian neighborhood of Mezquitán. As the pilgrims left the city behind, they were joined by a dozen dance troops, dressed in their colorful costumes, and led through the countryside near the Colomos water pumping station along the automobile road to Zapopan. Followed by a long line of cars, the crowd sang and prayed and the dancers danced. Their arrival at Zapopan was greeted by a sea of people crowded alongside the road, in the plazas, on the rooftops, in and around the atrium and church building. All awaited the triumphant arrival of the Queen, under the abiding peal of church bells.[125]

8. José Guadalupe Zuno and the Collapse of Public Space

THE EARLY TWENTIES was a period of almost constant conflict in Jalisco. The points of tension were several, including local struggles over revolutionary legitimacy and governance, conflict between local politicos and the central government in Mexico City, and an ongoing war of position between Catholics and revolutionaries over the loyalties of the masses and public space in an emerging civil society. In all of these arenas, José Guadalupe Zuno played a central role, as agitator, defender of local autonomy, state-builder, and revolutionary iconoclast. In one way or another, the history of early post-revolutionary Jalisco, and the run up to the 1926 religious rebellion were deeply conditioned by this young revolutionary.

José Guadalupe Zuno Hernández was born in 1891 near La Barca, Jalisco. He studied at the Liceo de Varones in Guadalajara, from whence he was expelled after participating in the 1910 Maderista marches. As the revolution moved from Madero's reforms toward civil war, Zuno emerged as a young artist of some promise, studying painting with José Clemente Orozco and founding a salon in Guadalajara called the Centro Bohemio. While his younger brother Alberto joined the Carrancista fight against Villa's army, Zuno painted and exhibited. Once the 1917 constitution reestablished formal government, Zuno moved openly into politics, first as a federal congressman, then as mayor of Guadalajara in 1922, and as governor of Jalisco in 1923. From this point until President Calles forced him out of the governor's palace, Zuno made his most important contribution to post-revolutionary statecraft.[1]

The historical significance of Zuno is tied to the emerging mass politics of post-revolutionary Mexico, born of a highly mobilized society and the different national projects that clashed during the presidencies of Álvaro Obregón

(1920–1924) and Plutarco Elías Calles (1924–1928). Obregón was the revolution's greatest military caudillo, and Calles would soon emerge as the institutional architect of the new regime.[2] From Guadalajara, Zuno played his hand with the caudillo and tried to channel Jalisco politics in step with Obregón's project to consolidate state power and close the period of armed conflict that had characterized Mexican politics during the previous decade. But he would also show a strong interest in shaping the institutions of government in Jalisco, a predilection that would lead him to clash with Calles over the balance of political power between Mexico City and Guadalajara.[3] And yet, despite his ties of loyalty to Obregón, Zuno's style of politics was really more akin to that of Calles. Obregón is often described as a conciliator, Calles an authoritarian.[4] Zuno shared with Obregón a populist political style, but he was not interested in conciliation; to the contrary, he was intransigent. And regardless of the rivalry that emerged between them, Zuno and Calles followed a similar path in their dealings with political Catholicism. Often, in fact, Zuno was a step ahead of his Sonoran counterpart, as with his decision in 1923 to proscribe confessional unions from the Jalisco labor code. Both understood early on that they could profit from controlling organized labor, that political Catholicism was a threat, and that the new politics was a phenomenon of the organized masses.

In the waning months of the Obregón presidency, the Sonoran clique came to blows over the succession. Adolfo de la Huerta, Obregón's treasury minister, was a popular candidate with strong support in the military. He had led the Sonoran rebellion against President Carranza in 1920 and had served as provisional president between June and December that year. But Interior Minister Calles controlled the political machinery of government and emerged as Obregón's likely successor. Soon after declaring his candidacy, in December 1923 General De la Huerta rebelled.[5] In Jalisco, Generals Manuel M. Diéguez and Enrique Estrada both fielded troops in his favor. They were defeated at Ocotlán, Jalisco, a battle that proved to be the turning point of the rebellion. Subsequently, De la Huerta and Estrada were exiled to the United States, but Diéguez was less fortunate; having taken sides with Carranza against Obregón in 1920, he had already been pardoned once. He fled south through Guerrero and Oaxaca, but loyalist troops caught up with him in Chiapas, and Obregón ordered him shot at Tuxtla Gutiérrez on April 21, 1924.[6] In the end, the rebellion was short-lived and its failure seemed to mark the end of caudillo politics and the beginning of a period of institutions.[7]

Zuno avoided public entanglements during the rebellion. The US consul wrote that Zuno had fled Guadalajara when the rebellion broke out, and only reappeared after the federal army had defeated the rebels.[8] The historian Jaime Tamayo says he left Guadalajara at the outset for Ameca, where he armed agrarista peasant leagues. But he then offers no more data on Zuno's activities until after the rebellion.[9] Jean Meyer says Zuno went to Mexico City to convince Obregón and Calles that Archbishop Orozco y Jiménez was behind the rebellion,[10] but that the president was not convinced. These scenarios are mutually plausible, but there is also a paucity of evidence regarding the governor's whereabouts during those difficult weeks. In any case, Zuno reemerged in February 1924 with his hand strengthened by the state of exception in Jalisco. Taking advantage of the conjuncture, he forced out town mayors across the state and replaced them with men who were loyal to him. The Callista faction in Mexico City was keen on implicating Zuno in the rebellion. Interior ministry informants wrote at great length about the intrigues of the Zuno administration. An early theory was that he had played both sides of the rebellion, but informants eventually came to the conclusion that the governor had supported the De la Huerta rebellion. They also investigated, in late 1924, whether Zuno actively plotted the murder of communications minister and union boss, Luis N. Morones.[11] By early 1926, the congress took steps to dissolve his government, effectively forcing him to step down as governor in March.[12] The senate voted to suspend his right to hold office for a seven-year period, thereby officially barring him from formal political participation. And by June, the congress removed the substitute governor, the state legislature, and a majority of the town councils in the state of Jalisco, all of which were zunista bulwarks.

However, it was the religious conflict that most clearly shaped the history of Jalisco and its capital city Guadalajara. This regional phenomenon marked the entire decade and conditioned the formation of the central state. In 1926, President Calles ordered strict application of the constitution as it pertained to religious practice. This decree, known as the Calles Law, prompted the Mexican bishops to suspend public worship and shut down church buildings across the nation. The 1926 clerical strike was a watershed in modern Mexican history, and immediately generated portentous—if isolated—acts of violence, followed eventually by a generalized popular rebellion. The Cristero Rebellion enveloped much of Jalisco and parts of Colima, Michoacán, Guanajuato, Durango, Aguascalientes, and Zacatecas.[13] It lasted for three years, consuming the Calles presidency and destroying the civic movement that formed the backbone of political Catholicism. The competing armies fought to a stalemate before US ambassador Dwight Morrow brokered a 1929 settlement acceptable to the bishops and president Emilio Portes Gil. The bishops were not in a position to demand a cessation of hostilities, but they did control the church buildings. And in June 1929, they ordered the churches reopened in a gamble to end the fighting.[14] Mostly, the gamble paid off, and the rebels returned to their homes.

This chapter traces the events that led to the rebellion. Zuno played an important role as did Francisco Orozco y Jiménez, the archbishop of Guadalajara. However, the main argument examines Catholic militants, and the ways they acted and reacted in confrontation with rivals. The narrative is divided in two main parts, and proposes an analytical division in which I argue that anticlerical politics evolved from less formal to more formal modes as statesmen like Zuno and Calles consolidated power and outlined strategies for containing the religious conflict. In a third and final section, I argue that Zuno's policies choked off civic protest by closing down the spaces in which Catholics organized and voiced their opposition. Tension mounted, conventional vehicles of protest disappeared, and without civic or nonviolent means available, rural Catholics from western Mexico turned eventually to armed rebellion in late 1926.

Unscripted Anticlericalism, 1920–1922

Following the return of the Guadalajara archbishop from exile in the fall of 1919, Catholic politics became dynamic and assertive: lay associations aimed to seize control of new spaces and regain those lost in previous years. Organized laity founded workers' centers, women's and youth groups, schools, newspapers, cooperatives, and labor unions. Religious leaders returned from exile and lay leaders made their names. Meanwhile, President Obregón (1920–1924) attempted to consolidate his power after the 1920 Agua Prieta rebellion, and showed a willingness to negotiate with diverse factions in an effort to end the revolution. His first overture to the Catholics was the return of church buildings, revoking closure decrees imposed between 1914 and 1919.[15] State power remained relatively weak, and anticlericalism often took the form of *ad hoc* vandalism, rioting, shootings, and bombings. To some extent, this violence was independent of government policy, carried out by proxies such as *cromistas*[16] and militant agrarians.

The massification of both Catholic and revolutionary politics prompted serious clashes on the streets. The year 1921 saw three important dynamite attacks,[17] and serious acts of vandalism and affray. In Mexico City, an early morning dynamite attack on the archbishop's home caused considerable damage in February. There were no injuries, but Catholic organizations staged public protests and posted civilian sentinels around the clock at the home.[18] The attack has been interpreted as a response to the Virgin of Zapopan coronation, which concluded about ten days earlier.[19] In Guadalajara on Labor Day (May 1), pro-government workers marched on the cathedral and flew the red-and-black anarcho-syndicalist flag from the bell tower. Led by Miguel Gómez Loza, a law student and union leader, Catholics confronted the intruders. Gómez Loza forced his way into the belfry, where he was beaten up. For this valor, he was celebrated as a fearless defender of the Catholic cause. The Knights of Columbus decorated him and he, like Anacleto González Flores, became part of a new lay leadership espousing combative, nonviolent action.[20] Fellow activist Vicente Camberos Vizcaíno narrated Gómez Loza's attempt to seize the flag with admiration and bestowed an epic quality on the event in his 1949 biography: although it must have been a brief episode, this retelling has become a classic of partisan Catholic historiography.[21]

Some days later in Morelia, a similar episode had more tragic consequences. Antonio Rius Facius, a member of the ACJM during the twenties, wrote that on May 7 a group of students paraded through the streets; one young man dressed in priest's clothing rode an ass and blessed the passersby with mocking solemnity.[22] The passage recalls Natalie Zemon Davis's descriptions of early modern charivaris.[23] The insult passed without causing an altercation, but served to heighten tensions among the most active on either side of the Church-state divide. Then, on the eighth, the CROM organized a rally in protest of clergy and landowners. Isaac Arriaga, Governor Mújica's "right-hand man" was among the main speakers.[24] As the rally turned into a cromista procession, a group of demonstrators made their way up to the bell tower at Morelia's cathedral to ring the bells and hang the red-and-black flag, as had been done a week earlier in Guadalajara. After the demonstrators left the cathedral, an ACJM militant, Joaquín Cornejo, took the flag down. That afternoon, a group of fifteen returned to take back the flag, convinced that the sacristan had taken it down. When he could not produce the flag, they beat him, and destroyed a painting of the Virgin of Guadalupe, making long crossing cuts in the canvas with a knife.[25]

The response was again to organize public protest. The Catholic Ladies Union called for a pilgrimage through downtown Morelia on the eighth, but was denied a march permit. Subsequently, the ACJM was able to secure a permit for a silent march on the twelfth, four days later. At three o'clock in the afternoon, the march set out from the sanctuary of the Virgin of Guadalupe in Morelia; it grew quickly, reaching approximately 7,000, and apparently was not silent. The demonstrators shouted slogans in favor of Christ the King and the Virgin of Guadalupe. As they approached the old aqueduct, they came face to face with a group of policemen and agraristas who intended to head off the march. The chief of police, Vicente Coyt, met the demonstrators and told them to disperse while Isaac Arriaga, the leader of the pro-government agrarian commission, pled with the crowd to disperse. When they did not, the police opened fire on the crowd. Among the initial victims was mister Cornejo, the young man who removed the anarchist flag from the bell tower. In death, Cornejo became a martyr to the cause.[26]

This time, Catholics fired back on their adversaries, killing Arriaga and three more on the pro-government side. Another of the pro-government casualties was José Martínez, the head of Police Special Services. There were as many as twelve pilgrim casualties, and another forty wounded, some fatally. The presence, and death, of Arriaga, Mújica's "right-hand man," is important because it raises the question of formal and informal policy. The presence among the police ranks of an armed civilian, leader of a pro-government social organization, seems ominous. However, Arriaga has been described as a moderate who could speak to the Catholic side, and might serve to temper the more radical and violent proclivities of police chief Coyt.[27] In any case, the presence of the agrarista group does not suggest formal policy so much as the informal arrangements born of patron-client ties. And yet, one might reasonably suppose that government at the highest levels was not clear of the event. Such was anticlerical hostility during the early Obregón regime, in this case, mediated by the Mújica administration's style of politics.[28]

As the shooting began, ACJM leader Julián Vargas drew a pistol and began firing at the police. His narration, apparently based on Ruíz Villaloz, is as follows:

> Julian has drawn a pistol, presenting the smallest target he can, and begins to fire, shouting Long Live Christ the King! At his side a man is down—a water carrier—shot through the heart. A few steps away, a lady steps onto the embankment and shouts Long Live Christ the King! Long Live Our Valiant Men! She is struck down shot right in the chest . . . Julian Vargas feels his legs go limp with pain, they no longer hold him upright, he's been hit; he sits down on the embankment and continues shooting. . . . Another

bullet strikes his arm and wrist and forces him to drop the pistol; he takes it up with his left hand and continues shooting. . . . An expansive bullet pierces Julian Vargas in the neck; he extends his arms, collapses on the ground and lets go of the pistol which falls next to his left hand. Not a bullet remains.[29]

Like Cambero's description of Gómez Loza fighting his way to the belfry, this narrative was written after the Cristero Rebellion, which explains the embellishment of certain details, such as the woman perched upon a traffic embankment and shot through the chest as she calls out, "Long Live Our Valiant Men!" as well as the epic, almost cinematographic staging. Nevertheless, Rius Facius's narrative and the body count help shed light on the increasing polarization of Catholic and pro-government forces. Morelia was essentially the first serious armed confrontation.

About the same time, a small explosive device was detonated at the Mexico City archbishop's residence. Then, a month later, on June 4, a bomb exploded at Orozco y Jiménez's residence in Guadalajara. Both explosions were purportedly set off by the CROM. In response, the ACJM formed a security team while various confessional groups organized demonstrations. These included the labor unions, Knights of Columbus, Catholic Ladies, and the Tomás de Kempis Society, a local devotional group named after the fourteenth-century German mystic.[30] More than 4,000 marched peacefully through the city center. The Union of Catholic Worker Syndicates (USOC) also organized a petition signed by the Guadalajara unions, demanding the ouster of the local chief of police.[31] In the highlands region of Jalisco, subsequently a stronghold of *Cristero* rebel activity, the San Julian ACJM organized a march with members of the local trade unions and Guadalupan study circles. The organizers in San Julian selected a symbolic site for the demonstration, concluding the march at a portal on the town plaza named after Agustín de Iturbide, Mexico's first emperor and an icon of Catholic nationalism.[32]

On November 14, a third bomb went off in the Basilica de Guadalupe, the most sacred site in Mexico.[33] Placed in a flower vase at the foot of the famous painting of Mexico's patron, it destroyed a bronze cross and the marble altar, although the painting survived. Amidst the destruction, the glass protecting the painting was not shattered, bolstering the popular verdict that the event constituted a miracle and strengthening the Virgin of Guadalupe cult. The perpetrator, Juan Esponda, would have been lynched by the crowd, were he not quickly arrested and evacuated by a group of soldiers. The bombing was denounced across the country, inciting new Catholic militancy. In Mexico City 20,000 faithful gathered at the Basilica in repudiation of the bombing, and Catholics declared the eighteenth a national day of mourning.[34] In Guadalajara the Catholic Women Workers Confederation (CCO), organized a pilgrimage to the sanctuary of the Virgin of Zapopan as an act of vindication, or *desagravio*, for the bombing. The event was scheduled for January 1922, in order to coincide with the anniversary of the 1921 coronation pilgrimage from Guadalajara to Zapopan, and the CCO ran a special campaign to involve women workers in the public demonstration of repudiation.[35]

After a year of bombings, shootings, and isolated rioting, the Mexican Social Secretariat (SSM) organizations continued to build their social bases and, in Jalisco at least, continued to prosper. All in all, the toll in Guadalajara was low: there had been no deaths since 1914–1915, the middle years of the revolution. But the recent bombing at the sanctuary of Guadalupe outside Mexico City left no doubt as to the seriousness of the conflict. Politics had begun to replace the logic of civil war, but sporadic acts of terror, intimidation, and political violence punctuated the landscape of post-revolutionary Mexico.

In the state of Jalisco, government was weak and unstable due to deep rifts among the groups that vied for power. Elected representatives often failed to serve out their terms, and governors, mayors, and city councils were often appointed through extraordinary fiat. On March 10, Guadalajara city councilmen supporting Governor Vadillo were involved in a scuffle with opposition councilmen aligned with José Guadalupe Zuno. A policeman named Jesús F. Gómez attempted to impede the opposition members from entering the building. Both sides ended up shooting at each other inside a government building. Gómez shot Luis C. Medina, a tailor by trade, labor leader, and municipal vice president.[36] In the melee, a former city councilman named Vitaliano Rivera was shot and killed, as was officer Gómez. Several others were wounded with non-life-threatening gunshot wounds as well.

Governor Vadillo was away from the capital at the time, but returned the following day to depose the Guadalajara mayor and dissolve the city council. In its place he named an eight-member council to govern Guadalajara for the remainder of the year. The local congress deliberated over how to respond and, in particular, whether to force the governor to step down and face criminal charges for the event that led to the shootings. They also requested that the national government provide the congress with armed protection, which they received in the form of an army detachment. José Guadalupe Zuno and several other members of the local congress sat as a grand jury on March 17 and forced the governor to step down. Antonio Valadés Ramírez, a federal congressman, replaced him by appointment of the grand jury. It also reinstated the city council but not the mayor, who belonged to the same political group as the ousted governor. In his place, the city council named a new mayor, Luis C. Medina, the opposition councilman who had survived a gunshot wound in the melee. With a new governor and mayor, Guadalajara was in a state of latent turmoil.[37]

———

In this context, less than a week after Medina assumed office, the anarcho-syndicalist Revolutionary Renter's Union demonstration on March 26 to protest the cost of housing. The early 1920s was an era of rent strikes, and Guadalajara produced movements similar to those in Orizaba and Mexico City.[38] Led by Jenaro Laurito, an Argentine anarchist, and Justo González, a Socialist Revolutionary Party (PRS) activist who was Guadalajara's former police chief, the city's *inquilinos* marched downtown, targeting their protest at specific sites. These included the offices of the liberal daily *El Informador*; the Catholic Union of Commercial Employees; the Catholic daily *Restauración*; the socially upscale Casino Jalisciense; and the "Club Atlas," home to a local soccer team. Along the way, the protesters forced bystanders to doff their hats to the scarlet-and-black flag.[39]

The final destination was San Francisco Gardens. There are several versions of what took place that Sunday, but the most common describes how rent strikers taunted Catholic workers as they left mass. In nearly all versions, the Catholics were unarmed and provided all the casualties. The numbers involved vary, and the highest figure was given by the US vice consul, who reported that 1,000 unarmed Catholics dispersed 100 armed inquilinos led by Laurito y González.[40] *El Obrero* published an extensive report a week after the events. In it, the paper reported that one of the protesters, Ascencio Cortés, rode on horseback and opened fire on the crowd, followed by Jenaro Laurito and others. A riot ensued. After the commotion, five Catholic workers lay shot dead, with another eleven seriously injured. Several of the injured subsequently died.[41] Some hours later, Laurito and González were arrested; but so was Miguel Gómez Loza. When his supporters demanded an explanation for his arrest, they were informed that he was simply wanted for questioning as a witness.

The reaction following the massacre was quick and massive, further polarizing the different actors involved in the conflict. On Monday, comrades of the slain workers brought the victims' bodies to the Union of Catholic Worker

Syndicates office and improvised a chapel there. At *Restauración*, employees mourned a newspaper boy, who had been shot while hawking the daily outside San Francisco church, then carried his body to the USOC office. At four o'clock that afternoon, the funeral procession made its way toward the municipal cemetery. The banners of all the Catholic unions were present. The homes along the route were decorated with large black bows in memory of the dead. *El Obrero* estimated 30,000 marched with the bodies of the slain. At the cemetery, a medical student spoke to the crowd, followed by a worker. The last speaker was Anacleto González Flores, who made an impassioned plea to the authorities, "as befitted the criminal bloodshed," for justice and future guarantees, insisting that they were living among outlaws. He emphasized the need for society as a whole to take a firm position against the continued spread of communism, and reminded the mourners that some in government continued to support those guilty of the massacre. A Catholic chronicle referred to González Flores's speech as a solemn and historical moment.[42]

The mounting violence was not restricted locally, but had national and international repercussions. In February 1921, Alfredo Robles Domínguez prepared to travel to Washington.[43] He had sent his family outside the country as a safety precaution, and would soon join another opposition leader, National Republican Party (PRN) president Rafael Ceniceros y Villareal, who was already lobbying officials of the US Republican Party. According to the chargé d'affaires of the US embassy in Mexico City, Robles Domínguez wanted to discuss a possible anti-Obregón movement in Mexico. According to the US embassy official, the recent bombing at the bishop's palace and president Obregón's response had made the talks possible.[44] As the attacks mounted, in Mexico City, Guadalajara, Morelia, and elsewhere, national newspapers speculated on the Catholic response. Days before the Sunday massacre in Guadalajara, an influential Mexico City daily had written that Catholics across the nation were building a sociopolitical organization to arrest the increasingly serious attacks of the radicals. The article noted the upcoming Catholic workers congress to be held in Guadalajara,[45] and in its editorial suggested that if it did not become a "clerical" movement, it should be welcomed.[46] Reports published in *El Universal* prompted official statements by Interior Secretary Calles to the effect that as far as the federal government was concerned, the Catholics were within their rights to participate in politics. Although Mexico's two main dailies, *El Universal* and *Excelsior*, applauded the interior secretary's moderation, *Excelsior* also editorialized that radicals like Mújica and Carrillo Puerto should not fret, as Calles's declarations were not to be taken seriously.[47]

The political intrigue of the era also took on international dimensions. Such was the case following an unannounced visit to the State Department in May 1922 by the Catholic bishop, Francis Clement Kelley.[48] An assistant secretary of state received Kelley, who had recently arrived from Guadalajara. The bishop warned that a revolution was brewing in Mexico and would be the work either of the "Bolsheviki" element in society or of conservative Catholics. In Guadalajara, he had learned that Catholics were extremely bitter toward the Obregón government, but that they were also too fearful to act openly on their feelings. Guadalajara was in political chaos, having gone through three city councils, three mayors, and three governors in a matter of only a few months. Such instability promoted terror, he insisted. Although the bishop confided his feeling that Obregón was an essentially well-intentioned man, he presided over a very weak government and was surrounded by traitors. Calles particularly was a nefarious character, he felt, adding that the whole of the Mexican people was most certainly disgusted with the current regime. Intervention, in his opinion, would be welcomed if people could be assured that it would be only in the interest of ensuring free and fair elections, and setting up a responsible government. He recommended employing a team of pilots to cover strategic areas within Mexico and drop pamphlets from airplanes stating the true purpose of the United States. In the meantime, the US government should stand firm on its demands of the Obregón government as a prerequisite to diplomatic recognition.[49]

Despite recent US Catholic Church policy vis à vis Mexico,[50] Bishop Kelley pushed for a broad interventionist strategy. He seemed oblivious to the deleterious effects that Wilson's 1914 occupation of Veracruz and Pershing's 1916 "punitive expedition" in search of Villa had produced.[51] First Kelley proposed that the United States use the Catholic Church across Latin America in order to dispel traditional fears and hatred felt toward the "colossus of the north." He described a meeting with the recently deceased steel baron and philanthropist Andrew Carnegie, whom he had asked to fund a project to educate Latin American priests in the United States. He noted, in this respect, that many Catholic priests had been exiled in the United States during the revolution of the past decade and had returned to Mexico with warm feelings toward their northern neighbor. Second, and more specifically pertinent to Mexico, the bishop spoke of the relationship between Obregón and Francisco Villa. Obregón needed Villa, Kelley reasoned, and had quietly commissioned him to protect the northern border from interventions.[52] Here the bishop was less than forthright regarding his motives, but clearly wished to convince his State

Department interlocutor that Villa was not the villain he was thought to be. Pancho Villa, he explained, had gone through a religious conversion. Kelley told a story in which Villa had recently called together his followers and told them that while he had taught them to kill and steal, he now wished them to reconsider. For this purpose he had built them a church. His desire was to be able to leave a bag of gold in the middle of an open field, and to return later to find it right where he had left it. This Villa, explained Bishop Kelley, was the most probable future leader of a conservative Catholic revolution in Mexico.[53]

Bishop Kelley's story about Villa seems apocryphal, and while the notion of US intervention will surprise few, Villa would certainly have been an unorthodox choice of leaders in 1922 for a US-sponsored revolution. After all, just five years had passed since General Pershing's futile expedition had marched around the arid mountains of northern Chihuahua looking to "punish" Villa for his raid on the New Mexican border town of Columbus. To the credit of the State Department, a Division of Mexican Affairs specialist read the memorandum and recommended that it would not be necessary to further interview Monsignor Kelley. The bishop's motives, whatever they might have been, were driven by his belief that a godless state was carrying out a religious persecution of biblical proportions in Mexico. But setting aside the issue of Kelley's motives, it is striking that in a period of about eighteen months, during which time the Mexican state had not publicly articulated a policy vis à vis the Catholic Church, the conflict had escalated to the point that local events had national, and potentially international repercussions.

Anticlericalism as State Formation, 1923–1926

By 1923, the Obregón administration headed toward crisis over who would be the next president. With the emergence of Calles as the likely successor, state policy became more openly anticlerical. Street violence of the sort the unions had generated in 1921 and 1922 waned, while governmental dispositions began to limit the Catholic Church and its affiliates. This had debilitating effects on the lay organizations. In effect, there were two independent but related processes unfolding. On one side, state and pro-government organizations evolved from an informal or unscripted policy of violence to a scripted anticlerical policy. In 1923, men like Calles and Zuno continued to react to a proactive Catholic movement, but began to act strategically against it. On the other side, the Catholic lay organizations were increasingly pressured to abandon their proactive tactics, retrench, and adopt a defensive strategy in reaction to state policy.

The change began in January 1923 at Cubilete Peak, in Guanajuato.[54] Located near the town of Silao, the *cerro* rises from a highland plateau to an altitude of 2,600 meters above sea level, and was considered by Catholics to be the geographical center of Mexico. The peak itself was private property, belonging to one of the signers of the 1917 constitution, José Natividad Macías. A moderate, Macías had agreed to permit construction of a monument on his property in commemoration of Christ the King, at the site of an old chapel. In under a year, the Church authorities had collected the money needed to fund the project. On January 11, 1923, nine years to the day after the ill-fated marches commemorating Mexico to Christ the King, a pilgrimage of 50,000 faithful walked up to the peak led by Emeterio Valverde y Téllez, bishop of León. Once the pilgrims reached the peak, Bishop Valverde said mass, and the Vatican delegate to Mexico, Bishop Ernesto Filippi placed the cornerstone.[55]

The government response to the pilgrimage is telling, and suggests the Mexican heads of state were still reacting to a proactive Catholic movement. First of all, Antonio Madrazo, the governor of Guanajuato, had been in contact with Emeterio Valverde and Francisco Orozco y Jiménez. The bishops had explained the objective of the pilgrimage to the governor, assuring him that the participants would be respectful of the law and that the act of worship would take place on private property. Second, Interior Secretary Calles received a written complaint from the National Anticlerical Federation prior to the pilgrimage, and effectively ceded jurisdiction to the state of Guanajuato, by assuring the plaintiffs that Governor Madrazo had everything under control. After the pilgrimage, Madrazo maintained that no law had been broken, but President Obregón ordered the Vatican delegate to leave the country, under Article 33 of the 1917 constitution, which prohibits foreigners from participating in Mexican politics. Although the government response seemed to reveal a degree of confusion, the deportation of Monsignor Filippi may be viewed as the founding moment of an emerging, scripted, strategic anticlerical policy. Filippi's deportation was the easiest channel through which government anticlericals could strike out at the Church at the moment; and although Mexican political Catholics took the blow seriously, even the bishops continued to move forward with plans under the cover of their constitutionally guaranteed right to worship. If the authorities would not permit a statue to Christ the King on Cubilete peak, Catholics would instead build a new and larger church building. Bishop Valverde needed no permit to do so, even though eventually a permit would be necessary to celebrate mass there.[56] Nevertheless, following the incident at Cubilete, government action would not be so much in response to

confessional politics, as designed to reshape and limit future Catholic participation in the political sphere.

This would be difficult, as was noted indirectly by the Mexican Anticlerical
Federation, a pro-government, Masonic offshoot founded in 1923 that lobbied
against the Cubilete project.[57] The organization's director, Manuel Bouquet Jr.,
was a former governor of Jalisco. He had served during the 1918 conflict over
Article 130 and the exile of archbishop Orozco y Jiménez. Jean Meyer noted
ironically that Mr. Bouquet was probably hardened by the humiliating defeat
that Catholics handed his administration. Apparently the federation had a
fairly broad presence, with sections in the capital cities of Coahuila, Durango,
Jalisco, Michoacán, Puebla, San Luis Potosí, Veracruz, and Yucatan—cities
that had hosted Liberal Party clubs since Porfirian times. This presence reflects
revolutionary political dominance in the capital cities, but does not necessarily
reflect deep popular support. Most interesting, perhaps, was the federation's
take on women and the masses of Mexican faithful, a position expressed in the
organization's mission:

> [The Federation] considers itself center and union of all those who recog-
> nize in the Catholic clergy a common enemy. . . . The bloody struggle that
> during the past ten years we have sustained . . . looking to establish a true
> democracy, a reign of justice and the solution to our latent social problems,
> made us lose sight of the reactionary work of the eternal enemies of liberty
> . . . we didn't realize the resistance of clericalism, until after it had moved
> into the field of offensive action. . . . For such action it counts on the fanati-
> cism of the masses . . . and on woman.[58]

The Mexican Anticlerical Federation reflected the political polarization of
the times, but it clearly was faced with a difficult situation. By a sweeping reification of women as "woman" and plebian culture in general as "masses"—
which might easily include Villistas, Zapatistas, as well as future Cristero rebels—the Federation was left with severely depleted possibilities for its social
base. Perhaps the organization would have drawn a base of support from some
among urban professionals, artisans, industrial workers, and, especially, government bureaucracy. But by dismissing most of society as the dupes of evil
friars, there was little room for recruitment and still less for political compromise. The pamphlet offers a colorful example of the state of political speech,
and is indicative of substantial polarization that existed at the time.

This polarization would permeate the highest levels of state and national government. Carranza had avoided irretrievable clashes with the Church, and Diéguez had followed his example in 1919, in spite of his aversion to the cloth. Obregón had attempted to set a course of moderation. By contrast, Calles and Zuno both sought confrontation with their Catholic rivals and refused to negotiate. In May 1923, Zuno entered the governor's palace in Guadalajara and proceeded to apply constitutional Article 123 through legislation proscribing confessional unions.[59] State policy in Jalisco prefigured or foreshadowed what was to come from the national government during the Calles presidency. Zuno closed Catholic schools, convents, seminaries, union offices, and youth centers. In response, thousands of Catholic activists faced off against pro-government labor unions and anticlerical politicos. As the crisis grew, revolutionaries such as Governor Zuno, Communications Minister Morones, and Interior Minister Calles designed actions that obeyed an institutional logic of state power. Their goal was to shut down the public space that permitted opposition politics, and their authority determined the theater: Zuno in Jalisco, Morones through the CROM, and Calles in his quest for the presidency.

As 1923 drew to a close, the religious conflict was momentarily thrust to the back burner by Adolfo de la Huerta's rebellion. While the rebels held Guadalajara, Zuno went to Mexico City to try and implicate the Catholics in the rebellion.[60] Although the story did not take, similar rumors had circulated in the capital. One such flyer circulated on the eve of the rebellion, purported to link Cooperatist Party (PNC) leaders like Jorge Prieto Laurens with General De la Huerta and militant Catholics:

> Warning, Citizens! Reaction, Bureaucracy, Treason, cowardly and scheming cooperatist politicians—Prietistas—are gathered in the shadow of the masked one, Don Adolfo de la Huerta, to the cry of Long Live Christ the King.[61]

Such rumors were not necessarily false or unfounded. Following the De la Huerta rebellion, President Calles would be vigilant of the evolving oppositions around the country, and his spies were surprisingly efficient at collecting data on several fronts. In October 1924, an interior ministry agent intercepted a letter that Jorge Prieto Laurens sent to Adolfo de la Huerta in New York. He photographed the letter in the United States and then allowed it to reach De la Huerta. In the letter Prieto Laurens wrote that he had secured financial backing in England for a revolution through a Mr. Lyman Chatfield & Company.[62]

This information was echoed a couple of months later, rightly or wrongly, when a former congressman and De la Huerta supporter spoke to a government spy about a rumored plot. Juan Pastoriza described a plan, supported by the United States and England, in which a new government would be installed under the auspices of Francisco León de la Barra, Félix Díaz, and Adolfo de la Huerta. In this rumor, the National Cooperatist Party would play a supporting role.[63] In subsequent reports, government agents were interested in establishing the relation between the events surrounding the pilgrimage to Cubilete, the De la Huerta rebellion, and groups of Catholics in the southwestern United States. The ties were not borne out; however, Agent F. De la Garza offered one clearly stated conclusion: US Catholic clergy, and Bishop Kelley of Oklahoma in particular, had refused to commit any support to antigovernment elements looking to topple the Calles administration. This is a revealing change of opinion, given Kelley's interview in Washington three years earlier.[64]

On his return to Guadalajara, Zuno treated the Catholic organizations as rebel sympathizers, which some certainly had been. He closed down the ACJM weekly, *Atalaya*, as well as *Restauración*, Guadalajara's Catholic daily, second in circulation to *El Informador*. In the case of *Restauración*, Zuno was angry that the paper had written enthusiastically about the rebellion. In retaliation, his supporters sacked and looted the building where the daily was located, and several employees were arrested without charge. He also closed down Guadalajara's main daily, *El Informador*, of moderate liberal editorial stance. In this case, although its news coverage had been strictly neutral, the paper was tainted through family ties, the owner's brother having been a De la Huertista general.[65]

In March 1924, Zuno moved against the lay associations, distributing a memorandum to the municipal presidents across the state, instructing them to prohibit all meetings of the Catholic Association of Mexican Youth (ACJM), the Knights of Columbus (CC), and the *Sindicato de Agricultores* [*sic*]. Zuno charged them with conspiracy to rebel against his government.[66] In Guadalajara, the ACJM offices were confiscated by the *Comisión Interventora de Bienes de Rebeldes*, the government office in charge of expropriating the property of those who participated in the De la Huerta rebellion. In response, the ACJM declared that they had nothing to hide, and challenged Zuno by moving their meetings to San Francisco Gardens, the public park in downtown Guadalajara where a group of Catholic workers had been gunned down two years earlier. The open challenge to revolutionary and government authority was risky, but the battle for public space was a fundamental part of Catholic militancy in the twenties. In this case, the ACJM was able to persuade a judge to grant an injunction against the confiscation of their offices, which were returned to the organization.[67] Under the local leadership of Salvador Chávez Hayhoe, a partisan lawyer, the group was able to resist the initial acts of government anti-clericalism, but they were being forced to the defensive.[68]

But was there a point of confrontation in which revolutionaries and political Catholics could not turn back? The issue is complex and difficult to address for several reasons. For one thing, Church hierarchy had not supported the De la Huerta rebellion. In Guadalajara, Federal Agent Sanchez Aldana made a habit of presenting himself, incognito, as an enemy of the government in order to gain opposition favor. Still, he reported that his informant had spoken twice to the archbishop, who had been unequivocal in refusing his support for the uprising.[69] Calles himself had told the press that was the case.[70] But was there perhaps a moment or event that marked the breakdown of political relations between Catholics and the state? In this sense, Rius Facius placed great importance on the Second National Eucharistic Congress, celebrated in Mexico City in 1924, as a turning point in Church-state relations, setting the stage for armed resistance.[71] He saw Catholic militancy, especially ACJM example, as foreshadowing the subsequent armed conflict. Writing in the 1950s, he invoked the right to resort to armed rebellion, and ultimately, martyrdom. But his argument is apologetic, and suffers from the teleological inertia that comes with an explanation of history as leading invariably to a single heroic event.[72] Meyer appropriated aspects of this argument, but incorporated them in a more convincing interpretation.[73] Rius Facius and Meyer both note that the Eucharistic Congress was originally planned in early 1923, and set for early 1924, a date that was postponed out of prudence, due to the De la Huerta rebellion. For Meyer, the congress was an extension of the Cubilete incident, in which the Catholics decided to bring the conflict from Guanajuato to Mexico City, and place it at the doorstep of the revolutionary state.

There is certainly a degree of continuity in Catholic tactics, and the congress was indeed a provocation. Whether it was the key confrontation that led to the breakdown between Church and State is less evident. For one thing, government reaction was somewhat muted at the time. Some writers refer to government repression following the congress. Rius Facius referred to brutal persecution, although he seems to have been thinking ahead to the Cristero

Rebellion. Meyer argued that the congress had provoked a series of events that led in slippery slope fashion to the rebellion. In Spanish, he uses the term *engranaje*, which suggests a succession of events in which one triggers the next in a mechanical way or a causal relationship. In this relationship, the congress was the confrontation that set up the succession of events.[74] A delegate to the congress pointed to Miguel Palomar y Vizcarra's speech as the catalyst that pushed the government to action.[75] Yet the congress concluded pretty much without incident. The final event, a theater adaptation of Sor Juana Inés de la Cruz's "El divino Narciso," was canceled after the CROM-controlled union that staffed the theater where it was to be held refused to work the event.[76] The interior ministry opened up an investigation to decide if the reform laws had been violated, but this was nothing new for Catholics.

In fact, the content of the congress was often quite reserved in terms of its political implications. There were several speeches given on the importance of the Holy Eucharist in children's education; the acclaimed Catholic historian, Mariano Cuevas, SJ, spoke on the first recorded mass in Mexican history (celebrated at Cozumel in 1518);[77] and Luis Mier y Teran, *l'enfant terrible* of the ACJM, railed against the conspiring doctrines of liberalism and positivism.[78] Neither were the congress conclusions particularly inflammatory: they focused on the clergy, education, children, and the sick. There were interesting aspects to the conclusions, such as the foundation of some new associations, like the Central Eucharistic Secretariat, the League of Christian Modesty, and the Struggle against Pornography. The congress established December 31 as a national day of reparation, or *desagravio*, and January 1 as the official day for national prayer for Divine Providence in search of more favorable religious legislation. And finally, the congress voted to redouble efforts to get the faithful out for the important pilgrimages, such as the December 12 *romería* to the Tepeyac sanctuary.[79] All in all, such efforts were significant, but suggest introspection and spiritual practice rather than the combative politics common to the ACJM or the workers' movement.

This suggests that the congress was considered subversive less for what people said, than for what it actually was: a very large, open meeting of Catholics, organized under the aegis of Archbishop Leopoldo Ruiz y Flores (Michoacán), Bishop Emeterio Valverde y Tellez (León), and the Jesuit Joaquín Cardoso. The guest list included six foreign bishops, thirty-three Mexican bishops, many lower clergy, Catholic lay leaders and intelligentsia. It had active corporate support of the Knights of Columbus (CC), Catholic Ladies (UDCM), Catholic Youth (ACJM), and Catholic Workers (CNCT), and several key Mexico City unions undertook specific tasks in the congress organization, including twenty-one members of the Catholic Union of Commercial Employees (twelve men and nine women), and fourteen members of the Catholic Carpenters Union.[80] The organizing committee used the state bureaucracy to assure the proper visas for foreign guests months prior to the celebration of the congress, an indication of the open, public manner in which they worked.[81] They secured public, nonreligious venues. Yet the main stage was adorned with a memorable symbol of Mexican Catholic nationalism, an enormous Mexican flag with the white Eucharist resting over it, shining golden with the aura of holiness and the image of the crucifix in the middle.[82] The organizers scheduled the congress to coincide with *el día de la Raza*, the October 12 celebration of Hispanic culture and the arrival of Catholicism to Mexico. However, eucharistic congresses had been held on both sides of the Atlantic, attracting international participation. The next international congress of this nature was currently in the early organizational stages in Chicago, where it would take place in June 1926.[83] Dozens, perhaps hundreds, of foreigners, including a considerable Mexican contingent, attended that congress, which was celebrated without the least bit of Church-state tension. But that was Chicago. For Mexican social Catholics, the 1924 congress was a bold statement of position; by the Calles administration, it must have been interpreted as an open threat. But was there really a subversive message contained in the many speeches given?

If there was, it found expression in the speech delivered by Miguel Palomar y Vizcarra. Historians have noted several aspects of the speech. Meyer, for example, referred to Palomar's confrontational tone, when he told Catholics that the best way to lose the war was to run from the battle. "A people may perish," he challenged, "not because they are weak, but because they are cowardly." His point of reference was Jalisco, where he had fought many battles, and where Catholics had defeated revolutionary anticlericalism in 1919. But his prescription was directed at Catholic Mexicans as a people. The central organizing element of his speech, indeed the most interesting aspect, was contained in the title: "The Eucharist as an Essentially Virile Sacrament."[84] Rius Facius mentioned it, which should come as no surprise, as he had lived through the period, and had belonged to the Mexican Association of Catholic Youth (ACJM), which took the issue of masculine honor in struggle very seriously. This is an important trope, if historians are to understand the religious significance of Catholic militancy. The word virile, *viril*, had two meanings, both of which are deployed here, creating a metaphoric image of great importance. The more common form, the adjective, refers to the attributes of men, often constructed as strength and vigor. In the 1883 *Diccionario General Etimológico de la Lengua Española*, it is simply understood as that which belongs to, or is proper of a man, without examples.[85] But *viril* was also a noun, derived from the Latin word for glass, as the Spanish, *vidrio*. It referred to the glass pane that formed part of the monstrance, a usually golden container with a transparent glass front that was used to publicly exhibit and protect the host; it was the smaller container in turn stored in the tabernacle, and the emphasis is dual: the *viril* permits the host to be seen publicly at the same time that it protects it.[86] This is the essence of Man's role in the Eucharist. Man is a transparent, public custodian, *custodia*, which defends and protects the Holy Eucharist, thus preserving the corresponding sacrament as religious practice.[87] One is reminded of Miguel de la Mora's 1910 formulation "[men] accustomed to every kind of danger, with neither fear in their hearts, nor respect for the enemy.[88] For Palomar y Vizcarra, these are the custodians of the Eucharist.

Over a year before the congress, the Jesuit Joaquín Cardoso had gotten in touch with Palomar on behalf of the organizing committee, and asked him specifically to develop the theme of manliness and communion. Cardoso suggested the title of the speech.[89] But Palomar gave it meaning, context, and power. He wrote out the central phrases in capital letters over and over again in his drafts. It was an open challenge, designed to awaken deep feelings of belonging, and shame Catholic men into action. State-sanctioned violence marked the early twenties: riots, shootings, bombings, vandalism, and deportations had been the response to the Catholic presence in the emerging civil society outlined in the 1917 constitution. He spoke to this reality in the language of a persecuted but unbroken people. As he spoke, over thirty Mexican bishops sat and listened, as well as many of his comrades, men and women with whom he had worked for over twenty years. More than a few must have felt the sting of his words, as they echoed throughout the theater.

> "I have not come to tell you that men should take Communion; for me, that is a given, and for many of you, thank God, it is already achieved. I have not come to tell you that men should take Communion because they are men, but that because they take Communion, they ought to act like men ... THE EUCHARIST IS AN ESSENTIALLY VIRILE SACRAMENT."[90]

Catholics had often referred to the Church as the wife of Jesus Christ. But in the heat of battle, that trope was joined by others in Palomar's deployment of religious imagery: to be a Catholic man was to accept the sacrifice of the Eucharist, to risk crucifixion at the hands of the Caesar, and to embrace the defense of Church with Christ's valor. Masculinity was characterized as energetic, noble, virile, integral, and courageous. Palomar contrasted these attributes with a religion perceived by anticlerical revolutionaries as practiced by cowards who feared struggle and did not appreciate liberty. The struggle he referred to must be understood first in terms of the individual conscience against the rights of state, and could only be made through great sacrifice. Catholics must realize that state authority had to be based on the common good; legitimacy could only be achieved through government in the interest of society as a whole, and there could be no monopoly of rights in favor of any one group in society. Under liberalism they lived enslaved:

> We think we fulfill magnificently our responsibilities, confining ourselves to our homes and our churches; in them we organize splendid gatherings, and we file through with devotion, a peaceful gaze on our faces, our heads bowed, hands clasped, we move about softly; after receiving the Bread of the Strong, and tasting the Wine of those who struggle, we would like [to live in tranquility] . . . because we are afraid to think, love and live. . . . we must have the courage to leave the sacristy and go to the people. . . . [91]

According to Palomar, Catholics must learn the teachings of the Church regarding property; the role of work in social relations; how to associate in order to constitute the social and economic organization of the fatherland; and they must defend the right to educate their children according to the dictates of their conscience. If the family was being destroyed; if woman was being prostituted; if the "Shepherd's Immaculate Wife"—the Church—was in danger of enslavement or annihilation; if Jesus was not permitted "to parade his divine royalty through the city streets and countryside of the nation founded by Christianity"; if the Host could not be broken on the volcano's snowy peaks; if a priest must disguise himself, as if he were a criminal, before venturing out into the street in order to visit the ill; it was because men who took Communion had no notion of their corresponding civic duty, and had not done their part courageously, as men.

The way Palomar contextualized it was certainly dramatic, but the main idea was relatively simple: as citizens, Catholics had a civic duty. Palomar wanted his "countrymen," especially the men, to organize around certain themes, including elections, social welfare, access to public office, and the right to freely and publicly exercise religious liberty. He told his audience to look to the inspiring leadership of other Catholic struggles, such as Daniel O'Connell in Ireland, Count Montalambert and Albert de Mun in France; Ludwig Windthorst and Hermann von Mallinckrodt in Germany, Gabriel García Moreno in Ecuador, and Monsignor Schaepman in the Netherlands. All had persevered through moments of bitter defeat, and successfully defended the "holy" and "sacred" cause. Their struggles ought to be considered side by side with Mexico's own, which had its moment of glory in Jalisco. There, Palomar reminded his audience, the faithful had courageously faced persecution, had endured the bitterness of deciding, along with their priests, to abandon their churches. The night before they closed the churches, *el Santísimo*, the Holy Eucharist was distributed to the children of the faithful in a massive demonstration of resolve: they did not know when they might once again be able to return to their churches, or receive the sacraments, but confronting uncertainty they would defend their children. This defense was as extraordinary as it was immaterial: in their moment of despair, the parents had preemptively graduated their young in the Church by extending to them the Sacrament of the Eucharist. They had persevered, had triumphed, and their persecutors had been defeated. Palomar mentioned no names, but this last reference was to Manuel M. Diéguez, the revolutionary who had been responsible for the anticlerical policy that triggered the 1918 crisis. Only months earlier, Diéguez had been executed for his role in the De la Huerta rebellion.

In closing, Palomar told his audience that if Mexico were to commit apostasy, he would sooner prefer to see its dormant volcanoes come to life creating a terrible cataclysm that would engulf the "fatherland," causing it to disappear once and for all. This was an intriguing choice of words. *Apostasy* is derived from the Greek word for revolt. Palomar, in turn, foreshadowed the anti-apostate revolt to come.

The Tipping Point

The 1924 congress was a rallying cry for political Catholics, but was it *el punto de quiebre*, the tipping point? Not exactly. It was more specifically a public manifestation of the highly polarized state of Catholic politics. Calles, Zuno, and others responded in time. Following the congress, they began to systematically attack the lay associations and shut down the spaces in society where they operated. The first clear indicator of the new balance of power came early in 1925, when agents of the CROM founded a schismatic church, a Gallican-style Mexican Catholic

Church designed to compete with Roman Catholicism. Mexico had seen schismatic churches before; there had been more than one attempt in the nineteenth century, and Calles had made a brief attempt while governor of Sonora.[92] Mimicking the Knights of Columbus, the schismatics called themselves the Knights of Guadalupe or, more formally, the Order of Guadalupan Knights. Although the Mexican Catholic Apostolic Church (known by its Spanish acronym, ICAM) was at best a limited success,[93] the Calles administration supported it and Roman Catholics in Mexico took it quite seriously.

On February 21, 1925, 100 CROM members and Knights of Guadalupe occupied Mexico City's La Soledad church and forced the pastor to flee.[94] When neighborhood Catholics attempted to fight their way back into the occupied church building, the fire and police departments took the side of the schismatics and broke up the riot. In one photograph, taken on February 23, 1925, firemen used large hoses to break up an attempt to recover the church building.[95] The following week, a similar attempt at the famous Saint Marcos church in Aguascalientes led to a bloody showdown. Again the schismatics numbered about 100, again they were composed of Morones supporters. In this case, the pro-government crowd was forced to retreat when local Catholics defended their church. Reinforced by 200 soldiers and three machine gunners, the schismatics returned. In the confrontation there were scores of dead, hundreds of wounded, and subsequently some 400 Catholics were banished from the state. At the sedition trial, the court was presented with two pistols, a bunch of knives and a sack of stones.[96]

In response to the Mexican schismatic church, Catholics organized the National Religious Defense League (LNDR). But the civilian anger was not limited to the militant faithful. In the days following the schism, an interior ministry agent reported a conversation with Liborio Espinosa, a former congressman affiliated with the moderate liberal National Cooperatist Party (PNC). Espinosa spoke bitterly to the agent regarding the Calles presidency, and made specific reference to a "National Catholic League," certainly a reference to the nascent LNDR. He said this new league was busy organizing a rebellion in response to the government's overt protection of the schismatic Church. The clergy would use its influence from one end of the country to the other, he felt, to channel religious fervor in support of the League, promising recompense in the afterlife. If there were no modern saints, like those of antiquity, it was because there were no Mexican martyrs. Espinosa finished by saying, surprisingly, that he was not a religious man, but that he would follow such a movement as a sworn enemy of President Calles.[97]

The forging of the schism ratcheted up the political tension and initiated a gradual collapse of public political space. This collapse became apparent in four distinctive, but clearly related, ways. First, by putting church buildings at the heart of the conflict, the schism forced Catholics to retreat into these redoubts of their faith and defend them. The schism upped the ante and terrified Catholics because it meant not merely the punitive expropriation of churches, but their redistribution on sectarian criteria. The stakes were no longer rendered in terms of the closure of church buildings, but more starkly, in terms of who might effectively—in the state's view—dispose of them. In Mexico City, the faithful of La Soledad—a real *barrio bravo*—responded by rioting and reoccupying the church, which Calles then closed: it was a measure of the schism's odiousness to Catholic opinion that this reversion to earlier anticlerical precedent was seen as the lesser of two evils.

In Jalisco, both rumored and actual state actions affected Catholic militants, who heard the news from Mexico City, Aguascalientes, and elsewhere, and who watched as Governor Zuno began to expropriate the properties that housed their associations. They reacted with violent indignation to the suggestion that it was the CROM—implicitly the federal regime—that backed the schismatic, or revolutionary, clergy in its church seizures.[98] Here, too, the key struggle was over church buildings. Guadalajara Catholics were particularly troubled by rumors that the city's three most politically active parish churches—Mexicaltzingo, La Merced, and the Santuario de Nuestra Señora de Guadalupe—would be given to the schismatics. The fact that a project to expropriate these and other city churches had existed since 1918—the Ayuntamiento considered the above parishes particular bastions of "fanaticism"—lent weight to such rumors.[99]

If revolutionaries were unable to expropriate these parish churches, this was due to the massive protests that city Catholics made in their defense. The conflicts were now siege-like, centering on physical churches (*templos*) not pastors, as an interior ministry agent reported in Guadalajara in August 1925; and it was in these spaces that Catholics now set their defense:

> Among the clergy there is much alarm because it is rumored . . . that the Schismatics are going to take some churches, among them El Santuario, La Merced, and Mexicalcingo [*sic*], and in all of them they [the Catholics] have people on daily watch, both day and night.[100]

The agent reported that the Knights of Columbus and Union of Catholic

Porters were protecting El Santuario with neighborhood backing: it had been agreed that the militants would communicate news of an attack by ringing the church bells, a signal that would call parishioners to go "violently" to defend the faith, wherever required.[101] The church building had become a living, material extension of the faith.

Second, the assault on church buildings was part of a broader state politics, the aim of which was to secure control of the infrastructure that allowed Catholic organizations to function. Throughout the year following the Mexico City schism, Zuno and Jalisco's state government acted to close and expropriate dozens of Catholic properties. Besides churches, the policy affected convents, schools, union headquarters, seminaries, and association offices.[102] This campaign lasted from July 1925 until governor Zuno was forced out office late in March 1926.[103] It caused a substantial increase in cases of Catholic affray and protest against the government, and it was matched by the widespread arrest of Catholic students and clergy, and the expulsion of seminarians, priests, and religious.[104]

The confiscation of property that housed Catholic associations was a clear sign of the reduction of public political space. For Zuno, it was a question not merely of public order, but of driving Catholic politics to the margins: Zuno did not hesitate to order police to disperse Catholics by shooting over their heads, or to have firemen disperse them with powerful cannonades of water. He also closed the preparatory and theological seminaries in the neighborhood of Analco, *on grounds of hygiene*, a move meant to humiliate his adversaries.[105] The suggestion was that seminarians were unclean, a charge that turned the basic sacred-profane binary on its head. Catholics resisted: a new theological seminary was improvised as well as a preparatory seminary. Once these seminaries were opened, Zuno again ordered the police to dislodge the seminarians and confiscate the properties: resistance was met with beatings, gunshots, and water blasts from the city's firemen.[106] The Mexican Association of Catholic Youth reacted to the loss of its Guadalajara office, located in the city center, with public protest: the *acejotaemeros* moved their activities to the San Francisco Gardens, turning their day-to-day business into a public demonstration with clear political intentions.[107] The closing of Catholic schools in Guadalajara and rural Jalisco was dealt with creatively, as may be seen in the case of Mezquitán, where Father García wrote that classes had become clandestine, under the tree-cover of a sprawling riverbed bordering the ancient village, and in the houses of the faithful.[108]

Third, a reduction in the space available for public communication

FIGURE 12. Laity with José Garibi Rivera, Cloister of San Francisco, Guadalajara, ca. 1925. First row seated on floor: Luis Padilla (first on left), J. Trinidad Flores y Flores (third from left), Agustín Yañez (sixth from left); Second row seated: José Garibi Rivera (fifth from left), Anacleto González Flores (sixth from left); Third row standing: Ignacio S. Orozco (second from left); Maximiano Reyes (third from left); Fourth row standing: Miguel Gómez Loza (ninth from left). Source: Luis Padilla Family Collection.

accompanied the policy of controlling Catholicism's formal sites. In 1925, Catholic newspapers were closed: the National League of Religious Defense (LNDR),[109] founded on March 14, responded by cultivating good relations with newspapers considered neutral or sympathetic;[110] and by publishing posters, flyers, and bulletins. Jalisco's Popular Union (UP) defense league published *Gladium*, a clandestine newsletter that distributed 100,000 copies and found its way to the most remote areas of the region.[111] Zuno's closing of pro-Catholic newspapers had pushed the confessional opposition press underground; likewise, the surprisingly vocal national press would also be partially gagged by the middle years of the Calles presidency.[112]

To this anticlericalism, fourth, should be added a growing intolerance, born perhaps of the delahuertista rebellion, and intended—as in 1914—to eliminate the revolution's political rivals. In early 1926, an interior ministry agent described Zuno's political consolidation in terms of murders, incarcerations, extortion, and corruption. Agrarian communities that disobeyed the regime, for instance, might find their seeds sequestered, or their leaders locked up, and then either fined or bribed with cash gifts. According to the report, if they resisted Zuno's pressure, one or two agrarians would be shot, and the leaders called in to restate their obedience. The tightest political control was employed in Guadalajara, the agent wrote, where "all oppositionist [sic] political activity to C[itizen] Governor Zuno has been suffocated."[113] It bears repeating that these were not the words of a Catholic militant but of an agent of the interior ministry.

Detentions of clergy and laity associated with political Catholicism were also common.[114] The immediate Catholic response was to organize defense committees, but these would turn out to constitute the first step toward larger scale organizations. The first to grow out of the religious defense committees was the Jalisco UP, six months prior to the Mexico City Liga. The UP quickly achieved a presence throughout central and west central Mexico.[115] These two organizations would work together to a degree and, according to Antonio Gomez Robledo, the Liga in Jalisco was constituted by the UP. In his biography of Anacleto González Flores, Gómez Robledo wrote that the Liga initially attempted to absorb the UP, and therefore constitute itself as the only Catholic mass organization nationally, but the deep popularity of the UP made such a development impossible. The Liga could only exist to the extent that the UP supported it, and therefore, González Flores and the UP leadership also represented the Liga in Jalisco.[116]

In Mexico City, the men who founded the Liga saw it as a vanguard movement. It would provide a national leadership, separate from clergy, capable of directing a massive grassroots movement.[117] In general, the Liga would be closely tied to the ACJM, the Catholic organization most respected for its combative membership. In Guadalajara, González Flores and the UP also had ties to the ACJM, but with a completely different ideology and organizational structure. The UP relied on no such vanguard organization; instead it mobilized local leaders in a highly decentralized fashion, inspired by the German Volksverein.[118] Although the two organizations coexisted in Jalisco, there was tension. Antonio Gómez Robledo,[119] who was a teenage member of the Guadalajara Popular Union and a follower of González Flores, later described the relation between the two organizations:

> The Union and the Liga held each other in suspicion. The Liga . . . tried to absorb the Union as it expanded. It was impossible, though, because by

that time [González Flores's] name had become a sacred symbol, and the problem was avoided temporarily by uniting both organizations under one person. But one could already observe in Jalisco vehement protests against the mistakes of the Mexico City organization, the spirit and attitude of its delegates clashed openly with the austerity of the province.[120]

One of the ways the representatives of these two cities, organizations, and lifestyles clashed was through their ideas of how the UP and Liga should be organized. The ACJM was accustomed to a formal protocol that, according to Antonio Gómez Robledo, reflected an elite, class-based view of politics and organization.[121] In Jalisco, the UP had no such formal leadership, and although it relied on the speaking skills and combative attitude of the local ACJM, it did not follow the ACJM organizational model. This is perhaps not surprising, and comes into focus in an account given by a collaborator of González Flores, an ACJM activist and future Jesuit, Heriberto Navarrete. In his memoir on the period, Navarrete wrote of a lively debate at the ACJM over who should be the next president of the Guadalajara chapter. Jorge Padilla nominated Anacleto González, who was quite popular, but Pedro Vázquez Cisneros had the support of the local elite, men like Efraín González Luna, the Chávez Hayhoe brothers, and Gabriel Ortíz García. When it looked as if González would not be elected, Padilla remarked that the reason was that he was of humble origins. In other words, it was a problem of status directly related to social class.[122] In considering the UP's organizational structure, it is pertinent then to ask whether or how class mattered.

Anacleto González Flores shaped the Popular Union to focus on three basic issues: catechism, schools, and press. These issues, he felt, could be easily accepted by a broad cross-section of society. In all three cases, the UP argued that the state was proscribing the basic rights of Mexican citizens, to worship, to educate their children according to their own personal dictates, and to freely express their opinions. However, González Flores began from an evaluation of Catholic practice, which he saw as weak and superficial. In the midst of crisis he reasoned, adapting the popular adage, *Él que mucho abarca poco aprieta*, which might translate as "Don't bite off more than you can chew."

The solution to this problem is the inimitable key to solving all others. Once resolved, naturally and spontaneously we will arrive at the solution of the rest. Schools, catechism, press and organization: from these will flow the rest, imperceptibly, inevitably.[123]

This philosophy guided UP actions, which focused on the most basic aspects of organization, leaving for subsequent battles the more explicitly political goals of party and union.

For Gómez Robledo, the UP philosophy was summed up in three ideas: simplicity, universality, and flexibility.[124] Simplicity of goals dictated UP appeal to basic needs, and simplicity of form characterized its structure. Neighbors chose their leaders on a block-by-block basis. Several blocks made up a zone, and the block leaders designated the zone leader. Each parish might contain several zones, and the zone leaders decided on their parish head, a layman or woman, whose authority was separate from the parish as an ecclesiastical jurisdiction.[125] There were no careful archives, nor formal ceremonies. The UP developed no ritualized protocol for executing tasks. There were no written orders or memos sent back and forth, and everything was done locally, in the most decentralized manner possible. The UP was built on the basic premise of the efficacy of personal links:

> Block, zone, parish: the person responsible for each of these constituencies [circunscripciones] was in close contact with his subordinates and his immediate superior. Ceremony, solemnity, and protocol were absent; there were almost no books, nor were letters sent. Paperwork was replaced by the efficacy of personal communication.[126]

In addition to its simplicity, according to Gómez Robledo, the UP was universal in its appeal because it was radically democratic. It excluded nobody, and would recruit its leadership without respect to class or sex. "One had to feel the novel enchantment of the first meetings of parish leaders, in which the equality of function grouped the cobbler with the lawyer."[127] It also grouped men with women. The UP-coordinating committee, elected by the parish leaders, provided a window into this equality. The December 1926 election ratified Anacleto González Flores as chief, Miguel Gómez Loza as treasurer, Heriberto Navarrete as general secretary, and three counselors: Silvestre Arias, María Ocampo, and Joséfina Zuloaga. These five comprised the committee that would advise González Flores.[128] This was not a quota, but a reflection of leadership in the ranks. With respect to membership activity, women were involved in every way, equal to men to the extent that they participated. In practice, women's participation was a major aspect of the Popular Union. In the same manner, women and men of working-class status held leadership roles bestowed by and through their peers.

Along with its simplicity and universality, the UP was characterized by its flexibility. González Flores referred to this as a big tent approach, an extension of the defense of the faith from church and home to the different spaces of society: newspapers and broadsheets, schools, block leaders and propagandists, the workshop and factory. In the tradition of the nineteenth-century Volksverein, the UP took its defense to the different points of conflict. González Flores referred to the UP as a school of hope, optimism, and encouragement.[129] As in its reaction to the schismatic church, Catholic neighbors were organized for immediate response:

How? The Popular Union—which is present everywhere, by virtue of its structure and organization, and which takes the fight to every front: the workshop, the factory, at home, in school, anywhere an expression of individual or social life appears—is the calling that will generalize the struggle for God.[130]

This flexibility made possible the step from popular front tactics of civilian defense to guerrilla warfare.

Months prior to the January 1927 insurrection that swept Jalisco and neighboring states, President Calles ordered the churches to be inventoried. Rather than comply, the bishops decided to close the churches, as the Guadalajara Archdiocese had done in 1918. On the last day of July 1926, all across Mexico pastors turned the churches over to the faithful. In many places, as the shepherd departed, his flock moved into the churches in an act of self-defense. The priests left the churches, turning them over to laity as caretakers. While worship became clandestine and informal, in the tradition of the catacombs, the churches became the living, breathing center of social life, a point of constant reunion, around the clock. The faithful occupied the churches, their bell towers, atriums, and adjacent parks. Archbishop Orozco y Jiménez circulated instructions to the Catholics of Guadalajara, declaring that the Popular Union representatives were the only people authorized to take up monetary collections in the name of needy priests and other demands related to the current circumstances, and that they would carry a credential signed by the archbishop himself. Just as they had occupied the churches, the Popular Union also took over the administrative tasks of the clergy.[131]

By the end of 1926, the confrontation had destroyed the political spaces in which Catholics organized themselves, and erased the practical distinction between militants and neutrals. In this context, it made sense to a growing

FIGURE 13. Crowd protecting el Santuario de Nuestra Señora de Guadalupe, August 1926. Source: Archivo Histórico de la Arquidiócesis de Guadalajara.

number of Catholic militants to take the step from politics to rebellion. Heriberto Navarrete, the UP secretary and one of González Flores's closest confidants, described the decision to rebel. In December 1926, local UP leaders from across Jalisco met to elect a new leadership for 1927. A strict secrecy was imposed:

> The convocation was made through special envoys, and the instruction sent to the Parish Chiefs (those who would have legal representation), included an absolute prohibition of any communication regarding the motive of their trip to Guadalajara, not even to their own pastors.[132]

At the general assembly, which was held clandestinely, a Liga motion to rebel against Calles was discussed. Leaders were asked to return to their parishes, consult with their subordinates, and decide whether to heed the call to arms. However, this presented a problem because the Popular Union was founded as a civic organization; its mission directed the organization to abstain from military activity. For Secretary General Navarrete, it was quickly apparent that a distinction between civic and armed resistance was untenable. If there were to be a rebellion, the UP would be swept into civil war by its social base. In the most memorable passage of his memoir, Navarrete recounted a conversation with a local leader. Navarrete was at pains to explain that the UP officers were legally bound to work through civic, nonviolent means. To this, his interlocutor responded: "I don't get it, you mean we are going to fight, while you watch us? Is it because you are scared?" Apparently, this appeal to Navarrete's sense of manly honor and duty was irresistible. By his account, Navarrete soon convinced González Flores that if the UP's local leadership went to war, then there was no other path for its directorate but to follow suit.[133]

———

The events of this chapter mark the final cycle of Catholic politics during the revolutionary period. Worker associations expanded their activities and reach during the early twenties, with the support of youth and women's groups. After 1921, they found greater organizational infrastructure through the umbrella coverage provided by Alfredo Méndez Medina and the Mexican Social Secretariat. By 1923, however, the tide began to turn against the proponents of a Catholic alternative in post-revolutionary Mexico. Anticlerical legislation and politics in zunista Jalisco marked the pace for broader developments nationally, and the rise of Plutarco Elías Calles brought a new emphasis on government through a strict prohibition on confessional politics. Deepening tension between rival groups pitted against each other along a Church-state cleavage produced violent confrontations.

The darkening mood was reflected in the writing of Anacleto González Flores. In 1926 he wrote frenetically, producing material of a deeply pessimistic outlook that was widely distributed through *El Obrero*, *La Época*, and *Gladium*. His views on religious liberty evolved from a rallying cry for combative civics to a call for sacrifice:

> We will vote with the blood of our arms tied to the rock of the persecuted, with the blood of our bound lips, with the blood of our children, our women, our elderly who, in agony, will lift up their hands in a sign of protest.[134]

His pen frequently centered on the issue of spiritual fortitude for an oppressed people. As his mood became increasingly apocalyptic, a theme emerged above others in his writing, the idea of martyrdom. Through the concept of a martyred people, his writing found its way back to a more idealistic outlook. The Apocalypse, after all, was the ultimate trial for a faithful people.

Death did not discourage him, but rather gave him a stronger sense of purpose. In this way he offered his body, and called on his supporters to do the same.[135]

The summer of 1926 provided the tipping point. On one side, President Calles forced the states to legislate and apply constitutional Article 130. State legislatures would license priests, limit their numbers, confiscate church buildings deemed unnecessary and redeploy them for use as schools, museums, and workshops. Governor Garrido Canabal of Tabasco is famous for legislating that only married men could legally officiate mass; as a result, his state was essentially emptied of clergy.[136] In Mexico City and points south along the gulf coast, the ICAM competed for faithful with the Roman Catholics.[137] In Jalisco, Zuno's anticlericalism recrudesced through the spring, and the Popular Union flourished through the summer. In Guadalajara, the local congress established that the capital city would be permitted to license no more than sixty-five priests; Ciudad Guzman, ten; Tepatitlán and Lagos de Moreno, five apiece.[138] To avoid the political implications of licensing their priests with the state, the bishops collectively opted out of the system. They decided to close all the churches and enact a clerical strike. Drawing directly from Jalisco's 1918 experiences, they attempted to institutionalize what had been essentially a social movement, and promote it on a national scale. However, Mexico was not Jalisco.

The cleavage created by Zuno's use of expropriation, the *Ley Calles*, and a nationwide clerical strike effectively collapsed public space and pushed political Catholics over the edge. The 1918 clerical strike in Jalisco had been part of a broad arsenal of tactics that directed popular discontent through civic channels. It was inspired, paradoxically, by the rights enshrined in the new constitution. By contrast, the 1926 clerical strike did not have a national leadership, and belonged to no clear strategy. The Mexico City Liga aspired to a national leadership role. But having grown out of an elitist clique, its leaders did not have a broad social base. On the opposite end of the spectrum, Jalisco's Popular Union had a broad social base, but Anacleto González Flores and other Guadalajara leaders had already ceded authority to local chiefs. With a radically decentralized leadership, the Unión Popular became more militant. And by the end of the year, local UP chiefs in rural Jalisco, Guanajuato, Michoacán, and Colima opted for rebellion. This shift in leadership carried the organizational locus of political Catholicism from Guadalajara to scores of villages. With time they would come together around a few military leaders and civilian governors, but always tied to the towns and villages where the rebels had their homes. Guadalajara was lost, urban leaders like González Flores and Gómez Loza would flee the city, and the rebellion would be an essentially rural affair.

9. Anacleto González Flores and the Martyrs' Plebiscite

They [pilgrims] follow the paradigm of the *via crucis*, in which Jesus Christ voluntarily submitted his will to the will of God and chose martyrdom rather than mastery over man, death *for* the other, not death *of* the other.

—VICTOR AND EDITH TURNER

The Martyrdom of Anacleto

In the early hours of the first day of April 1927, soldiers surrounded a house in Guadalajara's Sanctuary district.[1] They secured the escape routes at street level as well as the adjacent rooftops. Then they broke down the front door at the Tepeyac drugstore and simultaneously climbed into the house from the azotea, which they reached from neighboring roofs. Inside they found the Vargas González family stumbling around in the dark in a state of confusion. They also found the head of Jalisco's Popular Union, Anacleto González Flores, whom the family had been hiding.[2] The soldiers apprehended Anacleto, who was thirty-nine years old, along with three of the Vargas González kids, Ramón, Jorge, and Florentino.[3] At about the same time, soldiers also raided the nearby apartment of another young Catholic militant, Luis Padilla.[4] Apparently searching for Anacleto, they found only Padilla, whom they arrested. All five prisoners were taken to the *Cuartel Colorado* military barracks on the eastern edge of the city.

Once in custody, General Jesús Ferreira accused them of sedition and court-martialed the five that same morning. Ferreira later released a statement in which he defended the arrest of González Flores and the others based on military intelligence gathered from rebels captured in the Jalisco highland region. He also reported that his men had confiscated printed material of a seditious nature at the Vargas González household. On the basis of this information, he explained, he had been able to link González Flores and three of the others to another Catholic militant, Miguel Gómez Loza, who was still at large. Anacleto, Jorge, Ramón, and Luis were treated as Cristero rebels, armed religious fanatics that fought the Mexican army in the highlands and elsewhere across western Mexico.

Anacleto González Flores was interrogated and tortured in the presence of the others, all of whom were his subordinates in the Popular Union and the Catholic Association of Mexican Youth (ACJM). General Ferreira ordered him hung by his thumbs and whipped. During the ordeal, he interrogated his captive as to the whereabouts of Archbishop Orozco y Jiménez, as well as the locations, leadership, and plans of the rebels. González Flores remained steadfast and serene, refusing to offer any information. His mates watched the soldiers flay the bottom of his feet. After several hours he collapsed, his disjointed hands unable to sustain the weight of his body. At this point, he addressed his tormenters:

> I have worked selflessly to defend the cause of Jesus Christ and his Church. You will kill me, but the cause will not perish. Many stand behind me, willing to defend it to the death. I leave, but with the conviction that soon I will see from heaven the triumph of religion in my fatherland.[5]

When González Flores finished speaking, Ferreira signaled to a soldier, who plunged a bayonet through his back. The soldiers of the 30th Battalion finished off the others more quickly, executing them by firing squad. The bodies were displayed to the public later that afternoon. Florentino Vargas was spared execution, and all versions of these events rely on his initial relation.[6]

The original sources for these events are testimony, written at the time of the executions by Catholics who participated in the Popular Union movement. The description attributed to Florentino Vargas González is unique, and while the execution is fact, it is impossible to corroborate the details. Information surrounding the Vargas González testimony was reported by Catholic and independent press at the time of the executions, and verified by thousands who filled the streets in a conscious tactic of public witness. In a hybrid practice that incorporated the postcard tradition, popular in the early twentieth century, and the older tradition of distributing religious relics, portable photographs of the martyred bodies circulated for generations following the executions.[7]

FIGURE 14. Anacleto González Flores, posthumous portrait, April 1, 1927. Source: Archivo Histórico de la Arquidiócesis de Guadalajara.

FIGURE 15. Jorge and Ramón Vargas González, posthumous portrait, April 1, 1927. Source: Archivo Histórico de la Arquidiócesis de Guadalajara.

Here I have relied on two documents. The author of the first document gave it a title, "*Narración sobre algunos de los martires ejecutados en Guadalajara en Abril de 1927.*" It chronicled the events of April 1 and 2 on two legal-sized, single-spaced, typewritten pages. At several points the author lapsed into the familiar language of personal correspondence, adopting the first person and speaking personally to his reader. The author was assuredly a Jesuit, judging from the end of the letter, which carries the initials "A M D G," *Ad majorem Dei gloriam*, the Society of Jesus motto. The names of the four victims are handwritten next to the title, an addendum that was likely included some time later to clearly identify the subject of the letter. Unfortunately, the letter is not signed; and while it does not indicate a recipient either, it was likely written for and sent to Miguel Palomar y Vizcarra.[8]

The author of the second document refers to it as an *opusculum*. It is signed by Crisanto del Valle, a pseudonym, is titled "*Anacleto González Flores. Semblanza*," and is dated 1927. A header on the cover page reads, "*Mártires de la persecución mejicana*," suggesting that the author intended to write about others as well. And a legend at the foot of the cover page reads "*Mártires los llamamos sin prevenir el juicio de la Santa Iglesia*," a point that emphasizes the historical gravity of the execution as well as the immediate sense that it was transcendent. It is a much longer document, extending seventeen pages and offering a fuller treatment of González Flores's life and death. Like the first, it was made at the time of the executions, a point that is clear in the final paragraphs, where the author exhorts his or her reader to reproduce the document, publish it where possible, and generally get the word out. In style and content, it prefigures a 1928 ACJM-produced opúsculo attributed to ACJM founder Luis Beltrán y Mendoza.[9]

The "Narración" offered important details regarding the reception and mourning vigil of the executed. "*Yo fui como todo el mundo*," the author wrote: "Everyone went to see," hinting at the general commotion surrounding the arrests. Given the level of organization and communication that the Popular Union achieved, it is not surprising that a huge crowd formed to mourn the victims, a circumstance corroborated by *El Informador*, the Guadalajara daily.[10] Florentino Vargas was released at the Municipal Medical Section offices, where the bodies of the others were put on public display. The Jesuit witness who wrote to Palomar y Vizcarra described Anacleto's corpse as "smiling, both rows of teeth . . . plainly visible, as one who smiles frankly with joy, his eyes [were] open and his expression evoked serenity."[11] The crowd that received him soaked cotton in his bloody wounds, an ancient ritual by which the martyr's final act of devotion bestowed miraculous relics.

Later, his bloodied clothing was cut into small pieces and distributed to the faithful as well.

That evening, thousands mourned him, spilling from his humble home and filling the streets outside. His widow and two children accompanied him, along with many followers, in what Crisanto del Valle described as an air of triumph rather than sadness. When asked about his father, González Flores's eldest, his three-year-old son, responded: "Some bad men killed him because he loved the child Jesus too much."[12] On the following day, a throng escorted his body to the municipal cemetery near the old Indian pueblo of Mezquitán. Along the way they chanted his well-known deprecation, "Queen of martyrs, pray for us and the Popular Union." Agustín Yañez, the celebrated novelist— and a Guadalajara native—wrote of Anacleto's cortège:

> Saturday 2 April 1927, Guadalajara—on its shoulders—bloodstained and shaken, brings him to his burial and even his adversaries have been moved and come to breathe new life into him, a myth-making new life that will never expire.[13]

At the cemetery, González Flores was eulogized. Among the speakers were the Huerta brothers, Salvador and Ezequiel, who were active in the Catholic movement. A third brother, Eduardo Huerta, was the local priest at Sweet Name of Jesus parish. After the funeral, Salvador and Ezequiel were arrested and summarily executed, their bodies immediately buried. The only notification that their families received was a burial ticket indicating the gravesite. Salvador, a mechanic, left ten children; Ezequiel, a cantor, left eleven.[14]

These acts of exemplary violence speak to the collapse of political space. What they do not reveal is the acute tension between repression, understood by many Catholics as religious persecution, and religiously inspired violence, understood by President Calles, the Mexican Army, and some in local government as open rebellion. Although the motives and expectations of each side were arguably more complex than this, it is safe to say that both perceptions were reasonable. This slide into rebellion is the topic of this final chapter. To frame it, I will focus initially on the life and writings of González Flores; then I will shift to a discussion of the rebellion itself.

From Civics to Martyrdom: The Storm and the Advancing Desert

In his time, Anacleto González Flores was quite well known, the public face of a mass movement. Friend and foe alike recognized him as an outstanding

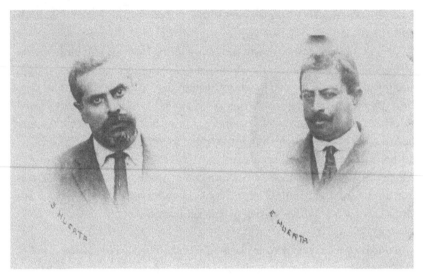

FIGURE 16. Salvador and Ezequiel Huerta. Source: Archivo Histórico de la Arqui-diócesis de Guadalajara.

orator, and he was a prodigious writer who graced his craft with an expansive sense of letters and history. He was an avid reader, who was equally comfortable quoting holy scripture, as Ibsen's *Hedda Gabler*. He drew inspiration broadly, including from Emmeline Pankhurst—an English socialist, feminist, and suffragist—and Terence MacSwiney, the Lord Mayor of Cork, Ireland—uncommon figures in the cultural transcript of his readers.[15] Today, eighty-five years hence, Anacleto, Ramón, Jorge, and Luis are *beatos*, making their way through the proper Vatican channels toward canonization. They are now creatures of the elusive realm of the miracle: a liminal space in which the devoted must sing their praise and the Vatican must sanction their song.[16] Anacleto—whom the faithful often refer to by his first name alone, or by the nickname *Cleto*—is considered quite miraculous.

Much of what we know about the young González Flores is through his first biographer, Antonio Gómez Robledo. As a young man, Gómez Robledo was a student of González Flores and a close follower in the Popular Union. He was nineteen years old when Anacleto was murdered. Ten years later he wrote a sympathetic biography of his martyred teacher, initially published under the pseudonym Demetrio Loza. That effort remains today the standard work on Anacleto's life.[17] Gómez Robledo was arrested in 1927, following the murder of

González Flores, but avoided a firing squad due to the intervention of his uncle, Juan de Dios Robledo, a signer of the 1917 constitution.[18]

Anacleto González Flores was born in 1888, in the highland town of Tepatitlán. Of his childhood, we know little more than that he was raised in poverty by his parents, was the second of twelve children, that his father got in trouble with Porfirian authorities, and that he was taught to be a weaver. His father, Valentín González, participated in a failed rebellion—Death to the Bad Government!—and was sentenced to prison for two years at San Juan de Ulúa, Veracruz, and a work camp in Quintana Roo. He contracted malaria, which ruined his health, but eventually returned home to toil the rest of his days. In the meantime, Anacleto learned to work in his father's absence.[19]

The historian Ramón Jrade has suggested that Anacleto's youth and family were not Catholic in any exceptional way.[20] This observation is only vaguely demonstrated and seems at any rate obtuse. More to the point, Gómez Robledo wrote that Anacleto was converted to active Catholicism by a missionary from Guadalajara who arrived at Tepatitlán to preach to the field hands and laborers there. Anacleto was seventeen, according to his biographer, and was hooked from that point on. At age twenty, he enrolled at the San Juan de los Lagos diocesan seminary, "Jalisco's convent," where he studied for five years. A 1912 trip to Maderista Mexico City fascinated him, though he was apparently critical of Francisco León de la Barra as well as Francisco Madero. On his return to San Juan, he became involved with the National Catholic Party, helping to strengthen its presence in the towns near the seminary. In the summer of 1913, he declined the invitation to travel to Rome and continue his studies; the prize was offered to him as the most outstanding student of his graduating class. Instead, he moved to Guadalajara and enrolled as a law student at the Catholic Free School of Law.[21]

It is pretty clear that 1914 was a watershed year for González Flores. The first twenty-five years of his life transpired in the small towns northeast of Guadalajara. He had lived in poverty as a child, and the seminary had opened up new possibilities for him. He moved to Guadalajara in time to begin his law studies that September. He rented a room in an old house at 682 Sor Juana Inés de la Cruz Street in the center of town.[22] The owner of the house was an elderly lady called Gerónima, and half a dozen students from the Jalisco highland towns rented rooms in her house. She charged 30 centavos a day for room and a meal, and the boarders called her *Doña Giro*. In this spirit, González Flores christened the house *la Gironda*, after the Girondists of the French Revolution. There was a guitar at la Gironda, and it became *Carlota Corday*, after the

Girondist sympathizer who was executed by guillotine for murdering the Jacobin leader, Jean-Paul Marat, in 1793. Anacleto and his mates saw themselves as
latter-day *Girondinos*. Such details are impressionistic, but help the historian
to understand the political imaginary of González Flores and other provincial
Catholics. They appear as "children of the revolution," rather than partisans of
the old regime.[23]

When the Constitutionalist army took Guadalajara in July 1914, the military government installed by General Obregón shut down Catholic places of
worship, as well as schools, newspapers, seminaries, convents, and other official buildings and residences. Anacleto's law studies were rendered null and
void, and like many young Catholics, he was forced to reconsider his plans.
Practically destitute, he traveled to the southern Jalisco town of Concepción
de Buenos Aires, where he sought the help of his brother. The new year found
him there when a group of revolutionaries, nominally followers of Pancho
Villa, passed through. Their chaplain was Father Pérez Rubio, the Tepatitlán
priest who baptized Anacleto as an infant, and had later been a sort of spiritual
advisor for him. Anacleto was handy with a quill, and joined the group in the
role of secretary to General Antonio Delgadillo, Villista governor of the state
of Colima.

This adventure lasted no more than a few days. In January 1915, the group
was cornered in Poncitlán, near Lake Chapala, by General Julián Medina,
Villa's main surrogate in Jalisco. It turned out that Delgadillo was a former
Federal Army officer, and that there was bad blood between him and Medina.
Medina's soldiers executed Delgadillo, Pérez Rubio, and several others, allow-
ing the rest of the group to go free.[24] Anacleto had been spared, but witnessing
the execution of his hometown pastor had a devastating effect on him and
drove him to renounce violence.[25] Back in Guadalajara he made ends meet as
a teacher and private tutor, resettled at the boarding house on Sor Juana Inés
de la Cruz Street. From that point on he became gradually more involved with
the causes of political Catholicism. As revolutionary violence waned in the
region, and civilian life reemerged, González Flores participated in the 1916
foundation of the Catholic Association of Mexican Youth (ACJM), Guadalajara chapter.[26] As in Mexico City, the Guadalajara ACJM quickly became an
institutional support for Catholic politics, and one way in which this new lay
politics expressed itself was through the founding and dissemination of confessional newspapers.

By June of 1917, González Flores founded the first of several Guadalajara
newspapers that would feature his editorial voice. *La Palabra*, a weekly

four-page confessional newspaper, appeared for two years. Subsequently, he would be partially responsible for founding *La Época*, *El Obrero*, and *Gladium*, In addition, he collaborated with several dailies, including *Restauración*, *El Tiempo*, and *El Heraldo* in Guadalajara, and *El País* in Mexico City.

In the following pages I will analyze several topics that emerge in the writing of González Flores; but first, a caveat. His contemporaries, both friends and foes, as well as his biographers and historiographers, have all emphasized that a central aspect of the public identity of González Flores was his reputation as an outstanding orator. He was also a prolific writer, of journalism, history, sociology, politics, and literary critique. This circumstance creates a dilemma for the historian, who must construct, order, evaluate, and interpret documentary evidence of one sort or another. All of this, in the end, can be read as testimony. This testimony was written, at some point, and became documents. The dilemma is dual. On one hand, González Flores's oratory is beyond my reach as a historian. It was almost always ephemeral, and did not endure, except through passing testimony of those whom he addressed. As such, I am left only with his written work in the task of interpreting his life, a circumstance that only throws into relief the fragmentary nature of representation.

My writing hopes to represent a historical figure through his writing, which was only one facet of his complex life. This I take as a call for prudence. On the other hand, my own interpretation of González Flores's writing is that he was guided by a principle of classical Roman and Athenian culture; he believed that the art of oratory was superior to memory, and by extension, writing. In 1926, less than a year prior to his death, González Flores published an essay evoking the blacksmith's forge as a metaphor for the training of militant public speakers. In this essay he writes about education and political participation. His language is intensely religious, though he never speaks directly to the issues of Catholic faith. The word, he writes, is the legacy of the writer. However, in the case of the speaker, "it is inexact to say that his word works the miracle of action on others; it is more logical, more exact to say that the speaker himself is responsible, because he himself is the eloquent word, he is his word."[27] In a sense, this is the dilemma of all historiography: it generates secondhand sources. But in the case of González Flores, this circumstance takes on greater significance to the extent that in his public life he not only privileged speech over writing, but all indications are that speech as action profoundly determined his relation to his comrades and followers.

Nevertheless, from my trench as a writer, it seems important to reflect on the written word that González Flores left to posterity. Perhaps not all, but

the great majority of his written work was produced subsequent to the signing of the 1917 constitution, and in one way or another, it presented itself
always in dialogue with the constitution and its defenders. González Flores
often published in newspapers, as an editorialist, and he acted as the directing editor of *La Palabra* from 1917 until 1919, and *Gladium* in 1926 and 1927.[28]
Beyond his writing for the periodical press, there are written versions of
some of his speeches, ostensibly his oratory transformed into writing.
Themes include the tactics of working-class struggle and the dangers of
worker emigration to the United States. He published a book in 1920 on "the
religious question" in Jalisco, closely following the classic nationally focused
study on the nineteenth-century liberal reform in Mexico by the Jesuit Régis
Planchet. At the time of his execution, González Flores was working on one
last book, a final call to young Catholics, on activism and the importance to
remain young in spirit.[29]

In order to get a more nuanced view of González Flores, I want to look more
carefully at his writing as it reflected several important moments during that
last ten years of his life. To a large extent, the events to which I will refer are
covered in earlier chapters of this book. Therefore, I will be brief in describing
them and will focus on his writing as a reflection of his views as they evolved
during the years between the signing of the new constitution and the downward spiral into religious rebellion. The themes that I will discuss are the social
question, religious liberty, and martyrdom.

THE SOCIAL QUESTION

In mid-1917, González Flores spelled out his interpretation of the social question in the early issues of *La Palabra*, the weekly newspaper that he edited and
published. The historical moment is critical in order to understand his ideas.
González Flores wrote against the backdrop of the new constitution, the
crowning achievement of the Mexican Revolution. The constitution is his
interlocutor, and there are three issues that dominate his attention. First, Articles 27 and 123 interpret the contemporary problems of peasants and workers
solely in terms of class conflict. Second, Articles 5, 24, 27, 103, and 130 radical-
ize the anticlerical policies of the nineteenth century, reduce the legal space of
the Catholic Church in society, and criminalize public displays of worship and
devotion, such as pilgrimages. This is public space "emptied of God," in the
words of Charles Taylor.[30] Third, although the new status quo is more difficult,
Articles 8 and 9 establish a public space and mechanisms that may be used to

protest the policies of the new regime. This is the context of his ideas on the social question.

For González Flores, the point of departure for his thoughts on the social question was an intellectual dispute with socialists over its character. He saw the socialist position as reductionist, viewing everything in terms of "the more or less perfect distribution of wealth." To the contrary, he argued that the root of the problem lay in social imbalances that contained a spiritual dimension as well as a material one. In his mind, the issue could only be understood by identifying the multiple aspects of "social energy," which could be religious, political, moral, or legal, as well as economic.[31] In his analysis, the "imbalance," or "disorientation," was the result of two factors. The first was the profound discrepancy that characterized the nineteenth-century society right up to the present. This is a reference to what contemporary scholarship often calls secularization. However, alongside the discrepancies of the times, he saw a second factor: a misunderstanding about the destiny of human life impeded the necessary balance between the political, legal, and economic relations that formed society. His argument juxtaposed antiquity to modern society, where the later referred generally to Christianity. González Flores used Aristotle as a point of reference, because he was a widely admired figure. For Aristotle, slavery was natural; in marriage, a woman could not rise to the level of companionship in her relation to her husband; a father might exercise the privilege of life and death over his children. In this antiquity, characterized by many inequalities, González Flores saw the roots of the social question. In his writing, it was through the life and thought of Jesus of Nazareth that the idea of social equality was born. In González Flores's thought, the equality of the soul was the foundation of equality in society.[32] Therefore, Christianity could be seen as the basis for the fraternal bonds that held a nation, a people, or a society together.[33]

But it was not only socialism that drew his attention. For González Flores, the liberal regimes and capitalist economies of his time had shown absolute scorn for working people. "Alone, abandoned, and defenseless, [the worker] must consider his lot, his present and his future." In light of an interpretation that favors the production of wealth over all else, the worker has been reduced to the status of a machine, and has lost his most basic dignity. Liberalism, he concluded, is guilty of fomenting an erroneous notion regarding the meaning of human life, and in that sense, he emphasized the religious nature of the social question.[34]

In June 1918, a legal reform forced González Flores to confront his ideas regarding the social question in the political arena. The Jalisco state legislature passed a law in keeping with the spirit of Article 130 of the 1917 constitution. The new law sharply reduced the number of priests who could legally work in the state and expropriated more than half of the Catholic churches in and around Guadalajara. In preparation for the reform, the military arrested Archbishop Francisco Orozco y Jiménez, boarded him on a northbound train, and escorted him to exile in the United States. For over a year, the archbishop followed the conflict from his exile in the city of Chicago, while González Flores led the resistance back home in Jalisco.[35]

The struggle played out over many months, but finally, in January 1919, the state legislature met, pressured by governor Manuel M. Diéguez, and overturned the law.[36] And following months of negotiation between the archbishop, the Mexican interior minister, and the governor's office in Guadalajara, Orozco y Jiménez returned in October to a hero's welcome. The success of the Jalisco resistance ushered in a period of growth for Catholic lay organizations, and a relative détente with the revolutionary governments in Guadalajara and Mexico City. González Flores and other leaders hoped the lay movement would achieve a national presence. Central among the groups that benefited from this period of political apertura, were the Catholic unions. Their method of organization and activism mirrored González Flores's holistic vision of society that saw the religious, political, economic, legal, and moral aspects of community as essential to a shared form of struggle and life.

RELIGIOUS LIBERTY

The resistance of 1918 informed González Flores's ideas on religious liberty. In 1920 he wrote that the struggle had made a national impact in the sense that it sent a signal that local organization could defeat unpopular legislation, and because it set the basic positions of Catholics and revolutionaries regarding freedom of conscience.[37] Following the 1918 campaign, he went about developing his ideas on religious liberty. His writing on the issue fed subsequent movements led by the Popular Union, the National League in Defense of Religious Liberty, and the armed groups that fought after 1926 under the leadership of the Ejército Libertador. But his ideas were first clearly presented in January 1921, in reference to the coronation ceremony of the Virgin of Zapopan. This occasion was the result of the 1918 campaign.

Anacleto González Flores wrote on the topic of religious liberty in a philosophical context, set in relation with his ideas about government and freedom. Specifically, a government that impeded religious worship was properly considered tyrannical, and a people deprived of this basic freedom were essentially slaves. The worst tyranny, in his view, was that which imposed itself between a people and their God, because this relationship constituted the supreme aspiration of human energy. When a tyrant limits a people's quest for religious liberty and worship, he leaves them no other choice than the sacrifice of living for the state. González Flores looked to ancient Rome for example, arguing that although Roman citizens exercised the right of life and death over their slaves, memory afforded no instance in which they imposed their will between the gods and the "obscure soul of the slave." Furthermore, for the faithful, God represented the path of the thirsty traveler toward light and respite, the hope of the weak and the miserable. For this reason, the soul of a people must calmly oppose the tyrant and demand religious liberty. Its only weapons in this struggle are "the idea and the word."[38]

Thought and word were basic to his view of political protest, and they extended beyond the issue of religious liberty to a view of civil rights. In "The Sword and the Gag," González Flores writes, "The respect of opinion is the corner stone of democratic life."[39] Then he anchors this idea by arguing that it has generally been a failure in Latin countries. His reasoning is that instead of enshrining free speech, the trend has been government by gag, that is, by suppression of the political speech of Catholics. It is true, he adds, that government is made more difficult by the clamor of opinion, and that the spoken or written word may be used as a force against an opposing force, as a form of resistance or defiance. In effect, public opinion may be harnessed against the interest of government. But when public opinion simply reflects the views of a people, *el pueblo*, the foundation of all modern systems of rule, then government is obliged to listen. As of 1793, nobody has the right to govern against the will of "the people." Government does have, in fact, recourse to violence, to draw the sword and strike, but this act is in open conflict with the principles of modern democracy that, whether good or bad, have enshrined the proclamation of popular sovereignty. In the end, the sword is powerless to defeat the word. González Flores evokes the nineteenth-century Italian poet Giosué Carducci—who was also known for his anticlerical politics—when he compares government suppression of free speech to a *cintarazo en el vacío*, the blow of a sword that misses its mark.

The suppression of free speech, wrote González Flores, was an antiquated weapon in the age of popular sovereignty. He referred to it as the "sling of the chimera," an illusory weapon against the modern arms of thought and word that form public opinion. Against the armor of the word, the violence of the sword cannot fail but to make a martyr with ardent followers; it will reproduce one hundredfold the word of he who is felled for his thought. Nor can public opinion be imprisoned. González Flores evokes here the nineteenth-century French historian Jules Michelet, who referred to the Bastille as *la cárcel del pensamiento*, the prison of thought. The Bastille, he then reminds his readers, was demolished with the opening eruption of revolution. He concludes the piece with an admonition that government listen, rather than strike or gag.

Anacleto's ideas on political speech were grounded in philosophy and theology, as can be seen in his article "Speechless," which hints at the link between ideas and his activist agenda. "Each word is an incomplete action," he wrote. Cryptic, it announces a further idea. "This explains, for one, the decisive influence that the word has had and will always have, but also the need to put alongside the word a serious effort to arrive at the just fulfillment of the thought."[40] This initial couplet is then joined by a further idea, that the importance of the word is often understated, even disdained, when compared to the importance afforded to action. We celebrate the energy of the ironsmith who works at the forge, while we receive the poet with a shrug of the shoulders. Ibsen, he paraphrases, has one of his characters say that an action is worth a million words. In the 1865 dramatic poem, *Brand*, the protagonist is an idealistic priest who is set on saving humanity and is driven by his uncompromising fanaticism to tragic end.[41]

González Flores takes issue with such rigid distinctions and counters that an action is nothing more or less than a word "severely cast in the molten crucible of body and thought, and mounted precisely where the soul joins the heart." In this phrase, he seems to offer an analogy: the heart is to the body as the soul is to thought. If the heart is the vital organ that gives the body life, so, too, does the soul serve as the foundation of thought. This is an important idea for understanding the religious center of his political philosophy. And the word provides a radical unity, not only of thought but also of identity. This is the Word understood as it appears in the first chapter of the gospel of John. To this end, Matthew Henry's commentary (1708–1710) reasons that "there is the *word conceived*, that is, *thought*, which is the first and only immediate product and conception of the soul (all the operations of which are performed by *thought*), and it is one with the soul. And thus the second person in the Trinity is fitly called *the Word*; for he is the *first-begotten of the Father*, that eternal essential Wisdom which *the Lord possessed*, as the soul does its thought, *in the beginning of his way*."[42] González Flores invokes the word as a point of communion, and renders it through the Lord's Prayer: "Our Father in heaven . . ."

In his thought this is a radically democratic statement, the idea that we are all brothers and sisters. He chides whites for the othering of blacks, and augers a moment in which all hands will come together, above and beyond difference: race, color, wealth, talent, honor, and noble rank.[43]

In his time, González Flores saw the written word as undervalued. In times of conflict, he wrote, we tend to rush to action. Words are at a discount when it comes to defending thought, conscience, and citizenship from revolutionary paroxysm. This is a mistake, he argued: the pamphlet, book, broadside, and especially the periodical press should play a central role in the defense of speech. The rush to action would only lead to a savage idyll, he warns, invoking Mexico's celebrated poet, Manuel José Othón, and would surely beget catastrophe: "the desert, the desert, the desert."[44]

There is a hint of vanguard in this idea. The written word will act as the compass for future action, and the written word, of course, is the realm of teachers and intellectuals like González Flores. He sees this as a strategy of reconquest; today we might see it as a clear sign of the ultramontane teachings of his day. But he also manages to see it in terms of modern political struggle, even national liberation. Thus, the Lord's Prayer is a foundational thought that, in the prose of González Flores, enables the weak to stand up to the strong, the beggar to kings, the shack before the palace, and even, in reference to the geopolitics of the day, the Malays to the English. This last example can be seen as a variation on a broader theme of Catholic liberation from Protestant Imperialism, and González Flores often used the Irish Revolution in the same manner. The Lord's Prayer arms the speechless with the voice and words they will use to stand up to their oppressors.[45]

But prayer alone, even as political speech, was insufficient. In Mexico, the fight for religious liberty was unequal, and Catholics were armed with outdated weapons. There is an interesting mixture of martial language and politics here. First, the author refers to combat and arms, and explains that, as Catholics, he and his readers belong to the army of God and the Church. He then continues to argue that the battles they must join are battles for ideas, words, and organization. The battlefield—in this metaphor—is constituted by the new systems, resources, and means of dissemination that may be mobilized with the objective of reaching out to and conquering the masses of modern society. In the past, such work was much more difficult, extension was limited, and results were poor. But now, in twentieth-century Guadalajara, one might have an idea, invent a new system or program, write it down and print it using newspaper or the pages of a book as a platform, and in a matter of days reach out to a vast auditorium. In post-revolutionary Mexico, students all carried books and newspapers under their arms. And victory belonged to those who recognized the novelty of this new circumstance, and trusted in its power of persuasion.[46]

Meanwhile, lamented González Flores, the Catholics of Mexico continued to organize governed by a siege mentality, an outdated strategy predicated on denouncing their enemies and preaching to the converted. They fought without recourse to the periodical press, literature, schools, organizations, political pamphlets, or the theater of public opinion. There is hyperbole here to be sure. At the very least, the Guadalajara Catholics had been successful at printing newspapers, maintaining schools (at times clandestinely), founding organizations, and printing literature. But things were certainly more difficult beyond Guadalajara. And in Anacleto's prose, they had been humiliated. In order to prevail, they would need to procure and learn to use these and all licit modern arms. González Flores refers to them as "the modern and noble arms of civilization."[47] But they must also abandon the mentality of throwing stones at an enemy armed with machine guns. This attitude would only lead to the tyranny of slavery.

In 1926, the situation recrudesced, and González Flores focused his writing on the figure of the tyrant. In the lead-up to the 1927 rebellion, it enunciated a theological justification for tyrannicide and just war, and it appeared in conjunction with another idea, that of sacrifice. The sacrifice required when faced with tyranny, following Christian tradition, was martyrdom.

MARTYRDOM

The concept of martyrdom was present in his early work, for example, in his reference to Jesus Christ as the Great Martyr.[48] The topic seems to have interested him as historical and theological precedent, prior to the political crisis that would produce a swing in his writing toward martyrdom. His topics prior to the twenties focused on political participation, while martyrdom raised the issue of withdrawal from the political sphere, of sacrifice, the ultimate sacrifice, as an antipolitics. This position was also clearly political: González Flores had forged his own identity with Jesus as a model, and martyrdom became central to his writing in the last year of his life.

In González Flores's imaginary, the suicide of the Roman soldier and statesman, Cato of Utica, represented an honorable death. Cato lived during the century prior to the birth of Christ, and he took his life after losing in battle to

Julius Caesar's army. The death of Cato had a dual meaning for González Flores. First, he was unwilling to live in a world ruled by Caesar. Second, he refused to concede to Caesar the power of pardon, because Caesar's pardon would have made Cato beholden to the tyrant. This resistance, in González Flores view, was exemplary, but ultimately, it did not precisely reflect the political context of his time. There was simply too much distance between Roman antiquity and revolutionary Mexico. In contrast, the examples of Emmeline Pankhurst and Terence MacSwiney, both of whom were his contemporaries, represented a distinct and more tangible, even intimate, possibility. In these two cases, the sacrifice made in opposition to the tyrant was offered in the form of a hunger strike. This, thought Anacleto, would become the political tactic of the modern pariah.[49]

I want to dwell on the cases chosen by González Flores, because they are an indicator of his broadmindedness. Emmeline Pankhurst was a British suffragist and a socialist.[50] She used the hunger strike on numerous occasions in the struggle for women's rights and equality, beginning as early as 1913, according to her biographer.[51] Although her example was extraordinary, it was ultimately surpassed, in the writing of González Flores, by that of Terence MacSwiney, Lord Mayor of the Irish port city of Cork. A militant Republican, MacSwiney was jailed in 1920, during the Irish Revolution, on the charge of possessing printed material of a seditious nature. He immediately declared a hunger strike in protest of his imprisonment, to no avail. The strike dragged on for seventy-four days, finally taking his life. The fundamental value in his example resides in his intransigence, his rejection of the tyrant's political arrangements. However, what González Flores found most convincing was the reaction that the strikers incited in their respective societies.[52] Thousands of women rallied around Pankhurst. But MacSwiney represented the ideal example, because of the religious overtones in the Irish political struggle against the British Empire. In this case, the martyr's sacrifice of the Catholic Republican, his death by hunger strike, mobilized the Irish against the Protestant English in the context of a revolution that was contemporaneous with the one in Mexico.

In connection with his writing on the theme of the hunger strike, González Flores developed one other idea, that of the desert "that will emerge and extend itself in every direction: the plaza, the street, movie houses, theaters, walkways, vehicles, commercial establishments, business centers, they will all encounter the arrival of the desert." Here he deploys two distinct notions of desert. Public space will be as a desert: that is, empty, void, lifeless; but more importantly, the text makes reference to desertion, the act of abandoning. In this way, it also refers to the hunger strike. González Flores characterized the death of MacSwiney, slow and deliberate, as a desertion from the plenitude of youth.[53] As he abandoned the course of life, he became a specter, leaving the author to pose the question, "Is there anything more inoffensive and passively rebellious than a specter?"[54] In this text, the specter joins with the notion of the desert in that it embodies the act of abandon, inflicted on the body itself: the deserted body as desert.

In González Flores's writing, the mayor of Cork represented something more complex than a role model or hero; he represented the new tactics of political struggle that might be adopted in confrontation with the enemy, the tyranny of the revolutionary state. Based on his experience in Jalisco in 1918, he believed in the boycott, the rigorous black of mourning, and in civil disobedience: the massive desertion of Catholics as a campaign capable of defeating the anticlerical politics of the revolution.[55] But in 1926, although the Catholics of Jalisco were highly disciplined, the Bishops' attempt at a national boycott proved a failure. In this context, González Flores was forced to recognize that his thought and writing would not be enough to defeat the tyrant. Accordingly, his writing reached beyond the current arsenal of tactics, to argue for the martyr's sacrifice.[56] However, at the same time he witnessed a transformation in the movement that he led: peaceful opposition ceded to armed rebellion.

In an extraordinary passage, penned some ten years later, Heriberto Navarrete related the details of a secret meeting called by the organization leadership and attended by men and women who represented the towns and parishes across a large part of Jalisco and adjoining regions.[57] Toward the end of 1926, about 100 local chiefs met in Guadalajara by cover of night, without fanfare, in secrecy. They were under strict orders not to speak of their reason for traveling to Guadalajara, not even to their local chaplains or priests.[58] At the meeting, González Flores read a missive sent by the Mexico City leadership of the National League for the Defense of Religious Liberty (LNDLR). The League proposed that the Popular Union join in armed rebellion against the Mexican government. According to Navarrete, González Flores hoped the Popular Union would continue to pursue change by peaceful means, but requested that each town or parish decide for itself whether to adhere to the rebellion.[59] As it turned out, adherence to the rebellion was general. It was impossible to maintain peaceful resistance in the context of generalized violence. This he had referred to as a "blood vote."[60]

The theme of martyrdom should be seen as deriving from the particular circumstance of oppression suffered at the hands of the tyrant. This is how

González Flores understood it. With the generalized move toward rebellion in January 1927, he remained in hiding as dozens of Jalisco towns, one by one, rose up in open rebellion. In Guadalajara, González Flores found himself severely limited. He moved frequently between safe houses under the protection of a network of Popular Union militants, and he spent long hours writing. It was during these final months of his life that he wrote *Tú Serás Rey*, a book that speaks specifically to young people about political commitment in public life, the power of the written word, the eloquence of oratory, and the value of the press to social movements, activism, and advocacy. The book ends with a reflection on the activism and advocacy of Daniel O'Connell, the Irish nationalist and political leader who won a seat to the House of Commons, thus forcing the British to reform the political system in colonial Ireland in 1829.[61] Referred to by the British as "the king of the beggars," O'Connell achieved the franchise for Ireland, the basis for modern citizenship. It also turned him into one of the most beloved figures in all of Irish history. In this way, González Flores saw him as the beggar who became king, and suggested his readers follow in O'Connell's footsteps. However, in the dire secrecy of 1927, González Flores himself seemed to honor another Irish Republican, the martyr MacSwiney.

There is a tension just below the surface of González Flores's writing and activism during these final months. Many of his followers, especially those who came from the towns and villages of rural Jalisco, chose the path of armed rebellion; meanwhile, he recommended to his readers, often the Guadalajara followers of the Catholic Association of Mexican Youth, the path of Daniel O'Connell, the path of political reform. They had prayed, attended mass, and lived as Catholics at home, he wrote. Meanwhile, Christ was absent in the streets, in the plazas, in the schools, in the legislature, in books, in the universities; Christ was missing generally from public and social life. By contrast, Satan governed all of these places and spaces. Catholics must leave the safety of their churches and homes, and take Christ to the public sphere. Catholics must fill the streets with prayer, where, he warned, they would be met with the pike, sword, bayonet, and clenched fist of the executioner.[62] This was a politics of social movement, and yet, in his personal life, he chose the desert, the path of martyrdom, a sacrifice at once religious and political.

A Martyr's Plebiscite?

What, ultimately, is the connection between Anacleto González Flores and the Catholic rebellion that spread across western and northwestern Mexico

between 1926 and 1929? González Flores was an altogether modern thinker; he saw the teachings of the Holy Scripture through the lens of contemporary society. Martyrdom became the hunger strike, the boycott, and the politics of mass witness: forms of sacrifice intended to make an exemplary statement in the here and now. Social movement ought to be channeled through religious motivation toward contemporary political goals. This was the message of his most famous essay, "The Martyrs' Plebiscite." Here González Flores incorporated an archaic understanding of martyrdom, not strictly defined in terms of those who die in the name of their religious belief, but rather, those who suffer the tribulations of religious persecution. Again the modernist, González Flores saw in this sacrifice the collective identity of a movement that would challenge the authoritarian politics and sectarian violence of the Mexican Revolution. *The martyrs' plebiscite* fused the identities of citizen and believer in a simple but powerful trope. However, contemporary historiography demands a closer look at the idea of the rebellion as plebiscite.

Jean Meyer argued that the suspension of worship detonated the rebellion, and that it belonged to a series of tactics made by the Catholic hierarchy in its struggle against the Calles administration.[63] Yet his considerable oeuvre always pointed to the importance of looking beyond the institutional prerogatives of Church and state, to the militants in Guadalajara and scores of towns and villages who were at the center of the conflict. The closing of the churches was a political gambit in a larger game of chess. That chess match, I have argued, was ultimately over the legitimate parameters of political participation. In other words, it was a fight over the construction of secularity in the Mexican Revolution.[64] Thus, the suspension of worship, the closing of the temples, is properly seen as a metaphor for the collapse of the political sphere, the point at which negotiations over the acceptable uses of public space by Catholics broke down.

González Flores explained this in terms of an advancing desert.[65] In his view, the defense of religion was properly sought through political protest; and in the harsh circumstance of early 1926, political suicide/sacrifice was appropriate.[66] González Flores explained this modern martyrdom in terms of the folded hand: in opposition to the open hand that accepts life, he evoked Terence MacSwiney, who closed his hand, abandoning the comfort and very sustenance of material life. In Anacleto's Christological thought, from martyrdom came rebirth. Thus, González Flores called on Catholic Mexicans to sacrifice themselves as MacSwiney had:

By our hands—millions will cease to open themselves to the river of life, and will close as tightly as possible under the weight of consternation—will come resurrection, which is more assured, stronger, more certain than martyrdom itself, than persecution itself. We may not be the emaciated specter of the mayor of Cork, but if we clench our fists tightly and refuse to open them in the vital torrent to the best of our ability, we may eventually appear quite like him.[67]

However, the religious militants of western Mexico abandoned civic parades in favor of armed rebellion. It would be inexact to speak of spontaneous rebellions, because they only seemed so from the perspective of the Mexican army and, perhaps, the vantage point of the Church. To the contrary, each town and village deliberated and decided when and how to enter the fray. Meyer has described the descent into war as a civic phenomenon. It took months for the initial event to produce a conflict between belligerents. In any case, the second half of 1926 saw one town after another rise up against the Federation and President Calles.[68] Generally, the rebellions were not coordinated. There was no leadership, other than the individuals in whose hands each town put their trust and their lives. By the end of 1926, towns had rebelled across much of Jalisco, Colima, west Guanajuato, north Michoacán, and regions to the southwest of Mexico City. In the north, there were uprisings in Aguascalientes, Zacatecas and Durango.[69] Plotted on a map, the spatial distribution follows roughly the "geopolitical axis of Catholic restoration" proposed by Ceballos Ramírez for 1910.[70] And Jalisco is indisputably in the center of the rebellion.[71]

The December 1926 call, for each town to deliberate over whether to join in open rebellion, set the stage for an intensified and expanded area of conflict in 1927.[72] Scores of towns rebelled in a region stretching from León in the east, to Colima in the south, and Tepic to the west. The rebels were enthusiastic, but poorly armed and trained. The conflict was bloody and one-sided, with tremendous casualties among the rebels. However, those who survived—and learned to adopt guerrilla tactics and asymmetric modes of warfare—generally counted on a vast civilian population in their conflict with the better-armed, conventional forces of the Mexican army.[73] Again, we owe Jean Meyer the overarching narrative: during 1927 and 1928, Enrique Gorostieta and others organized a rebel army from the many guerrillas that had formed across western Mexico. While the National League for the Defense of Religious Liberty (LNDLR) attempted to call the shots from Mexico City, regional rebel government emerged in the areas controlled by Gorostieta's forces, under Aurelio Acevedo (Zacatecas), Miguel Gómez Loza (Jalisco), and others.[74]

However, a more recent generation of scholars shifted the focus of study from the grand narrative of religious rebellion as epic poem—the Christiad as a modern day Iliad—toward a more precise consideration of the local reasons and ways of rebellion. Ramón Jrade was perhaps the first scholar to order, categorize, and typify the literature.[75] He criticized Meyer for his loose application of social science methods and his romanticized view of the rebels as rural Catholic mystics. But he recognized that Meyer's was the first study to ground analysis of the rebellion in the lives and motives of the rebels themselves. Jrade also saw the importance of the emerging argument that the rebels were motivated by material conditions (the land question), more than ideological ones (the religious question).[76] His own work built on this argument by fleshing out the ways the consolidation of state power in revolutionary Mexico impacted "specific forms of rural community organization" in towns representative of differentiated regions within the state of Jalisco. It was important, he argued, not to assume that the rebellion was a direct consequence of Church-state conflict; instead, he saw it as the outcome of "class divisions and power struggles that developed in sections of the countryside following the revolution."[77]

Jennie Purnell argued that the difference between Cristero and *agrarista* communities in Michoacán lay in their respective histories of land tenure as much as it did religious identity. For Purnell, the key was to understand how specific communities reacted to the twin revolutionary policies of agrarian reform and anticlericalism.[78] She didn't doubt the religious identity of the Cristero rebels, but questioned whether religious practice was substantially different from that of armed peasants who defended the agrarian reform and fought against the Cristeros. The key was not in the long-term religious legacies of towns, which might be similar, but in the recent or conjunctural impact of modernization. In particular, Michoacán towns like Zacapú or Patzcuaro were left land poor at the end of the nineteenth century, and were therefore receptive to agrarian reform in the post-revolution. By contrast, coastal villages, like Aquila, those of the Purépecha highlands, such as San Juan Parangaricutiro, as well as the rancher communities of northwestern Michoacán, such as San José de Gracia, survived the Porfirian era with their lands intact. For all of these villages, Purnell was interested in the play between land, religious practice, and local political authority.[79] But ultimately, she argued that the difference lay in the way specific communities reacted to relevant state policy as it impacted local histories, creating political Catholics and others who were not.

Julia Preciado Zamora followed the comparative methodology of Jrade and Purnell by choosing Cristero, agrarista, and neutral (*pacífico*) communities on the Jalisco-Colima border.[80] In her findings, Suchitlán Colima, a land-poor community that received land during the earliest years of the agrarian reform (1919), proved a loyal pro-government element throughout the period and fought against the Cristero forces between 1927 and 1929. Preciado Zamora explicitly compared Suchitlán to Purnell's study of San Juan Parangaricutiro.[81] Although she sees both towns as examples where locals bought into the agrarian reform and forged loyalties with the new state, she reads one aspect of Purnell's argument against the grain. Purnell argued that case studies should distinguish between historical and conjunctural factors, following Steve Stern's work on consciousness and peasant rebellion in the Andes.[82] For Purnell, religious affiliation belongs to a historical legacy, while agrarian concerns ought to be understood conjuncturally.[83] But Preciado Zamora argued that agrarian conflict was essential to the historical legacy of Suchitlán, while passing over the importance of religious identity. In any case, the town of Suchitlán seems to have played the role of cannon fodder in the rebellion. Suchitlán suffered over sixty casualties among their troops, and the Tonila rebels burned down the town in June 1929, leaving the survivors displaced as refugees in Colima city.[84]

By contrast, the Cristero stronghold of Tonila offers a more complex picture than the ones we have seen in previous studies.[85] Tonila is a town built in the foothills of the Colima Volcano. It belonged to the state of Jalisco, but to the Dioceses of Colima. Like Suchitlán, a group from Tonila requested land through the early agrarian reform. The petition was not, however, resolved quickly. Ten years later, in the mid-1920s, the community was offered land, but many rejected it. The municipal seat at Tonila became staunchly Cristero, and also received the implicit support of Bishop Velasco and his diocesan council, who abandoned the city of Colima to wait out the rebellion there. By contrast, La Esperanza, a small town some three kilometers distant from Tonila, remained neutral, joining neither of the belligerent forces. The families of La Esperanza served as retainers for the hacienda of the same name; they were essentially a town of peons, and they remained neutral throughout the conflict at the behest of the hacienda owner. Although the town was pacífico, Zamora wrote that its inhabitants discreetly supported the Tonila Cristero rebels.[86] These cases suggest a historical legacy of Catholicism, but they also suggest a long-term land problem, as well as a conjunctural circumstance that favored religious identity during the rebellion, in the case of Tonila, while it favored neutrality inspired by economic concerns, in the case of La Esperanza.

Most recent studies, in this manner, beg the question of how to understand the construction of religious identity and practice, as well as how it constitutes historical agency. Most every major study published after Jean Meyer's ground-breaking work seems to suggest that scholars can, perhaps ought, to understand religion through other elements, whether land or local politics. In this way, Matthew Butler's work has proved a healthy revision of prior literature. He took Meyer's insight regarding the religious motivation of Cristero rebels and went to work trying to understand how it happened, what were its forms and operations. Then he went about trying to construct more precise case studies through his research in eastern Michoacán state.[87]

What he found is that Catholicism was not a constant, but that it was constructed in multiple ways, and impacted political identities in equally complex manners. Cristeros and agraristas were both likely to be Catholics, but this should not be seen as a reason to pass over religious identity as a factor in the construction of political identity. To the contrary, scholars must map political identity onto religious identity. Using the same data Purnell cited from the 1910 census, Butler points out that the nine states with the highest density of priests map out the geography of the revolt. From this point he hypothesizes that more clericalized areas will more likely be supportive of the revolt. This is not to characterize it as a clerical revolt, but it does lead Butler to look at particular parishes for distinguishing forms of religious practice.[88] The context of his study recognized a variety of religious practices and a diverse spiritual landscape ranging from "the ultraclericalized catholicity of the Jalisco highlands and the Zamora Bajío to the syncretic and relatively declericalized religions of the Tarascan and Otomí sierras." This continuum was also shaped by diverse local devotions, some orthodox and others less so, the Methodist and Presbyterian pockets of southern Jalisco and eastern Michoacán, and perhaps even the incipient Church of the Light of the World, founded in Guadalajara in 1926.[89] He concluded that ideology, place, land, and religion were all basic aspects of the political-religious identities of both Cristeros and agraristas. However, the rebellion was not a religious war in the sense of sixteenth-century Reform-era Europe.[90] It was rather a war about religion, about the ways twentieth-century Mexican peasants and townsfolk might relate to their respective churches and clergy, in short, a war over the relationship between religious practice and the public sphere.

This sense of the religious conflict is front and center in the writing of Anacleto González Flores. A product of the "churchy, sacramental, clericalized"[91] towns of the Jalisco highlands, he saw the conflict as a plebiscite over how much control the central government might exercise over local customs. His was a political Catholicism in the sense outlined in the introduction of this book: a phenomenon that depended on the tactics of mass politics. This basic element would also characterize the rural bands that turned to armed rebellion in and after 1926. In this sense, political action and warfare were both Catholic in inspiration.[92]

———

This chapter opened with a story about the execution and martyrdom of Anacleto González Flores. Situated in the final chapter of the book, the event serves as a metaphor for a broader Catholic political struggle. Then, through a careful reading of Anacleto's journalistic writing on key topics—the social question, religious liberty, and martyrdom—I have argued that his vision narrowed and hardened in the context of the political closure that accompanied the emergence of the revolutionary state in the decade of 1920. The broader argument, however, continues to be that this was a politics born of the Mexican Revolution; it was not counterrevolutionary. It attempted to confront the state through legitimate channels of protest, and in the face of certain violence, called for patience and perseverance. The argument gains perspective in the context of recent historiography on the Cristero Rebellion, both in the sense of a contrast with arguments that are very different, and in comparison with recent work that has carefully teased out the complex forms in which religious belief informed the politics of rebellion. But in the end, this book is not primarily about Anacleto González Flores. He belongs to a bigger picture, that of modern political Catholicism as a historical phenomenon born prior to the Mexican Revolution and consumed after 1926 in the brutal battles of the Cristero Rebellion. In this sense, the epigraph on the *via crucis* highlights the paradox of martyrdom in this chapter. When applied to the life of González Flores, it rings true, as he did offer up his life, a death *for* the other. But the same cannot be said of the villagers and townsfolk who took up the fight in 1926. They, too, offered up their lives, perhaps, but the rebellion was always more about the death *of* the other. The collapse of the political sphere dictated precisely such a resolution.

Conclusion
Politics and Religion in the Mexican Revolution

THIS BOOK HAS described and analyzed political behavior, both collective and individual, in terms of culture. For the purposes of the book, culture has been interpreted broadly, but one very important aspect of the cultural context I have sought to portray is the role of religious practice in social life. Here, religious practice has not been limited to prayer, worship, or the celebration of the sacraments; it has also encompassed social activities undertaken in the spirit of religious liberty and political speech. In this sense, religious practice may be seen as quintessentially modern.

The decision to understand religious practice as social reflects the mentality of the social Catholics who populate the pages of the book. For them religion was not just about Sunday mass; to the contrary, it was about how they lived their lives. Catholicism was a civic religion in the way described by Jean-Pierre Bastian for Protestantism.[1] It informed practices that ordered and gave reason to their lives beyond the temple, in house and street, school, workshop and fields, union and party. They lived by the vow of "establishing all in Christ," and it only makes sense to look for religious inspiration in daily life.

I have also pushed at the definition of politics and have tried to look beyond the narrow corridors of presidential and parliamentary power. I have placed great emphasis on the role of anonymous, collective actors, and their leadership. Although the book is fundamentally about Catholicism, most historical agency has been sought among laity. I have been interested in understanding how laity and clergy interact, but also in how laity acts at the margins of clerical tutelage or control. From this methodological strategy, a picture has emerged of middle and working-class people, Mexican Roman Catholics, who were central to the relations between Church and state. More importantly still, they were central to the unfolding of the Mexican Revolution. In order to understand their political practice, I have chosen to look outside the generally drawn boundaries of the Mexican Revolution, in order to catch a glimpse of how the great social upheaval of 1910 changed Catholicism.

In conceptual terms, I have argued that the central tension in this story is that of citizen and believer. The historiographic riddle posed by this tension is how to understand the limits of each, and the overlap they inevitably present. Another way to frame this issue is to ask where politics ends and religion begins. It turns out that careful analysis advises against such binary views, and pushes the reader to consider the many ways that politics and religion not only coexist, but are invariably entangled. Conventional histories of Church and state have generally imposed an analytical separation of politics and religion on empirical data, looking to understand the motives of one or the other. Here, I have asked instead how politics constitutes religion and vice versa. In posing this question, I have been motivated by the basic hypothesis that religion and devotion are no less important to understanding modernity than politics. I have tried to show throughout each chapter that historians must discard the idea that religion is somehow pre-modern, a residual leftover that has no place in the world of science, politics, and law.

In order to understand the play of politics and religion, I have argued that one must consider the constantly changing terms of secularity that character- ize society. In other words, modern society reflects an ever-shifting relation- ship between religion and politics, one that can be observed and measured qualitatively in the ways public space is used, and in terms of the evolving limits to and acceptance of religious practice in society. The limits—the condi- tions of secularity—may be seen differently by local populations and agents of the state. This is the question at the heart of all secularization theory; however, seen through a historical lens, it becomes richer, less linear and more robust. Furthermore, this phenomenon has much to tell us about the kinds of conflict and coexistence that characterized the revolutionary era in Mexico.

Empirically, social Catholicism or Catholic social action was a basic aspect of the practices I identified at the outset of the book. In Mexico, liberal Cathol- icism characterized Church politics during the long administration of Presi- dent Díaz, but by the final ten years of the regime, social Catholicism was ascendant and liberal Catholicism waned. This phenomenon was the result of a generational renovation in Catholicism. Social Catholics and Christian Democrats invested in a politics of laity gradually displaced liberals who had dominated a period of clerically driven elite politics.[2] In this sense, the birth of a modern laity transformed the logic of Church-state relations. One current within social Catholicism favored Christian democracy, particularly the idea that the Catholics ought to have a political party, and ought to participate openly in politics as Catholics. But this was not a universally popular idea. Some intellectuals subscribed to ideas of Christian democracy prior to 1911, but a movement would not begin to take shape until the fall of the Díaz regime. In this trepidation one can see the tensions between the social and the political. Eventually, the power vacuum of the initial year of revolution would bring out the full potential of social action as a politics of religious identity.

Prior to 1911, social action was debated, shaped, and prescribed by a group of Catholic intellectuals composed of both clergy and laity. Constructed by a broad group of activists, it was characterized by some important internal contradictions that would later appear in practice. In particular, there were disagreements over what to do about social problems rooted in class difference. Most activists recognized the reasons for class conflict, but there were differences of opinion regarding how to treat it. Another area in which there were internal contradictions to the movement had to do with the role of women in society. It is important to recall here that early social Catholicism, and the national gatherings of Catholic thinkers in particular, were strictly male affairs. In this context, a Catholic elite—male, mostly urban, professional, and mestizo—wrote and debated about women in a manner similar to the way they addressed issues of workers, peons, or Indians. In all of these cases the construction was unstable, and meaning changed through the Mexican Revolution, as a distinctly political Catholicism displaced Catholic social action.

Meetings such as the 1906 Guadalajara congress or the 1910 Mexico City retreat were the source of modern politics, and tactics such as the pilgrimage, which later would become important to political Catholicism and the movements it inspired. In late Porfirian Mexico, social action was discussed as a program, and executed as a parish-level pedagogy of Christian civility and socio-religious progress. Yet it was constructed as a self-consciously apolitical social theology. Catholic leadership, including clergy and laity, purposely maneuvered so as to consciously avoid its political implications. However, during the last couple of years prior to the Madero revolution, particularly after the 1908 Creelman interview, some Catholics began to consider more seriously the political potential of social Catholicism.

The political transition in Mexico commenced several years prior to the fall of Porfirio Díaz. During this period, an urban political opposition emerged in a political sphere still dominated by the government of President Porfirio Díaz. This initial aperture, roughly spanning the years 1908–1910, was of great importance in shaping the political forces that would characterize the Madero regime.[3] During the Porfirian *fin de régimen*, the emerging political opposition experimented using different tactics to marshal discontent with the regime. Although these movements were not necessarily successful—the attempt to draft Bernardo Reyes as President Díaz's vice president is the obvious example—they were notable for providing a sort of school where many trained who had not participated previously in the political sphere. In this sense, both Reyismo and the Anti-Reelectionist clubs provided such experience.

In this period and context, Catholic activists organized quickly, developing social action networks. From the parishes, they constructed an organizational framework and a disciplined militancy. The parish system offered a common ground and an institutional base for the Operarios Guadalupanos and others who had participated in the many seminars, congresses, and other meetings inspired by social Catholic theology. This experience would facilitate greatly the move from social action to the explicitly political movement that crystallized in the form of the National Catholic Party. This was the point of departure for Christian democracy in Mexico, and the lens through which we can see the emergence of a distinctly modern, political Catholicism.

The fin de régimen saw the formation of opposition political movements that mined the once solid control of the state. But with the fall of President Díaz, systemic political control dissolved, ceding power to the regions. In practice, this created a vacuum, and an aperture in which opposition groups could compete for power. Some of the fiercest political competition developed in Jalisco, where it pitted liberals against Catholics in a battle that the latter would initially win.

The collapse of the regime was achieved through armed rebellion, although it was unevenly distributed, with broad scope and intensity in the Sierra Madre Occidental region of northern Mexico and in Morelos, south of Mexico City. While rebellion was part of the repertoire of tactics in Jalisco, its scope and intensity were limited. It was less successful, and more contained, in this state than elsewhere. By contrast, political competition and reform flourished in the uncontrolled context of Maderista Jalisco. There, opposing groups, including remnants of the Díaz administration, supporters of Francisco Madero, and an emerging group of political Catholics all sought to participate in the fast-changing electoral landscape.

The rise of the National Catholic Party (PCN) in Jalisco was built on the parish network, and as a result was more thorough and widespread than the campaigns of other political parties. As the PCN grew, and won local and statewide elections, Jalisco became the center of a prototypical Christian democracy movement, a phenomenon with no real precedent in Mexico. PCN activists faced off with liberal candidates, but also with Porfirian caciques and other entrenched local interests in rural Jalisco. Their organizing tactics were both new and old. PCN promoters scoured the state trying to spread the word about the new party, town by town, and they faced adverse circumstances in doing so. But they also mobilized captive groups in support of their cause, as in the case of ranch hands sent to vote, or parish worker circles who took on the task of organizing the party locally. Although the quality of this democratic experience was uneven, the level of mobilization and enthusiasm is noteworthy, and, again, the effort was unprecedented.

National Catholic Party government has left a mixed legacy, one remembered mostly for the tactics and opportunism of the Mexico City leadership, which threw its support to the Huerta dictatorship following the assassination of President Madero and Vice President Pino Suárez. It is necessary to consider the PCN within this context, because it shaped the history of the nation. The PCN gained little from the Huerta government, and in return brought on its own demise. However, while the party elite maneuvered in Mexico City in search of state power, the Jalisco PCN had won open and competitive elections, and attempted to govern the state. This experiment was only a partial success, in part due to the inexperience of the PCN legislators. It was also limited in time, to 1912 and 1913. But the tenor of the period is worth consideration. They did not think in terms of revolutionary fiat, but rather deliberative democracy. The 1912 legislature, dominated by the Catholic Party, sought moderate social reforms and promised to govern as centrists, in the tradition of the popular Belgian Catholics. They legislated proportional representation in the local congress, made it easier for government to recognize the studies of those who attended Catholic schools, and tried to implement a policy of social welfare for the rural and urban poor. When the Constitutionalist army prevailed, the PCN was swept away as a relic of the counter-revolution, but that narrative does not stand up to empirical scrutiny.

In west-central Mexico, the years 1914 and 1915 were characterized by the final demise of the old regime. January began with the "Christ the King" marches in Guadalajara, Mexico City, and other cities. Huertistas saw them as an affront to the regime, while Carrancistas received them as a display of counter-revolutionary sentiment. Two weeks later Huerta called governor

López Portillo y Rojas to Mexico City to join the presidential cabinet, and general José María Mier was installed as governor of Jalisco. The main threat to the dictator was military, rather than political, posed by Obregón's army that approached Guadalajara from Tepic. Nevertheless, Huerta's authority in question, civilian government was suppressed in favor of military rule; to little avail. This new collapse of the political sphere was followed during the summer of 1914 by renewed civil war, this time between the followers of Francisco Villa and Venustiano Carranza, opposing leaders within the revolutionary ranks.

The Jalisco Catholic Party was not the only casualty of the 1914 civil war, and in Guadalajara the northern revolutionaries made a point of inflicting a measure of symbolic violence against targets they associated with the Church, or with Catholic culture in general. Guadalajara was not unique in this sense. In this city, Manuel M. Diéguez had the effigies of saints removed from plazas, markets, and towns, while in Monterrey, Antonio Villarreal caused quite a spectacle by ordering them shot. In mock ceremony, soldiers lined up bronze, ceramic, and wooden statues observing the practice of pelotón and paredón, and, faithful to the idiom of violence of the day, executed them. Revolutionary iconoclasm was part of an ideological struggle, the imposition of northern anticlericalism on a recalcitrant population.

The civil war also brought large armies, revolutionary violence, and a share of terror to Guadalajara. By and large, Catholics supported Villa over Carranza both out of a sense that he would be less intolerant toward their religion, and because he did not impose outsiders on them. His governor in Jalisco, Julián Medina, was from Hostotipaquillo, and was more accepting of local customs, even though he was neither part of, nor particularly interested in, political Catholicism. Perhaps the most important example of symbolic violence meted out against Guadalajara's Catholic population was the January 1915 execution of a local priest. To be sure, it was not symbolic, but very real to those who witnessed it, and to Father Galván, who was shot. But it was an act of revolutionary terror, in the tradition of the French Revolution. A priest was shot to make an impression on the population, thus its symbolic importance. The paredón where the execution took place was immediately transformed into a space of reverence and religious devotion. This devotion has lasted through the years, and today the Vatican recognizes David Galván as a saint, and a martyr to the cause. Thus an act of violence committed against a young priest, a man of little stature publicly or within the Church, has generated a completely different context historically.

In the wake of the civil war, the winners drafted a new constitution, which decreed tough anticlerical policies. The move to impose these policies was accompanied by the detention and banishing of Guadalajara's archbishop, Francisco Orozco y Jiménez. In response, Catholics in Jalisco mobilized, and although they had no effective political representation, they preserved the organizational network that had made the PCN successful. In a matter of months they mobilized much of Jalisco's Catholic population through public protest, written petition, and a strategy of nonviolent noncooperation. They applied tight economic sanctions against mechanized forms of transportation (including the city's trolley system), selected businesses, and media. They adopted a self-imposed state of mourning, dressing in black, rejecting all forms of fiesta, dance, theater, movies, and other expressions of leisure. The scope and focus of the movement, and their ability to mobilize the rural population alongside urban Catholics, made for a massive and sustained protest. Its breadth was all the more impressive due to the discipline of the protesters, and the amount of time they were able to sustain it. Between June 1918 and January 1919 the campaign was sustained, and in February, the government saw fit to abandon the anticlerical measures. By June 1919 the archbishop had returned to Mexico from his Chicago exile. In Guadalajara he was received as a hero.

The resurgent movement of 1918–1919 demonstrates how a politically excluded group can challenge the limits of the political sphere. Having been successful in their 1918 campaign against the anticlerical policies of the Jalisco state government, political Catholics turned again to founding new lay organizations. They were assured of their ability to mobilize rural and urban populations around issues pertaining to the preservation of worship and the defense of their ecclesiastic authorities. In 1919 they began to form new organizations that would carry the campaign much further. As with the PCN nearly a decade before, lay leaders began to project a role for Christian democracy as the principal organizing medium of civil society. The vehicle through which they planned to achieve this would be a labor union movement. But the scope would reach much further, encompassing factory and workshop, church and home. In the words of the Jesuit Alfredo Méndez Medina, the union would be the workers' extended family network.

In practice, the union movement in Jalisco was as dense and popular as the parish network on which it was built. But the unions functioned in a manner different from that which the 1906 social Catholics had imagined. First of all, women were as fundamental to the movement as men. Second, and of equal importance, the rigid leadership hierarchy plotted out by the 1906 delegates was not implemented. The unions were invariably tied to the Catholic Church, and a cadre of advisors traveled around the archdiocese training local lay leadership. This Catholic vanguard was a mixture of clergy and laity; of middle-class professionals, factory workers, and artisans; of men and women. Political Catholicism was rooted in local leadership, needs, and interests. But it was also tied to a national network of organizations through the Guadalajara-based National Confederation of Catholic Workers, and the Mexico City–based Mexican Social Secretariat.

The 1918 campaign taught lay leaders that public protest in large numbers, out in the street, was a vital tactic that generated unity, a shared or common experience, and constantly reminded civil government of the popular base and widespread resolve of Catholics. To reach a deeper, more solid unity, activists shifted from the tactic of public protest to procession and pilgrimage, foregrounding faith as the main link, and effectively transgressing the boundaries between the religious and the political. Tens of thousands of peaceful Catholics could be effectively assembled in the street in a nonviolent political tactic characterized by collective prayer. The result was a combative, intransigent Catholic identity, and a mentality of sacrifice, or even martyrdom. In his most famous writing, Anacleto González Flores asked his supporters to join *the martyr's plebiscite*. The revolution was afraid, he told them, and the time was at hand for Catholics to take back the public sphere. Catholic blood would be spilt, but he assured his readers that a martyr's death was the most noble, as it immortalized the cause of Catholic Mexico.[4] By 1927 he had died as he had instructed others to live, and in death became one of the most famous martyrs to the Catholic cause in Mexico, surpassed only, perhaps, by Miguel Agustín Pro.

This was fundamentally a message about secularity and public religion. The martyr's plebiscite was an open challenge to state power over public space emptied of God, to recall Taylor's phrase.[5] Secularity was always about negotiating the acceptable parameters of devotion and religious worship. And these were always already grounded in social practice. Thus, the plebiscite, martyred or not, was a story about the privatization of religion and the manner in which the faithful might seek to push devotion back out into public space. It is, at the same time, a story about what themes and interests might be broached in Habermas's famous public sphere, and who would be allowed to enunciate them.[6]

The Catholic union movement fit more thoroughly the concept of Christian democracy than any other aspect of political Catholicism over the first twenty-five years of the century, including the Catholic Party. By 1924 it was excluded and formally proscribed from the political sphere, but overshadowed it by encompassing society as a whole. This was due to the emphasis placed on organizing all aspects of life as part of a unified system. In this sense, the movement had an underlying corporatist character. It unified the family, workplace, church, school, market, band, and theater within a single, flexible, all-encompassing and multitudinous group. It competed with the pro-government unions for membership. But it also pushed religious issues to the forefront through secular means.

Finally, the most important characteristic of the Catholic union movement was its flexibility. It was mounted on the parish system, the way the PCN had been. This permitted it a wide acceptance, and a practical link to the family and church. It also created the means by which the union movement might change. By 1925 state policy began to reflect a recrudescent anticlericalism that was aimed, in particular, at the lay organizations associated with the Catholic Church. As state and federal government acted to close down the spaces where confessional associations operated, the movement was transformed. Mexico City militants formed the National League for the Defense of Religious Liberty (LNDLR), modeled as a vanguard organization for Catholic politics. But at the same time, Anacleto González Flores and others in Jalisco formed the Popular Union, and used the union structure to do it. As the channels for political compromise failed, the decentralized leadership of the Popular Union grew impatient with the tactics of political struggle. In the impasse created by the Calles Law and the clerical strike of 1926, the LNDLR called for rebellion, and leaders of the Popular Union decided to rebel. Silently, the local leaderships of the union movement switched from a civilian to a military mode of organization, and the union movement, as such, disappeared. It became something else.

Through three long years of rebellion, west-central Mexico was transformed, and the Cristiada was constructed: religious rebellion as popular epic. Following the rebellion, Church and state would achieve a new understanding, a new *modus vivendi*. Catholic townsfolk called it *los arreglos*, "the arrangement," an allusion to dark and cynical backroom deals struck between the powerful. For laity, the catharsis of rebellion consumed political Catholicism and the social movements that had underwritten it. For Christendom, as of 1931 a new theology would replace social Catholicism, more oriented toward clerical-controlled relationships focused strictly on spiritual affairs.[7] In Mexico, laity would continue to organize, but without the benefit of the parish network, which was restricted to pastoral control. A new generation would grow up in a Catholic Mexico in which politics was restricted to a single party, and outside the party there was little legitimacy. There would be attempts to carve out an opposition politics, such as the left-wing Mexican Communist Party and the right-wing National Synarchist Party. The 1939 foundation of the National Action Party would bring some tenets of Christian democracy to the post-revolutionary *polis*. But the rebellion had effectively mounted a fundamental challenge to revolutionary legitimacy, and in response political resolve was hardened. The post-revolutionary state would cultivate a distinct authoritarian character that has survived the twentieth century.

In dramatic terms, the rebellion was the climax of a Mexican secularization narrative, while the 1928 State of the Union address, delivered by President Calles, announced the denouement.[8] It would materialize months later with the foundation of the National Revolutionary Party, and a formal end to the rebellion in June 1929. The Cristero Rebellion is the climax not simply because of the objectives, focus, and scope of the movement, but because it crystallized, and eventually consumed, the efforts of a generation of Catholic activists that had organized and participated politically. The rebellion belonged to the era of mass politics, and would have been impossible half a century earlier when priests were stripped of their citizen's rights. In a paradox of the Mexican Revolution, religious rebellion effectively destroyed political Catholicism as a movement with national aspirations.

This becomes clear with the drama's denouement: the institutionalization of the revolution, the birth of a state party and its invitation to the *reactionaries*: "We want the reactionaries as our enemy. . . . So that the institutional life of our country can be realized, it is necessary for those who see themselves as conservatives, to honestly hoist the banner of their principles and oppose the revolutionaries."[9] These are the words of Luis L. León, and while the oratory is his, the ideas are not original; they come from President Calles's final State of the Union address.[10]

The irony of the moment is better understood if we take into consideration political Catholicism. The 1928 State of the Union address became the cornerstone of the new state, the foundation of the "institutionalized revolution,"[11] that is, the consolidation of a new order and cultural hegemony. In 1929 this did not yet exist; but it had been imagined, and Calles worked tirelessly to herd the fractured revolutionary family, including his own Labor Party followers and those of the rival Liberal Constitutionalist Party. His goal was to include them in a governing party acceptable to all. The initial irony is rhetorical and sarcastic. In the address, Calles called for the participation of reactionaries and conservatives, at the same time that he imagined a revolutionary future in which there was no room for a conservative power base or legislation.[12] But the greater irony appears through the words of Calles and León, in their call for the enemy to raise the banner of its principles. In 1928, the greatest enemy was political Catholicism, which had been proscribed from the law and had successfully fought the Mexican army to a draw. Calles said he wanted a rival, but through legal maneuvering he, along with regional chiefs like Zuno, made clear that the new order would repress the only serious competitor at that point capable of disputing state power and their national project.

The consolidation of the revolutionary state, a new spatial and political relationship between government and governed, was founded on a strategic exclusion prior to the birth of the new system of political representation in which, eventually, all Mexicans would participate. At the same time, the birth of the system also depended on an act of collective political suicide—or martyrdom—committed by the Catholic movements that joined the Cristero Rebellion. The tragedy of this story is that, by choosing armed rebellion, these movements made sure that any possibility of a confessional politics, as remote as it may have been in 1924 or 1925, would in the future be impossible. They spent their cartridges in the war. Subsequently, other movements would emerge, but no confessional movement would approach the magnitude achieved by political Catholics prior to the rebellion.

Notes

Chapter 1

1. This and the following paragraphs are based on a memoir written by Heriberto Navarrete, SJ. His is the only version of the event, for which there is no corroborating evidence to this day; it is, literally, his word. See *"Por Dios y por la patria": Memorias de mi participación en la defensa de la libertad de conciencia y culto, durante la persecución religiosa en México de 1926 a 1929*, 3rd ed. (México: Editorial Jus, 1973), 102–8.

2. "Uno de los de la *jota eme*," in the original, is a reference to the ACJM, the Catholic Association of Mexican Youth. Its members were male, unmarried lay Catholics, often students, who were literate and took over the role of clergy in "reading" mass to the faithful, a way of reproducing a basic sacrament in the absence of priests; Navarrete, *Por Dios*, 107.

3. The opening vignette is a story told by Heriberto Navarrete in his memoir on the religious rebellion of the 1920s. In this sense, it is a representation of his own historical memory. He wrote it in the final months of 1939, twelve years after the events portrayed. Navarrete was born in Etzatlán, Jalisco, in 1903, where he spent his childhood until his family moved to Guadalajara in 1910. In 1920 he joined the Mexican Association of Catholic Youth (ACJM), where he met Anacleto González Flores, with whom he became a close friend. He studied engineering but failed to complete his degree. In 1926 he became general secretary of the Popular Union (UP) in Jalisco. He was detained in Mexico City on April 2, 1927, the day after the arrest and execution of González Flores, and was imprisoned at Islas Marías penal colony for several months. Upon release, he joined the Catholic rebellion as a soldier and secretary to General Enrique Gorostieta. When the rebellion ended in July 1929, Navarrete returned to Mexico City and went to work as a civil engineer at the Ministry of Agriculture and Public Works (*Fomento*). In October 1933, he joined the Society of Jesus, where he took his vows two years later in 1935.

4. The italics are the author's original writing; see R. Scott Appleby, *The Ambivalence of the Sacred: Religion, Violence, and Reconciliation*, foreword by Theodore M. Hesburgh (New York: Rowman & Littlefield Publishers, 2000), 29.

5. Cited in Appleby, *The Ambivalence of the Sacred*, 28; see also Rudolph Otto, *The*

Idea of the Holy: An Inquiry into the Non-Rational Factor in the Idea of the Divine and Its Relation to the Rational, trans. John W. Harvey (Oxford: Oxford University Press, 1923), 12–13.

6. Emile Durkheim, *The Elementary Forms of Religious Life*, trans. Karen E. Fields (New York: Free Press, 1995); see also Mustafa Emirbayer, ed., *Emile Durkheim: Sociologist of Modernity* (Oxford: Blackwell Publishing, 2003), 109–22.

7. Emirbayer, *Emile Durkheim*, 134–38, reprints a fragment of Sewell's article; the original is William H. Sewell Jr., "Historical Events as Transformations of Structures: Inventing Revolution at the Bastille," *Theory and Society* 25 (1996): 864–71; see also, William H. Sewell Jr., *Logics of History: Social Theory and Social Transformation* (Chicago: University of Chicago Press, 2005), 248–50.

8. Martin Conway, "Introduction," in *Political Catholicism in Europe, 1918–1965*, ed. Tom Buchanan and Martin Conway (New York: Oxford University Press, 1996), 1–33.

9. William B. Taylor, *Magistrates of the Sacred: Priests and Parishioners in Eighteenth-Century Mexico* (Stanford, CA: Stanford University Press, 1996), 35–40.

10. K. Aaron Van Oosterhout, "Confraternities and Popular Conservatism on the Frontier: Mexico's Sierra del Nayarit in the Nineteenth Century," *The Americas* 71, no. 1 (2014): 101–30.

11. The diocese of Tepic was erected in 1891 and included the general area of the Tepic territory, subsequently established as the state of Nayarit in 1917. Two parishes in the territory, La Yesca and Amatlán de Cañas, remained attached to the Guadalajara archdiocese, while four parishes located in the state of Jalisco were included in the new diocese: Mascota, Talpa, San Sebastián and Guachinango.

12. Fernando Cervantes, "Mexico's 'Ritual Constant': Religion and Liberty from Colony to Post-Revolution," in *Faith and Impiety in Revolutionary Mexico*, ed. Matthew Butler (New York: Palgrave MacMillan, 2007), 57–73.

13. Taylor, *Magistrates of the Sacred*, 40.

14. Taylor, *Magistrates of the Sacred*, 40.

15. Revolutionary iconoclasm has been the topic of much quality work of late. See Ben Fallaw, "Varieties of Mexican Revolutionary Anticlericalism: Radicalism, Iconoclasm, and Otherwise, 1914–1935," *The Americas* 65, no. 4 (2009): 481–509; Alan Knight, "The Mentality and Modus Operandi of Revolutionary Anticlericalism," in *Faith and Impiety in Revolutionary Mexico*, ed. Matthew Butler (New York: Palgrave MacMillan, 2007), 21–56; Adrian A. Bantjes, "The Regional Dynamics of Anticlericalism and Defanaticization in Revolutionary Mexico," in *Faith and Impiety in Revolutionary Mexico*, ed. Matthew Butler (New York: Palgrave MacMillan, 2007), 111–30; Adrian A. Bantjes, "Burning Saints, Molding Minds: Iconoclasm, Civic Ritual, and the Failed Cultural Revolution," in *Rituals of Rule, Rituals of Resistance: Public Celebrations and Popular Culture in Mexico*, ed. William H. Beezley, Cheryl English Martin, and William E. French (Wilmington, DE: SR Books, 1994), 261–84; Marjorie Becker, "Torching La Purísima, Dancing at the Altar: The Construction of Revolutionary Hegemony

in Michoacán, 1934–1940," in *Everyday Forms of State Formation: Revolution and the Negotiation of Rule in Modern Mexico*, ed. Gilbert M. Joseph and Daniel Nugent (Durham, NC: Duke University Press, 1994), 247–64; and Carlos Martínez Assad, *El laboratorio de la revolución: el Tabasco Garridista* (México: Siglo XXI, 1984).

16. The classic work is Adrien Dansette, *Religious History of Modern France*, trans. John Dingle, vol. 2 of *From the Revolution to the Third Republic* (New York: Herder and Herder, 1961); see also, Norman Ravitch, *The Catholic Church and the French Nation, 1589–1989* (London: Routledge, 1990); Ivan Strenski offers an interesting twist on the transformation of the Catholic Church in revolutionary France by arguing that the concept of sacrifice that anchored the Republic was rooted in Catholic thought; see *Contesting Sacrifice: Religion, Nationalism, and Social Thought in France* (Chicago: University of Chicago Press, 2002).

17. S. William Halperin, *The Separation of Church and State in Italian Thought from Cavour to Mussolini* (Chicago: University of Chicago Press, 1937).

18. José Casanova, *Public Religions in the Modern World* (Chicago: University of Chicago Press, 1994), particularly chapters 1 and 2; René Rémond, *Religion and Society in Modern Europe*, trans. Antonia Nevill (Oxford: Blackwell, 1999).

19. Patrick Granfield, "The Church as Societas Perfecta in the Schemata of Vatican I," *Church History* 48, no. 4 (1979): 431–46; and Patrick Granfield, "Auge y declive de la 'societas perfecta,'" *Concilium* 177 (1982): 10–19.

20. Stathis N. Kalyvas, *The Rise of Christian Democracy in Europe* (Ithaca: Cornell University Press, 1996); Micheal Fogarty, *Christian Democracy in Western Europe, 1820–1953* (London: Routledge & Kegan Paul, 1957).

21. Roger Aubert et al., *La Iglesia en el mundo moderno (1848 al Vaticano II)*, vol. 5 of *Nueva historia de la Iglesia*, 2nd ed., trans. T. Muñoz Sciaffino (Madrid: Ediciones Cristiandad, 1984), 44–64.

22. Leo XIII, *Two Basic Social Encyclicals: "On the Condition of Workers," Leo XIII and Forty Years After, "On Reconstructing Social Order," Pius XI* (Washington, DC: Catholic University of America Press, 1943).

23. On the influence of *Rerum Novarum* in Mexico, see Manuel Ceballos Ramírez, *El catolicismo social: un tercero en discordia*, Rerum Novarum, *la "cuestión social" y la movilización de los católicos mexicanos (1891–1911)* (Mexico: El Colegio de México, 1991).

24. Jorge Adame Goddard, *El pensamiento político y social de los católicos mexicanos, 1867–1914* (Mexico: UNAM, 1981), 42–50.

25. Dino Bigongiari, ed., *The Political Ideas of St. Thomas Aquinas* (New York: Hafner Press, 1953), vii–xxxvii.

26. Umberto Eco, "Elogio de Santo Tomás," *Nexos*, March 1, 1998, accessed November 10, 2017, https://www.nexos.com.mx/?p=3096.

27. Leo XIII, *Two Basic Social Encyclicals*, 21.

28. Kalyvas, *The Rise of Christian Democracy*; Fogarty, *Christian Democracy*; on Germany, see Noel D. Cary, *The Path to Christian Democracy: German Catholics and*

the Party System from Windthorst to Adenaur (Cambridge, MA: Harvard University Press, 1996).

29.   In spite of the limited spread of party politics, nineteenth-century Spanish history was in many ways forged by the antiliberal, Catholic social movement known as Carlism. See Jordi Canal's important work on the topic, *El carlismo: dos siglos de contrarrevolución en España* (Madrid: Alianza Editorial, 2000).

30.   Kalyvas, *The Rise of Christian Democracy*, 1–3, 63–75; see also, Aubert et al., *La Iglesia en el mundo moderno*, 78–114.

31.   Martin Conway, "Catholic Politics or Christian Democracy? The Evolution of Interwar Political Catholicism," in *Political Catholicism in Europe, 1918–45*, ed. Wolfram Kaiser and Helmut Wohnout, vol. 1 (London: Routledge, 2004), 236–41.

32.   Of course, here Casanova invokes St. Augustine, *The City of God*, trans. Marcus Dods (Chicago: Encyclopaedia Britannica, Inc., 1952).

33.   Casanova, *Public Religions*, 14–15.

34.   Bigongiari, ed., *The Political Ideas*, xxxiii–xxxiv.

35.   Saint Thomas Aquinas, *The Summa Theologica of St. Thomas Aquinas*, II–II, Q60, A6, 2nd and revised ed., literally translated by Fathers of the English Dominican Province (1920).

36.   Casanova, *Public Religions*, 15.

37.   Karen Armstrong, *A History of God: A 4,000-Year Quest of Judaism, Christianity and Islam* (New York: Ballantine Books, 1993), 293.

38.   Reinhart Koselleck, *Futures Past: On the Semantics of Historical Time*, trans. with an introduction by Keith Tribe (New York: Columbia University Press, 2004), chapters 1, 6, 13, and 14.

39.   My translation; Alfonso Mendiola, "El giro historiográfico: la observación de observaciones del pasado," *Historia y grafía* 14 (2000): 185.

40.   Andres Lira, "El Estado liberal y las corporaciones en México (1821–1859)," in *Inventando la nación: Iberoamérica. Siglo XIX*, ed. Antonio Annino and François-Xavier Guerra (México: Fondo de Cultura Económica, 2003), 381–85; Antonio Annino, "Pueblos, liberalismo y nación en México," in *Inventando la nación: Iberoamérica, siglo XIX*, ed. Antonio Annino and François-Xavier Guerra (México: Fondo de Cultura Económica, 2003), 399–430.

41.   Michel Foucault, *Discipline and Punish: The Birth of the Prison*, trans. Alan Sheridan (New York: Vintage Books, 1979).

42.   Cervantes, "Mexico's 'Ritual Constant.'"

43.   Elisa Cárdenas Ayala, "Hacia una historia comparada de la secularización en América Latina," in *Ensayos sobre la nueva historia política de América Latina, siglo XIX*, ed. Guillermo Palacios (México: El Colegio de México, 2007): 202.

44.   Cárdenas Ayala, "Hacia una historia comparada"; on laicity and its derivations, see Adrian A. Bantjes, "Mexican Revolutionary Anticlericalism: Concepts and Typologies," *The Americas* 65 no. 4 (April 2009): 469 and passim.

45.   For Europe, see René Rémond, *Religion and Society in Modern Europe*, trans.

Antonia Nevill (Oxford: Blackwell, 1999); Andrew C. Gould, *Origins of Liberal Dominance: State, Church, and Party in Nineteenth-Century Europe* (Ann Arbor: University of Michigan Press, 1999); Kalyvas, *The Rise of Christian Democracy*; for an attempt to link Europe and Latin America, see Jean-Pierre Bastian, ed., *La modernidad religiosa: Europa latina y América Latina en perspectiva comparada* (México: Fondo de Cultura Económica, 2004).

46. Rémond, *Religion and Society*.

47. Fortunato Mallimaci, "Catolicismo y liberalismo: las etapas del enfrentamiento por la definición de la modernidad religiosa en América Latina," in *La modernidad religiosa: Europa latina y América Latina en perspectiva comparada*, ed. Jean-Pierre Bastián (México: Fondo de Cultura Económica, 2004), 19–44.

48. Jean Baubérot, "Los umbrales de la laicización en la Europa latina y la recomposición de lo religioso en la modernidad tardía," in *La modernidad religiosa: Europa latina y América Latina en perspectiva comparada*, ed. Jean-Pierre Bastián (México: Fondo de Cultura Económica, 2004), 94–110.

49. Elisa Cárdenas Ayala has discussed these arguments in Cárdenas, "Hacia una historia," 203–7.

50. Annick Lempérière, "De la república corporativa a la nación moderna," in *Inventando la nación. Iberoamérica, siglo XIX*, ed. Antonio Annino and François-Xavier Guerra (México: Fondo de Cultura Económica, 2007), 316–46.

51. Casanova, *Public Religions*, 20–25.

52. Bastian, ed., *La modernidad religiosa*.

53. Taylor, *Magistrates of the Sacred*, 13–14.

54. Elías J. Palti, "La transformación del liberalismo mexicano en el siglo XIX. Del modelo jurídico de la opinión pública al modelo estratégico de la sociedad civil," in *Actores, espacios y debates en la historia de la esfera pública en la ciudad de México*, ed. Cristina Sacristán and Pablo Piccato (México: Instituto Mora / Universidad Nacional Autónoma de México), 81.

55. Fernando Escalante Gonzalbo, *Ciudadanos imaginarios: memorial de los afanes y desventuras de la virtud y apología del vicio triunfante en la república mexicana: tratado de moral pública* (México: El Colegio de México, 1993), 155.

56. Jürgen Habermas, *The Structural Transformation of the Public Sphere: An Inquiry into a Category of Bourgeois Society*, trans. Thomas Burger with the assistance of Frederick Lawrence (Cambridge, MA: MIT Press, 1989), 5–14; Joan B. Landes refers to an "absolutist public sphere"; see *Women and the Public Sphere in the Age of the French Revolution* (Ithaca: Cornell University Press, 1988).

57. Lempérière, "De la república corporativa," 329–30.

58. This is a conjectural periodization. It draws from Enrique Semo, who has imagined an anticlerical revolution between 1854 and 1867, and Roberto Blancarte, who has emphasized the year 1873 as the indisputable moment of Church–state separation; see Enrique Semo, *Historia mexicana: economía y lucha de clases* (México: Era, 2008), 288; and Roberto Blancarte, "Laicidad y secularización en México," in *La modernidad*

religiosa: Europa latina y América Latina en perspectiva comparada, ed. Jean-Pierre Bastian (México: Fondo de Cultura Económica, 2004), 52, 54, 59.

59. Gyan Prakash, "Subaltern Studies as Post-Colonial Criticism," *American Historical Review* 99, no. 5 (1994): 1485.

60. Jean-Pierre Bastian, *Los disidentes: sociedades protestantes y revolución en México, 1872–1911* (México: Fondo de Cultura Económica / El Colegio de México, 1989), 162.

61. Bastian, *Los disidentes*, 17.

62. Bastian, ed., *La modernidad religiosa*, 9.

63. François-Xavier Guerra made this argument nearly thirty years ago; see *México: del Antiguo Régimen a la Revolución*, trans. Sergio Fernández Bravo, 2 vols. (México: Fondo de Cultura Económica, 1988), especially volume 1.

64. Twentieth-century Mexico was often characterized by communitarian politics, from the revolutionary era and the Cristero Rebellion, to the emergence of the 1994 Zapatista rebellion in Chiapas. If anything, the past twenty years have seen a boom in antiliberal, communitarian politics, as many rural and indigenous populations have demanded recognition of ancestral territories and the right to govern according to local tradition. For an apt critique of the "traditional," see Dipesh Chakrabarty, *Provincializing Europe: Postcolonial Thought and Historical Difference* (Princeton: Princeton University Press, 2000), 11–16.

65. See, for example, Chakrabarty, *Provincializing Europe*, 27–46.

66. Here my thinking is influenced by Saurabh Dube. See his trilogy, *Sujetos subalternos* (México, El Colegio de México, 2001); *Genealogías del presente* (México, El Colegio de México, 2003); and *Historias esparcidas* (México, El Colegio de México, 2007).

67. I am not suggesting historians abandon such terms, but that we must always interrogate our own presuppositions regarding what they do and do not mean and explain if we are to deploy them.

68. Charles Taylor, *A Secular Age* (Cambridge, MA: Belknap Harvard, 2007), 1–22, 423–26, 530–35.

69. Casanova, *Public Religions*, 19–39.

70. Taylor, *A Secular Age*.

71. Casanova, *Public Religions*, 35–39.

72. Jean-Marie Mayeur and Madeleine Rebérioux, *The Third Republic from Its Origins to the Great War, 1871–1914*, trans. J. R. Foster (Cambridge: Cambridge University Press, 1987), 227–40.

73. Ceballos Ramírez, *El catolicismo social*.

74. Edward Wright-Rios, *Revolutions in Mexican Catholicism: Reform and Revelation in Oaxaca, 1887–1934* (Durham, NC: Duke University Press, 2009); Edward Wright-Rios, "Envisioning Mexico's Catholic Resurgence: The Virgin of Solitude and the Talking Christ of Tlacoxcalco, 1908–1924," *Past and Present* 195 (2007): 197–239; José Alberto Moreno Chávez, *Devociones políticas: cultura política y politización en la Arquidiócesis de México, 1880–1920* (México: El Colegio de México, 2013).

75. J. Samuel Valenzuela and Erika Maza Valenzuela, "The Politics of Religion in a Catholic Country: Republican Democracy, *Cristianismo Social* and the Conservative Party in Chile, 1850–1925," in *The Politics of Religion in an Age of Revival*, ed. Austen Ivereig (London: ILAS, 2000), 220; Sol Serrano, ¿*Qué hacer con dios en la república? Política y secularización en Chile, 1845–1885* (México: Fondo de Cultura Económica, 2008); Sol Serrano, "La estrategia conservadora y la consolidación del orden liberal en Chile, 1860–1890," in *Constitucionalismo y orden liberal. América Latina, 1850—1920*, ed. Marcello Carmagnani (Nova americana—otto editore, 1988), 126.

76. Roberto Di Stefano, *El púlpito y la plaza: clero, sociedad y política de la monarquía católica a la república rosista* (Buenos Aires: Siglo Veintiuno Editores Argentina, 2004), 153–237; Roberto Di Stefano and Loris Zanatta, *Historia de la Iglesia argentina: desde la Conquista hasta fines del siglo XX* (Buenos Aires: Mondadori, 2000).

77. Roberto Di Stefano, "En torno a la Iglesia colonial y del temprano siglo XIX. El caso del Río de la Plata," *Takwá* 8 (2005): 49–65.

78. Stephen J. C. Andes, *The Vatican & Catholic Activism in Mexico & Chile: The Politics of Transnational Catholicism, 1920–1940* (Oxford: Oxford University Press, 2014).

79. Karl Schmitt, "Church and State in Mexico: A Corporatist Relationship," *The Americas* 40, no. 3 (1984): 349–76.

80. Robert J. Knowlton, *Church Property and the Mexican Reform, 1856–1910* (DeKalb: Northern Illinois Press, 1976).

81. Mariano Cuevas, SJ, *Historia de la Iglesia en México*, vol. 5 (México: Editorial Porrúa, S. A., 1928), 283–336.

82. Blancarte, "Laicidad y secularización."

83. The concept of decline explains a circumstance, by definition, beyond state policy; it explains the phenomenon of secularization in society as manifested through the loss of the faithful, the falling numbers of believers in society; Casanova, *Public Religions*, 25–35. More recently, there is now evidence of religious decline in Ireland, even prior to the 2009 allegations of mass rape and beatings in the most recent scandal involving Church abuse of schoolchildren. On decline, see Noel Barber, SJ, "Religion in Ireland: Its State and Prospects," in *Christianity in Ireland: Revisiting the Story*, ed. Brendan Bradshaw and Dáire Keogh (Dublin: Columba Press, 2002), 287–97. On the allegations, see Henry McDonald, "Endemic rape and abuse of Irish children in Catholic care, inquiry finds," *The Guardian*, May 20, 2009.

84. Wright-Rios, *Revolutions in Mexican Catholicism*, does this for the Oaxaca Archdiocese. Along the way, it provides a much-needed rethinking of the revolution as revolutionary Mexico—a historical moment rather than a discrete event.

85. Bantjes, "Mexican Revolutionary Anticlericalism," 476–79.

86. Reprinted in Plutarco Elías Calles, *Pensamiento político y social. Antología (1913–1936)* (México: Instituto de Estudios Históricos de la Revolución Mexicana/ Fideicomiso Archivos Plutarco Elías Calles y Fernando Torreblanca/Fondo de Cultura Económica, 1988), 190–95.

87. This idea inspired the important collection of essays edited by Gil Joseph and Daniel Nugent. Here I am pushing it in a somewhat different direction. See Joseph and Nugent, *Everyday Forms.*

88. Jean Meyer, *La cristiada*, trans. Aurelio Garzón del Camino, 3 vols. (México: Siglo XXI, 1973–74); Jean Meyer, *The Cristero Rebellion: The Mexican People between Church and State, 1926–1929*, trans. Richard Southern (Cambridge: Cambridge University Press, 1976); Ceballos Ramírez, *El Catolicismo Social.*

89. My views on how this system of political representation was constructed are influenced by Mary Kay Vaughan, *Cultural Politics in Revolution: Teachers, Peasants, and Schools in México, 1930–1940* (Tucson: University of Arizona Press, 1997).

90. Anacleto González Flores, *El plebiscito de los mártires*, 50th anniversary edition (Morelia: Impresos FIT, 1980), 272.

91. Two important studies treat these years from the state of Jalisco. Laura O'Dogherty examines the rise and fall of the National Catholic Party (PCN), and Elisa Cárdenas Ayala considers the broader political sphere—including the PCN—in a study that makes sense of the fall of the old regime and the making of revolutionary Jalisco. See Laura O'Dogherty Madrazo, *De urnas y sotanas: El Partido Nacional Católico en Jalisco* (México: Regiones/CONACULTA, 2001); and Elisa Cárdenas Ayala, *El derrumbe: Jalisco, microcosmos de la revolución Mexicana* (México: Tusquets, 2010).

92. To the extent that a politics of Christian Democracy developed, it happened along very different lines. I recognize the influence of Christian Democrats like Efraín González Luna in the 1939 founding of the National Action Party. Nevertheless, it is noteworthy that Mexican Christian Democrats did not found such a party openly, as their colleagues in many parts of continental Europe had done. This was surely a legacy of the Mexican Revolution. On National Action, see Soledad Loaeza's pioneering work, *El Partido Acción Nacional: la larga marcha, 1939–1994* (México: Fondo de Cultura Económica, 1999); on Christian Democratic ideology, see Jorge Alonso, *Miradas sobre la personalidad política de Efraín González Luna* (Guadalajara: Universidad de Guadalajara/CUCSH, 2003).

93. Di Stefano, *El púlpito.*

94. This volume features new research on religion in contemporary Mexican history by two generations of writers, including Alan Knight, Fernando Cervantes, Jean-Pierre Bastian, Keith Brewster, Claire Brewster, Adrian A. Bantjes, Robert Curley, Matthew Butler, Kristina A. Boylan, Jean Meyer, Ben Fallaw, Massimo De Giuseppe, Edward Wright-Rios, and Benjamin Smith. See Matthew Butler, ed., *Faith and Impiety in Revolutionary Mexico* (New York: Palgrave MacMillan, 2007).

95. *The Americas, Special Issue: Personal Enemies of God: Anticlericals and Anticlericalism in Revolutionary Mexico, 1915–1940* 65, no. 4 (2009); The contributing authors are Adrian Bantjes, Ben Fallaw, Robert Curley, Matthew Butler, Benjamin Smith, and Roberto Blancarte.

96. Robert Curley, "Transnational Subaltern Voices: Sexual Violence, Anticlericalism, and the Mexican Revolution," in *Local Church, Global Church: Catholic Activism*

in Latin America from Rerum Novarum *to Vatican II*, ed. Stephen J. C. Andes and Julia G. Young (Washington, DC: The Catholic University of America Press, 2016); Yolanda Padilla Rangel, *Los desterrados: Exiliados católicos de la Revolución Mexicana en Texas, 1914–1919* (Aguascalientes: Universidad Autónoma de Aguascalientes, 2009).

97. Eduardo J. Correa, *El Partido Católico Nacional y sus directores. Explicación de su fracaso y deslinde de responsabilidades* (México: Fondo de Cultura Económica, 1991); José Saldaña, a Monterrey *cronista*, journalist and politician, attributed this to one of Villareal's officers. In any case, it was committed in July 1914, when Villareal had become military governor of the state. One of his first acts in this office was to close the city's churches. I thank César Morado Macías at Universidad Autónoma de Nuevo León for his help on this.

98. Luis González, "La Revolución Mexicana desde el punto de vista de los revolucionados," *Historias* 8–9 (1985): 5–13.

99. The classic work on the rebellion is Meyer, *La cristiada*. However, there has been excellent revisionist work published recently including Matthew Butler, *Popular Piety and Political Identity in Mexico's Cristero Rebellion: Michoacán, 1927–1929* (Oxford: The British Academy/Oxford University Press, 2004); Julia Preciado Zamora, *Por las faldas del volcán de Colima: Cristeros, agraristas y pacíficos*, (México: Centro de Investigaciones y Estudios Superiores en Antropología Social/Archivo Histórico del Municipio de Colima, 2007); and Julia Preciado Zamora and Servando Ortoll, eds., *Los mochos contra los guachos: Once ensayos cristeros* (Morelia: Editorial Jitanjáfora, 2009).

100. Robert Curley, "Avanza el desierto: Espacio público y suicido político en el imaginario cristero," in *Los mochos contra los guachos*, eds. Julia Preciado Zamora and Servando Ortoll (Morelia: Editorial Jitanjáfora, 2009), 45–59.

101. González Flores, *El plebiscito*, 115–22.

102. Ivan Strenski constructs an interpretive architecture, culled from French history, to unpack the meanings of Catholic sacrifice. What strikes the reader, leaving aside the French periodization (Reformation; Rococo; Revolution; Restoration), is how often the points of reference were common to Mexican Catholic history, too. Tridentine theology, the devotion to the Sacred Heart, the writings of Joseph de Maistre, the intransigence of the Syllabus: all were familiar to Anacleto González Flores; Strenski, *Contesting Sacrifice*, chapter 2.

103. Paul Vanderwood has been an inspiration for me in my evolving view of Catholic politics; see *The Power of God Against the Guns of Government: Religious Upheaval in Mexico at the Turn of the Nineteenth Century* (Stanford: Stanford University Press, 1998).

Chapter 2

1. Early twentieth-century Catholic intellectuals used the term "Catholic sociology." My use simply reflects their language.

2. Manuel Ceballos Ramírez, *El catolicismo social: un tercero en discordia*. Rerum

Novarum, *la ʾcuestión social" y la movilización de los católicos mexicanos (1891–1911)* (México: El Colegio de México, 1991), 175–251; Jorge Adame Goddard, *El pensamiento político y social de los católicos mexicanos, 1867–1914* (México: UNAM, 1981), 197–204.

3. Jean Meyer, "El catolicismo social en México hasta 1913," *Colección "Diálogo y Autocrítica"* 1 (México: IMDOSOC, 1985).

4. Joan W. Scott, *Gender and the Politics of History* (New York: Columbia University Press, 1988), 59.

5. The construction of Catholic identities was equally mediated by questions of ethnicity, although such considerations were mostly absent at the Third Catholic Congress. However, the proceedings of the Fourth Catholic Congress, held in Oaxaca in 1909, put the ethnic question in the fore; see *Cuarto Congreso Católico Nacional Mexicano* (Oaxaca: Tip. de la Casa de Cuna, 1913).

6. There is a vast historiography on these topics. An excellent general survey is Alan Knight, *The Mexican Revolution*, 2 vols. (Cambridge: Cambridge University Press, 1986), vol. 1, chap. 2.

7. *La Libertad*, October 27, 1906, 2.

8. As with the term *Catholic sociology*, these categories were set and named by the organizers. I simply adopt them as descriptive terms.

9. They were published as *Congreso tercero católico nacional y primero eucarístico*, 2 vols. (Guadalajara: Imprenta de El Regional, 1908), vol. 2; (henceforth, *3CCN*).

10. The distinction between liberal and social Catholics stretches back to the early nineteenth century, and my understanding relies on the work of Manuel Ceballos Ramírez. Liberal Catholics took a conciliatory view of the social and political changes of the times, including enlightenment thought, as well as liberalism in the economy, politics, and society. Social Catholics, like traditionalists and Democrats, were characterized as intransigents. There were differences between these three factions, but they generally agreed on a basic program of reconquest. They sought to restore the Church to its former importance as a social institution, reject liberal reform, and held that Christianity and modernity were incompatible. Their differences were reflected in the following positions: traditionalists tended to be monarchists; social Catholics accepted republicanism, and sought social change actively through mutualist societies, worker circles, the press, schools, sports, and civic associations; Democrats were convinced that political change was necessary, sought popular mobilization, and worked to develop confessional labor unions. All of these groups, it should be added, rejected the program of class struggle (Ceballos Ramírez, *El catolicismo social*, 22–26).

11. In this hypothesis, the presence of religious themes is attributed to liberal Catholics, and counterbalances the themes of the social Catholics (Ceballos Ramírez, *El catolicismo social*, 202–3).

12. *La Libertad*, October 19, 1906, 2.

13. A recent study of Oaxacan Catholics does an excellent job of placing Archbishop Gillow historically and geographically; see Edward Wright-Rios, *Revolutions*

in Mexican Catholicism: Reform and Revelation in Oaxaca, 1887–1934 (Durham, NC: Duke University Press, 2009).

14. Ceballos Ramírez, *El catolicismo social*, 48–49, 202–16.

15. Ceballos Ramírez, *El catolicismo social*, 202, 205.

16. Terrazas was editor of *La Revista Católica*, a newspaper of the Diocese of Chihuahua from 1896, according to François-Xavier Guerra. According to Margarita Terrazas Perches, her father continued managing the *Revista Católica* until 1910. At the same time he had a cultural magazine, *La Lira Chihuahuense*. Terrazas acquired *El Correo de Chihuahua*, the newspaper for which he is best known, in January 1899. The *Correo* was published, despite closures and occasional imprisonment, until 1935. In 1913 he became the civilian administrator of Francisco Villa's army. See François-Xavier Guerra, *México: del Antiguo Régimen a la Revolución*, trans. Sergio Fernández Bravo, 2 vols. (México: Fondo de Cultura Económica, 1988), vol. 2, 345–457; Silvestre Terrazas, *El verdadero Pancho Villa* (México: Ediciones Era, 1985), 218; Friedrich Katz, "Pancho Villa, los movimientos campesinos y la reforma agraria en el norte de México," in *Caudillos y campesinos en la revolución mexicana*, ed. David Brading (México: Ediciones Era, 1985), 86–105.

17. *3CCN*, vol. 2, 705.

18. Fondo Palomar y Vizcarra, box 38, folder 263, 134–35; (henceforth, citations will appear separated by diagonals, for example, FPyV, 38/263/134–35).

19. FPyV, 40/273/2101, 2111, 2120, and 2130, José María Soto to Miguel Palomar y Vizcarra, Morelia, March 20, April 12, May 12, and June 16, 1909.

20. FPyV, 40/273/2072, 2078, and 2083, J. Refugio Galindo to Palomar y Vizcarra, Tortugas-Temascalillos, June 9, September 9, and December 6, 1907.

21. FPyV, 40/285/2284–87, Arnulfo Castro to Palomar y Vizcarra, Hastings, Great Britain, June 21, 1911.

22. *3CCN*, vol. 2, 361–648; 689–708.

23. Adame Goddard, *El pensamiento político*, 49.

24. This was in agreement with contemporary Vatican writing, in which the grounds for family relationships were sought in natural law and sacred history. In the same sense, society is organized on the model of the family, which predates organized society. Needless to say, there is a reified vision of *family* in play here. See *Rerum Novarum*, § 19–20, New Advent, accessed December 18, 2015, http://www.newadvent.org/library/docs_le13rn.htm.

25. The author refers to the "edificio social," or social structure, which was a common equivalent for the "cuerpo social," or social body. Both share the analogy of reciprocity, in which each part plays a particular role in the function of the whole (Perfecto Méndez Padilla, "La santidad del Matrimonio y del hogar mediante el Sacramento Eucarístico," in *3CCN*, vol. 2, 411).

26. These ideas concerning the relations of everyday life reflect Paul's Epistle to the Ephesians, 5–6. Méndez Padilla, "La santidad," in *3CCN*, vol. 2, 414.

27. Ireneo Quintero, "La santidad del Matrimonio y del hogar mediante el Sacramento Eucarístico," in *3CCN*, vol. 2, 382.

28. This reification of *woman*, though at least as old as the scripture from which Méndez Padilla quoted, probably had more recent roots in European Enlightenment thought; for eighteenth- and nineteenth-century examples, see Denise Riley, *"Am I That Name?": Feminism and the Category of "Women" in History* (Minneapolis: University of Minnesota Press, 1988), 18–43; and Scott, *Gender and the Politics*, 139–140. See also Carol Pateman, *The Sexual Contract* (Stanford: Stanford University Press, 1988), 1–18.

29. Quintero, "La santidad," in *3CCN*, vol. 2, 378.

30. Agustín G. Navarro, "La dignidad de la mujer y la divina Eucaristía," in *3CCN*, vol. 2, 361–62; Michel Foucault, *The History of Sexuality, Volume 1: An Introduction*, trans. Robert Hurley (New York: Vintage Books, 1980), 73, 113–14, 158–59.

31. Genesis, 3:19; Leo XIII quotes this in *Rerum Novarum* to indicate the character of work; the force a worker expends in exchange for assuring the basic necessities for reproduction of life; *Rerum Novarum*, § 62, New Advent, accessed December 18, 2015, http://www.newadvent.org/library/docs_le13rn.htm.

32. I point out the interpretation because in a rural economy work did not necessarily mean a man's absence, and much small-scale farming employed the reciprocal duties of men and women, or more to the point, an extended family. The interpretation at hand, in other words, seems more proper to urban circumstances, and even in a city like Guadalajara, most men and women did not work in factories, but at artisan trades and petty commerce, often located in the home.

33. Navarro, "*La dignidad*," in *3CCN*, vol. 2, 368–69.

34. Navarro, "*La dignidad*," in *3CCN*, vol. 2, 372.

35. Ephesians 5; Quintero, "*La santidad*," in *3CCN*, vol. 2, 374.

36. Quintero, "*La santidad*," in *3CCN*, vol. 2, 382.

37. *Rerum Novarum*, § 48, New Advent, accessed December 18, 2015, http://www.newadvent.org/library/docs_le13rn.htm.

38. *Rerum Novarum*, § 28, New Advent, accessed December 18, 2015, http://www.newadvent.org/library/docs_le13rn.htm.

39. Antonio Quagliani, "Catolicismo social," in *Diccionario de Política*, ed. Norberto Bobbio et al. (México: Siglo XXI, 1984), 228–32.

40. Luciano Achiaga, "Grandes bienes que reportan los caballeros cristianos que se inscriben y cumplen su deber en las Asociaciones Eucarísticas," in *3CCN*, vol. 2, 466.

41. For a similar argument developed in the French case, see William H. Sewell Jr., *Work and Revolution in France: The Language of Labor from the Old Regime to 1848* (New York: Cambridge University Press, 1980); for Mexico, see François-Xavier Guerra's definition of the collective actor; Guerra, *México: del Antiguo Régimen*, vol. 1, 126–81.

42. Therein lies the subtitle of Manuel Ceballos Ramírez's book. One way to translate this is "tie-breaker." However, in use, the tercero en discordia refers to a judge—or perhaps a teacher—who offers a third way out of a two-sided conflict.

43. *El Tiempo*, May 27, 1891; quoted in Ceballos Ramírez, *El catolicismo social*, 36.

44. In the original text Macías referred to "*hombres de letras,*" or "literate men." I have translated "men of culture" in the sense argued by William Rowe and Vivian Schelling. The sharp contrast between "high" and "popular" culture was perhaps not so evident in early twentieth-century thinking, although it certainly was implicit. Not until after the Mexican Revolution were the terms developed in the sense that they are generally understood today. Still, the sort of example cited here corresponds to what might today be termed "high culture." See Rowe and Schelling, *Memory and Modernity: Popular Culture in Latin America* (London: Verso, 1991), 197.

45. Luis Macías, "Métodos económicos y prácticos para establecer en las parroquias las Sociedades de Obreros," in *3CCN*, vol. 2, 500–504.

46. Three large bound volumes (from the period) comprise the file of correspondence, session records, and press of the First National Catholic Congress, held in 1903, at Puebla. They are held at the Secretariado Social Mexicano library in Mexico City. For information pertaining to the workers circles in Puebla, see the record of the fifth session and related documents, February 25, 1903, 178.

47. Macías, "Métodos económicos," in *3CCN*, vol. 2, 500, 514; *Rerum Novarum*, § 76, New Advent, accessed December 18, 2015, http://www.newadvent.org/library/docs_le13rn.htm.

48. Macías, "Métodos económicos," in *3CCN*, vol. 2, 506.

49. Manuel F. Chávez, "La expansión del capital mediante la caridad y el trabajo en favor de los pobres," in *3CCN*, vol. 2, 522.

50. Manuel F. Chávez, "La expansion del capital," in *3CCN*, vol. 2, 521.

51. Today Palomar y Vizcarra is remembered as a pioneer of rural credit institutions in Mexico. In addition to his participation in Puebla, see Miguel Palomar y Vizcarra, *Las Cajas Raiffeisen* (Guadalajara: El Regional, 1907); and two serialized articles published in series by *Restauración Social*, between November 1910 and November 1911, numbers 11, 14, 16, 18, 19, 20, 21, 23, and his conference presented to delegates of the Zapopan Social Agrarian Seminar, in January 1921, FPyV, 38/263/217–52, pp. 217–52. Recent discussions include Ceballos Ramírez, *El catolicismo social*, 382–392; Francisco Barbosa Guzmán, *La caja rural católica de préstamos y ahorros en Jalisco (1910–1914 y 1920–1924)* (Mexico: IMDOSOC, 1996); Enrique Lira Soria, *Biografía de Miguel Palomar y Vizcarra, Intelectual Cristero (1880–1968)* (bachelor's thesis, UNAM, 1989); and Tania Hernández Vicencio, "Revolución y Constitución: Pensamiento y acción política de Miguel Palomar y Vizcarra," *Historia y Grafía* 42 (2014): 159–92. See also below, chapter 4.

52. Chávez, "La expansión del capital," in *3CCN*, vol. 2, 525.

53. *Rerum Novarum*, § 63, New Advent, accessed December 18, 2015, http://www.newadvent.org/library/docs_le13rn.htm.

54. Faustino Rosales, "Obligación de los patrones de atender física y moralmente a las necesidades de los trabajadores," in *3CCN*, vol. 2, 545–46.

55. Nicolás Leaño, "Juicio del anterior trabajo," in *3CCN*, vol. 2, 551.

56. Rosales, "Obligación de los patrones," in *3CCN*, vol. 2, 547. Regarding this, Rosales asserts that "family" refers to an "ordinary family," that is, of three children.

57. Positions varied from free market advocates to those who favored government intervention to assure the family wage. For early twentieth-century Europe, the different stances are summarized in Luis Irurzun Muru, *El Catolicismo Social y el Socialismo al Desnudo. O los Problemas de Carne y Hueso* (Barcelona: La Hormiga de Oro, 1919), 115–28. See also chapter 2.

58. Their view that women should not work did not exist in a vacuum. In fact, the family wage was based on the idea that women *and* children should not work, and this was the position of Catholics and liberals alike. On this and other similarities between the Catholic labor proposals and those written into the 1917 constitution, see Jorge Adame Goddard, "Influjo de la doctrina social católica en el artículo 123 constitucional," *Colección "Diálogo y Autocrítica"* 8 (México: IMDOSOC, 1994).

59. FPyV, 40/273/2111, 2120 and 2130, Soto to Palomar y Vizcarra, Morelia, April 12, May 12, and June 16, 1909.

60. *Restauración Social* 2 and 3, nos. 1–19.

61. Chávez, "La expansión del capital," in *3CCN*, vol. 2, 526.

62. Chávez, "La expansión del capital," in *3CCN*, vol. 2, 523–25.

63. Rosales, "Obligación," in *3CCN*, vol. 2, 547.

64. Chávez, "La expansión del capital," in *3CCN*, vol. 2, 523–25; On commutative and distributive justice, see Thomas Aquinas, *The Summa Theologica of St. Thomas Aquinas*, II-II, Q61, 2nd and rev. ed., literally translated by Fathers of the English Dominican Province (1920).

65. Chávez, "La expansión del capital," in *3CCN*, vol. 2, 523–25.

66. Ceballos Ramírez, *El catolicismo social*, 210–14, narrates this event.

67. Rosales, "Obligación," in *3CCN*, vol. 2, 547; Leaño, *"Juicio,"* in *3CCN*, vol. 2, 551.

68. Leaño, "Juicio," in *3CCN*, vol. 2, 553.

69. Leaño, "Juicio," in *3CCN*, vol. 2, 553.

70. FPyV, 40/273/2164–65, memorandum issued by Miguel Palomar y Vizcarra, September 12, 1909. The other members were José Tomás Figueroa, Félix Araiza, Gilberto Ramos, and Luis B. de la Mora; on the Operarios Guadalupanos, see chapter 4.

71. Thanks to Grady Miller for assistance in the translation. Needless to say, the original text, in Spanish, is ultimately more eloquent. My analysis is based on the original text, not the translation. The original text reads:

> Es la primera hora de la mañana, esa hora en que alborozada despierta la vida enmedio de una incomparable actividad, que se traduce en trinos y gorgeos, en rumores vagos y murmullos cristalinos, en brisas juguetonas y aromas deliciosos. La maga de los crepúsculos ha volcado en la región oriental del cielo todas las ánforas de sus variados y brillantes colores, y ha encendido con ardiente llama los girones de nube, que flotan sobre las lejanas crestas de los montes azules, como si quisiera preparar docel espléndido y suntuoso arco de triunfo al Rey de la luz, que se avecina.
>
> A esa hora tan fresca y tan bella sale del pueblecillo X. . . . un ejército singular. Son doscientos ginetes, que marchan de dos en fondo, formando compañías

de diez en diez bajo la dirección y presidencia de un cabo. A la vanguardia marcha un Sacerdote, radiante de júbilo, no sin marcial continente; y a la izquierda del tonsurado Jefe, avanza el abanderado que lleva entre sus callosas manos de labrador de la tierra, á guiza de militar enseña, una imagen de la Santísima Virgen María, Refugio de Pecadores. . . .

¿Qué significa ese tan desusado ejército? Si queréis saberlo, servíos acompañar a los noveles soldados por esos campos amenos y apacibles, de girasoles rojos emperlados de rocío y de sencillas flores de Santa María, de penetrante y agradable perfume. No tengáis miedo, que no perturbarán la paz hombres armados de rosarios y combatientes cuyo grito de guerra son las alabanzas de la Madre de Dios, entonadas con voz robusta y sonora.

Miradlos: ya llegan a la cabecera de la parroquia y entran por las modestas calles, guardando el más profundo silencio de sus labios, más notable por el ruido que producen los cascos de los corceles, al pisar en los burdos empedrados.

Al llegar al templo parroquial, todos, a una señal del General en jefe, ó sea, del Párroco, echan pie á tierra, y dejando los caballos al cuidado de sus compañeros, avanza cada compañía, de rodillas, por el atrio primeramente, y después por el pavimento sagrado de la casa de Dios, hasta el altar mayor, luciente como una ascua, por la multitud de cirios encendidos y coronado graciosamente por la amada Refugiana.

Junto al altar espera ya el Párroco, revestido con el alba sobrepelliz carrujada y con la estola de flecos de oro. El continente del sacerdote es grave y solemne, como que ha de asistir en el nombre mismo de Dios, á un acto serio y trascendental. Llega por fin la primera compañía, guiada por su cabo, al pie del altar santo, y allí, aquellos hombres del campo, avezados á toda clase de peligros, sin miedo en el corazón, ni respeto al enemigo, humillan su cerviz, y, delante del cielo y de la tierra, escoltados por invisible cohorte de ángeles, que contemplan regocijados aquel sublime cuadro, en la presencia adorable de Dios, cuyo ministro lo representa visiblemente, prometen abstenerse por dos o tres años, del alcohol que envenena el cuerpo y envilece el alma, y lo prometen con el fin de glorificar á la Santísima Virgen María, su tierna Madre, honrar el nombre de cristianos, dar buen ejemplo á sus familiares y cooperar á la santa reforma de las costumbres sociales. Todas las compañías hacen sucesivamente lo mismo.

Si quisiérais permanecer en el templo algunas horas más, veríais á esos aldeanos volver, después de haber dejado sus caballos en la casa de algún vecino o en alguna de las posadas del pueblo, para confesar sus pecados y confirmar con una fervorosa comunión sus formales promesas de hombres que no saben faltar á su palabra.

72. Miguel M. de la Mora, O.G., "El estudio de Sociología en los Seminarios," conference delivered at the Second Mexican Social Catholic Seminar, October 22, 1910; *Restauración Social* 3, no. 16 (1911): 176–87, and 3, no.17 (1911): 225–32.

73. Etienne Gilson, *The Christian Philosophy of St. Thomas Aquinas* (Notre Dame: University of Notre Dame Press, 1994) 7–15.

74. James C. Livingston, *Modern Christian Thought: From the Enlightenment to Vatican II* (New York: Macmillan, 1971), 388–91.

75. The pastor's moral authority and the strengthening of the parish as a social institution are aims outlined in the Plenary Council of Latin America (1899), held in Rome. See Laura O'Dogherty, "El concilio plenario latinoamericano," paper presented at the XVII Coloquio de Antropología e Historia Regionales: La Iglesia Católica en México (Zamora: El Colegio de Michoacán, 1995).

76. For a colonial example see William B. Taylor, *Magistrates of the Sacred: Priests and Parishioners in Eighteenth-Century Mexico* (Stanford, CA: Stanford University Press, 1996), 47–73.

77. *Memoria del Segundo Congreso Católico de México y Primero Mariano* (Morelia: Talleres Tipográficos de Agustín Martínez Mier, 1905), 369.

78. *Memoria del Segundo Congreso Católico*, 371.

Chapter 3

1. Until recently, the historiography was based on these excellent contributions: Francisco Banegas Galván, *El por qué del Partido Católico Nacional* (México: Jus, 1960); Jean Meyer, "El catolicismo social en México hasta 1913," *Colección "Diálogo y Autocrítica"* 1 (México: IMDOSOC, 1985); Manuel Ceballos Ramírez, *El catolicismo social: un tercero en discordia. Rerum Novarum, la "cuestión social" y la movilización de los católicos mexicanos (1891–1911)* (México: El Colegio de México, 1991).

2. Robert Curley, "Los laicos, la Democracia Cristiana y la revolución mexicana (1911–1926)," *Signos Históricos* 7 (2002): 149–70.

3. Michael Fogarty, *Christian Democracy in Western Europe, 1820–1953*, 2nd ed. (London: Routledge & Kegan Paul, 1966).

4. Fogarty, *Christian Democracy*, 5.

5. Fogarty, *Christian Democracy*, 7.

6. Ceballos seems not to have written with Fogarty in mind and does not include the book in his bibliography; for reference to a "Catholic geopolitical axis," see Ceballos Ramírez, *El catolicismo social*, 16 and *passim*.

7. Stathis N. Kalyvas, *The Rise of Christian Democracy in Europe* (Ithaca: Cornell University Press, 1996).

8. Kalyvas, *The Rise of Christian Democracy*, 2.

9. Kalyvas, *The Rise of Christian Democracy*, 1–2.

10. Talal Asad, *Genealogies of Religion: Discipline and Reasons of Power in Christianity and Islam* (Baltimore: The Johns Hopkins Press, 1993), 27–54.

11. Bernardo Reyes, one of President Díaz's closest confidants, was a powerful general, former governor of the state of Nuevo León, and war secretary from 1900 to 1904, and was responsible for the modernization of the Mexican army.

12. Ceballos Ramírez, *El catolicismo social*, 322, 326.

13. Banegas Galván, *El por qué*, 31–32; Curley, "Los laicos," 151–52.

14. Roger Aubert, *Catholic Social Teaching: An Historical Perspective* (Milwaukee, WI: Marquette University Press, 2003), 121–23.

15. Leo XIII, *Graves de Communi Re*, § 7, The Holy See, accessed December 18, 2016, http://w2.vatican.va/content/leo-xiii/en/encyclicals/documents/hf_1 -xiii_ enc_18011901_graves-de-communi-re.html.

16. Henry Edward Manning's life pretty well spanned the nineteenth century. He was a close ally of Pope Leo XIII, and his views on Catholic social justice were influential in the writing of Pope Leo's most famous encyclical, *Rerum Novarum*. Manning was the head of the Catholic Church in England, and a central figure in the settling of the 1889 London dock strike. He died in 1892.

17. Óscar Alzaga, *La primera democracia cristiana en España* (Barcelona: Editorial Ariel, 1973), 21–22.

18. The encyclical also treats the larger issue of beneficence, or philanthropy, and has quite a bit to say regarding the charity of the well-to-do, which is seen as part of the same order of things. The underlying position is that society ought to be understood in corporatist terms, as is pointed out by Alzaga. A thread of analysis not taken in this article, but all the same important, is how and in what ways this sort of thinking would eventually predispose political Catholics in many countries to support fascist regimes. See Alzaga, *La primera*, 23. This connection is explicitly made by franquista intellectuals Miguel Sancho Izquierdo, Leonardo Prieto Castro, and Antonio Muñoz Casayús of the Universidad de Zaragoza in 1937. Their treatise on corporatism looks into the models offered by Italian, Portuguese, and German varieties, and links the idea directly to Pope Leo XIII. See Miguel Sancho Izquierdo, Leonardo Prieto Castro y Antonio Muñoz Casayús, *Corporatismo: Los movimientos nacionales contemporáneous. Causas y realizaciones* (Zaragoza: Editorial Imperio, 1937), 14–15, 87–88.

19. Leo XIII, *Graves de Communi Re*, § 7.

20. Leo XIII, *Graves de Communi*, § 4.

21. This is an important distinction that relies on the basic understanding that papal encyclicals could not promote a particular kind of government. Christian democracy, thus, would have to take on local expressions contingent upon each particular society or nation-state.

22. See, for examples, three letters written by Francisco Traslosheros to Miguel Palomar y Vizcarra, on March 24 and 26, and April 29, 1908; Fondo Palomar y Vizcarra, box 38, folder 263, documents 144–46, 147–49, and 155–60 (henceforth, citations will appear separated by diagonals, for example, FPyV 38/263/144–46, 147–49, and 155–60).

23. FPyV 40/273/2149–50, Operarios Guadalupanos, monthly newsletter, August 8, 1909.

24. Antonio Rius Facius, *De Don Porfirio a Plutarco, Historia de la ACJM* (México:

Jus, 1958), 8; and Antonio Rius Facius, *Bernardo Bergoend, SJ: guía y maestro de la juventud mexicana* (México: Editorial Tradición, 1972), 20.

25. Kalyvas, *The Rise of Christian Democracy*, 1–20.

26. Mariano Cuevas, SJ, *Historia de la Iglesia en México*, vol. 5 (México: Editorial Porrúa, S. A., 1928); On Catholic publishing, see Manuel Ceballos Ramírez, *Historia de Rerum Novarum en México (1867–1931)* (México: IMDOSOC, 2004), 157–214.

27. The best analysis of the cycle of conferences is Ceballos Ramírez, *El catolicismo social*, chapter 5.

28. FPyV, 40/273/2154–55, Traslosheros to Palomar y Vizcarra, Mexico City, August 27, 1909.

29. Ceballos Ramírez, *El catolicismo social*, 312–41.

30. The founding members were: Dr. J. Refugio Galindo (Tulancingo), Antonio de P. Moreno (Villa de Guadalupe), Father José María Soto (Morelia), Francisco Villalón (Morelia), Silvestre Terrazas (Chihuahua), and Miguel Díaz Infante (León). Palomar y Vizcarra would likely have been among this group had he attended the Oaxaca congress, and in fact, he was the first person formally invited to join the others. FPyV, 40/273/2086, 2094, and 2095, Galindo to Palomar y Vizcarra, Tortugas-Tamascalillos, January and February, 1909.

31. Manuel Ceballos Ramírez, "Los Operarios Guadalupanos: intelectuales del catolicismo social mexicano, 1909–1914," in *Las instituciones*, ed. Manuel Ceballos Ramírez, vol. 2 of *Catolicismo social en México*, (México: IMDOSOC / AIH, 2005), 97.

32. Manuel González Ramírez, *Las ideas—La violencia*. Vol. 1, 31–33, of *La revolución social de México*. México: Fondo de Cultura Economica, 1960.

33. FPyV, 38/263/144–49, Traslosheros to Palomar y Vizcarra, Pacho, March 24, 1908.

34. As in John Womack's interpretation of *sufragio efectivo, no reelección*, "a real vote and no boss rule." See John Womack Jr., *Zapata and the Mexican Revolution* (New York: Vintage Books, 1970), 55.

35. Silvio Zavala, *Apuntes de historia nacional, 1808–1974* (México: El Colegio Nacional—Fondo de Cultura Económica, 1999), 112.

36. At the time of Traslosheros's letter on the Creelman interview, March 1908, Madero was busy writing *La sucesión presidencial en 1910*. It would be out by the end of the year.

37. FPyV, 40/284/2197, Operarios Guadalupanos, monthly newsletter, June 12, 1910.

38. It is unclear who individually or collectively wrote the analysis, although it would have to be somebody close to Refugio Galindo. FPyV, 40/284/2198–2200, Operarios Guadalupanos, monthly newsletter, June 12, 1910.

39. FPyV, 40/273/2149–50, Operarios Guadalupanos, monthly newsletter, August 8, 1909; FPyV, 40/273/2181–82, Operarios Guadalupanos, monthly newsletter, October 8, 1909; and FPyV, 40/284/2200–2201, Operarios Guadalupanos, monthly newsletter, June 12, 1910.

40. FPyV, 40/273/2149–50, Operarios Guadalupanos, monthly newsletters, July 8 and August 8, 1909.

41. FPyV, 40/273/2131, Galindo to Palomar y Vizcarra, June 22, 1909.

42. Ceballos Ramírez, *El catolicismo social*, 313–15, 318.

43. FPyV, 40/273/2149–50, Operarios Guadalupanos, monthly newsletter, August 8, 1909. The early newsletters, such as the one cited here, were typewritten by Dr. J. Refugio Galindo and mimeographed. He would then write in the name of the member to whom it was to be sent, and in the case of Miguel Palomar y Vizcarra, would often handwrite a note at the end, containing information that was not for broader consumption. Newspaper circulation data is primarily from Ceballos Ramírez, "Los Operarios Guadalupanos," 77.

44. FPyV, 40/273/2164–65, memorandum circulated by Palomar y Vizcarra, Guadalajara, 12 September, 1909.

45. Debates regarding salary and the family wage were important on the eve of the Mexican Revolution in 1910. For differing opinions expressed by members of the Operarios Guadalupanos, see *Restauración Social* 2, no. 11–12, and 3, no. 13–19. All of these articles originated as speeches delivered to the Second Catholic Social Week, celebrated in Mexico City in October 1910.

46. Ceballos Ramírez, *El catolicismo social*, 319, 322, and 326; Elisa Cárdenas Ayala, *Le laboratoire démocratique: Le Mexique en révolution (1908–1913)* (Paris: Publications de la Sorbonne, 2001), 50–69.

47. FPyV, 40/273/2059–65, De la Mora to Palomar y Vizcarra, Monterrey, July 11, 1909.

48. FPyV, 40/273/2059–65.

49. Miguel Palomar y Vizcarra, *El sistema Raiffeisen* (México: Antigua Imprenta de Murguia, 1920); Francisco Barbosa Guzmán, *La caja rural católica de préstamos y ahorros en Jalisco (1910–1914 y 1920–1924)* (México: IMDOSOC, 1996); Ceballos Ramírez, *El catolicismo social*, 382–92.

50. Miguel Palomar y Vizcarra, *In memoriam de Don José Palomar* (Guadalajara: Linotipografía Guadalajara, 1944); another characterization is Jaime Olveda, "José Palomar: prototipo del empresario preburgués," *Relaciones* 9, no. 36 (1988): 33–56.

51. In the case of Arandas, for which there are detailed records, loans were made at 8 percent interest; Barbosa, *La caja rural católica*, 52–61.

52. Refugio Galindo, O.G., "El salario," *Restauración Social* 2. no. 12 (1910): 427; J. Félix Araiza, O.G., "El salario real y el Estado," *Restauración Social* 3, no. 15 (1911): 120.

53. Benigno Arregui, O.G., "Insuficiencia de los sueldos o salarios," *Restauración Social* 2, no. 11 (1910): 402.

54. Juan Torres Septién, O.G., "La Iglesia Católica en todos los tiempos ha sido la defensora y conservadora de los intereses de la sociedad," *Restauración Social* 3, no. 13 (1911): 6.

55. J. Ascención Reyes, O.G., "El Salario Real," *Restauración Social* 3, no. 16 (1911): 166–75.

56. Reyes, "El Salario Real," 166–75.

57. Galindo, "El salario," 430–34.

58. Tomás F. Iglesias, O.G., "¿Es posible que el obrero goce de un salario justo y qué tiempo debe trabajar?" *Restauración Social* 3, no. 13 (1911): 21.

59. See chapter 1.

60. Galindo, "El salario," 422–35.

61. Reyes, "El salario real," 166–75.

62. Iglesias, "¿Es posible que el obrero . . . ?" 21.

63. Iglesias, "¿Es possible que el obrero . . . ?" 19, 21.

64. Galindo, "El salario," 428.

65. Carlos A. Salas López, O.G., "Influencia del Estado en el aumento del salario real," *Restauración Social* 3, no. 13 (1911): 9–17.

66. Salas López, "Influencia del Estado," 16.

67. Miguel M. de la Mora, O.G., "Normas para juzgar acerca de la intervención del Estado en la solución de la cuestión obrera," *Restauración Social* 3, no. 13 (1911): 50–51.

68. Reyes, "El salario real," 168.

69. Araiza, "El salario real," 119–27.

70. José Tomás Figueroa, O.G., "El salario," *Restauración Social* 2, no. 12 (1910): 443.

71. Torres Septién, "La Iglesia Católica," 2–8.

72. Salas López, "Influencia del Estado," 9–17.

73. Galindo, "El salario," 422–35; Reyes, "El salario real," 166–75.

74. Friedrich Katz, *The Life and Times of Pancho Villa* (Stanford: Stanford University Press, 1998), 107–111; Roque Estrada, *La revolución y Francisco I. Madero* (México: INEHRM, 1985), 469–71.

75. The executive committee was: Fernández Somellera, president; Amor and de la Hoz, vice presidents; García Pimentel, treasurer; Díez de Sollano and García, secretaries; Martínez del Campo, subsecretary. Sánchez Santos refused to be included in the executive committee, probably as an act of protest against the designation of Fernández Somellera as president.

76. The program was drawn up by De la Hoz, Sánchez Santos, and Amor.

77. FPyV, 40/285/2284–87, Arnulfo Castro, SJ, to Palomar y Vizcarra, June 21, 1911.

78. Facius, *Bernardo Bergoend*, 19–24.

79. Eduardo J. Correa, *El Partido Católico Nacional y sus Directores. Explicación de su fracaso y deslinde de responsabilidades* (México: Fondo de Cultura Económica, 1991), 74–75.

80. See the final chapter and especially the conclusion of Stephen J. C. Andes fine new comparative study of transnational Catholicism, *The Vatican and Catholic Activism in Mexico and Chile: The Politics of Transnational Catholicism, 1920–1940* (Oxford: Oxford University Press, 2014). There is a solid, if limited, argument to be made that by 1940, the incipient Partido Acción Nacional (National Action Party, or PAN) offered a secular, Christian-inspired, politics independent of Church tutelage. The most obvious limit to this argument is that the PAN was unable to win the presidency, or most other elections, for another sixty years. One can see the roots of Christian Democracy in the

PAN through the founding participation of Efraín González Luna; see Jorge Alonso, *Miradas sobre la personalidad política de Efraín González Luna* (Guadalajara: Universidad de Guadalajara/CUCSH, 2003).

81. The one exception was the idea that those who served in the judicial branch should have special guarantees vis à vis the executive branch in order to safeguard their independence. The telegram is reproduced in Banegas Galván, *El por qué*, 50.

82. Correa, *El Partido Católico Nacional*, 102–103.

83. *El Luchador Católico* (Ciudad Guzmán, Jalisco), November 24, 1912, p. 2.

Chapter 4

1. Laura O'Dogherty Madrazo's pioneering work on the topic is an obvious and important point of reference for this chapter; see *De urnas y sotanas: El Partido Nacional Católico en Jalisco* (México: Regiones/CONACULTA, 2001).

2. Eduardo J. Correa, *El Partido Católico Nacional y sus directores. Explicación de su fracaso y deslinde de responsabilidades* (México: Fondo de Cultura Económica, 1991), 94–95.

3. José Antonio Serrano Ortega, "Reconstrucción de un enfrentamiento. El Partido Católico Nacional, Francisco I. Madero y los maderistas renovadores (julio de 1911–febrero de 1913)," *Relaciones* 58 (1994): 176–96.

4. José C. Valadés, *Historia general de la revolución mexicana*, 2nd ed., vol. 2 (México: Editorial del Valle de México, 1979), 231.

5. José M. Meza, "Primera clarinada o el desprestigio del Gobierno, o el triunfo del P. Católico," *La Libertad*, June 24, 1912, 2; Luis Manuel Rojas, "Vamos al fracaso," *La Libertad*, October 4, 1912, 1; see also *La Libertad*, August 21, 1912, 1–2; and *La Libertad*, August 23, 1912, 1–2.

6. *La Libertad*, September 17, 1912, 2; *La Libertad*, September 23, 1912, 1–3.

7. The idea of revolution at the margins comes from Elisa Cárdenas's excellent book; Elisa Cárdenas Ayala, *El derrumbe: Jalisco, microcosmos de la revolución Mexicana* (México: Tusquets, 2010).

8. Alejandro Tortolero Villaseñor, *El agua y su historia. México y sus desafíos hacia el siglo XXI* (México: Siglo XXI, 2000).

9. Friedrich Katz, *The Life and Times of Pancho Villa* (Stanford: Stanford University Press, 1998).

10. François-Xavier Guerra, *México: del Antiguo Régimen a la Revolución*, trans. Sergio Fernández Bravo, 2 vols., vol. 2 (México: Fondo de Cultura Económica, 1988), 409, 447.

11. Valadés, *Historia General*, vol. 2, 231–32.

12. O'Dogherty Madrazo, *De urnas y sotanas*; Cárdenas Ayala, *El derrumbe*; Elisa Cárdenas Ayala, *Le laboratoire démocratique: Le Mexique en révolution (1908–1913)* (Paris: Publications de la Sorbonne, 2001); and Robert Curley, "Slouching Towards Bethlehem: Catholics and the Political Sphere in Revolutionary Mexico" (PhD diss., University of Chicago, 2001).

13. Laura O'Dogherty, "Dios, Patria y Libertad. El Partido Catolico Nacional," in *Las instituciones,* ed. Manuel Ceballos Ramírez, vol. 2 of *El catolicismo social en México* (México: IMDOSOC / Academia de Investigación Humanística, 2005), 143–45.

14. Guerra, *México: del Antiguo Régimen,* vol. 2, 395.

15. Correa, *El Partido Católico Nacional,* 198, 202, 208–210.

16. Correa, *El Partido Católico Nacional,* 203.

17. The obvious exception was José López Portillo y Rojas, PCN candidate for governor, who was very much a part of the Porfirian cultural and political elite. However, he did not belong to the PCN and was presented simply as an honest citizen of Jalisco, around whom everybody might rally. See for example, Fondo Miguel Palomar y Vizcarra, box 40, folder 287, document 2405, Form letter circulated by the PCN-Jalisco Executive Electoral Committee, 1912 (henceforth, citations will appear separated by diagonals, for example, FPyV, 40/287/2405).

18. Maximiano Reyes, PCN secretary for Mezquitán, reported that most party leaders in that Indian neighborhood were brickmakers; see FPyV, 41/291/2782, Reyes to Miguel Palomar y Vizcarra, April 7, 1913. Further evidence of this may be found by comparing the lists of party candidates with a 1904 military census taken in Guadalajara that lists occupation; see FPyV, 40/287/2407, Candidaturas de electores, Partido Católico Nacional, Centro de Jalisco, Municipalidad de Guadalajara, June 1912; and Archivo Municipal de Guadalajara (henceforth, AMG), Padrón de Servicio Militar, décimo cuartel, 1904.

19. Correa, *El Partido Católico Nacional,* 202.

20. On Ciudad Guzmán, see O'Dogherty Madrazo, *De urnas,* 112–13; on Cocula, FPyV, 40/288/2467, Corcuera to Palomar y Vizcarra, Hacienda de San Diego, January 23, 1912; on "sociabilidades tradicionales," see Guerra, *Del Antiguo Régimen,* vol. 1, chapter 3, especially132–39.

21. O'Dogherty Madrazo, *De urnas,* 165, 167.

22. On poor organization in La Barca and Jamay, see FPyV, 40/286/2373, Arrieta Vizcayno to Palomar y Vizcarra, Jamay, November 28, 1911; for Talpa, see 40/289/2577–78, Quintero to Palomar y Vizcarra, Mascota, August 20, 1912.

23. A longer view qualifies this argument, as some of the towns she names became strongholds of the Union Popular by the 1920s. See O'Dogherty Madrazo, *De urnas,* 165.

24. FPyV, 41/291/2793–94, Juan Medina to Palomar y Vizcarra, San Cristóbal de la Barranca, April 23, 1913.

25. Guerra, *México: del Antiguo Régimen,* vol. 1, 39.

26. Guerra, *México: del Antiguo Régimen,* vol. 1, 40.

27. *El Obrero, Organo de la Convención Obrera Electoral* appeared from June 1906 until the end of the year, and is held at the Biblioteca Pública del Estado de Jalisco, in Guadalajara.

28. The activists were Ireneo and Francisco de Sales Quintero; FPyV, 40/289/2577–78, Quintero to Palomar y Vizcarra, Mascota, August 20, 1912.

29. The delegate was Agustín Navarro Flores; FPyV, 40/290/2693–96, Navarro Flores to Palomar y Vizcarra, Tototlán, December 26, 1912; and 40/290/2697, Rubalcava to Palomar y Vizcarra, Tototlán, December 26, 1912.

30. FPyV, 40/288/2463–64, J. Jesús Aviña to Palomar y Vizcarra, Zapotitlán, January 12, 1912.

31. FPyV, 40/288/2482, Reynoso to Palomar y Vizcarra, Tepatitlán, April 2, 1912.

32. FPyV, 41/295/3069, Reynoso to Palomar y Vizcarra, Tepatitlán, February 27, 1914; and 41/295/3067–68, Hernández Sánchez to Palomar y Vizcarra, Tepatitlán, February 27, 1914.

33. FPyV, 40/288/2484–85, Manuel M. González to Palomar y Vizcarra, Tonalá, February 13, 1912.

34. On the 1899 Council, see Jerónimo Thomé da Silva, Arzobispo de San Salvador, Primado del Brasil, et al., *Carta Sinodal que los Arzobisbos y Obispos Congregados en Roma para el Concilio Plenario de la América Latina dirigen al Clero y a los Fieles de sus Diocesis* (Colima: Imp. del Comercio, 1899).

35. FPyV, 41/291/2790, Flores to Palomar y Vizcarra, Tenamaztlan, April 23, 1913.

36. FPyV, 41/2912744–46, Santana to Palomar y Vizcarra, Ayutla, March 3, 1913.

37. FPyV, 41/296/3183–84, Preciado to Palomar y Vizcarra, Tapalpa, June 23, 1914.

38. One party activist, unconvinced by indirect elections, wrote to Miguel Palomar asking how he could be sure the opposition would not pay the PCN electors to vote for liberal candidates. See FPyV, 40/286/2352, Lomelí to Palomar y Vizcarra, El Salto, September 19, 1911.

39. FPyV, 40/287/2406, "Partido Católico Nacional, Centro de Jalisco, Candidatos para electores que propone el partido para la municipalidad de Guadalajara," n.d.

40. Archivo Histórico de la Arquidiócesis de Guadalajara (henceforth, AHAG), Box SMM, 1907, Estadística de la Arquidiócesis de Guadalajara, Parroquia de Jesus.

41. FPyV, 40/286/2315, Salazar and Cisneros to Palomar y Vizcarra, Fábrica de Atemajac, September 2, 1911.

42. FPyV, 40/287/2436–37, Rodríguez to Palomar y Vizcarra, Tamazula, March 29, 1912.

43. FPyV, 20/288/2466, Hueso to Palomar y Vizcarra, Tapalpa, January 22, 1912.

44. FPyV, 40/288/2552–53, Navarro Flores to Palomar y Vizcarra, Tamazula, July 1, 1912; 40/290/2660, Martínez to Palomar y Vizcarra, Hostotipaquillo, November 20, 1912; 40/289/2569, de la Torre to Palomar y Vizcarra, Tepatitlán, August 6, 1912; and 40/289/2629, de la Torre to Palomar y Vizcarra, Tepatitlán, October 16, 1912.

45. FPyV, 40/288/2344–45, Martínez to Palomar y Vizcarra, Arandas, July 19, 1912; and 41/292/2879–82, Official Minutes of the Municipal Electoral Commission, Municipal President José Jesús Mojica, July 19, 1912.

46. Ceballos Ramírez, *El catolicismo social*, 303–9.

47. FPyV, 40/285/2312, "Algunas razones," Guadalajara, January 1912.

48. FPyV, 40/284/2211, Galindo to Palomar y Vizcarra, Tortugas-Temascalillos, August 20, 1910; 40/284/2212, Palomar y Vizcarra to Galindo, Guadalajara,

August 20, 1910; 40/285/2284–87, Castro, SJ, to Palomar y Vizcarra, Hastings, Great Britain, June 21, 1911; *Restauración Social* 3, no. 20, August 15, 1911, 392.

49.   For an early twentieth-century description of the Volksverein, one that likely reflects the movement as it was understood by Mexican Catholic intellectuals, see Joseph Lins, "Volksverein," in *The Catholic Encyclopedia. An International Work of Reference on the Constitution, Doctrine, Discipline, and History of the Catholic Church*, ed. Charles G. Herbermann, Edward A. Pace, Condé B. Pallen, Thomas J. Shahan, and John J. Wynne, vol. 15 (New York: Robert Appleton Company, 1912).

50.   Knight, *The Mexican Revolution*, vol. 1, 402.

51.   FPyV, 40/289/2635–37, "Decreto #1461"; 41/291/2752, "Instrucciones sobre la Ley de representación proporcional en los Ayuntamientos y en la Legislatura"; Aldana Rendón, *Del reyismo*, 180.

52.   Prior to the middle nineteenth century, Catholic schools should not be considered private either. Schooling had been entirely Catholic, and therefore, the doctrine of educational freedom sought to create private education as part of the same process of secularization that sought institutional differentiation of Church and state. However, subsequent legislation would attempt to marginalize and limit Catholic education.

53.   Francisco Barbosa Guzmán, "De la manera cómo los diputados católicos ejercieron la libertad de educación en Jalisco 1912–1914," *Estudios Sociales* 11 (1991): 65–85.

54.   FPyV, 35/248, "Entrevista realizada por la Srta. Alicia Olivera con el Sr. Lic. Miguel Palomar y Vizcarra, Mexico, DF, 15 de agosto de 1960," 10–11.

55.   The first case I found was from late August 1912; the last was in late June 1914. There were several cases in which the decrees referred to groups of individuals whose studies were validated without naming individuals, suggesting a universe closer to 200 cases; see Archivo del Congreso de Jalisco (henceforth, ACJ), Decrees Passed, 2nd 23rd Legislature (Mar. 1 de 1912–Ene. 31 de 1913) and 24th Legislature (Feb. 1 de 1913–1914).

56.   It also merits mention that most of the women were from towns in rural Jalisco; ACJ, 2nd 23rd Legislature, decree 1527, "Revalida los estudios de instrucción primaria elemental y superior que hicieron las señoritas María Dolores y Sabina Casillas, en la Escuela de Nuestra Sra. del Rosario, de Autlán (Jalisco)," December 11, 1912; ACJ, 24th Legislature, decree 1667, "Revalida a la Srita. María de Jesús Casillas los estudios que hizo en la Segunda Escuela Parroquial (Guadalajara)," October 4, 1913; ACJ, 24th Legislature, decree 1673, "Revalida a la Srita. María Esther Busto los estudios que hizo en la segunda escuela parroquial de niñas (Guadalajara)," October 7, 1913; ACJ, 24th Legislature, decree 1791, "Revalida a las Sritas. Constanza, Marías [sic] de Jesús y María del Refugio Córdova los estudios de Instrucción Primaria que hicieron en el Colegio del Sagrado Corazón de Jesús de Atotonilco el Alto (Jalisco)," April 17, 1914.

57.   ACJ, 24th Legislature, decree 1679, "Revalida al joven Joaquín Rosado Peña, los estudios que hizo en el Colegio Internacional (Guadalajara)," October 24, 1913; ACJ, 24th Legislature, decree 1658, "Revalida a D. Arturo N. Corona los estudios que hizo

en la Escuela López Cotilla (Guadalajara)," September 30, 1913; ACJ, 24th Legislature, decree 1714, "Revalida a D. Angel Reinaga los estudios de Instrucción Primaria que hizo en la Escuela López Cotilla (Guadalajara)," February 11, 1914.

58. ACJ, 24th Legislature, decree 1657, "Revalida a D. Federico Barba González y a D. Silvano del mismo apellido los estudios que hizo en el Seminario Auxiliar de San Juan de los Lagos," September 29, 1913; ACJ, 24th Legislature, decree 1680, "Revalida a Don Enrique Díaz de León los estudios que hizo en el Seminario Conciliar (Guadalajara)," October 24, 1913.

59. FPyV, 40/296/3172-96, "Colección de los decretos, circulares y ordenes de los poderes legislativo, ejecutivo, y judicial arreglado por el encargado del Archivo General del Gobierno, tomo XXVI, Legislación de Julio de 1912 a Junio de 1914"; 41/291/2890, Araiza to Palomar y Vizcarra, July 26, 1913.

60. *La Gaceta de Guadalajara*, April 11, 1912, 1.

61. They compared the state laws of Texas, Nebraska, Missouri, Florida, Wisconsin, Louisiana, Mississippi, Vermont, and New Jersey; see Biblioteca Pública del Estado de Jalisco (henceforth, BPE), Miscelánea 752/1, "El Bien de Familia," April 1912, 16–19. Also for a copy of the law, see FPyV, 40/288/2531-38, "Legislación social," typewritten document, May 26, 1928.

62. See chapter 1.

63. They do not mention divorce or bigamy, but neither do they establish marriage as a requisite. In the case of a two-family parent, they assume that a widow or widower might establish a new family, and ought to have the right to protect each one; BPE, Miscelánea 752/1, 16.

64. In this sense it was different from homesteads in the United States; it was not a land grant, but recognition of the status of inalienability conferred on a small property already acquired.

65. BPE, Miscelánea, 752/1, 18, 22–23.

66. BPE, Miscelánea, 752/1, 19.

67. Barbosa Guzmán, *La Caja Rural*, 62–70.

68. This opinion is common in the correspondence regarding the credit unions. If the priest was not involved, people would not join.

69. FPyV, 41/296/3152-53, Preciado to Palomar y Vizcarra, April 24, 1914.

70. The confederation was constituted by credit unions at El Refugio (1920), San Antonio Juanacastle (1922), Zapotlanejo (1921), and Santa Fe, Zapotlanejo (1921). The other seven founded during the period were located at San Julián (1919), Cuquío (1920), Tuxcueca (1920), Jocotepec (1921), Etzatlán (1921), Tototlán (1922), and Ciudad Guzmán (1923); Barbosa Guzmán, *La Caja Rural*, 89–105.

71. FPyV, 40/288/2478, "A ellos . . . ¡los jacobinos! . . . la porra," Guadalajara, n.d. The intent is satirical, and Navarro is appropriating the rowdy slang of the lower-class revolutionaries whom he and other Catholic Party members routinely referred to as "the mob." At the bottom of the sheet, under the name T. Tumbo, Palomar y Vizcarra wrote out "Lic. Agustín Navarro Flores 1912."

72.   Apparently, unbeknownst to the Catholics, Robles Gil initially put off the elections at Madero's request. However, Madero was concerned by the rebellion of Pascual Orozco, and Robles Gil put off the elections out of distaste for Catholic Party electoral success; see O'Dogherty Madrazo, *De urnas*, 176.

73.   BPE, Miscelánea, 752/1, 7.

74.   Manuel F. Chávez, "La expansión del capital mediante la caridad y el trabajo en favor de los pobres," in *3CCN*, vol. 2, 522.

75.   Michael C. Meyer, *Huerta: A Political Portrait* (Lincoln: University of Nebraska Press, 1972), 60–61.

76.   Friedrich Katz, *The Secret War in Mexico, Europe, the United States and the Mexican Revolution* (Chicago: University of Chicago Press, 1981), 119–23.

77.   José María Muriá, *Jalisco: Una Historia Compartida* (Guadalajara: Gobierno del Estado de Jalisco, 1987), 517.

78.   The *New York Times*, August 1, 1913. Woodrow Wilson was sworn in as president of the United States on March 4, 1913; see also Meyer, *Huerta*, 112–17, on President Wilson's reasoning and decision-making process.

79.   John Womack Jr., *Zapata and the Mexican Revolution* (New York: Vintage Books, 1970), 167–70.

80.   Luis Liceaga, *Félix Díaz* (México: Editorial Jus, 1958), 301–2.

81.   Lozano spoke on Huerta's behalf from the Congress, Robles Gil joined his cabinet as development secretary, and Lopez Portillo y Rojas joined as foreign secretary; see Meyer, *Huerta*, 143–44.

82.   The Casino Jalisciense was a salon governed by the membership of Guadalajara's bourgeois elite. It was located in the city's historic center and, as a symbol of privilege, was occasionally the target of popular or working-class protest.

83.   Archivo Histórico de Jalisco (henceforth, AHJ), Ramo G.1.913, unnumbered folder, Box G-125.

84.   Amado Aguirre, *Mis memorias de Campaña* (México: INERHM, 1985), 29; a Constitutionalist general, Aguirre was chief of staff to Manuel M. Dieguez. His memoir, written in the 1930s, is an unusually candid and balanced reflection on the period of the armed revolution.

85.   Aguirre, *Mis memorias*, 26–33.

86.   Meyer, *Huerta*, 140–42, 145–46.

87.   The assassination of Belisario Domínguez and the dissolution of Congress have been amply treated in the literature. See Manuel González Ramírez, *La revolución social de México, tomo 1, Las ideas—la violencia* (México: Fondo de Cultura Económica, 1960), 396–97; and Meyer, *Huerta*, 146–47. Better assessments of Catholic Party involvement are found in Correa, *El Partido Católico Nacional*, 165–67; and O'Dogherty Madrazo, *De urnas y sotanas*, 239–40.

88.   Here the correspondence of the German consul, Paul von Hintze, is revealing. See Katz, *The Secret War in Mexico*, 122.

89.   Subsequently Tamariz took a post in the Huerta administration as Agriculture

Secretary, plausibly a reward for his support in the Congress; Correa, *El Partido Católico Nacional*, 177–79.

90. Correa, *El Partido Católico Nacional*, 177.

91. FPyV, 41/295/3059–60, Traslosheros to Palomar y Vizcarra, February 20, 1914.

92. FPyV, 41/295/3053, Traslosheros to Palomar y Vizcarra, February 15, 1914.

93. Correa, *El Partido Católico Nacional*.

94. Moisés González Navarro, *Cristeros y agraristas en Jalisco*, vol. 1 (México: El Colegio de México/Centro de Estudios Históricos, 2000), 171.

95. There are two exceptions: first, the Huichol, or Wixarika nation located in the southern reaches of the Sierra Madre Occidental, beyond the reach of most mestizo society; and second, Coca and Tecueje pueblos located in the Guadalajara region. These did have complaints regarding land, and participated actively in the early agrarian reform. See Laura Gomez Santana, "Identidades locales y la conformación del Estado mexicano, 1915–1924. Comunidades, indígenas y pobres en el reparto agrario en Jalisco central" (PhD diss., Universidad de Guadalajara, 2009).

96. On the modest origins of Jalisco land tenure patterns, see, François Chevalier, "Acerca de los orígenes de la pequeña propiedad en el Occidente de México. Historia Comparada," in *Después de los latifundios (la desintegración de la gran propiedad agraria en México)*, 3–12 (paper presented at the 3rd Coloquio de Antropología e Historia en México, El Colegio de Michoacán, 1982).

97. This had not always been the case. In 1810, when Hidalgo's army marched through southern Jalisco (fleeing failure in central Mexico), they found communities like Zacoalco more than ready to join in the fight. At that time local haciendas and communities were much more polarized; see William B. Taylor, "Banditry and Insurrection: Rural Unrest in Central Jalisco, 1790–1816," in *Riot, Rebellion, and Revolution: Rural Social Conflict in Mexico*, ed. Friedrich Katz (Princeton: Princeton University Press, 1988), 216–25.

98. O'Dogherty, *De urnas y sotanas*, 220–21.

99. Robert E. Quirk, *The Mexican Revolution and the Catholic Church, 1910–1929* (Bloomington and London: Indiana University Press, 1973), 25.

100. Mary Kay Vaughan, *Cultural Politics in Revolution: Teachers, Peasants, and Schools in México, 1930–1940* (Tucson: University of Arizona Press, 1997), especially chapter 1.

101. Correa, *El Partido Católico Nacional*. This argument runs throughout the book, but is perhaps most forcefully stated in chapter 19, "El fracaso y la culpa," 195–211.

102. FPyV, 41/291/2786, Correa to Palomar y Vizcarra, April 18, 1913.

103. Correa, *El Partido Católico Nacional*, 198–200, 210–11.

104. Correa, *El Partido Católico Nacional*, 198–200, 210–11.

105. O'Dogherty, *De urnas y sotanas*, chapter 5, especially 249–53.

106. Arnaldo Córdova, *La política de masas del cardenismo* (México: Era, 1974).

107. Gilbert M. Joseph and Daniel Nugent, "Popular Culture and State Formation in Revolutionary Mexico," in *Everyday Forms of State Formation: Revolution and the*

Negotiation of Rule in Modern Mexico, ed. Gilbert M. Joseph and Daniel Nugent (Durham, NC: Duke University Press, 1994), 17.

108.   One could credibly argue that Catholics knew this long before the advent of mass politics, as a cursory evaluation of local historical archives reveals. In the case of Jalisco, for example, one can document recurring public marches, pilgrimages, parades, and other religious representations in towns across the state subsequent to the 1867 republican restoration and right up until the 1910 revolution. The reform laws did not successfully root out local religious practice, which could frequently be governed by local arrangements, a sort of moral economy of rural social relations; see Briseida Gwendoline Olvera Maldonado, "Catálogo del Ramo de Gobernación, Asunto Iglesia (1867–1911), Archivo Histórico de Jalisco" (Bachelor's thesis, Universidad de Guadalajara, 2002).

109.   Vicente Camberos Vizcaíno, *Francisco el Grande. Mons. Francisco Orozco y Jiménez. Biografía* (México: Editorial Jus, 1966), 246.

110.   Francisco Orozco y Jiménez, *Segunda carta pastoral del Ilmo. y Revmo. Sr. Dr. y Mtro. D. Francisco Orozco y Jiménez, 5o Arzobispo de Guadalajara con motivo de la solemne consagración de la república mexicana al sacratísimo corazón de Jesús* (Guadalajara: Tip. de El Regional, 1913).

111.   Antonio Rius Facius, *De Don Porfirio a Plutarco, Historia de la A.C.J.M.* (México: Jus, 1958).

112.   The Mexican bishops asked Pius X to consecrate Mexico to the Sacred Heart in 1913, a petition that deserves some added context. The devotion to the Sacred Heart of Jesus emerged as a common practice in the Catholic world in the context of expanding secularity during the second half of the nineteenth century. A central component of the devotion is the love of Jesus Christ as an act of reparation or amends. In theological terms, the devotion manifests itself as a disdained or reviled love, a reflection of the persecution of the first Christians. It is in this sense that the Sacred Heart devotion constitutes an act of reparation or atonement. After 1850, it became common, and France is an exemplary case, for congregations as well as sovereign states to consecrate themselves to the Sacred Heart. But it was not until 1875 that Pius IX extended the devotion to all of Christendom. Following in this trend, Leo XIII issued *Annum Sacrum* in 1899 in which he consecrated humanity in the name of the Sacred Heart. The devotion continued to be popular during the early decades of the twentieth century, and King Alfonso XIII dedicated Spain in 1919. In his important study of religious rebellion in the Mexican state of Michoacán, Matthew Butler found that it was common among the rebels, a demographic cohort born in the late nineteenth century, to carry Sacred Heart as a second or middle name; see John Pollard, *Catholicism in Modern Italy: Religion, Society and Politics since 1861* (London: Routledge, 2008), 29; Thomas A. Kselman, *Miracles & Prophecies in Nineteenth-Century France* (New Brunswick, NJ: Rutgers University Press, 1983), 125–27; Matthew Butler, *Popular Piety and Political Identity in Mexico's Cristero Rebellion: Michoacán, 1927–1929* (Oxford: The British Academy / Oxford University Press, 2004), 204; Mary Vincent, *Catholicism in*

the Second Spanish Republic: Religion and Politics in Salamanca, 1930–1936 (Oxford: Clarendon Press, 1996), 92.

113.   FPyV, 41/295/3043, Traslosheros to Palomar y Vizcarra, January 28, 1914.

114.   In this usage, the reference is to the extrinsic solemnity of annual religious fiestas, marked by the decoration of a church or of the adjoining streets and houses, ringing of bells, and often, public pilgrimage or parading of religious figures. On solemnity, see Francis Mershman, "Solemnity," in *The Catholic Encyclopedia. An international Work of Reference on the Constitution, Doctrine, Discipline, and History of the Catholic Church*, ed. Charles G. Herbermann, Edward A. Pace, Condé B. Pallen, Thomas J. Shahan, and John J. Wynne, 15 vols., vol. 14 (New York: Robert Appleton Company, 1912).

115.   Fernando A. Gallo Lozano, comp., *Compilación de leyes de reforma* (Guadalajara: Congreso del Estado de Jalisco, 1973), 131–36, 152–63.

116.   *Chamula* is a general term that may refer to diverse Mayan ethnic groups that live in the Chiapas Sierra, including the Tzotzil, Tzeltal, Mame, Tojolabal, and Chol peoples. The Chamulas were seen by the white Chiapas elite as uncultured or uncivilized. They derided the archbishop in this manner because they felt he identified too strongly with the indigenous poor in the diocese.

117.   Francisco Orozco y Jiménez was exiled to Rome and the United States between 1914 and 1916, to the United States in 1918, and again to Rome, following the end of the Cristero Rebellion in 1929. There he spent his final years, only returning to Mexico on permission granted by President Lázaro Cárdenas in 1935. He died the following year at the age of seventy-two. Camberos Vizcaíno, *Francisco el Grande*, is the most extensive biography on Orozco y Jiménez; see also J. Ignacio Dávila Garibi, *Apuntes para la historia de la Iglesia en Guadalajara*, 7 vols., vol. 5 (México: Editorial Cultura, 1977), which offers a combination of biographical data and reproductions of some documents pertinent to the archbishop's life and work.

118.   Camberos Vizcaíno, *Francisco el Grande*, 251.

119.   *El Diario de Occidente*, January 14, 1914.

120.   "Por su patria y por su dama," *El Diario de Occidente*, January 15, 1914.

121.   Gavroche was the Parisian street urchin of Victor Hugo's *Les Miserables*. He was shot and killed while trying to smuggle ammunition to the revolutionaries from behind National Guard lines during the 1832 student uprising. He is also an agent of Parisian *argot*, the slang of the dangerous classes, a reference point that is significant here on account of Gavroche's editorial, entitled "Malediciencias," which may be translated "murmurings."

122.   Gavroche, "Maledicencias," *El Diario de Occidente*, January 14, 1914.

123.   *El Correo de Jalisco*, February 9 and 13, 1914.

124.   FPyV, 41/295/3079, Luis Álvarez to Palomar y Vizcarra, March 6, 1914.

125.   FPyV, 41/295/3082, Francisco de Sales Quintero to Palomar y Vizcarra, March 9, 1914.

126.   FPyV, 41/295/3098, Miguel Loza to Palomar y Vizcarra, March 18, 1914.

127.   FPyV, 41/296/3152–53, José Encarnación Preciado to Palomar y Vizcarra, April 24, 1914.

128.   For examples from Jalostotlan and Tepatitlan, see FPyV, 41/296/3158–59, Francisco de Sales Quintero to Palomar y Vizcarra, April 27, 1914, and 41/296/3160, Sabás G. Gutiérres to Palomar y Vizcarra, May 2, 1914.

Chapter 5

1.   The Sierra Volcánica Transversal is an extension of the Sierra Madre Occidental and the North American Rocky Mountains. It is considered separately, however, and is the only mountain range in the Americas that runs west-east instead of north-south. It is the same range that stretches through central Mexico, including Colima, Popocatépetl, and Orizaba peaks, all of which are currently live volcanoes. Like the Sierra Madre Occidental and Oriental, the Volcánica Transversal was covered with forest in the early twentieth century, making it difficult to cross; Jorge A. Vivó, *Geografía de México*, 4th ed. (México: Fondo de Cultura Económica, 1958), 53–54.

2.   Álvaro Obregón, *Ocho mil kilometros en campaña*, vol. 1 (México: Editorial del Valle de México, 1980), 229–39; J. Ángel Moreno Ochoa, *Semblanzas revolucionarias: compendio del movimiento de liberación en Jalisco* (Guadalajara: Talleres Berni, 1965), 36–45.

3.   Alan Knight, *The Mexican Revolution*, vol. 2 (Lincoln: University of Nebraska Press, 1986), 272.

4.   Manuel Aguirre Berlanga, *Génesis legal de la revolución constitucionalista, Revolución y reforma* (Mexico: INEHRM, 1985 [1918]), 32.

5.   Cristero and Reguer Collection, Dr. Jorge Villalobos Padilla, S. J. Library, ITESO (henceforth, CRC), José Mora y del Río, Arzobispo de México, et al., *Carta Pastoral Colectiva a los Católicos Mexicanos sobre la actual Persecución Religiosa* (1914).

6.   José Bravo Ugarte, *México, I, Independencia, caracterización política e integración social*, vol. 3, part 1 of *Historia de México* (México: Jus, 1944), 488.

7.   Fondo Miguel Palomar y Vizcarra, box 41, folder 296, document 3188–91, Fernández Somellera to Palomar y Vizcarra, August 9, 1914 (henceforth, citations will appear separated by diagonals, for example, FPyV 41/296/3188–91). For mention of threats against Fernández Somellera and his departure from México, see FPyV 41/295/3053, Traslosheros to Palomar y Vizcarra, February 15, 1914.

8.   *El Diario de Occidente*, January 12, 1914, 1, 4; January 15, 1914, 1; February 7, 1914, 2. Father Correa was a parish priest at Our Lady of Guadalupe between November 1909 and July 1914.

9.   Will B. Davis, *Experiences and Observations of an American Consular Officer During the Recent Mexican Revolutions* (Los Angeles: Wayside Press, 1920), 118.

10.   FPyV, 41/297/3198, Ramos Praslow to Palomar y Vizcarra, Guadalajara, June 2, 1915.

11. State Department Papers Relating to the Internal Affairs of Mexico, Record Group 59, File 812.00 (Political Affairs) document 13760, Davis to the Secretary of State, November 5, 1914 (henceforth, citations will appear separated by diagonals, for example, SD, 812.00/13760).

12. FPyV, 41/297/3214, de la Mora to Palomar y Vizcarra, Guadalajara, October 9, 1918.

13. Luis González, "La Revolución Mexicana desde el punto de vista de los revolucionados," *Historias* 8–9 (1985): 5–13.

14. SD, 812.00/12591, Hanna to the Secretary of State, Monterrey, July 23, 1914; SD, 812.00/12634, Canada to the Secretary of State, Veracruz, July 27, 1914; SD, 812.00/12885, Hamm to the Secretary of State, Durango, August 8, 1914; SD, 812.00/12959, Canova to the Secretary of State, México, August 21, 1914; SD, 812.00/12983, Sillman to the Secretary of State, México, August 24, 1914; SD, 812.00/27431, H. L. Hall to Davis, México, October 1, 1914; SD, 812.00/13720, Davis to the Secretary of State, Guadalajara, October 31, 1914; SD, 812.00/14090, Canada to the Secretary of State, December 13, 1914.

15. Eduardo J. Correa, *El Partido Católico Nacional y sus directores. Explicación de su fracaso y deslinde de responsabilidades* (México: Fondo de Cultura Económica, 1991), 208.

16. Biblioteca Pública del Estado de Jalisco, Universidad de Guadalajara, Fondo Miscelánea 783/7 (henceforth, BPEJ, Misc. 783/7), "Memorial del cabildo metropolitano y clero de la arquidiócesis de Guadalajara, al C. Presidente de la República Mexicana, Dn. Venustiano Carranza; y voto de adhesión y obediencia al Ilmo. y Revmo. Sr. Arzobispo, Dr. y Mtro. Dn. Francisco Orozco y Jiménez," April 1918, 4, (henceforth, *Memorial*). In addition to the schools, Alvarado commented on the damaging effects of the occupation of hospitals, rest homes, and other charitable institutions, as well as libraries and laboratories administered by the Catholic Church and closed by the Constitutionalist army during the occupation of Guadalajara.

17. The reference to the Bishop of Tehuantepec is from Meyer, *La Cristiada*, vol. 2, 77. The closing of the churches was reported in the *Boletín Militar*, July 22, 1914, 1; July 23, 1914, 1; July 24, 1914, 1; July 26, 1914, 2; July 29, 1914, 2.

18. BPE, 783/7, *Memorial*, 6. Alvarado placed the release of the priests nine days after the initial detention, on July 30. See also *Boletín Militar*, July 29, 1914, 1; Meyer, *La Cristiada*.

19. Francis Clement Kelley, *Blood-Drenched Altars: Mexican Study and Comment*, with documentation and notes by Eber Cole Byam (Milwaukee: The Bruce Publishing Company, 1935), 250.

20. *Boletín Militar*, July 29, 1914, 2; August 4, 1914, 1; August 18, 1914, 2.

21. For a contrasting interpretation, see Mario Aldana Rendón, *Del reyismo al nuevo orden constitucional, 1910–1917*, vol. 1 of *Jalisco Desde la Revolución* (Guadalajara: Gobierno del Estado/Universidad de Guadalajara, 1987), 218–21.

22. BPE, 783/7, *Memorial*, 6.

23. Amado Aguirre, *Mis memorias de Campaña* (México: INERHM, 1985 [1953]), 62–65.

24. BPE, 783/7, *Memorial*, 6.

25. Perhaps the most famous case was that of Father David Galván, who rode his bicycle out to the battlefield in early 1915 to administer the sacrament of Extreme Unction to the fallen soldiers of either army, and who was executed in such circumstances east of the old San Miguel de Belén Hospital (near the corner of Leña and Hospital streets) on January 31 that year. San David Galván, martyr, was canonized on May 21, 2000. On the recent canonization, See Ramiro Valdés Sánchez and Guillermo Maria Havers, *Tuyo es el reino: mártires mexicanos del siglo XX* (Guadalajara: Libros Católicos, 2000); *Proceso* 1224 (April 16, 2000): 50–56.

26. *Boletín Militar*, August 6, 1914, 1.

27. BPE, 783/7, *Memorial*, 8.

28. BPE, 783/7, *Memorial*, 10.

29. BPE, 783/7, *Memorial*, 8.

30. This situation is not new with the revolution; see chapter 2.

31. Aguirre, *Mis memorias*, 70.

32. Knight, *The Mexican Revolution*, vol. 2, 197.

33. *México Libre*, August 24, 1914, 1 and September 2, 1914, 3; *El Reformador*, August 24, 1914, 2. Like Huejuquilla in 1912, an Orozquistas guerrilla force attempted to sack San Julián in 1914.

34. Knight, *The Mexican Revolution*, vol. 2, 272.

35. See for example, José Guadalupe Zuno Hernández, *Historia de la Revolución en el Estado de Jalisco* (México: Biblioteca del Instituto Nacional de Estudios Historicos de la Revolución Mexicana, 1964), 91–94.

36. Davis, *Experiences and Observations*, 123–29; Aldana Rendón, *Del reyismo*, 257–61.

37. Davis, *Experiences and Observations*, 55.

38. Decree 28 was issued on September 2, while Decree 39 was issued on October 7; they and all of the 1914–1915 Jalisco Constitutionalist legislation are reprinted in José Parres Arias, *Estudio de la legislación constitucionalista de Jalisco y sus decretos constitutivos, 1914–1915* (Guadalajara: Universidad de Guadalajara/Instituto Jaliscience de Antropología e Historia, 1969). There were many protests from across the state resulting from these decrees; for example, see Archivo Histórico de Jalisco (henceforth, AHJ), T-1-914, folders 547, 548, 555, 578, 564, and 260.

39. SD, 812.00/13720, Davis to Secretary of State, Guadalajara, October 31, 1914; SD, 812.00/13913, Howard to Secretary of Navy, USS *San Diego*, November 25, 1914; SD, 812.00/14094, Davis to Secretary of State, Guadalajara, December 8, 1914; see also M. Cuzin, *Journal d'un français au Mexique, Guadalajara, 16 novembre 1914–6 juillet 1915* (Editions J. -L. Lesfargues, 1983), 72.

40. SD, 812.00/14020, Davis to Secretary of State, Guadalajara, December 9, 1914; SD, 812.00/14094, Davis to Secretary of State, Guadalajara, December 12, 1914; SD, 812.00/14087, Davis to Secretary of State, Guadalajara, December 15, 1914; SD, 812.00/14088, Davis to Secretary of State, Guadalajara, December 17, 1914.

41.   Luis Ángel Vargas Reynoso, *La presencia del Villismo en los Altos de Jalisco* (Guadalajara: Congreso del Estado de Jalisco, 2009).

42.   Friedrich Katz, *The Life and Times of Pancho Villa* (Stanford: Stanford University Press, 1998), 448.

43.   M. Cuzin, *Journal d´un français*, 66, 68; Aguirre, *Mis memorias*, 193; Antonio Gómez Robledo, *Anacleto González Flores: El Maestro*, 2nd ed. (México: Editorial Jus, 1947), 61–62.

44.   Davis, *Experiences and Observations*, 130. The other case that scandalized Guadalajara´s upper class was the execution of the wealthy landowner, Joaquín Cuesta Gallardo, ordered by Villa.

45.   Vicente Camberos Vizcaíno, *Un hombre y una época, apuntes biográficos* (México: Jus, 1949), 220.

46.   Gómez Robledo, *Anacleto González Flores*, 27–28.

47.   M. Cuzin, *Journal d´un français*, 68, 76.

48.   FPyV, 40/290/2660, Martínez to Palomar y Vizcarra, Hostotipaquillo, November 20, 1912.

49.   Katz, *The Life and Times*, 441.

50.   Davis, *Experiences and Observations*, 71–72; Aguirre, *Mis memorias*, 33; Moreno Ochoa, *Compendio del movimiento*, 114; Cuzin, *Journal d´un français*, 73.

51.   Aguirre, *Mis memorias*, 121.

52.   SD, 812.00/14482, Davis to Secretary of State, Guadalajara, January 19, 1915; Cuzin, *Journal d´un français*, 93; Luis Páez Brotchie, who would become the official chronicler of Guadalajara some years later, wrote that he was at the train station that afternoon; quoted in Moreno Ochoa, *Compendio del movimiento*, 133–37.

53.   Cuzin, *Journal d´un français*, 92–93.

54.   Archivo de la Palabra, Programa de Historia Oral (henceforth, PHO), 4–41, Daniel Cazés/Apolinar González, Ajijic, Jalisco, March 1961, 5.

55.   SD, 800.12/15551, Davis to Secretary of State, Guadalajara, June 19, 1915; Cuzin, *Journal d´un français*, 94.

56.   SD, 800.12/16835, Davis to Secretary of State, Guadalajara, November 9, 1915; Camarena quoted in Moreno Ochoa, *Compendio del movimiento*, 68–71.

57.   Diéguez informed his chief of staff that their losses had been under thirty, and that Medina's losses had been under fifty. Cuzin, the French merchant and consulate employee, reported dead Carrancista soldiers everywhere; Aguirre, *Mis memorias*, 134; Cuzin, *Journal d´un français*, 120–21.

58.   *Proceso* 1224 (April 16, 2000), 54.

59.   Anacleto González Flores, *La cuestión religiosa en Jalisco* 2nd ed. (México: ACJM, 1920), 285; see also, *El Obrero*, January 31, 1920, 1; February 7, 1920, 1; January 29, 1921, 1; February 5, 1921, 1; February 5, 1922, 3; June 11, 1922, 1.

60.   Camarena and Páez Brotchie quoted in Moreno Ochoa, *Compendio del movimiento*, 71, 137–38; Cuzin, *Journal d´un français*, 120–21; Camberos Vizcaíno, *Un hombre*, 219.

61. Several of the recent canonizations include similar martyrdom story scenes where the soon-to-be martyr comforts the earthly complaints of one who accompanies him, by appealing to the hereafter.

62. According to the story, Vera had attempted to seduce and rape, *seducir y raptar*, a young woman, and Galván had gotten in the way by telling her that Vera was not a good choice for a husband as he was already married. From that day on, the story goes, Vera hated Galván; Valdés Sánchez and Havers, *Tuyo es el reino*, 19–23.

63. González Flores, *La cuestión religiosa*, 285.

64. Cuzin, *Journal d'un français*, 95–97; Moreno Ochoa, *Compendio del movimiento*, 137.

65. Davis quotes a Catholic American living in Guadalajara: "That fathers Galván, Navarro, Araiza, Rameriz [*sic*], and another priest, were executed by the military here, there can be no doubt. . . ." However, I have no other evidence of the last four cases, and in the particular case of Araiza, there are reports to the opposite, as already mentioned. Davis, *Experiences and Observations*, 116.

66. SD, 812.00/14486, Davis to the Secretary of State, February 2, 1915; Davis, *Experiences and Observations*, 81–92.

67. SD, 812.00/14486, Davis to the Secretary of State, February 2, 1915; SD, 812.00/14492, Davis to Secretary of State, Guadalajara, February 19, 1915; Davis, *Experiences and Observations*, 81–92.

68. SD, 812.00/14491, Davis to Secretary of State, Guadalajara, February 15, 1915.

69. Aguirre, *Mis memorias*, 143–50, 175; Aldana Rendón, *Del Reyismo*, 249; Moreno Ochoa, *Compendio del movimiento*, 80–84.

70. Friedrich Katz, *The Secret War in Mexico, Europe, the United States and the Mexican Revolution* (Chicago: University of Chicago Press, 1981).

71. Katz, *The Secret War*, chapter 5; Knight, *The Mexican Revolution*, vol. 2, 160–62.

72. Alan Knight has written that violent reaction was most commonly directed against the symbols of US government, but rarely against the Americans themselves. See Knight, *The Mexican Revolution*, vol. 2, 162–71. See also, Charles C. Cumberland, "Huerta y Carranza ante la ocupación de Vercruz," *Historia Mexicana* 6, no. 4 (1957): 534–47. For a firsthand account see Davis, *Experiences and Observations*, 18–24.

73. Emphasis in the original; Antonio Ortíz y Gordoa, "Ante el enemigo," *El Correo de Jalisco*, April 22, 1914.

74. This episode seems to be unrelated to the Madero revolution, which was several weeks away at the time; see SD, 812.00/438, Magill to Secretary of State, Guadalajara, November 15, 1910; SD, 812.00/615, Magill to Secretary of State, Guadalajara, December 26, 1910; Servando Ortoll and Avital H. Bloch, "Xenofobia y nacionalismo revolucionario, los tumultos de Guadalajara, México, en 1910," *Cristianismo y sociedad*, 86 (1985): 63–78.

75. Davis, *Experiences and Observations*, 38.

76. Knight, *The Mexican Revolution*, vol. 2, 159–60.

77. FPyV, 41/296/3158–59, Francisco de Sales Quintero to Palomar y Vizcarra, Jalostotitlan, Jalisco, April 27, 1914.

78.   FPyV, 41/296/3160, Gutiérrez to Palomar y Vizcarra, Pegueros (Tepatitlan), Jalisco, May 2, 1914.

79.   Fondo José María Mier, C1–8, Hynojosa to Mier, May 13, 1914. The original reads: "Por la pte hago saber a Ud que los Sres Florentino Parra, Patricio Ornelas, Cecilio Sotomayor, Manuel Ermosillo, se espresan muy mal del Gobierno en sus frecuentes borracheras que se ponen en la cantina del Limoncito, han dicho varias veces que todos los que handan dando de patriotas no son mas de ridiculos y estupidos y que la tal intervencion es del vandido y asesino Huerta, nada mas que una medida estratégica para envabucar a tanto pendejo y llevarlos con los rebolucionarios para durar mas en el poder y robar mas a la nacion y que la verdadera intervencion de los americanos es para derrocar a este gobierno de perros vandidos y asesinos. Sin mas Su afmo Atto y S. S. Gumercindo Hynojosa (El Limonsito es en la cuadra de la 4ª Zona)."

80.   James P. Gaffey, *Francis Clement Kelley and the American Catholic Dream*, vol. 2 (Bensenville, IL: The Heritage Foundation, 1980), 8.

81.   Archive of the Archdiocese of Oklahoma City, Kelley Papers, box 10, folder Mexican Question, document 122, Francis P. Joyce to Henry A. Constantineau, Veracruz, September 29, 1914; Kelley Papers, box 10, folder Mexican Question, document 126, Henry A. Constantineau to Francis P. Joyce, Galveston, October 23, 1914; Kelley Papers, box 10, folder Mexican Question, document 57, Signed affidavit taken by Emilio Ledas Rivera, Veracruz, October 28, 1914.

82.   Jacques Lafaye, *Quetzalcóatl y Guadalupe: La formación de la conciencia nacional en México*, trans. Ida Vitale and Fulgencio López Vidarte (México: Fondo de Cultura Económica, 1992), 161–78.

83.   CRC, José Mora y del Río, Arzobispo de México, et al., *Carta Pastoral Colectiva a los Católicos Mexicanos sobre la actual Persecución Religiosa*, November 1914; J. Ignacio Dávila Garibi, *Apuntes para la historia de la Iglesia en Guadalajara*, vol. 7 (México: Editorial Cultura, 1967), 310–24.

84.   Based on sixty-one letters included among the US State Department Consular dispatches; see SD, 812.00/16415, microfilm roll 49.

85.   Robert E. Quirk, *The Mexican Revolution and the Catholic Church*, 69. A similar opinion was also expressed by one correspondent who argued in favor of recognition, saying that most Americans were in favor, even though they did not have a "regular letter-writing corps" to do their bidding; see SD, 812.00/16425, Dodge to Lansing, Ruskin Tennessee, November 2, 1915.

86.   Letters were sent by Irish, Lithuanian, German, Bohemian, and Slavic groups, which were careful to also identify themselves as "American citizens." In addition, although the American Federation of Catholic Societies (AFCS) was not an ethnically specific organization, one of its main stated objectives was the destruction of bigotry. Like many such associations, the AFCS was founded in the period following *Rerum Novarum*, in 1899.

87.   SD, 812.00/16425, Union Constitutionalists to President Wilson, Los Angeles, October 5, 1915.

88. SD, 812.00/16425, Dorethy to Lansing, Rochester N.Y., October 18, 1915.

89. SD, 812.00/16425, Dodge to Lansing, Ruskin Tennessee, November 2, 1915.

90. Davis, *Experiences and Observations*, 179.

91. SD, 812.00/16415, Shields to President Wilson, Brooklyn, October 11, 1915; Mathews to President Wilson, Kenton, October 6, 1915; Frep to President Wilson, New York, October 6, 1915; Vasiliauskas to President Wilson, October 5, 1915; McLaughlin to President Wilson, October 11, 1915.

92. SD, 812.00/16415, Ledvina to Wilson, Chicago, October 5, 1915.

93. SD, 812.00/16415, Collins to Wilson, Jackson, MO., October 9, 1915. It bears mentioning that Collins's commentary regarding funerals and cemeteries is not supported by law, which, in fact, characterized such circumstances as outside the public sphere. The key legislation was the November 27, 1874, circular that reformed a decree signed by Sebastian Lerdo de Tejada on May 13, 1873. The legislation compared the separate plots of a cemetery to apartments in a large building, in which the particular religious customs of the inhabitants may be observed without harm to neighbors. It clearly stated that cemeteries were not to be considered public places; see Fernando A. Gallo Lozano, ed., *Compilación de leyes de reforma* (Guadalajara: Congreso del Estado de Jalisco, 1973), 152–54.

94. SD, 812.00/16415, Tumulty to Lansing, Washington, October 22, 1915.

95. Guadalajara's Rotunda for Illustrious Men was finally renamed the Rotunda for Illustrious Jaliscans in 2000, with the addition of its first famous woman, the educator Irene Robledo.

Chapter 6

1. Archivo Histórico de Jalisco (henceforth, AHJ), Gobernación, G-1–916, box G-128, unnumbered folder, 27 May, 1916.

2. Alan Knight, *The Mexican Revolution*, vol. 2 (Lincoln: University of Nebraska, 1986), 442.

3. Jeffrey W. Rubin, *Decentering the Regime: Ethnicity, Radicalism, and Democracy in Juchitán, Mexico* (Durham, NC, and London: Duke University Press, 1997).

4. Biblioteca Pública del Estado de Jalisco (henceforth, BPE), Miscelánea Pamphlet Collection 783/7, "Apuntes para la Historia: La Cuestión Religiosa en Jalisco," 1918; J. Ignacio Dávila Garibi and Salvador Chávez Hayhoe, *Colección de documentos relativos a la cuestión religiosa en Jalisco*, 2 vols. (Guadalajara: Tip. J. M. Yguíniz, 1920); Anacleto González Flores, *La cuestión religiosa en Jalisco* 2nd ed. (Mexico City: ACJM, 1920).

5. See Guillermo Raúl Zepeda Lecuona, *Constitucionalistas, Iglesia Católica y Derecho del Trabajo en Jalisco (1913–1919)* (Mexico City: INEHRM, 1997); Laura O'Dogherty, *De urnas y sotanas: El Partido Nacional Católico en Jalisco* (México: Regiones/CONACULTA, 2001).

6. *Carta Pastoral del Episcopado Mexicano sobre la Constitución de 1917* (Acordada, 1917), reprinted in J. Ignacio Dávila Garibi, *Apuntes para la historia de la Iglesia*

en Guadalajara, vol. 5 (México: Editorial Cultura, 1977), 310–21; "La Actitud de los Prelados Mexicanos ante la Nueva Constitución Política de la República," *Jalisco*, June 20, 1917; Luis C. Balderrama, *El Clero y el Gobierno de México: Apuntes para la Historia de la Crisis en 1926* (Mexico City: Editorial Cuauhtémoc, 1927), 19–32.

7. *Carta Pastoral.*

8. Orozco y Jiménez was born in 1864 and served as archbishop of Guadalajara from 1912 until his death in 1936. One Jesuit historian referred to him as an activist, *luchador*, a "Good Shepherd" who resisted the anticlerical surge of the revolution, whether through his leadership or by simply hiding out in the mountainous rural towns of the archdiocese so as not to abandon his flock; José Gutiérrez Casillas, *Historia de la Iglesia en México* (México: Editorial Porrúa, 1974), 455.

9. "Breve relación del regreso del Excmo. Sr. Arzobispo Orozco y Jiménez a la República Mexicana que firmado por él tuvo la gentileza de enviar por conducto particular al autor de estos Apuntes para la Historia de la Iglesia de Guadalajara," reprinted in Dávila Garibi, *Apuntes*, vol. 5, 300–10.

10. José Bravo Ugarte, *México, I, Independencia, caracterización política e integración social*, vol. 3, part 1 of *Historia de México* (México: Jus, 1944), 488.

11. On the eve of his arrival, he wrote to the parish priest, Cristóbal Magallanes from the Zacatecan town of Momax. He traveled with a passport under the name of Jesús Quiróz, the name with which he was baptized and his maternal grandmother's surname. He used another alias altogether to receive written correspondence, that of Higinio Renteria; Dávila Garibi, *Apuntes*, vol. 5, 301; Vicente Camberos Vizcaíno, *Francisco el Grande. Mons. Francisco Oroxco y Jiménez. Biografía* (México: Editorial Jus, 1966), 334.

12. José Cardinal Garibi Rivera was Archbishop of Guadalajara from 1936–1969. He was Guadalajara's first cardinal; see, "José *Cardinal* Garibi y Rivera," Catholic Hierarchy, accessed January 10, 2017, http://www.catholic-hierarchy.org/bishop/bgaribi. html.

13. Dávila, *Apuntes*, vol. 5, 323–24.

14. Orozco y Jiménez, Francisco. *Cuarta Carta Pastoral que el Ilmo. Y Rmo. Sr. Dr. y Mtro. D. Francisco Orozco y Jiménez, 5to Arzobispo de Guadalajara, Dirige a sus Diocesanos*, 1917, 1–5.

15. State Department Papers Relating to the Internal Affairs of Mexico, Record Group 59, File 812.00 (Political Affairs) document 20974, John Sillman to the Secretary of State, June 2, 1917 (henceforth, citations will appear separated by diagonals, for example, SD, 812.00/20974); Mario Aldana Rendón, *Del reyismo al nuevo orden constitucional, 1910–1917*, vol. 1 of *Jalisco desde la Revolución* (Guadalajara: Gobierno del Estado/Universidad de Guadalajara, 1987), 327.

16. On Diéguez, see Mario Aldana Rendón, *Manuel M. Diéguez y la revolución mexicana* (Guadalajara: El Colegio de Jalisco, 2006).

17. Alan Knight, *The Mexican Revolution* (Lincoln: University of Nebraska Press, 1986), vol. 2, 236–51.

18. The term refers to partisans identified with Ricardo and Enrique Flores Magón, Mexican precursors of the 1910 revolution, whose ideology was influenced by European anarchism, and whose political platform tended toward emancipation and self-government. On the Flores Magón brothers, their newspaper *Regeneración*, and the Mexican Liberal Party, see Claudio Lomnitz, *The Return of Comrade Ricardo Flores Magón* (New York: Zone Books, 2014); Ricardo Flores Magón et al., *Regeneración. 1900–1918. La corriente más radical de la revolución mexicana de 1910 a través de su periódico de combate*, prologue, selection, and notes by Armando Bartra (México: Era, 1977); John M. Hart, *Anarchism and the Mexican Working Class, 1860–1931* (Austin: University of Texas Press, 1987).

19. González Flores, *La cuestión religiosa*, 291, 317.

20. Adrian A. Bantjes, "Burning Saints, Molding Minds: Iconoclasm, Civic Ritual, and the Failed Cultural Revolution," in *Rituals of Rule, Rituals of Resistance: Public Celebrations and Popular Culture in Mexico*, ed. William H. Beezley, Cheryl English Martin, and William E. French (Wilmington, DE: SR Books, 1994), 273.

21. San Miguel Mezquitán, San José, Mexicaltzingo, Sweet Name of Jesus, San Francisco, and El Carmen were also closed. The detained priests were Miguel Cano, the archdiocesan secretary, and Lorenzo Altamirano; *Jalisco*, July 12, 1917; *El Occidental*, July 12, 1917; González Flores, *La cuestión religiosa*, 298.

22. González Flores, *La cuestión religiosa*, 299–300. Vicente Camberos Vizcaíno, *Un Hombre y una Epoca: Apuntes Biográficos* (Mexico City: Jus, 1949), 251.

23. SD, 812.00.21115, Silliman, Guadalajara, July 13, 1917.

24. González Flores, *La cuestión religiosa*, 300; Bonifacio Byrne, *Lira y Espada*, (Habana: Tipografía "El Fígaro," 1901), 14–15. The translation is mine; the original text is: "Dios de la misericordia: ya que existes / Del lado ponte de los pueblos tristes / y ellos acabarán con su verdugo. / Déjalos que, rompiendo su cadena / arranquen de su espíritu la pena. / Que se pongan de pie como valientes / y a Ti se elevarán sus bendiciones. / Y habrá sobre la tierra más leones, / pero habrá también menos serpientes."

25. Denise Riley, *"Am I that Name?": The Category of Women in History* (Minneapolis: University of Minnesota, 1988).

26. González Flores, *La cuestión religiosa*, 297–304; Camberos Vizcaíno, *Un Hombre*, 251.

27. *Jalisco*, July 13, 1917; *El Occidental*, July 13–14, 1917; *El Gato*, July 19, 1917.

28. *El Gato*, July 15, 1917; *El Occidental*, July 17, 1917.

29. The location referred to in each article is placed in parentheses; all dates are for 1917: *El Occidental*, July 20 (Orendaín), July 24 (Guadalajara), July 25 (Ciudad Guzmán), August 29 (Jesús María and Tenamaxtlán), September 25 (Tenamaxtlán), November 2 (Unión de Tula); *El Independiente*, July 22 (Guadalajara), July 26 (Tizapán and La Barca), September 6 (Cocula); *El Gato*, July 22 (San Miguel el Alto and Guadalajara), August 2 (Tapalpa), August 12 (Talpa), August 16 (Poncitlán and Guadalajara), August 19 (Zacoalco); and *El Radical*, September 3 (Arandas).

30. González Flores, *La cuestión religiosa*, 302.

31. AHJ, Ramo G.4.917, box G-340, unnumbered folder, Catholics to Governor, September 15, 1917, and Sector Juárez residents to Governor, September 1917.

32. *El Radical*, September 16, 1917; *El Paladín*, June 16, 1918.

33. Mario Aldana Rendón, ed., *Manuel M. Dieguez y el Constitucionalismo en Jalisco (documentos)* (Guadalajara: Gobierno de Jalisco, 1986).

34. Churches in villages east-northeast of the city (San Andrés, Tetlán, Huentitán el Alto, and Huentitán el Bajo) were presumably left open for worship. Archivo Municipal de Guadalajara (hereafter AMG), 1918, folder 139, Gobierno to Municipal President Rivera Rosas, February 1, and March 5, 1918.

35. AMG, 1918, folder 669, Gobierno to Municipal President, May 27, 1918.

36. AMG, 1918, folder 139.

37. Jorge Villaseñor, "Importante Iniciativa sobre la Reglamentación del Artículo 130 Constitucional," *El Occidental*, February 20, 1918.

38. Félix Navarrete and Eduardo Pallares, eds., *Colección de leyes y decretos relativos a la reducción de sacerdotes y la persecución religiosa en Méjico desde el punto de vista jurídico* (México, n.d.), 241–54; Dávila, *Apuntes*, vol. 5, 354–58. On July 15, 1918, forty-seven Catholic lawyers filed a lawsuit seeking to appeal Decree 1913.

39. On Porfirian occupational registers, see Robert Curley, "La Democratización del Retrato: Registro de Empleados Domésticos, 1888–1894," in *El Rostro de los Oficios*, ed. Arturo Camacho Becerra (Guadalajara: Editorial Amate, 2006), 23–36; Sergio González Rodríguez, *Los Bajos Fondos: El Antro, la Bohemia y el Café* (Mexico City: Cal y Arena, 1990).

40. *El Occidental*, June 1, 1918.

41. *El Informador*, July 25, 1918.

42. Dávila and Chávez, *Documentos*, vol. 1, 64–67.

43. According to statistics for 1967, the Guadalajara archdiocese had 1,640 priests and just over 4 million faithful, a ratio a 1:2,500; approximately 20 percent of priests in Mexico lived in the Guadalajara archdiocese. See José Bravo Ugarte, *México, II, Relaciones internacionales, territorio, sociedad y cultura*, vol. 3, part 2 of *Historia de México* (México: Jus, 1959), 430; and José Gutierrez Casillas, SJ, *Historia de la Iglesia en México* (México: Porrúa, 1974), 451.

44. *El Informador*, July 9 and 11, 1918.

45. BPE, Miscelánea 783/7, "Apuntes," 7–15; González Flores, *La cuestión religiosa*, 310–12; Antonio Rius Facius, *De Don Porfirio a Plutarco: Historia de la ACJM* (Mexico City: Jus, 1958), 103–6; Camberos Vizcaíno, *Un Hombre*, 254–55.

46. Francis Clement Kelley, *The Book of Red and Yellow: Being a Story of Blood and a Yellow Streak* (Chicago: The Catholic Church Extension Society of the United States of America, 1915).

47. David O'Brien, *Public Catholicism* (New York: Macmillan, 1989); José Casanova, *Public Religions in the Modern World* (Chicago: University of Chicago Press, 1994).

48. Alvarado is the first of 435 signatories, of whom over 90 percent are

archdiocesan clergy; BPE, Miscelánea 783/7, "Memorial del Cabildo Metropolitano y Clero de la Arquidiócesis de Guadalajara, al C. Presidente de la República Mexicana, Dn. Venustiano Carranza; y Voto de Adhesión y Obediencia al Ilmo. y Revmo. Sr. Arzobispo, Dr. y Mtro. Dn. Francisco Orozco y Jiménez," April, 1918.

49. Dávila and Chávez, *Documentos*, vol. 2, 45–49; *El Informador*, July 10, 1918.
50. Dávila and Chávez, *Documentos*, vol. 2, 36.
51. See María Teresa Fernández Aceves, "The Political Mobilization of Women in Revolutionary Guadalajara, 1910–1940," (PhD diss., University of Illinois, Chicago, 2000), 110–13. Gabriela Cano, "El Porfiriato y la revolución Mexicana: construcciones en torno al feminismo y al nacionalismo," *La Ventana* 4 (1996): 39–58.
52. Dávila and Chávez, *Documentos*, vol. 2, 27.
53. BPE, Miscelánea 783.7, Memorial, 31.
54. *El Informador*, July 19, 1918.
55. González Flores, *La cuestión religiosa*, 315; Rius Facius, *De Don Porfirio*, 104.
56. Rius Facius, *De Don Porfirio*, 108.
57. Fondo Miguel Palomar y Vizcarra box 41, folder 297, document 3207, Álvarez Tostado to Palomar y Vizcarra, 22–23 July 1918 (henceforth, citations will appear separated by diagonals, for example, FPyV, 41/297/3207); BPE, Miscelánea 783.7, "Apuntes," 19. *El Informador*, 23 July 1918, estimated more than 10,000.
58. FPyV, 41/297/3206, Álvarez to Palomar, July 22–23, 1918; González Flores, *La cuestión religiosa*, 321–23.
59. Archivo General de la Nación (henceforth, AGN), Presidentes, Estado Mayor Presidencial, vol. 340, 72, 58.
60. FPyV, 41/297/3207, Álvarez to Palomar, July 22–23, 1918.
61. Antonio Gómez Robledo, *Anacleto González Flores: El Maestro* 2nd ed. (México: Jus, 1947), 72.
62. González Flores, *La cuestión religiosa*, 322.
63. Antonio Gómez Robledo attributed the caption "*Le silence est, après la parole, la seconde puissance du monde*," to Félicité Robert de Lamennais (1782–1854), a French philosopher-priest who advocated democracy and church-state separation; see Gómez Robledo, *Anacleto González Flores*, 73. However, the idea seems to belong not to Lamennais, but to the French diplomat Charles-Maurice Talleyrand-Périgord (1754–1838), and may be found in his *La Confession de Talleyrand, V. 1–5, Mémoires du Prince de Talleyrand* (Paris: Sauvaitre), 1891.
64. Gómez Robledo, *Anacleto González Flores*, 73.
65. Dávila Garibi and Chávez Hayhoe, *Documentos*, vol. 1, 64–67, 74–78; *Colección de Leyes*, 241–54.
66. Rius Facius, *De Don Porfirio*, 111.
67. Decree 1913 stated that the legislation would first take effect in Guadalajara (August 1), then in the rest of the state (September 10); *Colección de Leyes*, 243.
68. These were not Anita Brenner's syncretic faithful with idols stashed behind altars; or, if they were, they also had a conventional interest in the sacraments that is

generally downplayed in the writing of Brenner's generation. See Anita Brenner, *Idols behind Altars* (New York: Payson and Clark, 1929).

69. González Flores, *La cuestión religiosa*, 331.

70. Dávila Garibi, *Apuntes*, vol. 5, 380–85.

71. BPE, Miscelánea 783.7, "Apuntes," 21.

72. González Flores, *La cuestión religiosa*, 332; Camberos Vizcaíno, *Un hombre*, 270.

73. Dávila Garibi and Chávez Hayhoe, *Documentos*, vol. 2.

74. González Flores, *La cuestión religiosa*, 333.

75. BPE, Miscelánea 783.7, "Apuntes," 91–92; Dávila Garibi and Chávez Hayhoe, *Documentos*, vol. 2, 200–6.

76. González Flores, *La cuestión religiosa*, 333.

77. Dávila Garibi and Chávez Hayhoe, *Documentos*, vol. 2, 209–211.

78. AHJ, Ramo Trabajo, T-2-918, box T-40 bis, unnumbered folder; and box T-9-918, unnumbered folder.

79. AHJ, T-2-918, Benito Gómez et al. to Manuel Bouquet, January 21, 1918.

80. AHJ, T-2-918, February 6, 1918.

81. AHJ, T-2-918, January 21, 1918.

82. AHJ, T-9-918, January 27, 1919.

83. AHJ, T-2-918, June 2, 1918, and another letter simply dated June 1918; on Vásquez Cisneros's role in the conflict of 1918, see Rius Facius, *De Don Porfirio*, 103–114.

84. *El Obrero*, June 7 and 28, 1919; August 16, 1919; November 22, 1919; July 3, 1920; September 17, 1921; October 29, 1921; December 13, 1921; March 12, 1922.

85. SD, 812.00/22456, Silliman, Guadalajara, December 28, 1918.

86. González Flores, *La cuestión religiosa*, 337.

87. *El Informador*, February 5, 1919.

88. Francisco Barbosa Guzmán, *La iglesia y el gobierno civil*, vol. 6 of *Jalisco desde la revolución* (Guadalajara: Gobierno del Estado/Universidad de Guadalajara, 1988), 231–33.

89. The text of both messages is reprinted in Dávila Garibi, *Apuntes*, vol. 5, 420–21.

90. Rius Facius, *De Don Porfirio*, 113–14.

91. The CCO was formed in 1919 and renamed the Confederación Católica del Trabajo (CCT) in 1920. In 1922 it was expanded and renamed the Confederación Nacional Católica del Trabajo (CNCT). From 1921 to 1922, another CCO—a women's organization called the Confederación Católica de Obreras—also existed. This organization eventually united with the CNCT, which included both men's and women's unions.

Chapter 7

1. His version of the events may be consulted in English through a memoir published by his host, Bishop Francis C. Kelley, president of the Chicago-based Catholic Extension Society; see Franciso Orozco y Jiménez, *Memoir of the Most Reverend*

Franciso Orozco y Jiménez, Archbishop of Guadalajara, Mexico, Being a True Account of His Life for the Ten Months after His Secret Return to His Diocese and the Incidents Connected with His Arrest and Expulsion; Also the Documents and Protests Connected with Same (Chicago: Extension Print, 1918).

2. Alfredo Méndez Medina, "Apuntes sobre el Congreso Obrero de Guadalajara," *Acción y fe* 1 (1921): 457–62.

3. J. Jesús Flores López, *Don Nacho. Ignacio S. Orosco "Don Nacho y la Confederación Nacional Católica del Trabajo"* (Guadalajara: printed by author, 1982).

4. *La Palabra* ran from 1917–1919 under the direction of Anacleto González Flores; *El Archivo Social* from 1921 to 1925 under the direction of the Jesuit Arnulfo Castro; and *El Obrero* from 1919 to 1925 with a diverse editorial staff, including Nicolás Leaño, F. Medina, Carlos Blanco, Anacleto González Flores, J. G. Cardona, and J. M. Navarro. Others who played an active role in this newspaper included Ignacio S. Orozco and J. Jesús López Flores.

5. The name changed over time in accordance with its changing objectives, from the Confederación Católica Obrera (CCO) in 1919, to the Confederación Católica del Trabajo (CCT) in 1920, and finally, the Confederación Nacional Católica del Trabajo (CNCT) as of 1922.

6. The Biblioteca Pública del Estado de Jalisco has an important partial collection, covering the first three years of publication, 158 issues published between June 1919 and July 1922.

7. Karen Arlette Flores Guizar, an undergraduate student of history at Universidad de Guadalajara, ordered, analyzed, and photographed the collection, creating an excellent database, searchable by key words, with embedded pdf files of every page of the newspaper. She used the Biblioteca Pública del Estado de Jalisco collection for this project.

8. Mario A. Aldana Rendón, *Desarrollo económico de Jalisco, 1821–1940* (Guadalajara: Universidad de Guadalajara, 1979); see also José María Muriá: *El territorio de Jalisco* (Guadalajara: Editorial Hezágono, 1991) and *Ensayos de historiografía jalisciense* (Guadalajara: Universidad de Guadalajara/Xalli, 1990).

9. Nevertheless, by 1927, some Huichol and Nauhua towns took up arms with the Cristeros, "in defense of religion."

10. This area would also develop strong pro-communist unions; see Jaime Tamayo, *Los movimientos sociales, 1917–1929*, vol. 4 of *Jalisco desde la revolución* (Guadalajara: Gobierno del Estado/Universidad de Guadalajara, 1988).

11. Manuel Ceballos Ramírez, "La enciclica *Rerum Novarum* y los trabajadores catolicos de la Ciudad de Mexico (1891–1913)," *Historia Mexicana* 129 (1983): 3–38.

12. Biblioteca Pública del Estado de Jalisco (henceforth, BPE), Miscelánea Pamphlet Collection 657/7, "Reglamento del Círculo Católico de Obreros Llamado Sociedad Alcalde," (Guadalajara: Imp. De T. Ramírez, 1895), 5–8.

13. Contrary to Anderson's argument, the formation of a Catholic nationalism cannot be explained primarily by the phenomenon of print capitalism, and clearly precedes

the era of literary mass consumption; see Benedict Anderson, *Imagined Communities: Reflections on the Origin and Spread of Nationalism*, rev. ed. (London: Verso, 1991).

14.   Pbro. Librado Tovar, *Primer Congreso Católico Regional Obrero* (Guadalajara: Tip. C. M. Sainz, 1921).

15.   Comité Diocesano de Acción Católica Social, *Curso Social Agricola Zapopano* (Guadalajara: Tip. Renacimiento, 1921).

16.   Junta Diocesana de Acción Católico-Social, *Primer Congreso Nacional Obrero: preparación, reseña, conclusiones aprobadas, modelos de estatutos para las agrupaciones confederadas*, (Guadalajara: Tip. Renacimiento, 1922).

17.   At the time, Morones was also secretary of industry, commerce and labor to President Calles, an indication of just how firmly pro-government the CROM in reality was. Seminario Conciliar Mexicano (henceforth, SCM), 30/C-III-9, Confederación Nacional Católica del Trabajo, *Carta abierta del Comité Central de la Confederación Nacional Católica del Trabajo—C.N.C.T.-al Sr. Luis N. Morones, Secretario de Industria, Comercio y Trabajo* (México: C.N.C.T., 1926), 4; Ceballos Ramírez, "El sindicalismo Católico en México, 1919–1931," *Historia Mexicana* 140 (1986): 656.

18.   Meyer credited Joaquín Márquez Montiel as the source of his data; see Jean Meyer, *La cristiada*, vol. 2, trans. Aurelio Garzón del Camino (México: Siglo XXI, 1991), 216; and Joaquín Márquez Montiel, *La doctrina social de la Iglesia y la legislación obrera mexicana*, 2nd ed. (México: Jus, 1958), 51. Meyer quoted from the rare first edition (Buena Prensa, 1939).

19.   Barry Carr, *El movimiento obrero y la política en México, 1910–1929* (México: Era, 1991), 216.

20.   Márquez Montiel, *La doctrina social*, 46; see also Joaquín Márquez Montiel, *La Iglesia y el Estado en México* (Chihuahua: Regional, 1950), 28–29.

21.   Méndez Medina, "Apuntes," 457–62. Márquez Montiel was familiar with this article; see Márquez Montiel, *La doctrina social de la Iglesia*, 52.

22.   The question is not academic, as Meyer has pointed out, because historians estimate that the anarchosindicalist Confederación General del Trabajo (CGT) counted about 15,000 members, while the CROM's figure of 400,000 members was likely inflated. Alan Knight has estimated that the CROM figure was more likely around 100,000, a number that would put into focus the seriousness of the Catholic threat; see Alan Knight, *The Mexican Revolution*, vol. 2 (Lincoln: University of Nebraska Press, 1986), 504; see also, Meyer, *La cristiada*, vol. 2, 216.

23.   Maximiano Reyes, "Circular del Comité Central de la C.N.C.T.," *El Archivo Social* 2, no. 25 (1922): 1–2.

24.   The congress recognized and admitted delegates from several kinds of groups. These included Catholic workers (1 delegate per 100 members), free workers (1 delegate per 100 members), religious associations with a majority working-class membership (1 delegate per 200 members), and workers attending from localities in which no formal organization existed (1 delegate per city, town, congregation, hacienda, or parish); Junta Diocesana de Acción Católico-Social, *Primer congreso nacional obrero:*

preparación, reseña, conclusiones aprobadas, modelos de estatutos para las agrupaciones confederadas (Guadalajara: Tip. Renacimiento, 1922), 15–17, 23.

25.   In the first CNCT report, published in November 1922, Reyes reported 67 unions that had been officially admitted, of which 63 reported a total of 7,540 members. Individual unions varied in their membership from 20 to 600 individuals, with an average of 100 to 120 per union. He also reported a sizeable backlog of applications that the CNCT administration had yet to process. In April 1923, Reyes reported 144 official member unions in an abbreviated report that did not detail their internal membership. However, assuming a continued average of 120 members per union, the 1923 figures would suggest somewhere in the neighborhood of 17,000 members. See Maximiano Reyes, "Primer Informe Semestral que el Comité Central de la C.N.C.T. rinde respetuosamente al Excmo y Rvmo Sr Arzobispo de México Dr. D José Mora y del Río, Presidente de la Acción Social Católica en la República, y a cada uno de los Ilmos y Rvmos Sres Arzobispos y Obispos de la República Mexicana," *El Archivo Social* 2, no. 34 (1922): 1–26; Maximiano Reyes, "Segundo Informe Semestral que rinde el Comité Central de la C.N.C.T.," *El Archivo Social* 2, no. 48 (1923): 1–8.

26.   In particular, the smaller sets of numbers (7,540–22,000) are consistent with specific reports of official applications and membership. The larger sets of data (600–800 delegates, 353 unions, 80,000 members) are harder to gauge in the absence of the CNCT archive.

27.   Miguel Palomar y Vizcarra, the Guadalajara lawyer, was responsible for the legal strategy. See in particular, Miguel Palomar y Vzcarra, "La Legalización del Sindicato y de sus instituciones filiales," *El Archivo Social* 2, no. 42 (1923): 13–20. This is the second of three parts in a serially published pamphlet. The others may be found in *El Archivo Social* 2, no. 40 (1923): 1–12, and *El Archivo Social* 2, no. 44 (1923): 21–41.

28.   See *El Archivo Social* and Junta Diocesana, *Primer Congreso Nacional*.

29.   The case in point involved the Catholic Unión Interprofesional de Obreros y Campesinos, which participated in a joint committee with the socialist and pro-government union locals at the "Dos Estrellas" mines of Tlalpujahua, Michoacán; see SCM, 30/C-III-9, "Carta abierta," 7.

30.   Ceballos Ramírez, "El sindicalismo Católico," 641.

31.   Jean-Marie Mayeur, "Los partidos católicos y demócrata-cristianos, intento de definición." *Colección "Diálogo y Autocrítica"* 6 (México: IMDOSOC, 1987), 4–5.

32.   John Pollard, *Catholicism in Modern Italy: Religion, Society and Politics since 1861* (London: Routledge, 2008), 59–61.

33.   José Andres-Gallego, *Pensamiento y acción social de la Iglesia en España* (Madrid: Espasa Universitaria, 1984), 398–99; see also, Tom Buchanan and Martin Conway, eds., *Political Catholicism in Europe, 1918–1965* (New York: Oxford University Press, 1996); Wolfram Kaiser and Helmut Wohnout, eds., *Political Catholicism in Europe 1918–1945*, vol. 1 (London: Routledge, 2004).

34.   Stathis N. Kalyvas, *The Rise of Christian Democracy in Europe* (Ithaca: Cornell University Press, 1996), 115.

35. There is some evidence that liberals successfully deployed the term to evoke negative change in society, as in the Swiss case, where the fear of "confessionalization" caused conservative politicians to distance themselves from Catholic initiatives during the inter-war period; see Kaiser and Wohnout, *Political Catholicism*, 70–72.

36. Kalyvas, *The Rise of Christian Democracy*, 2.

37. Fondo Miguel Palomar y Vizcarra box 40, folder 285, document 2285, Castro to Palomar y Vizcarra, Hastings Great Britain, June 21, 1911 (henceforth, citations will appear separated by diagonals, for example, FPyV, 40/285/2285).

38. Junta Diocesana, *Primer congreso nacional*; see also Pbro. Librado Tovar, *Primer Congreso Católico Regional Obrero* (Guadalajara: Tip. C. M. Sainz, 1921).

39. Stephen Andes has argued that there were other points of tension that led to Méndez Medina's ouster, including the Jesuit leadership's desire for Society members not to be involved in issues of an economic nature, where they were in charge of property or investments, and that he was accused of some indiscretion in the confessional; see Stephen J. C. Andes, "A Catholic Alternative to Revolution: The Survival of Social Catholicism in Postrevolutionary Mexico," *The Americas* 68, no. 4 (2012): 529–62.

40. The congress organizing committee read like a *who's who* of twentieth-century Guadalajara social Catholicism, including: Alfredo Morfín Silva, Luis and Salvador Chávez Hayhoe, J. M. Esparza, Nicolás Leaño, Arnulfo Castro, Luis B. de la Mora, José Gutiérrez Hermosillo, Jorge Padilla, José Toral Moreno, Anacleto González Flores, José Garibi Rivera, Carlos Blanco, Maximiano Reyes, Miguel Gómez Loza, Ignacio Orozco, Manuel Yerena, Rosendo Vizcaíno, Pedro Vásquez Cisneros, and Efraín González Luna. Along with Méndez Medina, the other main speakers were René Capistrán Garza, Arnulfo Castro, and Miguel Palomar y Vizcarra; see Junta Diocesana, *Primer congreso nacional*, 11–12 and 19–20.

41. Junta Diocesana, *Primer congreso nacional*, 6–7.

42. See chapter 8.

43. Méndez Medina, "Apuntes," 459–61.

44. Manuel Ceballos Ramírez, "El sindicalismo," 621–73.

45. This and subsequent quotations from the debate over confessionalism are from Méndez Medina, "Apuntes," 459–61.

46. Literally, till the uvula collapses.

47. Méndez Medina, "Apuntes," 462.

48. Bernardo García Díaz, *Textiles del valle de Orizaba (1880–1925): cinco ensayos de historia sindical y social* (Xalapa: Universidad Veracruzana, 1990), 220–22.

49. Martin Conway, "Introduction," in *Political Catholicism in Europe*, ed. Buchanan and Conway, 4.

50. There are many such examples in publications such as *La Palabra, El Archivo Social*, and *El Obrero*.

51. The decree, *Quemadmodum Deus*, was published December 8, 1870.

52. *El Obrero* 36 (February 7, 1920), 1.

53. Robert E. Quirk, *The Mexican Revolution and the Catholic Church*, 26.

54. Kalyvas, *The Rise of Christian Democracy*, 188–192; Gould, *Origins of Liberal Dominance*, 25–44; Martin Conway, "Belgium," in *Political Catholicism in Europe*, ed. Buchanan and Conway (New York: Oxford University Press, 1996) 187–218.

55. See chapter 1.

56. Andres-Gallego, *Pensamiento y acción social*, 418.

57. James Hennesey, SJ, *American Catholics: A History of the Roman Catholic Community in the United States* (Oxford University Press: New York, 1981), 228–29.

58. *El Obrero* 159 (June 18, 1922): 2.

59. Jaime Tamayo described them as scab unions; see Jaime Tamayo, *En el interinato de Adolfo de la Huerta y el gobierno de Alvaro Obregón (1920–1924)*, vol. 7 of *La clase obrera en la historia de México* (México: Siglo XXI / UNAM, 1987), 178–79, 181; and Jaime Tamayo, *Los movimientos sociales*, 80, 83.

60. Michael Snodgrass, *Deference and Defiance in Monterrey: Workers, Paternalism, and Revolution in Mexico, 1890–1950* (Cambridge: Cambridge University Press, 2003).

61. Tamayo, *En el interinato*, 176; García Díaz, *Textiles*, 221.

62. Ceballos Ramírez, "El sindicalismo católico," 639–45; Ceballos Ramírez, "La enciclica *Rerum Novarum*," 3–38; see also, Margarita Castro Palmares, Adriana Villa Michel, and Silvia Venegas Pacheco, "Indicios de las relaciones laborales en Jalisco," in *IV Concurso sobre derecho laboral Manuel M. Diéguez*, no editor listed (Guadalajara: Gobierno del Estado, 1982), 207–507.

63. William H. Sewell Jr., "How Classes Are Made: Critical Reflections on E. P. Thompson's Theory of Working-class Formation," in *E. P. Thompson: Critical Perspectives*, ed. Harvey J. Kaye and Keith McClelland (Philadelphia: Temple University Press, 1990), 72.

64. J. Ignacio Dávila Garibi, *Memoria histórica de las labores de la Asociación de Damas Católicas de Guadalajara* (Guadalajara: J. M. Iguíñiz, 1920), 143–44.

65. J. Jesús Flores López, "Ignacio S. Orozco," 18.

66. There were men involved in the UDC, but not as *Damas*. They tended to have an advisory role.

67. On Catholic notions of harmony and order, see Jorge Adame Goddard, *El pensamiento político*; for similar ideas in twentieth-century Argentine labor history, see Daniel James, *Resistance and Integration: Peronism and the Argentine Working Class, 1946–1976* (New York: Cambridge University Press, 1993), 47–48.

68. See chapter 1.

69. Adame Goddard, *El pensamiento*, 249–50.

70. On the nineteenth-century origins of Catholic thought on family, wages, and social degeneration, see Katherine A. Lynch, *Family, Class, and Ideology in Early Industrial France: Social Policy and the Working-Class Family, 1825–1848* (Madison: University of Wisconsin Press, 1988), 33–48.

71. José Toral Moreno, *El Sindicato Obrero y sus Instituciones Filiales*, 2 vols. (Guadalajara: Unión de Sindicatos Obreros Católicos de Guadalajara, 1923).

72. *El Obrero*, May 21, 1922, 2, and *El Obrero*, May 28, 1922, 3–4.

73.   SCM, 30/C-III-9, "Carta abierta," 5; FPyV, 38/265/308, Reyes to Palomar y Vizcarra, Guadalajara, May 12, 1922; Castro Palmares, Villa Michel, and Venegas Pacheco, "Indicios," 261–62.

74.   For comparative examples, there are many good studies on Mexican labor history. I have already mentioned Carr, *El movimiento obrero* and Snodgrass, *Deference*; see also, John Lear, *Workers, Neighbors, and Citizens: The Revolution in Mexico City* (Lincoln, NE: University of Nebraska Press, 2001). The classic source for material on such topics is *La clase obrera en la historia de México*, a multivolume set of monographs edited at the Universidad Nacional Autónoma de México under the supervision of Pablo González Casanova.

75.   *El Obrero*, December 24, 1921, 2.

76.   *El Obrero*, February 28, 1920, 1; and *El Obrero*, May 1, 1920, 1.

77.   *El Obrero*, June 28, 1919, 3; and *El Obrero*, August 6, 1921, 4.

78.   *El Obrero*, September 14, 1919, 1.

79.   *El Obrero*, January 31, 1920, 1; and *El Obrero*, February 14, 1920, 1.

80.   *El Obrero*, June 4, 1921, 1.

81.   *El Obrero*, April 9, 1922, 3.

82.   *El Obrero*, July 2, 1922, 1.

83.   *El Obrero*, June 14, 1919, 1.

84.   *El Obrero*, August 9, 1919, 1.

85.   *El Obrero*, January 22, 1921, 2.

86.   *El Obrero*, January 10, 1920, 1.

87.   *El Obrero*, February 14, 1920, 4.

88.   *El Obrero*, November 27, 1920, 1; and *El Obrero*, January 1, 1921, 1.

89.   This list was compiled from issues of *El Obrero* for the years 1919–1922, which are held at the BPE in Guadalajara. Surely it is not exhaustive.

90.   *El Obrero*, March 5, 1921, 4; and *El Obrero*, April 2, 1921, 2. The women's locals affiliated with the UCEC would be one of the initial recruiting bodies for the Saint Joan of Arc Women's Brigades during the Cristero Rebellion. See Jean Meyer, *The Cristero Rebellion*, 131–32.

91.   I have found relatively little biographical data on Maximiano Reyes, although his family was associated with the Atemajac textile mill going back a couple of generations. Two family members, Francisco Sr. (born in 1839) and Francisco Jr. (born in 1879), were registered in the 1904 military census, and both listed *industrial*, or factory worker, as their occupation. This was not so common in Mezquitán, where 50 percent of the male population were rural day laborers or tenant farmers, and another 25 percent were brickmakers; see Robert Curley, "La mira de los munícipes: el cabildo de Guadalajara y la modernidad a principios del siglo veinte," in *Vida y muerte entre la ciudad y sus barrios: Homenaje al Panteón Municipal de Guadalajara en su centenario, 1896–1996*, ed. Susana Pacheco Jiménez (Guadalajara: Ayuntamiento de Guadalajara/Ágata, 2000), 63–72.

92.   *El Obrero*, May 28, 1921, 2.

93. *El Obrero*, June 11, 1921, 2.

94. *El Obrero*, August 26, 1921, 1.

95. *El Obrero*, December 3, 1921, 1; *El Obrero*, December 17, 1921, 3; *El Obrero*, January 15, 1922, 2; *El Obrero*, February 12, 1922, 2; and *El Obrero*, March 19, 1922, 3.

96. *El Obrero*, May 14, 1922, 1.

97. Jürgen Elvert, "A Microcosm of Society or the Key to a Majority in the Reichstag? The Centre Party in Germany," in *Political Catholicism in Europe 1918–1945*, vol. 1, ed. Wolfram Kaiser and Helmut Wohnout (London: Routledge, 2004), 54.

98. Anacleto González Flores was connected to this phenomenon, whether by design or coincidence: the two newspapers in which I have found the publication of ex-votos are *La Palabra* (Guadalajara, 1917–1919) and *El Obrero* (Guadalajara, 1919–1925), which succeeded *La Palabra*. González Flores edited both papers.

99. *El Obrero*, December 24, 1921, 4.

100. *Votos de gracias* may be found in *La Palabra*, nos. 49, 51, 52, 56, 60, 66, 75, 76, 81, and 90. The saints change, but the general formula stays the same. The thankful include men as well as women.

101. *La Palabra*, November 10, 1918, 4.

102. *La Palabra*, June 2, 1918, 4.

103. Examples may be found in *El Obrero*, nos. 23, 99, 102, 107, 108, 110, 114, 129, 130, 134, 137, 147, 151, and 156.

104. *El Obrero*, July 12, 1919, 1; another example may be found at *El Obrero*, April 23, 1922, 1.

105. *El Obrero*, November 26, 1921, 3.

106. *El Obrero*, June 25, 1921, 2.

107. For the fifth anniversary commemoration of his death, see *El Obrero*, January 31, 1920, 1.

108. Anderson, *Imagined Communities*, 5–6, 34–35.

109. The Our Lady of the Pillar coronation has two interesting parallels with Mexico. First, the coronation was conceived as a counterweight to anticlericalism; second, it was followed by a 1908 celebration in which she received the full honors of captain-general, the highest military distinction; see William J. Callahan, *The Catholic Church in Spain, 1875–1998* (Washington, DC: The Catholic University of America Press, 2000), 263.

110. Wright-Rios, "Envisioning Mexico's Catholic Resurgence," 197–239.

111. Wright-Rios, "Envisioning"; *Cuarto Congreso Católico Nacional Mexicano* (Oaxaca: Tipografía de la Casa de Gama, 1913).

112. Comité Diocesano, *Curso Social*.

113. *El Informador*, January 17, 1921, 1; and *El Informador*, January 18, 1921, 1, 3, includes photographs.

114. John Goggin, "Pontifical Mass," in *The Catholic Encyclopedia. An international Work of Reference on the Constitution, Doctrine, Discipline, and History of the Catholic Church*, ed. Charles G. Herbermann et al., vol. 12 (New York: Robert Appleton Company, 1911).

115.   Although the obligations of each are not specified, a deacon may have read the gospel; a subdeacon may have carried the chalice with wine to the altar, prepared the accoutrements for the Eucharist, and read the Epistles; a presbyter may have assisted more generally; see Herbert Thurston, "Deacons," in *The Catholic Encyclopedia. An international Work of Reference on the Constitution, Doctrine, Discipline, and History of the Catholic Church*, ed. Charles G. Herbermann et al., 15 vols., vol. 4 (New York: Robert Appleton Company, 1908).

116.   *Album de la coronación de Ntra. Sra. de Zapopan* (Guadalajara: Impresores y Editores Juan Kaiser Sucs., S. En C., 1921), 47–59.

117.   *Album*, 70–73.

118.   *Album*, 10, 65.

119.   *Album*, 64–65.

120.   *Album*, appendix, 18.

121.   *El Informador*, January 19,1921, 1, 3, includes photographs; *Album*, 65–66.

122.   *Album*, 76; Luis Páez Brotchie, *Jalisco, historia mínima* (Guadalajara: H. Ayuntamiento Municipal, 1985), 363. Both of these sources quote *La Epoca* estimates of 20,000. *El Obrero*, January 22, 1921, 1–2, puts the number at 30,000. To put this into perspective, 30,000 would be equivalent to one in every five people living at that time in Guadalajara. By contrast, Barry Carr makes reference to a turnout of 40,000 in Mexico City for a CROM rally on the eve of the Cristero Rebellion (1926) and qualifies it as the largest of the decade. Proportional to the population, even 20,000 in Guadalajara would have been more formidable, as it was a much smaller city than Mexico. One must also take into account the excitement generated by the transient pilgrim population in Guadalajara expressly for the coronation. Carr, *El movimiento obrero*, 222.

123.   *Album*, 76; *El Informador*, January 19, 1921, 1, 3.

124.   Unlike Reyes and Díaz, Corona was assassinated in the prime of his political career. He was stabbed to death in Guadalajara at the age of 52, in 1889.

125.   *Album*, 74–75; *El Informador*, January 20, 1921, 1, 3, includes photographs; *Páez Brotchie, Jalisco*, 362–65; Meyer, *La Cristiada*, vol. 2, 113.

Chapter 8

1.   Zuno died in 1980, and it bears mentioning that from the early 1950s until the early 1970s, he wrote and published dozens of books and pamphlets on art, politics, and history, including his autobiography in four volumes. See José Guadalupe Zuno Hernández, *Reminiscencias de una vida*, 4 vols. (Guadalajara: no publisher given, 1956–1972).

2.   Arnaldo Córdova, *La Revolución en crisis. La aventura del maximato* (México: Cal y Arena, 1999).

3.   Jaime Tamayo, *La conformación del estado moderno y los conflictos políticos, 1917–1929*, vol. 2 of *Jalisco desde la revolución* (Guadalajara: Gobierno del Estado/Universidad de Guadalajara, 1988).

4. Jürgen Buchenau, *Plutarco Elías Calles and the Mexican Revolution* (Lanham, MD: Rowman & Littlefield Publishers, Inc., 2007), 146.

5. On the De la Huerta rebellion, see Georgette José Valenzuela, "Campaña, rebelión y las elecciones presidenciales de 1923 a 1924 en México," *Estudios de Historia Moderna y Contemporánea de México* 23 (2002): 55–111; Enrique Plascencia de la Parra, *Personajes y escenarios de la rebelión delahuertista, 1923–1924* (México: UNAM-Porrúa, 1998); Jaime Tamayo and Fidelina G. Llerenas, *El levantamiento delahuertista: Cuatro rebeliones y cuatro jefes militares* (Guadalajara: Universidad de Guadalajara, 1995); John W. F. Dulles, *Ayer en México. Una crónica de la Revolución (1919–1936)*, trans. Julio Zapata (México: Fondo de Cultura Económica, 1993 [1961]), 201–240; and J. Ángel Moreno Ochoa, *Semblanzas revolucionarias: compendio del movimiento de liberación en Jalisco* (Guadalajara: Talleres Berni, 1965).

6. Moreno Ochoa, *Semblanzas revolucionarias: compendio*, 149–53.

7. Córdova, *La Revolución en crisis*, 23–87.

8. State Department Papers Relating to the Internal Affairs of Mexico, record group 59, file 812.00 (Political Affairs) document 27035, McConnico to Secretary of State, Guadalajara, 12 February 1924 (henceforth, citations will appear separated by diagonals, for example, SD, 812.00/27035).

9. Tamayo, *La conformación del estado moderno*, 214–15, 226.

10. Jean Meyer, *El conflicto entre la Iglesia y el Estado, 1926–1929*, trans. Aurelio Garzón del Camino, vol. 2 of *La cristiada* (México: Siglo XXI, 1973), 131–33.

11. Archivo General de la Nación, Dirección General de Investigaciones Políticas y Sociales, box 1969-A/folder 2/24 pages, Report to Departamento Confidencial, Mexico, DF, 19–20 November 1924 (henceforth, citations will appear separated by diagonals, for example, AGN-DGIPS 1969-A/2/24).

12. *El Informador*, March 24, 1926, 1.

13. Jean Meyer provides excellent maps; see Jean Meyer, *La Cristiada, Obra Completa*, 2nd ed. (Mexico: Editorial Clio, 1999).

14. *El Informador*, June 30, 1929, 1–2.

15. Meyer, *La cristiada*, vol. 2, 111–12.

16. Members of the Regional Confederation of Mexican Labor (CROM), a client labor central.

17. Meyer, *La cristiada*, vol. 2, 113; Carr, *El movimiento obrero*, 217.

18. *El Obrero*, February 12, 1921, 1–2.

19. Meyer, *La cristiada*, vol. 2, 113. On the coronation, see chapter 7.

20. *El Obrero*, May 7, 1921, 1. Gómez Loza was executed in 1928. At the time he was the civilian governor of cristero-controlled areas in the state of Jalisco. *El Informador*, March 21, 1928. Like González Flores, he was recently beatified, and is one of several civilian martyrs from the 1920s that many Mexican Catholics hope will be canonized.

21. Vicente Camberos Vizcaíno, *Un hombre y una época, apuntes biográficos* (México: Editorial Jus, 1949), 306–7; Navarrete, *Por Dios y por la patria*, 32–35.

22. Rius Facius, *De Don Porfirio*, 192.

23. Natalie Zemon Davis has written of similar parody in seventeenth-century France; see *Sociedad y cultura en la Francia moderna* (Barcelona: Ediciones Crítica, 1993), 83–91.

24. Christopher R. Boyer, *Becoming Campesinos: Politics, Identity, and Agrarian Struggle in Postrevolutionary Michoacán, 1920–1935* (Stanford, CA: Stanford University Press, 2003), 104.

25. CROM organizers denied responsibility for the act of iconoclasm; see Rius Facius, *De Don Porfirio*, 193; Boyer, *Becoming Campesinos*, 105.

26. Alejandro Ruíz Villaloz, "Julián Vargas," *Criterio*, October 23, 1934.

27. Personal communication, Christopher R. Boyer, November 2010.

28. Christopher R. Boyer offers the highest, and most recent, casualty count. Jean Meyer accounted for ten pilgrims dead, eight men and two women. Rius Facius reported six Catholics, five men and one woman. Boyer, *Becoming Campesinos*, 106; Meyer, *La cristiada*, vol. 2, 116–17; Rius Facius, *De Don Porfirio*, 192–95.

29. "Julián ha sacado una pistola, presenta el menor blanco posible y empieza a tirar, a un tiempo que grita ¡Viva Cristo Rey! Junto a él, ha caído un hombre—un aguador—con el corazón atravesado, más adelante, una dama sube a una "luneta" . . . y grita ¡Viva Cristo Rey! ¡Vivan los hombres valientes! Cae fulminada por un tiro en pleno pecho. . . . Julián Vargas siente un dolor en las piernas, no puede sostenerse de pie, se las han atravesado; se sienta en la "luneta" y sigue disparando. . . . Un nuevo tiro le atraviesa el brazo y el antebrazo y lo hace soltar la pistola; la toma con la mano izquierda y sigue disparando. . . . Una bala expansiva atraviesa el cuello de Julián Vargas; abre los brazos, viene a dar contra el suelo y suelta la pistola que queda junto a su mano izquierda. La pistola estaba sin un sólo tiro." Rius Facius, *De Don Porfirio*, 194.

30. Tomás de Kempis (Thomas à Kempis, 1379–1471) was born in the diocese of Cologne. He is regarded as the author of the *Imitation of Christ*, a famous Christian study on devotion. In 1897, his remains were transferred to a St. Michaels Church of Zwolle, and enshrined in a reliquary that was paid for by donations from all over the world. This circumstance offers an indication of why he was a focus of devotion in early twentieth-century Mexico; see Vincent Scully, "Thomas à Kempis," in *The Catholic Encyclopedia. An international Work of Reference on the Constitution, Doctrine, Discipline, and History of the Catholic Church*, ed. Charles G. Herbermann et al., 15 vols., vol. 14 (New York: Robert Appleton Company, 1912).

31. *El Obrero*, June 11, 1921, 1, 3, 4.

32. According to the report, the turnout had been unfortunately low. Due to an early summer storm, about 550 marched. *El Obrero*, June 25, 1921, 2.

33. According to Rosendo Salazar, working class hero and pro-government labor historian, all three 1921 bombings were planned by the CROM at Luis Morones insistence; see Rosendo Salazar, *Civilismo y militarismo en la revolución* (México, 1958), 308. Carr, *El movimiento obrero*, 217, attributes both Mexico City bombings to the CROM, and cites an interview with José Petricioli in September, 1969.

34. *El Obrero*, November 19, 1921, 1; and *El Obrero*, November 26, 1921, 1–2. See also a letter of protest published in *El Obrero*, December 17, 1921, 2.

35. *El Obrero*, December 3, 1921, 1; *El Obrero*, December 17, 1921, 3; *El Obrero*, January 15, 1922, 2, 4.

36. SD, 812.00/25475, McConnico to Secretary of State, Guadalajara, 15 March 1922; SD, 812.00/25478, Summerlin to Secretary of State, Mexico, 14 March 1922, which reports three dead and five wounded.

37. In April, extraordinary elections were held to seat a new city council. The only party running was Zuno's Revolutionary Confederation. By May, the new city council was seated, Medina handed over the mayor's office to Zuno, and Medina went back to the post of vice mayor that he had held prior to the events of March. Tamayo, *La conformación del estado moderno*, 161–71.

38. On rent strikes in Mexico City, see John Robert Lear, *Workers, Neighbors, and Citizens: The Revolution in Mexico City* (Lincoln: University of Nebraska Press, 2001).

39. *El Informador*, March 27, 1922; *El Obrero*, April 2, 1922, 1, 3.

40. Navarrete, SJ, *Por Dios y por la Patria*; Moreno Ochoa, *Semblanzas revolucionarias, 1920–1930*, 39–45; Meyer, *La Cristiada*, vol. 2, 121; Jorge Durand, "El movimiento inquilinario de Guadalajara, 1922," *Encuentro* 2 (1984): 7–28; Jesús Gómez Fregoso, "Notas para la historia de los sindicatos católicos in Jalisco (1918–1924)," *Encuentro*, 3 (1984): 62; Ceballos Ramírez, "El sindicalismo Católico," 638; Jaime Tamayo, *Los movimientos sociales*, 135–36; Cuauhtémoc Medina Carrillo and Noe Figueroa Mendoza, *Luis C. Medina y el movimiento obrero en Jalisco* (Guadalajara: Gobierno de Jalisco, 1988), 63–83.

41. *El Obrero*, April 2, 1922, 1, 3.

42. *El Obrero*, April 2, 1922, 1, 3; *El Obrero*, April 9, 1922, 1; *El Obrero*, April 16, 1922, 1, 3, 8; *El Obrero*, April 23, 1922, 3; *El Obrero*, May 14, 1922, 1, 3, 4; *El Obrero*, June 18, 1922, 1.

43. Alfredo Robles Domínguez ran for the presidency as an opposition candidate against Obregón in 1920.

44. Obregón's official response had been that if the Catholic Church would have kept itself occupied with spiritual matters, instead of attacking the Bolsheviks, the bombing likely would not have occurred; SD, 812.00/24865, Summerlin to Secretary of State, Mexico, February 11, 1921; see also *El Obrero*, February 12, 1921, 2.

45. See chapter 7.

46. SD, 812.00/25479, Summerlin to Secretary of State, Mexico, March 14, 1922; SD, 812.00/25487, Summerlin to Secretary of State, Mexico, March 16, 1922.

47. SD, 812.00/25488, Summerlin to Secretary of State, Mexico, March 18, 1922.

48. SD, 812.00/25574, Adee to Hanna, Washington, May 3, 1922.

49. The report does not specify what the bishop meant by US government demands, but the most obvious of them regarded Article 27 of the Mexican constitution. The Harding administration, prior to the Bucareli agreements, was openly concerned about its possible application to US oil interests. Still one wonders if he did not

have in mind religious liberty, which had been an issue, albeit of lesser importance, during the Wilson administration.

50.   Following news of a Republican Party initiative promoting a US invasion of Mexico, the Chicago Church Federation voiced its opposition, reminding President Wilson that the Mexican bishops exiled in the United States during the revolution had called on American Catholics to oppose intervention; SD, 812.00/22899, Chicago Church Federation to President Wilson, Chicago, July 12, 1919. On recognition of the Obregón government, see SD, 812.00/24179, National Catholic War Council to Secretary of State Colby, Washington, June 4, 1920.

51.   The Veracruz occupation is treated in chapter 4. On Pershing's march through Chihuahua in 1916, see Friedrich Katz, *The Life and Times of Pancho Villa* (Stanford, CA: Stanford University Press, 1998), 566–82.

52.   Kelley seems misinformed on this count, as suggested by Villa's assassination the following year; see Katz, *The Life and Times of Pancho Villa*, 771–82.

53.   The State Department memorandum detailing Kelley's visit refers to him as Francis Canon Kelley, although it must have been Francis Clement Kelley, Oklahoma bishop and president of the Chicago-based Catholic Extension Society. *The Encyclopedia of American Catholic History* refers to Kelley as the principal publicist in the United States for the oppressed Mexican Catholic Church. Best known for *Blood-Drenched Altars: Mexican Study and Comment* (Milwaukee: The Bruce Publishing Company, 1935), a partisan interpretation of Mexican history, he was also host to Guadalajara Archbishop Francisco Orozco y Jiménez and other exiled Mexican Catholics after the fall of the Huerta regime, and again during the Cristero Rebellion. On Kelley's 1914 adventures, see Robert Curley, "Transnational Subaltern Voices: Sexual Violence, Anticlericalism, and the Mexican Revolution," in *Local Church, Global Church: Catholic Activism in Latin America from Rerum Novarum to Vatican II*, ed. Stephen J. Andes and Julia G. Young (Washington DC: The Catholic University of America Press, 2016), 91–116; a fairly exhaustive, if apologetic, biography of Kelley, is James P. Gaffey, *Francis Clement Kelley and the American Catholic Dream*, 2 vols. (Bensenville, IL: The Heritage Foundation, 1980).

54.   Valentina Torres Septién and Yves Solís, "De cerro a montaña santa: la construcción del monumento a Cristo Rey (1919–1960)," *Historia y grafia* 22 (2004).

55.   Rius Facius, *De Don Porfirio*, 223–24; Meyer, *La Cristiada*, vol. 2, 123.

56.   The interior ministry did, in fact, use legal and political means to block the plan, dragging out the process well into 1925. Today, a large statue of Christ the King is, in fact, located atop Cubilete peak, where thousands make the pilgrimage each year. The bishop of León defended the project in an ongoing official correspondence with high officials at the Interior Ministry. See Fondo Miguel Palomar y Vizcarra box 38, folder 256, document 312–19, Valverde Téllez to Valenzuela, August 22, August 31, and October 1, 1923 (henceforth, citations will appear separated by diagonals, for example, FPyV, 38/256/312–19).

57.   Meyer, *The Cristero Rebellion*, 28; see also Meyer, *La Cristiada*, vol. 2, 124–27.

58. *Estatutos de la Federación Anticlerical Mexicana* (México, 1923), 3, 7; also cited in Meyer, *La Cristiada*, vol. 2, 126–127.

59. Barbosa Guzmán, *La iglesia y el gobierno civil*, 272.

60. Meyer, *La Cristiada*, vol. 2, 132–33.

61. SD, 812.00/26480, Dawson to Secretary of State, Mexico City, October 15, 1923; see also, José Valenzuela, "Campaña."

62. AGN, DGIPS, 2053-A/2, Photograph of a letter, J. Prieto Laurens to A. De la Huerta, October 29, 1924.

63. AGN, DGIPS, 2053-A/2, Agente #1 to Gilberto Valenzuela, Mexico City, March 1925.

64. AGN, DGIPS, 2053-A/2, F. De la Garza to Secretaría de Gobernación, September 9, 1925, San Antonio, Texas.

65. SD, 812.00/27035, McConnico to Secretary of State, Guadalajara, February 12, 1924; SD, 812.00/27046, McConnico to Secretary of State, Guadalajara, February 21, 1924.

66. Meyer, *La Cristiada*, vol. 2, 134.

67. Rius Facius, *De Don Porfirio*, 270–71.

68. Chávez Hayhoe was the son of Manuel Chávez, former president of the Jalisco National Catholic Party. He was also co-editor, with J. Ignacio Dávila Garibi, of *Colección de documentos relativos a la cuestión religiosa en Jalisco*, 2 vols. (Guadalajara: Tip. J. M. Yguíniz), an invaluable 1920 compilation of primary sources; for discussion of these documents, see chapter 5.

69. AGN, DGIPS, 2053-A, Informe confidencial, Eduardo Sánchez Aldana to Francisco M. Delgado, Guadalajara, July 16, 1925.

70. *Excelsior*, March 20, 1924, 1.

71. The First National Eucharistic Congress was celebrated in Guadalajara in 1906; see chapter 1.

72. Rius Facius, *De Don Porfirio*, 299–303, especially 303.

73. Meyer, *La Cristiada*, vol. 2, 137–40.

74. Meyer, *La Cristiada*, vol. 2, 133.

75. Seminario Conciliar Mexicano, 86/A-VI-7, *Memoria del Congreso Eucarístico Nacional* (México, 1924), no page numbering (henceforth, SCM).

76. SCM, 86/A-VI-7, *Memoria del Congreso*, n.p.; Rius Facius, *De Don Porfirio*, 302; Meyer, *La Cristiada*, vol. 2, 138, refers to a CROM commando that interrupted the event.

77. This is significant in that it projects the Mexican nation backward to the conquest; see FPyV, 38/266/414–422, "Discurso pronunciado por el R. P. Mariano Cuevas de la Compañía de Jesús, miembro correspondiente de la Real Academia de la Historia," October 7, 1924.

78. FPyV, 38/266/436–448, "Discurso pronunciado por el joven pasante de derecho D. Luis Mier y Teran," October 9, 1924.

79. SCM, 86/A-VI-7, *Memoria del Congreso*, n.p.

80. FPyV, 38/265/342–344, Memorandum sent by the Rvdo. Padre Joaquín Cardoso, SJ, México, DF, Julio 24, 1924; FPyV, 38/265/345–347, Pablo Alexanderson Jr. to Miguel Palomar y Vizcarra, México, DF, July 31, 1924; FPyV, 38/266/349–353, 354–369 and 470–472, Protocolos eclesiásticos del congreso eucarístico, 1924.

81. FPyV, 38/265/342, Memorandum from Joaquín Cardoso, S. J., July 24, 1924.

82. The organizers used both the Olympia Theater and Lira Park; FPyV, 38/265/399, Lainé to Alexanderson, September 24, 1924; 38/265/379, Lainé to Alexanderson, September 1, 1924.

83. Cornelius Francis Donovan, *The Story of the Twenty-Eighth International Eucharistic Congress Held at Chicago, Illinois, United States of America, from June 20–24, 1926* (Chicago, 1927).

84. The speech is reproduced in SCM, *Memoria del Congreso Eucarístico Nacional* (México, 1924), no page numbering; see also Meyer, *La Cristiada*, vol. 2, 137, and Rius Facius, *De Don Porfirio*, 298–99.

85. Roque Bárcia, *Primer Diccionario General Etimológico de la Lengua Española*, 5 vols. (Madrid: Álvarez Hermanos, 1880–1883); 1.Viril. Adjetivo. Lo que pertenece al varón ó es propio de él. // . . . (Academia, *Diccionario de 1726*.) Etimología. *Varon*: latin, *virilis*.

86. Bárcia, *Primer Diccionario*, 1880–1883; 2. Viril. Masculino. Vidrio muy claro y transparente que se pone delante de algunas cosas para preservarlas ó defenderlas, deján- dolas patentes á la vista. Etimología. 1. Pudo formarse del nombre *vidrio*, cuasi vidril. (Academia, *Diccionario de 1726*.) 2. Viril 1, aludiendo á que ampara y defiende. 3. Viril. Masculino. La custodia pequeña que se pone dentro de la grande. Etimología. *Viril 2*.

87. *Custodia*, or custodian, is the Spanish for monstrance, emphasizing the notion that the host is at once publicly displayed and protected; see Bárcia, *Primer Diccionario*, 1880–1883; Custodia, Femenino. Guarda, por la acción y efecto de custodiar ó guardar alguna cosa. // Por antonomasia, la pieza de oro, plata ú otro metal en que se expone el Santísimo Sacramento á la pública veneración. // Anticuado. Tabernáculo. Etimología. *Custodio*: latin, Custodia.

88. See chapter 1, particularly the section entitled "Pilgrim and Soldier: The Paradox of Social Catholicism."

89. FPyV, 38/265/336, Cardoso to Palomar y Vizcarra, August 8, 1923.

90. Emphasis in the original text. "No vengo a decir que los hombres deben comulgar: ese deber, lo doy por supuesto, y, en muchos, a Dios gracias por cumplido. No vengo a decir aquí que los hombres deben comulgar, porque son hombres, sino que deben ser hombres porque comulgan . . . LA EUCARISTÍA ES UN SACRAMENTO ESENCIALMENTE VIRIL."

91. FPyV, 38/266/423–435, "Discurso pronunciado por el Sr. Lic. D. Miguel Palomar y Vizcarra, Caballero de la Orden de San Gregorio, Mexico City, October 9, 1924."

92. Pamela Voekel, "Liberal Religion: The Schism of 1861," in *Religious Cultures in Modern Mexico*, ed. Martin Austin Nesvig (Lanham: Rowman and Littlefield, 2007), 78–105; Arnulfo Hurtado, *El cisma mexicano* (México: Buena Prensa, 1956).

93. Matthew Butler's recent analysis of the Mexican Catholic Church does an excellent job of opening new space for debate and interpretation on this issue; see "*Sotanas Rojinegras*: Catholic Anticlericalism and Mexico's Revolutionary Schism," *The Americas* 65, no. 4 (2009): 531–54.

94. See Meyer, *The Cristero Rebellion*, 34; Butler, "*Sotanas Rojinegras*"; see also Mario Ramírez Rancaño, *El patriarca Pérez. La Iglesia Católica Apostólica Mexicana* (Mexico City: UNAM, 2006); and Mario Ramírez Rancaño, "La ruptura con el Vaticano. José Joaquín Pérez y la Iglesia Católica Apostólica Mexicana, 1925–1931," *Estudios de Historia Moderna y Contemporánea de México* 24 (2002): 103–42.

95. Rius Facius, *De Don Porfirio*, 305–14, the photograph is on 307; Meyer, *La cristiada*, vol. 2, 143–66.

96. Meyer, *The Cristero Rebellion*, 36–37.

97. AGN, DGIPS, 228/33, Oficial Primero to Secretaría de Gobernación, Mexico City, n.d. There is a second version of the report which seems to place it in March 1925; see AGN, DGIPS, 2053-A/2, Agent #1 to Secretaría de Gobernación, Mexico City.

98. AGN, DGIPS, 228/33/6, Agent #9 to Departamento Confidencial, Mexico City, June 26, 1925.

99. Archivo Municipal de Guadalajara (henceforth, AMG), 1918, folder 139, Gobierno to municipal president, Rivera Rosas, February 1 and March 5, 1918; AMG, folder 669, Gobierno to municipal president, May 27, 1918.

100. AGN, DGIPS, 244/10/11, Agent #24 (Eduardo Sánchez Aldana) to Departamento Confidencial, Guadalajara, August 16–22, 1925.

101. AGN, DGIPS, 244/10/11, 1925.

102. *El Informador*, December 19, 1924, 1; *El Informador*, December 23, 1924, 1, 3; *El Informador*, January 30, 1925, 1, 5; *El Informador*, July 28, 1925, 1, 6; *El Informador*, July 29, 1925, 1, 5; *El Informador*, July 31, 1925, 1; *El Informador*, August 19, 1925, 1, 6; *El Informador*, February 16, 1926, 1; *El Informador*, February 17, 1926, 1; *El Informador*, February 19, 1926, 1, 6; *El Informador*, February 21, 1926, 1–2; *El Informador*, February 24, 1926, 1; *El Informador*, February 25, 1926, 1, 8; *El Informador*, March 23, 1926, 1.

103. *El Informador*, March 24, 1926, 1.

104. *El Informador*, March 20, 1925, 1; *El Informador*, June 3, 1925, 1, 7; *El Informador*, July 30, 1925, 1–2; *El Informador*, August 2, 1925, 1, 8.

105. *El Informador*, December 23, 1924.

106. *El Informador*, July 28, 29, and 30, 1925.

107. Rius Facius, *De Don Porfirio*, 270–71.

108. Archivo Histórico de la Arquidiócesis de Guadalajara (henceforth, AHAG), Box San Miguel Mezquitán, Memorandum, García de Alba, September 13, 1925; further examples are offered by Rius Facius, *De Don Porfirio*, 321–22.

109. Early propaganda referred to the movement as the Liga Nacional de Defensa Religiosa (LNDR); in 1926, the acronym LNDLR (Liga Nacional Defensora de la Libertad Religiosa) was adopted.

110. AGN, DGIPS, 228/33/5, Agent #18 to Head of Departamento Confidencial, April 7, 1925, Mexico City; Meyer, *The Cristero Rebellion*, 36.

111. Meyer, *The Cristero Rebellion*, 33.

112. As Meyer reminds us, the press was quite free during the first two years of the Calles administration, as seen in the near-universal condemnation of the schism. After this, censorship became routine. Jean Meyer, *Historia de la revolución mexicana, 1924–1928: estado y sociedad con Calles* (Mexico City: El Colegio de México, 1977), 105–6.

113. AGN-DGIPS, 2046-C/5/10, report to Departamento Confidencial, Mexico City, February 11, 1926.

114. *El Informador*, June 3, 1925, 1, 7; and *El Informador*, July 30, 1925, 1–2.

115. For good maps, again Meyer, *Obra Completa*; see also Jean Meyer, *La guerra de los cristeros*, vol. 1 of *La Cristiada* (México: Siglo XXI Editores, 1974).

116. Gómez Robledo, *Anacleto González Flores*, 131–42, 185.

117. AGN, DGIPS, 228/33/5, Agent #18 to Head of Departamento Confidencial, Mexico City, April 7, 1925.

118. Gómez Robledo, *Anacleto González Flores*, 132; Meyer, *The Cristero Rebellion*, 33–34.

119. Antonio Gómez Robledo was born in 1908. As a high school student he participated in Catholic politics through the Popular Union, and subsequently described himself as González Flores's student. One of his first publications, quite different from the work to which he dedicated his professional life, was a biography of Anacleto González Flores. He began it in 1937, a decade following Anacleto's execution, and it was published in 1947. Today, it must still be considered the best biography of this Catholic writer and leader.

120. Gómez Robledo, *Anacleto González Flores*, 185.

121. Gómez Robledo, *Anacleto González Flores*, 136.

122. Gómez Robledo, *Anacleto González Flores*, 17–35; on class and status in the ACJM, see Navarrete, SJ, *Por Dios y por la patria*, 85–86.

123. Anacleto González Flores, "Él que mucho abarca," *El plebiscito de los mártires*, Edición en el 50º Aniversario (Morelia: Impresos FIT, 1980), 236–38.

124. Gómez Robledo, *Anacleto González Flores*, 134.

125. Navarrete, *Por Dios y por la patria*, 119.

126. Gómez Robledo, *Anacleto González Flores*, 135.

127. Gómez Robledo, *Anacleto González Flores*, 136.

128. Navarrete, *Por Dios y por la patria*, 121.

129. Gómez Robledo, *Anacleto González Flores*, 137; González Flores, "La vieja enfermedad," *El plebiscito*, 292.

130. González Flores, "Contra los tres," *El plebiscito*, 294.

131. AHAG, Section Gobierno, Series Obispos, Sr. Francisco Orozco y Jiménez, box 4, folder 20, August 19, 1926.

132. Navarrete, *Por Dios y por la patria*, 119.

133. Navarrete, *Por Dios y por la patria*, 122–23.

134. González Flores, "Un voto de sangre," *El plebiscito*, 272. Compare, for example, his editorial following the successful campaign to repeal Decrees 1913 and 1927; see *La Palabra*, February 2, 1919, 1.

135. See especially his final writing, which appeals to martyrdom as the ultimate fullfillment of youth; Anacleto González Flores, *Tú serás rey*, 3rd ed. (México: Comité Central de la ACJM), 1961.

136. Martínez Assad, *El laboratorio de la revolución*.

137. Matthew Butler, "*Sotanas Rojinegras*," 535–58.

138. *El Informador*, August 28, 1926, 1.

Chapter 9

1. Guadalajara's Sanctuary neighborhood was an artisan quarter characterized mostly by one-story houses built around open patios and flat contiguous *azoteas*, rooftop terraces where laundry was hung to dry in the morning sun. Workshops and storefronts commonly accented family homes, giving the barrio a bustling, commercial feel. At its heart was a notable pilgrimage site, the Sanctuary of Our Lady of Guadalupe. Fray Antonio Alcalde, the venerable bishop of Guadalajara, began construction of the temple in the 1770s and built 158 modest houses around it, in what was certainly one of Mexico's earliest subsidized housing campaigns for the poor. The temple was finished in 1781, and the barrio became host to the popular Guadalupe devotion celebrated every year on December 12. By the early twentieth century, the neighborhood stretched for blocks to the west, in the direction of Sweet Name of Jesus parish, and to the northwest, in the direction of the municipal cemetery, opened in 1896 on the edge of the old Mezquitán Indian pueblo. The Barranca de Belen, a sprawling riverbed with rocky, uneven terrain, framed the neighborhood's northern edge. To the east it was flanked by the Belen Hospital, a large panoptical institution equipped with a stately old cemetery no longer in use. Also built by Alcalde, it was nationalized in the nineteenth century by state-building liberals. To the south lay the city center.

2. Established in 1924, the UP, or Popular Union, was a Catholic lay association with a massive following in western Mexico. For more, see chapter 8.

3. Ramón and Jorge Vargas were medical students. Cristero and Reguer Collection, Dr. Jorge Villalobos Padilla, S. J. Library, Instituto Tecnológico de Estudios Superiores de Occidente, Guadalajara (henceforth, CRC), "Narración sobre algunos de los martires ejecutados en Guadalajara en Abril de 1927," Letter, signed AMDG, April 10, 1927; CRC, Crisanto del Valle, "Anacleto González Flores, Semblanza, Martires de la Persucución Mejicana," Typewritten document, 1927.

4. Luis Padilla (1899–1927) studied philosophy and theology at the Guadalajara and León seminaries, and served as president of the Catholic Association of Mexican Youth (ACJM) Guadalajara chapter, and as secretary of the Popular Union (UP). His story was widely publicized following his death through a pamphlet whose author opted for the precaution of a pseudonym; see Sitiens, "Esbozo de una biografía del

martir Luis Padilla, sacrificado en Guadalajara el viernes 1ro de abril de 1927," no Publisher, 56 pages (1929).

5. CRC, Crisanto del Valle, "Anacleto González Flores," 14.

6. CRC, "Narración," 1.

7. The images continue to circulate, through the new medium of the Internet. A simple search will turn up many images.

8. For one thing, the letter is part of a larger group of documents once belonging to Palomar y Vizcarra that are currently held by the Dr. Jorge Villalobos Padilla, S. J. Library at Guadalajara's Instituto Tecnológico de Estudios Superiores de Occidente (ITESO). Also, the document features the tell-tale shaky handwriting frequent on many of Palomar y Vizcarra's important papers, written when he was nearing death. Palomar y Vizcarra was conscientious about adding names, places, and dates to many documents in order to facilitate their identification subsequent to his passing. In this case, he simply wrote down the names of the executed, an addendum that offers little, given that the general story has since become quite well known. It was likely during the 1960s when he added to the original typewritten document. At that time, the future of these Catholic martyrs was much less certain.

9. I have preferred not to use the piece attributed to Beltrán y Mendoza, because I have only seen it through a recent transcription. Nevertheless, it is quite similar to the documents I have cited above; see Luis Beltrán y Mendoza, "In Memoriam (1928)," in *La Palabra. Edición homenaje al Maestro Anacleto González Flores*, ed. Tomás de Hijar Ornelas (Guadalajara: Arquidiócesis de Guadalajara, Sección Diocesana de Educación y Cultura, 2002).

10. *El Informador*, April 2, 1927, 1.

11. CRC, "Narración," 1.

12. CRC, Crisanto del Valle, "Anacleto González Flores," 15.

13. Agustín Yañez, *Imágenes y evocaciones* (México: El Colegio de Jalisco y Afaguara, 2003), 99.

14. CRC, "Narración," 2.

15. Anacleto González Flores, *El plebiscito de los mártires*, 115–22; on how these historical and literary figures influenced the author's ideas regarding politics and martyrdom, see Robert Curley, "Avanza el desierto," 45–59.

16. In between these two key elements stands the local Church, both parish and archdiocese. They must take up the cause and promote it. In this case, the Comisión Diocesana de Causas de Canonización de Guadalajara has collected evidence in support of the cause. Included in the evidence is Anacelto's oeuvre, which has been transcribed and is available online. See the *Causas de Canonización Guadalajara* blogsite for 2012 http://causasde canonizaciongdl.blogspot.mx/2012_11_01_archive.html, accessed April 2015.

17. Gómez Robledo, *Anacleto González Flores*.

18. Gómez Robledo left Guadalajara for Mexico City in 1927 and went on to have a long and celebrated life as a writer and teacher of philosophy, law, history, and letters.

He taught at the National University and other universities in Mexico and abroad, and served as Mexican ambassador to Italy (including Tunisia), Greece (including Cyprus), Brazil, Switzerland, and UNESCO. He published many books and articles and became an accomplished translator of Latin and Greek. He was a member of the Academia Mexicana de la Lengua and El Colegio Nacional. See Marta Morineau, "Antonio Gómez Robledo: vida y obra," *Anuario mexicano de historia del Derecho* (2005): 219–39; and Antonio Gómez Robledo, *Oratio doctoralis: últimos escritos* (Guadalajara: El Colegio de Jalisco, UNAM, CONACULTA, 1994).

19. Gómez Robledo, *Anacleto González Flores*, 26–27.

20. Ramón Jrade, "Inquiries into the Cristero Insurrection against the Mexican Revolution," *Latin American Research Review* 20, no. 2 (1985): 59.

21. Gómez Robledo, *Anacleto González Flores*, 25, 44–47; Ismael Flores Hernández, *Anacleto, líder católico. Génesis de la persecución religiosa en México* (Guadalajara: Folia Universitaria, 2005), 57, 60–61.

22. The street is known today as Santa Monica; see Tomás de Híjar Ornelas, "La Palabra," in *La Palabra. Edición homenaje al Maestro Anacleto González Flores* (Guadalajara: Arquidiócesis de Guadalajara, Sección Diocesana de Educación y Cultura, 2002); Flores Hernández, *Anacleto*, 61.

23. Gómez Robledo, *Anacleto González Flores*, 54–55; Robert Gildea, *Children of the Revolution, The French, 1799–1914* (London: Penguin Books, 2009).

24. M. Cuzin, *Journal d´un français au Mexique*.

25. Gómez Robledo, *Anacleto González Flores*, 28.

26. The Mexico City chapter was founded in 1913. On the ACJM, see Antonio Rius Facius, *De Don Porfirio*.

27. González Flores, *El plebiscito*, 45.

28. Much of this work can be read today because it was reprinted subsequent to his death; see González Flores, *El plebiscito*, which reprints his editorial writing basically from 1926, and De Híjar Ornelas, *La Palabra*, which is a facsimile edition of the entire two-year run of that newspaper, from 1917 to 1919.

29. Régis Planchet, *La cuestión religiosa en México* (México: ACJM, 1920); González Flores, *La cuestión religiosa*; and González Flores, *Tú serás rey*.

30. Taylor, *A Secular Age*, 2.

31. *La Palabra*, June 24, 1917, 1.

32. *La Palabra*, June 24, 1917, 1.

33. Thanks to Stephen Andes for pushing me on this issue.

34. *La Palabra*, July 1, 1917, 2.

35. These events are covered in chapter 5.

36. González Flores, *La cuestión religiosa*, 337.

37. González Flores, *La cuestión religiosa*, 316.

38. *La Palabra*, February 2, 1919, 1.

39. My translation. The original is titled "*Espadas y mordazas*." See González Flores, *El plebiscito*, 205–8.

40. My translation. The original is titled "*Sin palabras.*" See González Flores, *El plebiscito*, 59–65.

41. The 1914 English-language edition of *Brand* is in the public domain, and may be accessed online at http://babel.hathitrust.org/cgi/pt?id=mdp.39015030029758;view=1 up;seq=8, accessed May 15, 2014.

42. Matthew Henry, *An Exposition of the Old and New Testament*, 6 vols., 1st American edition (Philadelphia: Ed. Barrington & Geo. D. Haswell, 1828). See also http://www.biblestudytools.com/commentaries/matthew-henry-complete/john/1.html, accessed June 1, 2014. It is reasonable to suppose that González Flores would, in fact, not have read *An Exposition*, because Henry was a Presbyterian minister whose work circulated in Great Britain and the United States. Nevertheless, Henry's exegesis of John 1:1–5 seems quite pertinent to González Flores's writing. In fact, *The Catholic Encyclopedia* refers to *An Exposition* as "a practical commentary on the Old and New Testament." See Cornelius Aherne, "Commentaries on the Bible," in *The Catholic Encyclopedia. An international Work of Reference on the Constitution, Doctrine, Discipline, and History of the Catholic Church*, ed. Charles G. Herbermann, Edward A. Pace, Condé B. Pallen, Thomas J. Shahan, and John J. Wynne, 15 vols., vol. 4 (New York: Robert Appleton Company, 1908).

43. González Flores, *El plebiscito*, 61–62.

44. González Flores, *El plebiscito*, 63; Manuel José Othón, "Idilio salvaje," *Obras* (México, 1928).

45. González Flores, *El plebiscito*, 64–65.

46. González Flores, *El plebiscito*, 241–43.

47. González Flores, *El plebiscito*, 241–43.

48. *La Palabra*, June 10, 1917, 1.

49. González Flores, *El plebiscito*, 115–22.

50. A passing comment made by Nancy Cott may shed some light on why or how Anacleto González Flores became drawn to this socialist feminist. Cott wrote that she learned the most radical of her tactics from the Irish nationalist cause; see Nancy F. Cott, *The Grounding of Modern Feminism* (New Haven, CT: Yale University Press, 1987), 25–27; June Purvis, *Emmeline Pankhurst: A Biography* (London: Routledge, 2002), 40–41.

51. Purvis, *Emmeline Pankhurst*, 211, 217.

52. Joost Augusteijn, "Motivation: Why Did They Fight for Ireland? The Motivation of Volunteers in the Revolution," in *The Irish Revolution, 1913–1923*, ed. Joost Augusteijn (Hampshire, UK: Palgrave, 2002), 110; R. F. Foster, *Modern Ireland, 1600–1972* (Harmondsworth: Penguin Books, 1989), 499.

53. MacSwiney was born in 1879 and died in 1920.

54. González Flores, *El plebiscito*, 118.

55. See chapter 5.

56. González Flores, *El plebiscito*, 233–35, 243–45.

57. In 1926–1927, Heriberto Navarrete had been the secretary general to the Popular Union, and participated in the rebellion from September 1927 until July 1929.

Subsequently, he returned to his studies and graduated with an engineering degree in 1931. In 1933 he joined the Jesuits, and took his vows two years later. In the preliminary note that accompanies his memoir from the rebellion, he states that he began writing on October 3, 1939, about thirteen years after the meeting of Popular Union leaders in which the rebellion was discussed. See Heriberto Navarrete, SJ, *Por Dios y por la patria*, 13, 79.

58. Navarrete, SJ. *Por Dios y por la patria*, 119.

59. Navarrete, SJ. *Por Dios y por la patria*, 120.

60. González Flores, *El plebiscito*, 267–73.

61. González Flores, *Tú serás rey*, 149–53.

62. González Flores, *El plebiscito*, 243–45.

63. Meyer, *El conflicto entre la iglesia y el estado*, 261–85; and Meyer, *The Cristero Rebellion*, 48–58.

64. Taylor, *A Secular Age*.

65. Curley, "Avanza el desierto," 45–59.

66. González Flores, *El plebiscito*, 115–22.

67. González Flores, *El plebiscito*, 122.

68. Meyer, *The Cristero Rebellion*, 49–50.

69. Jean Meyer, *Los cristeros*, trans. Aurelio Garzón del Camino, vol. 3 of *La cristiada* (México: Siglo XXI, 1974), 101–9; and Meyer, *La Cristiada*, 55.

70. Ceballos Ramírez, *El catolicismo social*, 16.

71. Meyer, *La cristiada*, vol. 3, 102.

72. Navarrete, SJ. *Por Dios y por la patria*, 123.

73. Meyer, *The Cristero Rebellion*, 50.

74. Meyer, *La cristiada*, vol. 3, 134–201.

75. Jrade, "Inquiries," 53–69.

76. José Díaz and Román Rodríguez, *El movimiento cristero: sociedad y conflicto en Los Altos de Jalisco* (México: Editorial Nueva Imagen, 1979).

77. Jrade, "Inquiries," 64–66; and Ramón Jrade, "La organización de la Iglesia a nivel local y el desafío de los levantamientos cristeros al poder del Estado revolucionario," *Estudios del Hombre* 1 (1994): 65–80.

78. Jennie Purnell, *Popular Movements and State Formation in Revolutionary Mexico: The Agraristas and Cristeros of Michoacán* (Durham, NC: Duke University Press, 1999).

79. Purnell, *Popular Movements*, 18–19, 182–83.

80. Preciado Zamora, *Por las faldas del volcán*.

81. Preciado Zamora, *Por las faldas del volcán*, 150, 154, 156, 160–61.

82. Steve J. Stern, "New Approaches to the Study of Peasant Rebellion and Consciousness: Implications of the Andean Experience," in *Resistance, Rebellion, and Consciousness in the Andean Peasant World, 18th to 20th Centuries*, ed. Steve J. Stern (Madison: University of Wisconsin Press, 1987), 3–25.

83. Purnell, *Popular Movements*, 184.

84. Preciado Zamora, *Por las faldas del volcán*, 157.

85. Preciado Zamora, *Por las faldas del volcán*, 163–98.

86. Preciado Zamora, *Por las faldas del volcán*, 203–6.

87. Butler, *Popular Piety*.

88. Butler, *Popular Piety*, 106–8.

89. Butler, *Popular Piety*, 9–10.

90. Butler, *Popular Piety*, 215.

91. The phrase is Butler's; Butler, *Popular Piety*, 215.

92. Martin Conway, "Introduction," 1–33.

Conclusion

1. Bastian, *Los disidentes*.

2. Aubert, et al., *La Iglesia en el mundo moderno*; Ceballos Ramírez, *El catolicismo*.

3. Here it is important to distinguish the Madero regime from the rebellion that brought Madero to power. An almost exclusively rural rebellion brought down the Porfirian political class, but the urban political opposition replaced it. This contradiction had serious consequences, such as Pascual Orozco's decision to rebel in 1912, and the decision of Emiliano Zapata not to disarm, and eventually to resume his rebellion under the Plan de Ayala.

4. Anacleto González Flores, *El plebiscito*.

5. Taylor, *A Secular Age*.

6. Jürgen Habermas, *The Structural Transformation*.

7. Pius XI, *Quadragesimo Anno* (Rome, 1931).

8. Jürgen Buchenau, *Plutarco Elías Calles*, especially chapter 6.

9. Arnoldo Córdova, *La Revolución en crisis. La aventura del Maximato* (México: Cal y Arena, 1995), 71–72.

10. Plutarco Elías Calles, *Declaraciones y discursos políticos, cuadernos de la causa*, 12 vols., vol. 12 (México: Ediciones del Centro de Documentación Política, 1979) 165–79.

11. Luis Javier Garrido, *El partido de la revolución institucionalizada* (México: Siglo XXI Editores, 1982).

12. Calles, *Declaraciones y discursos políticos*, 172–74.

Bibliography

Archives

GUADALAJARA

Archivo de Instrumentos Públicos
Archivo Histórico de Jalisco
    —Ramo Gobernación, Asuntos
    —Ramo Trabajo y Previsión Social
Archivo Histórico del Arzobispado de Guadalajara
    —Parroquias
Archivo Municipal de Guadalajara
Archivo Parroquial, Dulce Nombre de Jesus
Archivo Parroquial, Santuario de Nuestra Señora de Guadalupe
Biblioteca Dr. Jorge Villalobos Padilla, SJ, Instituto Tecnológico de Estudios Superiores
    de Occidente
    —Cristero and Reguer Collection
Biblioteca Pública del Estado de Jalisco "Juan José Arreola"
    —Biblioteca Álvarez del Castillo y Fonoteca
    —Fondo Guadalajara
    —Fondo José María Mier
    —Fondo Miscelánea (Pamphlet Collection)
    —Hemeroteca Histórica
    —State Department Papers Relating to the Internal Affairs of Mexico, Record Group 59, 812.00 (Political Affairs, 1910–1929)

MÉXICO CITY

Archivo General de la Nación
    —Dirección General de Investigaciones Políticas y Sociales
Biblioteca Manuel Orozco y Berra, Instituto Nacional de Antropología e Historia
    —Archivo de la Palabra—Programa de Historia Oral

Biblioteca Nacional
    —Fondo Palomar y Vizcarra
    —Hemeroteca Nacional
Centro de Estudios de Historia de México Carso
    —Fondo Bernardo Reyes
    —Fondo Venustiano Carranza
Secretariado Social Mexicano
Seminario Conciliar Mexicano
    —Biblioteca Hector Rogel Hernández
Universidad Iberoamericana
    —Colección Porfirio Díaz
—Unión de Damas Católicas

CHICAGO

Archdiocese of Chicago, Archives and Records Center
    —Madaj Collection
Joseph Regenstein Library, University of Chicago
Northwestern University Library, Evanston
Richard J. Daley Library, University of Illinois

Maryland
National Archive and Record Administration
    —State Department Papers Relating to the Internal Affairs of Mexico,
    Record Group 59, File 812.00 (Political Affairs)
    —State Department Papers Relating to the Internal Affairs of Mexico,
    Record Group 59, File 812.404 (Religious Affairs)

OKLAHOMA

Archive of the Archdiocese of Oklahoma City
    —Francis Clement Kelley Papers

Periodical Collections

Acción. Guadalajara, 1914–1916
Acción y fé. Mexico City, 1922
Archivo Social, El (Organo del Comité Diocesano de Acción Social, subsequently
    Organo del Secretariado Regional de Acción Social Católica). Guadalajara,
    1921–1925

Boletín Militar. Guadalajara, 1914–1915
Chispa, La. Guadalajara, 1910–1911
Combate, El. Guadalajara, 1918
Correo de Jalisco, El. Guadalajara, 1910–1913
Criterio. Mexico City, 1934
Demócrata, El. Guadalajara, 1916
Diario de Occidente, El. Guadalajara, 1912–1914
Época, La. Guadalajara, 1918
Fígaro, El. Guadalajara, 1915
Gaceta de Guadalajara, La. Guadalajara, 1912
Gato, El. Guadalajara, 1917–1918
Informador, El. Guadalajara, 1917–1926
Jalisco. Guadalajara. 1916–1917
Labor Nueva (Organo de la Soberana Convención de Aguascalientes). Guadalajara, 1915
Luchador Católico, El. Ciudad Guzmán, 1912–1913
Malcriado, El. Guadalajara, 1911–1912
México Libre. Guadalajara, 1915
Nación, La. Mexico City, 1912–1914
Obrero, El. Guadalajara, 1919–1923
Occidental, El. Guadalajara, 1916–1917
Palabra, La. Guadalajara, 1917–1919
Paladín, El. Guadalajara, 1918
País, El. Mexico City, 1912–1914
Radical, El. Guadalajara, 1917
Reformador, El. Guadalajara, 1915
Regional, El. Guadalajara, 1910–1914
República, La. Guadalajara, 1914–1915
Restauración. Guadalajara, 1920
Restauración Social. Guadalajara, 1910–1912
Testigo, El. Guadalajara, 1909–1911

Primary Source Collections

Album de la coronación de Ntra. Sra. de Zapopan. Guadalajara: Impresores y Editores Juan Kaiser Sucs., S. En C. 1921.
Asociación Católica de la Juventud Mexicana. *Manual de la Asociación Católica de la Juventud Mexicana*, 3ra Edición. México: Comité General, ACJM 1922.
Asociación de Damas Católicas. *Reglamento de la Asociación de Damas Católicas de Guadalajara.* Guadalajara: Tip. El Regional. 1914.
Bárcia, Roque. *Primer Diccionario General Etimológico de la Lengua Española.* 5 vols. Madrid: Álvarez Hermanos. 1880–1883.

Carta Pastoral del Episcopado Mexicano sobre la Constitución de 1917. Acordada, 1917.

Colonia Jalisciense de la Ciudad de México. *La cuestión religiosa en Jalisco, apuntes para la historia.* México, DF, 1918.

Comité Diocesano de Acción Católica Social. *Curso Social Agrícola Zapopano.* Guadalajara: Tip. Renacimiento. 1921.

Confederación Nacional Católica del Trabajo. *Carta abierta del Comité Central de la Confederación Nacional Católica del Trabajo—CNCT-al Sr. Luis N. Morones, Secretario de Industria, Comercio y Trabajo.* México: CNCT 1926.

Congreso Eucarístico Nacional. México. 1924.

Congreso Tercero Católico Nacional y Primero Eucarístico. 2 vols. Guadalajara, Imprenta de El Regional. 1908.

Cuarto Congreso Católico Nacional Mexicano. Oaxaca: Tipografía de la Casa de Gama. 1913.

Dávila Garibi, J. Ignacio, and Salvador Chávez Hayhoe. *Colección de documentos relativos a la cuestión religiosa en Jalisco.* 2 vols. Guadalajara: Tip. J. M. Yguíniz. 1920.

Estatutos de la Federación Anticlerical Mexicana. México, 1923.

Junta Diocesana de Acción Católico-Social. *Primer Congreso Nacional Obrero: preparación, reseña, conclusiones aprobadas, modelos de estatutos para las agrupaciones confederadas.* Guadalajara: Tip. Renacimiento. 1922.

La Palabra. Edición homenaje al Maestro Anacleto González Flores. Guadalajara: Arquidiócesis de Guadalajara, Sección Diocesana de Educación y Cultura. 2002.

Mora y del Río, José, Arzobispo de México, et al. *Carta Pastoral Colectiva a los Católicos Mexicanos sobre la actual Persecución Religiosa.* 1914.

Navarrete, Félix, and Eduardo Pallares. *Colección de leyes y decretos relativos a la reducción de sacerdotes y la persecución religiosa en Méjico desde el punto de vista jurídico.* México, n.d.

Olveda, Jaime, Alma Dorantes, and Agustín Vaca, eds. *La prensa jalisciense y la revolución.* México: Instituto Nacional de Antropología e Historia. 1985.

Orozco y Jiménez, Francisco. *Cuarta Carta Pastoral que el Ilmo. Y Rmo. Sr. Dr. y Mtro. D. Francisco Orozco y Jiménez, 5to Arzobispo de Guadalajara, Dirige a sus Diocesanos.* 1917.

Orozco y Jiménez, Francisco. *Segunda carta pastoral del Ilmo. y Revmo. Sr. Dr. y Mtro. D. Francisco Orozco y Jiménez, 5o Arzobispo de Guadalajara con motivo de la solemne consagración de la república mexicana al sacratísimo corazón de Jesús.* Guadalajara: Tip. de El Regional. 1913.

Pius XI. *Quadragesimo Anno.* Rome, 1931.

Primer Congreso Agrícola de Tulancingo. México: Tip. Particular de la Sociedad Agrícola Mexicana. 1904.

Primer Congreso Nacional de la Unión de Damas Católicas Mejicanas. Tlalpan, DF: Imprenta del Asilo "Patricio Sanz." 1922.

Secretaría de Agricultura y Fomento. 1918. *Tercer censo de población de los Estados Unidos Mexicanos, verificado el 27 de octubre de 1910*, Estado de Jalisco. México: Oficina de la Secretaría de Hacienda, Departamento de Fomento. 1918.

Segundo Congreso Católico de México y Primero Mariano. Morelia: Talleres Tipográficos de Agustín Martínez Mier. 1905.

Silva, Jerónimo Thomé da, Arzobispo de San Salvador, Primado del Brasil, et al. *Carta Sinodal que los Arzobisbos y Obispos Congregados en Roma para el Concilio Plenario de la América Latina dirigen al Clero y a los Fieles de sus Diocesis.* Colima: Imp. del Comercio. 1899.

Tovar, Pbro. Librado. *Primer Congreso Católico Regional Obrero.* Guadalajara: Tip. C. M. Sainz. 1921.

United States Department of State, (Microfilm Collection). *Records Relating to the Internal Affairs of Mexico*, Washington, DC: National Archive and Records Administration. 1910–1929.

Vaca, Agustín, Alma Dorantes, and Jaime Olveda, eds. *Fuentes hemerográficas jaliscienses para el estudio de la revolución mexicana.* México: Instituto Nacional de Antropología e Historia. 1990.

Websites

New Advent, http://www.newadvent.org/library/docs_le13rn.htm.

Secondary Sources

Achiaga, Luciano. "Grandes bienes que reportan los caballeros cristianos que se inscriben y cumplen su deber en las Asociaciones Eucarísticas." In *Congreso Tercero Católico Nacional y Primero Eucarístico.* Vol. 2. Guadalajara: Imprenta de El Regional, 1908.

Adame Goddard, Jorge. *El pensamiento político y social de los católicos mexicanos, 1867–1914.* México: UNAM, 1981.

———. "Influjo de la doctrina social católica en el artículo 123 constitucional." *Colección "Diálogo y Autocrítica"* 8. México: IMDOSOC, 1994.

Aguilar Camín, Héctor. "Los jefes sonorenses de la revolución mexicana." In *Caudillos y campesinos en la revolución mexicana*, ed. David Brading, 125–60. México: Fondo de Cultura Economica, 1985.

Aguilar Camín, Héctor, and Lorenzo Meyer. *A la sombra de la Revolución Mexicana.* México: Cal y Arena, 1989.

Aguirre, Amado. *Mis memorias de Campaña*, México: INERHM, 1985 [1953].

Aguirre Berlanga, Manuel. *Genesis legal de la revolución constitucionalista, Revolución y reforma.* México: INEHRM, 1985 [1918].

Aherne, Cornelius. "Commentaries on the Bible." In *The Catholic Encyclopedia. An International Work of Reference on the Constitution, Doctrine, Discipline, and*

History of the Catholic Church, ed. Charles G. Herbermann, Edward A. Pace, Condé B. Pallen, Thomas J. Shahan, and John J. Wynne. 15 vols. Vol. 4. New York: Robert Appleton Company, 1908.

Alcantara Ferrer, Sergio. "La identidad cultural en el barrio del Santuario: Origenes." In *Capítulos de historia de la ciudad de Guadalajara*. Vol. 2, 169–92. Guadalajara: Ayuntamiento de Guadalajara, 1992.

Aldana Rendón, Mario. *Manuel M. Diéguez y la revolución mexicana*. Guadalajara: El Colegio de Jalisco, 2006.

Aldana Rendón, Mario A. *Del reyismo al nuevo orden constitucional, 1910–1917*. Vol. 1 of *Jalisco desde la Revolución*. Guadalajara: Gobierno del Estado/Universidad de Guadalajara, 1987.

———. *Desarrollo económico de Jalisco, 1821–1940*. Guadalajara: Universidad de Guadalajara, 1979.

———. *El campo jalisciense durante el porfiriato*. Guadalajara: Universidad de Guadalajara, 1986.

———, ed. *Manuel M. Dieguez y el constitucionalismo en Jalisco (documentos)*. Guadalajara: Gobierno de Jalisco, 1986.

Alexander, Sally. "Women, Class and Sexual Difference," *History Workshop* 17 (Spring 1984): 125–149.

Alonso, Jorge. *Miradas sobre la personalidad política de Efrain González Luna*. Guadalajara: Universidad de Guadalajara/CUCSH, 2003.

Alzaga, Óscar. *La primera democracia cristiana en España*, 21–22. Barcelona: Editorial Ariel, 1973.

Amaya, Luis Fernando. *La Soberana Convención Revolucionaria, 1914–1916*. Aguascalientes: Comisión Editorial de Aguascalientes, 1975.

The Americas. Special Issue: Personal Enemies of God: Anticlericals and Anticlericalism in Revolutionary Mexico, 1915–1940 65, no. 4 (2009).

Anderson, Benedict. *Imagined Communities: Reflections on the Origin and Spread of Nationalism*. Revised edition. London: Verso, 1991.

Anderson, Rodney. *Outcasts in Their Own Land: Mexican Industrial Workers, 1906–1911*. DeKalb, IL: Northern Illinois University Press, 1976.

Andes, Stephen, J. C. "A Catholic Alternative to Revolution: The Survival of Social Catholicism in Postrevolutionary Mexico." *The Americas* 68, no. 4 (April 2012): 529–62.

———. *The Vatican and Catholic Activism in Mexico and Chile: The Politics of Transnational Catholicism, 1920–1940*. Oxford: Oxford University Press, 2014.

Andrés-Gallego, José. *Pensamiento y acción social de la Iglesia en España*. Madrid: Espasa Universitaria, 1984.

Annino, Antonio. "Pueblos, liberalismo y nación en México." In *Inventando la nación: Iberoamérica, siglo XIX*, edited by Antonio Annino and François-Xavier Guerra, 399–430. México: Fondo de Cultura Económica, 2003.

Annino, Antonio, and François-Xavier Guerra, eds. *Inventando la nación:*

Iberoamérica, siglo XIX. México: Fondo de Cultura Económica, 2003.

Appleby, R. Scott. *The Ambivalence of the Sacred: Religion, Violence, and Reconciliation.* Foreword by Theodore M. Hesburgh. New York: Rowman & Littlefield Publishers, 2000.

Araiza, J. Félix, O.G. "El salario real y el Estado." *Restauración Social* 3, no. 15 (1911): 119–27.

Araiza, Luis. *Historia del movimiento obrero mexicano.* México City, 1964–1965.

Arias, Patricia. "La vida económica tapatía durante el siglo XX." In *Capítulos de historia de la ciudad de Guadalajara,* edited by Lina Rendón García. 2 vols. Vol. 2, 59–86. Guadalajara: Ayuntamiento de Guadalajara, 1992.

———. *Los vecinos de la sierra: microhistoria de Publo Nuevo.* Guadalajara: Universidad de Guadalajara & Centre d' Etudes Mexicaines et Centroaméricaines, 1996.

Armstrong, Karen. *A History of God: A 4,000-Year Quest of Judaism, Christianity and Islam.* New York: Ballantine Books, 1993.

Armstrong, Pat, and Hugh Armstrong. "Beyond Classless Sex and Sexless Class: Towards Feminist Marxism." *Studies in Political Economy* 10 (Winter 1983): 7–41.

Arregui, Benigno, O.G. "Insuficiencia de los sueldos o salaries." *Restauración Social* 2, no. 11 (1910): 397–406.

Asad, Talal. *Genealogies of Religion: Discipline and Reasons of Power in Christianity and Islam,* 27–54. Baltimore: The Johns Hopkins Press, 1993.

Aubert, Roger. *Catholic Social Teaching: An Historical Perspective.* Milwaukee, WI: Marquette University Press, 2003.

Aubert, Roger, J. Bruls, P. E. Cruncian, J. Tracy Ellis, J. Hajjar, and F. B. Pike. *La Iglesia en el mundo moderno (1848 al Vaticano II).* Vol. 5 of *Nueva historia de la Iglesia.* 2nd ed. Translated by T. Muñoz Sciaffino. Madrid: Ediciones Cristiandad, 1984.

Augusteijn, Joost. "Motivation: Why Did They Fight for Ireland? The Motivation of Volunteers in the Revolution." In *The Irish Revolution, 1913–1923,* edited by Joost Augusteijn. Hampshire, UK: Palgrave, 2002.

Augustine, St. *The City of God.* Translated by Marcus Dods. Chicago: Encyclopaedia Britannica, Inc., 1952.

Avila Espinosa, Felipe Arturo. "La sociedad mutualista y moraliizadora de obreros del Distrito Federal (1909–1911)." *Historia Mexicana* no. 169 (1993): 117–54.

Ayón Zester, Francisco. *Reyes y el reyismo.* Guadalajara: Editorial Font, 1980.

Baily, David C. "Revisionism and Recent Historiography of the Mexican Revolution." *Hispanic American Historical Review* no. 58 (1978): 62–79.

Balderrama, Luis C. *El Clero y el Gobierno de México: Apuntes para la Historia de la Crisis en 1926.* Mexico City: Editorial Cuauhtémoc, 1927.

Baldwin, Deborah, "Diplomacia cultural: escuelas misionales protestantes en México." *Historia Mexicana* no. 142 (1987): 287–322.

Banegas Galván, Francisco. *El por qué del Partido Católico Nacional.* México: Jus, 1960 [1915].

Bantjes, Adrian A. "Burning Saints, Molding Minds: Iconoclasm, Civic Ritual, and the Failed Cultural Revolution." In *Rituals of Rule, Rituals of Resistance: Public Celebrations and Popular Culture in Mexico*, edited by William H. Beezley, Cheryl English Martin, and William E. French, 261–84. Wilmington, DE: SR Books, 1994.

———. "Mexican Revolutionary Anticlericalism: Concepts and Typologies." *The Americas* 65, no. 4 (April 2009): 467–80.

———. "The Regional Dynamics of Anticlericalism and Defanaticization in Revolutionary Mexico." In *Faith and Impiety in Revolutionary Mexico*, edited by Matthew Butler, 111–30. New York: Palgrave MacMillan, 2007.

Barber, Noel, SJ. "Religion in Ireland: Its State and Prospects." In *Christianity in Ireland: Revisiting the Story*, edited by Brendan Bradshaw and Dáire Keogh, 287–97. Dublin: Columba Press, 2002.

Barbosa Guzmán, Francisco. "De la acción social católica a la cristiada." *Estudios Jaliscienses* No. 13 (1993): 5–21.

———. "De la manera cómo los diputados católicos ejercieron la libertad de educación en Jalisco 1912–1914." *Estudios Sociales* No. 11 (1991): 65–85.

———. *La caja rural católica de préstamos y ahorros en Jalisco (1910–1914 y 1920–1924)*. México: IMDOSOC, 1996.

———. *La iglesia y el gobierno civil*. Vol. 6 of *Jalisco desde la revolución*. Guadalajara: Gobierno del Estado/Universidad de Guadalajara, 1988.

Barcena, Mariano. *La 2. exposición de "Las Clases Productoras," y descripción de la ciudad de Guadalajara*. Guadalajara: Tip. de Sinforoso Banda, 1880.

Barrett, Michelle, and Mary McIntosh. "The 'Family Wage': Some Problems for Socialists and Feminists." *Capital and Class* 11 (1980): 51–72.

Barrón, Luis. *Historias de la Revolución mexicana*. México: CIDE/FCE, 2004.

Bastian, Jean-Pierre. "El paradigma de 1789. Sociedades de ideas y revolución mexicana." *Historia Mexicana* no. 149 (1988): 79–110.

———, ed. *La modernidad religiosa: Europa latina y América Latina en perspectiva comparada*. México: Fondo de Cultura Económica, 2004.

———. *Los disidentes: sociedades protestantes y revolución en México, 1872–1911*. México: Fondo de Cultura Económica / El Colegio de México, 1989.

Basurto, Jorge. *El proletariado industrial en México (1850–1930)*. México: Universidad Nacional Autónoma de México, 1975.

Baubérot, Jean. "Los umbrales de la laicización en la Europa latina y la recomposición de lo religioso en la modernidad tardia." In *La modernidad religiosa: Europa latina y América Latina en perspectiva comparada*, edited by Jean-Pierre Bastián, 94–110. México: Fondo de Cultura Económica, 2004.

Bazant Jan. "From Independence to the Liberal Republic, 1821–1867." In *Mexico since Independence*, edited by Leslie Bethell, 1–48. New York: Cambridge University Press, 1991.

———. *Los Bienes de la Iglesia en México (1856–1875)*. Mexico: El Colegio de México, 1971.

Beato, Guillermo. "La formación (y las relaciones familiares) de la burguesía de Jalisco durante el siglo XIX." Paper delivered to the VI Conference of Mexican and United States Historians, Chicago, Illinois, 10 September 1981.

Becker, Marjorie. "Torching La Purísima, Dancing at the Altar: The Construction of Revolutionary Hegemony in Michoacán, 1934–1940." In *Everyday Forms of State Formation: Revolution and the Negotiation of Rule in Modern Mexico*, edited by Gilbert M. Joseph and Daniel Nugent, 247–64. Durham, NC: Duke University Press, 1994.

Beezley, William H., Cheryl English Martin, and William E. French. *Rituals of Rule, Rituals of Resistance: Public Celebrations and Popular Culture in Mexico*. Wilmington DE: SR Books, 1994.

Beltrán y Mendoza, Luis. "In Memoriam (1928)." In *La Palabra. Edición homenaje al Maestro Anacleto González Flores*, edited by Tomás de Hijar Ornelas, no page numbering. Guadalajara: Arquidiócesis de Guadalajara, Sección Diocesana de Educación y Cultura, 2002.

Benjamin, Thomas, and Mark Wasserman, eds. *Provinces of the Revolution: Essays on Regional Mexican History, 1910–1929*. Albuquerque: University of New Mexico Press, 1990.

Bigongiari, Dino, ed. *The Political Ideas of St. Thomas Aquinas*, vii–xxxvii. New York: Hafner Press, 1953.

Black, Naomi. *Social Feminism*. Ithaca and London: Cornell University Press, 1989.

Blancarte, Roberto. "Laicidad y secularización en México." In *La modernidad religiosa: Europa latina y América Latina en perspectiva comparada*, edited by Jean-Pierre Bastian, 45–60. México: Fondo de Cultura Económica, 2004.

Boyer, Christopher R. *Becoming Campesinos: Politics, Identity, and Agrarian Struggle in Postrevolutionary Michoacán, 1920–1935*. Stanford, CA: Stanford University Press, 2003.

Brading, David A., ed. *Caudillo and Peasant in the Mexican Revolution*. Cambridge: Cambridge University Press, 1980.

Braudel, Fernand. *The Perspective of the World: Civilization and Capitalism, 15th–18th Century*, translated by Siân Reynolds. Vol. 3. Berkeley and New York: University of California Press, 1984.

Bravo Ugarte, José. *México, I, Independencia, caracterización política e integración social*. Vol. 3, part 1 of *Historia de México*. México: Jus, 1944.

———. *México, II, Relaciones internacionales, territorio, sociedad y cultura*. Vol. 3, part 2 of *Historia de México*. México: Jus, 1959.

Brenner, Anita. *Idols Behind Altars*. New York, 1929.

———. *The Wind That Swept Mexico: The History of the Mexican Revolution, 1910–1942*. Includes 184 historical photographs assembled by George R. Leighton. New York and London: Harper and Brothers Publishers, 1943.

Buchanan, Tom, and Martin Conway, eds. *Political Catholicism in Europe, 1918–1965*. New York: Oxford University Press, 1996.

Buchenau, Jürgen. *Plutarco Elías Calles and the Mexican Revolution*. Lanham, MD: Rowman & Littlefield Publishers, Inc., 2007.

Butler, Matthew, ed. *Faith and Impiety in Revolutionary Mexico*. New York: Palgrave MacMillan, 2007.

———. *Popular Piety and Political Identity in Mexico's Cristero Rebellion: Michoacán, 1927–1929*. Oxford: The British Academy/Oxford University Press, 2004.

———. "*Sotanas Rojinegras*: Catholic Anticlericalism and Mexico's Revolutionary Schism." *The Americas* 65, no. 4 (April 2009): 531–54.

Buttigieg, Joseph A. "Gramsci y la sociedad civil." In *Hegemonía, estado y sociedad civil en la globalización*, edited by Dora Kanoussi, 39–78. Translated by Cristina Ortega. Puebla: Benemérita Universidad Autónoma de Puebla-Plaza y Janés, 2001.

Byrne, Bonifacio. *Lira y Espada*. Habana: Tipografía "El Fígaro," 1901.

Calhoun, Craig, ed. *Habermas and the Public Sphere*. Cambridge, MA: The MIT Press, 1992.

———. "Introduction: Habermas and the Public Sphere." In *Habermas and the Public Sphere*, edited by Craig Calhoun, 1–48. Cambridge, MA: MIT Press, 1992.

Callahan, William J. *The Catholic Church in Spain, 1875–1998*. Washington, DC: The Catholic University of America Press, 2000.

Calvo, Thomas. *Poder, Religión y Sociedad en la Guadalajara del Siglo XVII*. Mexico: Centre D'Études Mexicaines et Centraméricaines/Ayuntamiento de Guadalajara, 1992.

Camberos Vizcaíno, Vicente. *Francisco el Grande. Mons. Francisco Orozco y Jiménez. Biografía*. México: Editorial Jus, 1966.

———. *Un hombre y una época, apuntes biográficos*. México: Editorial Jus, 1949.

Canal, Jordi. *El carlismo: dos siglos de contrarrevolución en España*. Madrid: Alianza Editorial, 2000.

Cano, Gabriela. "El Porfiriato y la revolución Mexicana: construcciones en torno al feminismo y al nacionalismo." *La Ventana* 4 (1996): 39–58.

Cárdenas Ayala, Elisa. *El derrumbe: Jalisco, microcosmos de la revolución Mexicana*. México: Tusquets, 2010.

———. "Hacia una historia comparada de la secularización en América Latina." In *Ensayos sobre la nueva historia política de América Latina, siglo XIX*, edited by Guillermo Palacios, 197–212. México: El Colegio de México, 2007.

———. *Le laboratoire démocratique: Le Mexique en révolution (1908–1913)*. Paris: Publications de la Sorbonne, 2001.

Carr, Barry. *El movimiento obrero y la política en México, 1910–1929*. México: Era, 1991.

Carrera Stampa, Manuel. *Los gremios mexicanos: la organización gremial en Nueva España, 1521–1861*. México: EDIAPSA, 1954.

Cary, Noel D. *The Path to Christian Democracy: German Catholics and the Party System from Windthorst to Adenaur*. Cambridge, MA: Harvard University Press, 1996.

Casanova, José. *Public Religions in the Modern World*. Chicago: University of Chicago Press, 1994.

Castro Palmares, Margarita, Adriana Villa Michel, and Silvia Venegas Pacheco. "Indicios de las relaciones laborales en Jalisco." In *IV Concurso sobre derecho laboral Manuel M. Diéguez*, no editor listed, 207–507. Guadalajara: Gobierno del Estado, 1982.

Ceballos Ramírez, Manuel. *El catolicismo social: un tercero en discordia*, Rerum Novarum, *la 'cuestión social" y la movilización de los católicos mexicanos (1891–1911)*. México: El Colegio de México, 1991.

———. "El sindicalismo Católico en México, 1919–1931." *Historia Mexicana* 140 (1986): 621–73.

———. *Historia de Rerum Novarum en Mexico (1867–1931)*. México: IMDOSOC, 2004.

———. "La enciclica *Rerum Novarum* y los trabajadores catolicos de la Ciudad de Mexico (1891–1913)." *Historia Mexicana* 129 (1983): 3–38.

———, ed. *Las instituciones*. Vol. 2 of *Catolicismo social en México*. México: IMDOSOC / AIH, 2005.

———. "Los Operarios Guadalupanos: intelectuales del catolicismo social mexicano, 1909–1914." In *Las instituciones*, edited by Manuel Ceballos Ramírez. Vol. 2, 97, of *Catolicismo social en México*. México: IMDOSOC / AIH, 2005.

Ceballos Ramírez, Manuel, and Alejandro Garza Rangel, eds. *Teoría, fuentes e historiografía*. Vol. 1 of *Catolicismo social en México*. Monterrey: Academia de Investigación Humanística, 2000.

Cervantes, Fernando. "Mexico's 'Ritual Constant': Religion and Liberty from Colony to Post-Revolution." In *Faith and Impiety in Revolutionary Mexico*, edited by Matthew Butler, 57–73. New York: Palgrave MacMillan, 2007.

Chakrabarty, Dipesh. *Provincializing Europe: Postcolonial Thought and Historical Difference*. Princeton: Princeton University Press, 2000.

Chávez, Manuel F. "La expansión del capital mediante la caridad y el trabajo en favor de los pobres." In *Congreso Tercero Católico Nacional y Primero Eucarístico*. Vol. 2. Guadalajara: Imprenta de El Regional, 1908.

Chevalier, François. "Acerca de los orígenes de la pequeña propiedad en el Occidente de México. Historia Comparada." In *Después de los latifundios (la desintegración de la gran propiedad agraria en México)*, 3–12. Paper presented at the 3rd Coloquio de Antropología e Historia en México, El Colegio de Michoacán, 1982.

———. "Un factor decisivo de la revolución agraria de Mexico: 'El Levantamiento de Zapata' (1911–1919)." *Cuadernos Americanos* 113 (1960): 165–87.

Cockcroft, James. "El maestro de primaria en la Revolución Mexicana." *Historia Mexicana* no. 64 (1967): 565–587.

———. *Intellectual Precursors of the Mexican Revolution*. Austin: University of Texas Press, 1968.

Collier, Ruth Berins, and David Collier. *Shaping the Political Arena*. Princeton: Princeton University Press, 1991.

Conway, Martin. "Belgium." In *Political Catholicism in Europe, 1918–1965*, edited by Tom Buchanan and Martin Conway, 187–218. New York: Oxford University Press, 1996.

———. "Catholic Politics or Christian Democracy? The Evolution of Interwar Political Catholicism." In *Political Catholicism in Europe, 1918–45*, edited by Wolfram Kaiser and Helmut Wohnout. Vol. 1, 236–41. London: Routledge, 2004.

———. "Introduction." In *Political Catholicism in Europe, 1918–1965*, edited by Tom Buchanan and Martin Conway, 1–33. New York: Oxford University Press, 1996.

Córdova, Arnaldo. *La ideología de la Revolución mexicana: La formación del nuevo régimen*. México: Ediciones Era, 1972.

———. *La política de masas del cardenismo*. México: Ediciones Era, 1974.

———. *La Revolución en crisis. La aventura del Maximato*. México: Cal y Arena, 1995.

———. *La revolución y el Estado en México*. México: Ediciones Era, 1989.

Correa, Eduardo J. *El Partido Católico Nacional y sus directores. Explicación de su fracaso y deslinde de responsabilidades*. México: Fondo de Cultura Económica, 1991.

Cott, Nancy F. *The Grounding of Modern Feminism*. New Haven, CT: Yale University Press, 1987.

Cuevas, Mariano, SJ. *Historia de la Iglesia en México*. Vol. 5, 283–336. México: Editorial Porrúa, S. A., 1928.

Cumberland, Charles C. "Huerta y Carranza ante la ocupación de Vercruz." *Historia Mexicana* no. 16 (1957): 534–47.

———. *The Mexican Revolution: The Constitutionalist Years*. Austin: University of Texas Press, 1972.

Curley, Robert. "Anticlericalism and Public Space in Revolutionary Jalisco." *The Americas* 65, no. 4 (2009): 507–29.

———. "Avanza el desierto: Espacio público y suicidio político en el imaginario cristero." In *Los mochos contra los guachos: Once ensayos cristeros*, edited by Julia Preciado Zamora and Servando Ortoll, 45–59. Morelia: Editorial Jitanjáfora, 2009.

———. "The First Encounter: Catholic Politics in Revolutionary Jalisco, 1917–19." In *Faith and Impiety in Revolutionary Mexico*, edited by Mathew Butler, 131–48. New York: Palgrave MacMillan, 2007.

———. "Honor y traición en el imaginario católico durante la revolución mexicana." In *Revolución, Resistencia y modernidad en Aguascalientes*, edited by Yolanda Padilla Rangel, 17–35. Aguascalientes: Universidad Autónoma de Aguascalientes, 2011.

———. "La Democratización del Retrato: Registro de Empleados Domésticos, 1888–1894." In *El Rostro de los Oficios*, edited by Arturo Camacho Becerra, 23–36. Guadalajara: Editorial Amate, 2006.

———. "La mira de los munícipes: el cabildo de Guadalajara y la modernidad a principios del siglo veinte." In *Vida y muerte entre la ciudad y sus barrios: Homenaje al Panteón Municipal de Guadalajara en su centenario, 1896–1996.* Edited by Susana Pacheco Jiménez, 61–83. Guadalajara: Ayuntamiento de Guadalajara/Ágata, 2000.

———. "La revolución mexicana de Alan Knight en Jalisco." *Caleidoscopio (Revista de Ciencias Sociales de la Universidad Autónoma de Aguascalientes)* no. 2 (1997): 181–86.

———. "Los laicos, la Democracia Cristiana y la revolución mexicana (1911–1926)." *Signos Históricos* 7 (2002): 149–70.

———. "'Los que subscribimos, indígenas de Mezquitán': comunidad y autoridad eclesiástica, 1894–1907." In *Vida y muerte entre la ciudad y sus barrios: Homenaje al Panteón Municipal de Guadalajara en su centenario, 1896–1996,* edited by Susana Pacheco Jiménez, 85–115. Guadalajara: Ayuntamiento de Guadalajara/Ágata, 2000.

———. "Pensar la revolución mexicana: El impulso revisionista y los temas de Jalisco, 1910–1920." *Revista del Seminario de Historia Mexicana* 1, no. 5 (2000): 117–43.

———. "Political Catholicism in Revolutionary Mexico, 1900–1926." The Helen Kellogg Institute for International Studies Working Paper Series, University of Notre Dame Working Paper No. 349 (2008).

———. "Religión, clase y género en el sindicalismo católico mexicano, 1919–1925." In *Las instituciones,* edited by Manuel Ceballos Ramírez, vol. 2, 297–338, of *El catolicismo social en México.* México: IMDOSOC / Academia de Investigación Humanística, 2005.

———. "Slouching Towards Bethlehem: Catholics and the Political Sphere in Revolutionary Mexico." PhD diss., University of Chicago, 2001.

———. "Sociólogos peregrinos: Teoría social católica en el fin-de-régimen porfiriano." In *Teoría, fuentes e historiografía,* edited by Manuel Ceballos Ramírez and Alejandro Garza Rangel, vol. 1, 195–237 of *El catolicismo social en México.* Monterrey: Academia de Investigación Humanística, 2000.

———. "Transnational Subaltern Voices: Sexual Violence, Anticlericalism, and the Mexican Revolution." In *Local Church, Global Church: Catholic Activism in Latin America from* Rerum Novarum *to Vatican II,* edited by Stephen J. Andes and Julia G. Young, 91–116. Washington DC: The Catholic University of America Press, 2016.

Cuzin, M. *Journal d'un français au Mexique, Guadalajara, 16 novembre 1914—6 juillet 1915.* Editions J. -L. Lesfargues, 1983.

Dansette, Adrien. *Religious History of Modern France.* Translated by John Dingle. 2 vols. New York: Herder and Herder, 1961.

Dávila Garibi, J. Ignacio. *Apuntes para la historia de la Iglesia en Guadalajara.* 7 vols. Vol 5. México: Editorial Cultura, 1977.

———. *Memoria histórica de las labores de la Asociación de Damas Católicas de Guada-lajara*. Guadalajara: J. M. Iguíñiz, 1920.

Davis, Natalie Zemon. *Sociedad y cultura en la Francia moderna*. Barcelona: Ediciones Crítica, 1999.

Davis, Will B. *Experiences and Observations of an American Consular Officer During the Recent Mexican Revolutions*. Los Angeles: Wayside Press, 1920.

De Certeau, Michel. *The Practice of Everyday Life*. Translated by Steven Rendall. Berke-ley: University of California Press, 1988.

De Giuseppe, Massimo. *Messico 1900–1930: Stato, Chiesa e popoli indigeni*. Brescia: Morcelliana, 2007.

De Híjar Ornelas, Tomás, ed. *La Palabra. Edición homenaje al Maestro Anacleto González Flores*. Guadalajara: Arquidiócesis de Guadalajara, Sección Dioc-esana de Educación y Cultura, 2002.

De La Brosse, Olivier, Antonin-Marie Henry, and Philippe Rouillard. *Diccionario del Cristianismo*. Translated by Alejandro Esteban Lator Ros. Barcelona: Edito-rial Herder, 1986.

De la Mora, Miguel M., O.G. "Normas para juzgar acerca de la intervención del Estado en la solución de la cuestión obrera." *Restauración Social* 3, no. 13 (1911): 50–51.

De la Peña, Guillermo. "Populism, Regional Power, and Political Mediation: Southern Jalisco, 1900–1980." In *Mexico's Regions: Comparative History and Development*, edited by Eric Van Young, 191–223. San Diego: Center for U.S.–Mexican Stud-ies, University of California, 1992.

Desan, Suzanne. "Crowds, Community, and Ritual in the Work of E. P. Thompson and Natalie Davis." In *The New Cultural History*, edited by Lynn Hunt, 47–71. Berkeley: University of California Press, 1989.

Díaz, José, and Román Rodríguez. *El movimiento cristero: sociedad y conflicto en Los Altos de Jalisco*. México: Editorial Nueva Imagen, 1979.

Díaz Ramírez, Manuel. *Apuntes sobre el movimiento obrero y campesino*. México: Edi-ciones de Cultura Popular, 1975 [1937].

Di Stefano, Roberto. *El púlpito y la plaza: clero, sociedad y política de la monarquíaa católica a la república rosista*. Buenos Aires: Siglo Veintiuno Editores Argen-tina, 2004.

———. "En torno a la Iglesia colonial y del temprano siglo XIX. El caso del Río de la Plata." *Takwá* 8 (2005): 49–65.

Di Stefano, Roberto, and José Zanca, comps. *Pasiones anticlericales. Un recorrido iberoamericano*. Bernal: Universidad Nacional de Quilmes Editorial, 2013.

Di Stefano, Roberto, and Loris Zanatta. *Historia de la Iglesia argentina: desde la Con-quista hasta fines del siglo XX*. Buenos Aires: Mondadori, 2000.

Donovan, Cornelius Francis. *The Story of the Twenty-Eighth International Eucharistic Congress Held at Chicago, Illinois, United States of America, from June 20–24, 1926*. Chicago, 1927.

Dorantes, Alma, and Agustín Vaca. "El pensamiento de la contrarrevolución en la prensa jalisciense, 1910–1920." In *IX Jornadas de Historia de Occidente: Revolución y Contrarrevolución en México. 27–29 noviembre, 1986*, no editor listed. Jiquilpan, Michoacán: Centro de Estudios de la Revolución "Lázaro Cárdenas," 1987.

Dube, Saurabh. *Genealogías del presente*. México: El Colegio de México, 2003.

———. *Historias esparcidas*. México: El Colegio de México, 2007.

———. *Sujetos subalternos*. México: El Colegio de México, 2001.

Dulles, John W. F., *Ayer en México, Una crónica de la Revolución (1919–1936)*. Translated by Julio Zapata. México: Fondo de Cultura Económica, 1993 [1961].

Durand, Jorge. "El movimiento inquilinario de Guadalajara, 1922." *Encuentro* 2 (1984): 7–28.

———. "La vida económica tapatía durante el siglo XIX." In *Capítulos de historia de la ciudad de Guadalajara*, edited by Lina Rendón García. 2 vols. Vol. 2, 39–58. Guadalajara: Ayuntamiento de Guadalajara, 1992.

———. *Los obreros de Río Grande*. Zamora, MI: El Colegio de Michoacán, 1986.

———. "Siglo y medio en el camino de la industrialización." In *Guadalajara, la gran ciudad de la pequena industria*, edited by Patricia Arias. Zamora, Mex: El Colegio de Michoacán, 1985.

Durkheim, Émile. *The Elementary Forms of Religious Life*. Translated by Karen E. Fields. New York: Free Press, 1995.

Eco, Umberto. "Elogio de Santo Tomás." *Nexos*. March 1, 1998. Accessed November 10, 2017. https://www.nexos.com.mx/?p=3096.

Elías Calles, Plutarco. *Declaraciones y discursos políticos, cuadernos de la causa*, 12 vols. Vol. 12. México: Ediciones del Centro de Documentación Política, 1979.

———. *Pensamiento político y social. Antología (1913–1936)*. México: Instituto de Estudios Históricos de la Revolución Mexicana/Fideicomiso Archivos Plutarco Elías Calles y Fernando Torreblanca/Fondo de Cultura Económica, 1988.

Elvert, Jürgen. "A Microcosm of Society or the Key to a Majority in the Reichstag? The Centre Party in Germany." In *Political Catholicism in Europe 1918–1945*, edited by Wolfram Kaiser and Helmut Wohnout, 46–64. London: Routledge, 2004.

Emirbayer, Mustafa, ed. *Émile Durkheim: Sociologist of Modernity*. Oxford: Blackwell Publishing, 2003.

Escalante Gonzalbo, Fernando. *Ciudadanos imaginarios: memorial de los afanes y desventuras de la virtud y apología del vicio triunfante en la república mexicana: tratado de moral pública*. México: El Colegio de México, 1993.

Estrada, Roque. *La revolución y Francisco I. Madero*. Guadalajara: Talleres de la Imprenta Americana, 1912.

Falcón, Romana. *El Agrarismo en Veracruz. La etapa radical (1928–1935)*. México: El Colegio de México, 1977.

———. "El revisionismo revisado." *Estudios Sociológicos de El Colegio de México* 5, no. 4 (1987): 341–51.

———. "¿Los origenes populares de la Revolución de 1910? El caso de San Luis Potosí." *Historia Mexicana* 114 (1979): 197–240.

———. *Revolución y caciquismo. San Luis Potosi, 1910–1938*. Mexico: Colegio de Mexico, 1984.

Falcón, Romana, and Soledad García. *La semilla en el surco: Adalberto Tejada y el radicalismo en Veracruz (1883–1960)*. México: El Colegio de México, 1986.

Fallaw, Ben. "Varieties of Mexican Revolutionary Anticlericalism: Radicalism, Iconoclasm, and Otherwise, 1914–1935," *The Americas* 65, no. 4 (2009): 481–509.

———. *Religion and State Formation in Postrevolutionary Mexico*. Durham, NC: Duke University Press, 2013.

Fanning, William H. "Chaplain." In *The Catholic Encyclopedia. An International Work of Reference on the Constitution, Doctrine, Discipline, and History of the Catholic Church*. Edited by Charles G. Herbermann, Edward A. Pace, Condé B. Pallen, Thomas J. Shahan, and John J. Wynne. 15 vols. Vol. 3. New York: Robert Appleton Company, 1908.

———. "Subdeacon." In *The Catholic Encyclopedia. An International Work of Reference on the Constitution, Doctrine, Discipline, and History of the Catholic Church*. Edited by Charles G. Herbermann, Edward A. Pace, Condé B. Pallen, Thomas J. Shahan, and John J. Wynne. 15 vols. Vol. 14. New York: Robert Appleton Company, 1912.

Fernández Aceves, María Teresa. "María Arcelia Díaz: la política laboral y de mujeres en Guadalajara, 1896–1939." In *Siete historias de vida. Mujeres jaliscienses del siglo XX*, edited by Anayanci Fregoso Centeno, 15–39. Guadalajara: Universidad de Guadalajara, 2006.

———. *Mujeres en el cambio social en el siglo XX mexicano*. México: Siglo XXI Editores/ Centro de Investigaciones y Estudios Sociales en Antropología Social, 2014.

———. "The Political Mobilization of Women in Revolutionary Guadalajara, 1910–1940." PhD diss., University of Illinois, Chicago, 2000.

Figueroa, José Tomás, O.G. "El salario." *Restauración Social* 2, no. 12 (1910): 436–44.

Florescano, Enrique. *El nuevo pasado mexicano*. México: Cal y Arena, 1991.

Flores Hernández, Ismael. *Anacleto, líder católico. Génesis de la persecución religiosa en México*. Guadalajara: Folia Universitaria, 2005.

Flores López, J. Jesús. *Don Nacho. Ignacio S. Orosco "Don Nacho y la Confederación Nacional Católica del Trabajo."* Guadalajara: printed by author, 1982.

Flores Magón, Ricardo, Práxedis Guerrero, Juan Sarabia, Enrique Flores Magón, and Librado Rivera. *Regeneración. 1900–1918. La corriente más radical de la revolución mexicana de 1910 a través de su periódico de combate*. Prologue, selection, and notes by Armando Bartra. México: Era, 1977.

Fogarty, Michael. *Christian Democracy in Western Europe, 1820–1953*. 2nd ed. London: Routledge & Kegan Paul, 1966.

Foster, R. F. *Modern Ireland, 1600–1972*. Harmondsworth: Penguin Books, 1989.

Foucault, Michel. *Discipline and Punish: The Birth of the Prison*. Translated by Alan Sheridan. New York: Vintage Books, 1979.

——. *The History of Sexuality, Volume 1: An Introduction.* Translated by Robert Hurley, 73, 113–14, 158–59. New York: Vintage Books, 1980..

——. *La arqueología del saber.* Translated by Aurelio Garzón del Camino. México: Siglo XXI, 1991.

Fowler-Salamini, Heather. *Agrarian Radicalism in Veracruz 1920–1937.* Lincoln: University of Nebraska Press, 1971.

Fowler-Salamini, Heather, and Mary Kay Vaughan, eds. *Women of the Mexican Countryside, 1850–1990: Creating Spaces, Shaping Transitions.* Tucson: University of Arizona Press, 1994.

Fraser, Nancy. *Unruly Practices: Power, Discourse, and Gender in Contemporary Social Theory.* Minneapolis: University of Minnesota Press, 1989.

Fregoso Centeno, Anayanci, coord. *Siete historias de vida. Mujeres jaliscienses del siglo XX.* Guadalajara: Universidad de Guadalajara, 2006.

Fregoso Rodríguez, Maria Dolores, José Alfonso Gómez Olvera, Susana Pacheco Jiménez, and Belén Guadalupe Zamudio Ríos. "Tabla cronológica de los gobernantes de Guadalajara: 1700–1992." In *Capítulos de historia de la ciudad de Guadalajara,* edited by Lina Rendón García. 2 vols. Vol. 2, 331–48. Guadalajara: Ayuntamiento de Guadalajara, 1992.

Gabayet Ortega, Luisa. "'Antes eramos mayoría . . .' las mujeres en la industria textil de Guadalajara." In *Mujeres y sociedad: salario, hogar y acción social en el occidente de México,* edited by Luisa Gabayet, Patricia García, Mercedes González de la Rocha, Silvia Lailson and Agustín Escobar, 91–105. Guadalajara: El Colegio de Jalisco/CIESAS, 1988.

Gaffey, James P. *Francis Clement Kelley and the American Catholic Dream.* 2 vols. Bensenville, IL: The Heritage Foundation, 1980.

Galindo, Refugio, O.G. "El salario." *Restauración Social* 2, no. 12 (1910): 422–35.

Gallo Lozano, Fernando A., comp. *Compilación de leyes de reforma.* Guadalajara: Congreso del Estado de Jalisco. 1973.

García Cantú, Gastón. *El socialismo en México.* México: Ediciones Era, 1969.

García Díaz, Bernardo. *Textiles del valle de Orizaba (1880–1925): cinco ensayos de historia sindical y social.* Xalapa: Universidad Veracruzana, 1990.

Garrido, Luis Javier. *El partido de la revolución institucionalizada.* México: Siglo XXI Editores, 1982.

Geertz, Clifford. *The Interpretation of Cultures.* New York: Basic Books, 1973.

——. *Local Knowledge: Further Essays in Interpretive Anthropology.* New York: Basic Books, 1983.

Gil Flores, Juan. "Tradiciones y costumbres de la Iglesia en Guadalajara." In *Capítulos de historia de la ciudad de Guadalajara,* edited by Lina Rendón García. 2 vols. Vol. 2, 149–68. Guadalajara: Ayuntamiento de Guadalajara, 1992.

Gildea, Robert. *Children of the Revolution, The French, 1799–1914.* London: Penguin Books, 2009.

Gilly, Adolfo. *La revolución interrumpida.* Mexico: Ediciones El Caballito, 1971.

——. "Fin de regimen, fin de epoca." *Nexos* 133 (1989).

Gilson, Etienne. *The Christian Philosophy of St. Thomas Aquinas.* Notre Dame: University of Notre Dame Press, 1994.

Goggin, John. "Pontifical Mass." In *The Catholic Encyclopedia. An international Work of Reference on the Constitution, Doctrine, Discipline, and History of the Catholic Church.* Edited by Charles G. Herbermann, Edward A. Pace, Condé B. Pallen, Thomas J. Shahan, and John J. Wynne. 15 vols. Vol. 12. New York: Robert Appleton Company, 1911.

Goldsmit, Shulamit, Alvaro Ochoa, and Graciela de Garay. *Contento y descontento en Jalisco, Michoacán y Morelos, 1906–1911.* México: Universidad Iberoamericana, 1991.

Gómez Fregoso, Jesús. "Notas para la historia de los sindicatos católicos in Jalisco (1918–1924)." *Encuentro* 3 (1984).

Gómez Fregoso, Jesús, Armando González, and J. Refugio Ramírez. "La Iglesia en Guadalajara: siglos XVI al XX." In *Capítulos de historia de la ciudad de Guadalajara,* edited by Lina Rendón García. 2 vols., 275–329. Guadalajara: Ayuntamiento de Guadalajara, 1992.

Gómez Robledo, Antonio. *Anacleto González Flores: El Maestro.* 2nd ed. México: Editorial Jus, 1947.

———. *Oratio doctoralis: últimos escritos.* Guadalajara: El Colegio de Jalisco, UNAM, CONACULTA, 1994.

Gomez Santana, Laura. "Identidades locales y la conformación del Estado mexicano, 1915–1924. Comunidades, indígenas y pobres en el reparto agrario en Jalisco central." PhD diss., Universidad de Guadalajara, 2009.

González, Fernando M. *Matar y morir por cristo rey. Aspectos de la cristiada.* México: Plaza y Valdés / U.N.A.M., 2001.

González, Luis. *Invitación a la microhistoria.* México: Clio / El Colegio Nacional, 1997.

———. "La Revolución Mexicana desde el punto de vista de los revolucionados." *Historias* 8–9 (1985): 5–13.

———. *San José de Gracia: Mexican Village in Transition.* Translated by John Upton. Austin: University of Texas Press, 1976.

González Flores, Anacleto. *El plebiscito de los mártires.* 50th Anniversary Edition. Morelia: Impresos FIT, 1980.

———. *La cuestión religiosa en Jalisco.* 2nd ed. México: ACJM, 1920.

———. *Tú serás rey.* 3rd ed. México: Comité Central de la A.C.J.M., 1961 [1927].

González Navarro, Moisés. *Cristeros y agraristas en Jalisco.* Vol. 1. México: El Colegio de México, 2000.

———. *Historia Moderna de Mexico, El Porfiritato: La Vida Social.* Mexico: Editorial Hermes, 1957.

González Ramírez, Manuel. *La revolución social de México.* 3 vols. México: Fondo de Cultura Economica, 1960–1966.

———. *Las ideas—La violencia.* Vol. 1, 31–33, of *La revolución social de México.* México: Fondo de Cultura Economica, 1960.

González Rodríguez, Sergio. *Los Bajos Fondos: El Antro, la Bohemia y el Café*. México: Cal y Arena, 1990.

González Trujillo, Maria de Lourdes. 1992. "Los gobiernos municipales de Guadalajara: 1910–1917." In *Capítulos de historia de la ciudad de Guadalajara*, edited by Lina Rendón García. 2 vols. Vol. 2, 239–73. Guadalajara: Ayuntamiento de Guadalajara, 1992.

Gould, Andrew C. *Origins of Liberal Dominance: State, Church, and Party in Nineteenth-Century Europe*. Ann Arbor: University of Michigan Press, 1999.

Gramsci, Antonio. *Selections from the Prison Notebooks*. Edited and translated by Quintin Hoare and Geoffrey Nowell Smith. New York: International Publishers, 1971.

Granfield, Patrick. "Auge y declive de la 'societas perfecta.'" *Concilium* 177 (1982): 10–19.

———. "The Church as Societas Perfecta in the Schemata of Vatican I." *Church History* 48, no. 4 (1979): 431–46.

Green, Marcus A. "Gramsci no puede hablar." In *Hegemonía, estado y sociedad civil en la globalización*, edited by Dora Kanoussi, 79–110. Translated by Cristina Ortega. Puebla: Benemérita Universidad Autónoma de Puebla-Plaza y Janés, 2001.

Gruening, Ernest. *Mexico and Its Heritage*. New York: The Century Company, 1928.

Guerra, François-Xavier. "La révolution mexicaine: d'abord une révolution minière." Annales, E. S. C. 36:5 (1981): 785–814.

———. *México: del Antiguo Régimen a la Revolución*. Translated by Sergio Fernández Bravo. 2 vols. México: Fondo de Cultura Económica, 1988.

Gutiérrez Casillas, José, SJ. *Historia de la Iglesia en México*. México: Porrúa, 1974.

Guzmán, Martín Luis. *Memorias de Pancho Villa*. México, 1964.

Haber, Stephen H. *Industry and Underdevelopment: The Industrialization of Mexico, 1890–1940*. Stanford: Stanford University Press, 1989.

Habermas, Jürgen. *Between Facts and Norms: Contributions to a Discourse Theory of Law and Democracy*. Translated by William Rehg. Cambridge, MA: MIT Press, 1996.

———. *The Structural Transformation of the Public Sphere: An Inquiry into a Category of Bourgeois Society*. Translated by Thomas Burger with the assistance of Frederick Lawrence. Cambridge, MA: MIT Press, 1989.

Hale, Charles. *Mexican Liberalism in the Age of Mora, 1821–1853*. New Haven: Yale University Press, 1968.

Halperin, S. William. *The Separation of Church and State in Italian Thought from Cavour to Mussolini*. Chicago: University of Chicago Press, 1937.

Hamilton, Nora. *The Limits of State Autonomy, Post-Revolutionary Mexico*. Princeton: Princeton University Press, 1982.

Haraway, Donna. "A Manifesto for Cyborgs: Science, Technology, and Socialist Feminism in the 1980s." In *Coming to Terms: Feminism, Theory, Politics*, edited by Elizabeth Weed, 173–204. New York: Routledge, 1989.

Hart, John M. "Albores y proceso de la Revolución Mexicana." *Historias* 8–9 (1985): 15–27.

———. *Anarchism and the Mexican Working Class, 1860–1931.* Austin: University of Texas Press, 1987.

———. *Revolutionary Mexico, The Coming and Process of the Mexican Revolution.* Berkeley: University of California Press, 1989.

Hennesey, James, SJ. *American Catholics: A History of the Roman Catholic Community in the United States.* New York: Oxford University Press, 1981.

Henry, Matthew. *An Exposition of the Old and New Testament.* 6 vols. 1st American edition. Philadelphia: Ed. Barrington & Geo. D. Haswell, 1828.

Hernández Chávez, Alicia. *Anenecuilco: memoria y vida de un pueblo.* México: Fondo de Cultura Económica, 1993.

———. "La defensa de los finqueros en Chiapas, 1914–1920." *Historia Mexicana* 111 (1978): 335–69.

Hernández Vicencio, Tania. "Revolución y Constitución: Pensamiento y acción política de Miguel Palomar y Vizcarra." *Historia y Grafía* 42 (2014): 159–92.

Hobsbawm, E. J. *Nations and Nationalism Since 1780: Programme, Myth, Reality.* Cambridge: Cambridge University Press, 1994.

Humpheries, Jane. "The Working Class Family, Women's Liberation and Class Struggle: The Case of Nineteenth Century British History." *Review of Radical Political Economics* 9, no. 3 (1977): 25–41.

Hunt, Lynn. *The New Cultural History.* Berkeley: University of California Press, 1989.

———. *Politics, Culture, and Class in the French Revolution.* Berkeley: University of California Press, 1984.

Hurtado, Arnulfo. *El cisma mexicano.* México: Buena Prensa, 1956.

Iglesias, Tomás F., O.G. "¿Es posible que el obrero goce de un salario justo y qué tiempo debe trabajar?" *Restauración Social* 3, no. 13 (1911): 18–21.

Irurzun Muru, Luis. *El Catolicismo Social y el Socialismo al Desnudo. O los Problemas de Carne y Hueso.* Barcelona: La Hormiga de Oro, 1919.

Jacobs, Ian. *Ranchero Revolt: The Mexican Revolution in the State of Guerrero.* Austin: University of Texas Press, 1982.

James, Daniel. *Resistance and Integration: Peronism and the Argentine Working Class, 1946–1976.* New York: Cambridge University Press, 1993.

Jones, Gareth Stedman. *Languages of Class: Studies in English Working Class History, 1832–1982.* Cambridge: Cambridge University Press, 1983.

José Valenzuela, Georgette. "Campaña, rebelión y las elecciones presidenciales de 1923 a 1924 en México." *Estudios de Historia Moderna y Contemporánea de México* 23 (2002): 55–111.

Joseph, Gilbert M., and Allen Wells. "Un replanteamiento de la movilización revolucionaria mexicana: los tiempos de sublevación en Yucatán, 1909–1915." *Historia Mexicana* 171 (1993): 505–46.

Joseph, Gilbert M., and Daniel Nugent, eds. *Everyday Forms of State Formation:*

Revolution and the Negotiation of Rule in Modern Mexico. Durham, NC: Duke University Press, 1994.

Jrade, Ramón. "Inquiries into the Cristero Insurrection against the Mexican Revolution." *Latin American Research Review* 20, no. 2 (1985): 53–69.

———. "La organización de la Iglesia a nivel local y el desafío de los levantamientos cristeros al poder del Estado revolucionario." *Estudios del Hombre* 1 (1994): 65–80.

Kaiser, Wolfram, and Helmut Wohnout, eds. *Political Catholicism in Europe 1918–1945*. Vol. 1. London: Routledge, 2004.

Kalyvas, Stathis N. *The Rise of Christian Democracy in Europe*. Ithaca: Cornell University Press, 1996.

Kanoussi, Dora, ed. *Hegemonía, estado y sociedad civil en la globalización*. Translated by Cristina Ortega. Puebla: Benemérita Universidad Autónoma de Puebla-Plaza y Janés, 2001.

Katz, Friedrich. "La doble jornada de la mujer en Guadalajara: 1910–1940." *Encuentro* 4 (1984): 41–64.

———, ed. *La servidumbre agraria en México en la época porfiriana*. México: Ediciones Era, 1980.

———. "The Liberal Republic and the Porfiriato, 1867–1910." In *Mexico since Independence*, edited by Leslie Bethell. New York: Cambridge University Press, 1991.

———. *The Life and Times of Pancho Villa*. Stanford, CA: Stanford University Press, 1998.

———. "Pancho Villa and the Attack on Columbus, New Mexico." *American Historical Review* 83, no. 1 (1978): 101–30.

———. "Pancho Villa, los movimientos campesinos y la reforma agraria en el norte de México." In *Caudillos y campesinos en la revolución mexicana*, edited by David Brading, 86–105. México: Ediciones Era, 1985.

———, ed. *Riot, Rebellion, and Revolution: Rural Social Conflict in Mexico*. Princeton: Princeton University Press, 1988.

———. *The Secret War in Mexico, Europe, the United States and the Mexican Revolution*. Chicago: University of Chicago Press, 1981.

Kelley, Francis C. *Blood-Drenched Altars: Mexican Study and Comment*. With documentation and notes by Eber Cole Byam. Milwaukee: The Bruce Publishing Company, 1935.

———. *The Book of Red and Yellow: Being a Story of Blood and a Yellow Streak*. Chicago: The Catholic Church Extension Society of the United States of America, 1915.

Keremitsis, Dawn. *La industria textil mexicana en el siglo XIX*. México: Sep Setentas/Secretaria de Educación Pública, 1973.

Kirk, Betty. *Covering the Mexican Front: The Battle of Europe versus America*. Norman: University of Oklahoma Press, 1942.

Knight, Alan. "La Révolution mexicaine: révolution minière ou révolution serrano?" *Annales, ESC* 38, no. 2 (1983): 449–59.

———. "The Mexican Revolution: Bourgeois? Nationalist? Or just a 'Great Rebellion'?"
    Bulletin of Latin American Research 4, no. 2 (1985): 1–37.

———. "The Mentality and Modus Operandi of Revolutionary Anticlericalism." In
    Faith and Impiety in Revolutionary Mexico, edited by Matthew Butler, 21–56.
    New York: Palgrave MacMillan, 2007.

———. *The Mexican Revolution.* 2 vols. Lincoln: University of Nebraska Press, 1986.

———. "Revolutionary Project, Recalcitrant People." In *The Revolutionary Process in
    México: Essays on Political and Social Change, 1880–1940*, edited by Jaime E.
    Rodríguez O. Los Angeles: University of California, 1990.

Knowlton, Robert J. *Church Property and the Mexican Reform, 1856–1910.* DeKalb:
    Northern Illinois Press, 1976.

Koselleck, Reinhart. Futures Past: *On the Semantics of Historical Time.* Translated and
    with an introduction by Keith Tribe. New York: Columbia University Press,
    2004.

Kselman, Thomas A. *Miracles and Prophecies in Nineteenth-Century France.* New
    Brunswick, NJ: Rutgers University Press, 1983.

Laclau, Ernesto, and Chantal Mouffe. *Hegemony and Socialist Strategy: Towards a Radi-
    cal Democratic Politics.* London: Verso, 1985.

Lafaye, Jacques. *Quetzalcóatl y Guadalupe: La formación de la conciencia nacional
    en México.* Translated by Ida Vitale and Fulgencio López Vidarte. México:
    Fondo de Cultura Económica, 1992.

Lancaster Jones, Ricardo. *Haciendas de Jalisco.* Guadalajara, 1962.

———. *La Hacienda de Santa Ana Apacueco.* Guadalajara, 1951.

Landes, Joan B. *Women and the Public Sphere in the Age of the French Revolution.*
    Ithaca: Cornell University Press, 1988.

Lau Jaiven, Ana. "Las mujeres en la revolución mexicana. Un punto de vista histo-
    riográfico." *Secuencia* 33 (1995): 85–101.

Leaño, Nicolás. "Juicio del anterior trabajo." In *Congreso Tercero Católico Nacional y
    Primero Eucarístico.* Vol. 2. Guadalajara: Imprenta de El Regional, 1908.

Lear, John Robert. *Workers, Neighbors and Citizens: The Revolution in Mexico City.*
    Lincoln: University of Nebraska Press, 2001.

Lears, T. J. Jackson. "The Concept of Cultural Hegemony: Problems and Possibilities."
    The American Historical Review 90. no. 3 (1985): 567–93.

Lempérière, Annick. "De la república corporativa a la nación moderna." In *Inventando
    la nación: Iberoamérica, siglo XIX*, edited by Antonio Annino and François-
    Xavier Guerra, 316–46. México: Fondo de Cultura Económica, 2007.

Leo XIII. *Graves de Communi Re*, § 7. The Holy See. Accessed December 18, 2016.
    http://w2.vatican.va/content/leo-xiii/en/encyclicals/documents/hf_1 -xiii_
    enc_18011901_graves-de-communi-re.html.

Leo XIII. *Two Basic Social Encyclicals: "On the Condition of Workers," Leo XIII and
    Forty Years After, "On Reconstructing Social Order," Pius XI*, 21. Washington,
    DC: Catholic University of America Press, 1943.

Liceaga, Luis. *Félix Díaz*. México: Editorial Jus, 1958.

Lins, Joseph. "Volksverein." In *The Catholic Encyclopedia. An International Work of Reference on the Constitution, Doctrine, Discipline, and History of the Catholic Church*. Edited by Charles G. Herbermann, Edward A. Pace, Condé B. Pallen, Thomas J. Shahan, and John J. Wynne. 15 vols. Vol. 15. New York: Robert Appleton Company, 1912.

Lira, Andres. "El Estado liberal y las corporaciones en México (1821–1859)." In *Inventando la nación: Iberoamérica. Siglo XIX, edited by* Antonio Annino and François-Xavier Guerra, 381–85. México: Fondo de Cultura Económica, 2003.

Lira Soria, Enrique. "Biografía de Miguel Palomar y Vizcarra, Intelectual cristero (1880–1968)." Bachelor's thesis, Universidad Nacional Autónoma de México, 1989.

Livingston, James C. *Modern Christian Thought: From the Enlightenment to Vatican II*, 388–91. New York: Macmillan, 1971.

Loaeza, Soledad. *El Partido Acción Nacional: la larga marcha, 1939–1994*. México: Fondo de Cultura Económica, 1999.

Lomnitz, Claudio. *The Return of Comrade Ricardo Flores Magón*. New York: Zone Books, 2014.

Lomnitz-Adler, Claudio. "Concepts for the Study of Regional Culture." In *Mexico's Regions: Comparative History and Development*, edited by Eric Van Young. San Diego: Center for U. S.—Mexican Studies, University of California, 1992.

———. *Exits from the Labyrinth: Culture and Ideology in the Mexican National Space*. Berkeley: University of California Press, 1992.

———. *Las salidas del laberinto: cultura e ideología en el espacio nacional mexicano*. Translated by Cinna Lomnitz. México: Joaquín Mortiz / Planeta, 1995.

Lomelí Suárez, Victor Hugo. *Guadalajara, sus barrios*. Guadalajara: Ayuntamiento de Guadalajara, 1982.

López Velarde, Ramón. *Obras*. Edition, prologue, and notes by José Luis Martínez. México: Fondo de Cultura Económica, 1994.

Lynch, Katherine A. *Family, Class, and Ideology in Early Industrial France: Social Policy and the Working-Class Family, 1825–1848*. Madison: University of Wisconsin Press, 1988.

Macías, Luis. "Métodos económicos y prácticos para establecer en las parroquias las Sociedades de Obreros." In *Congreso Tercero Católico Nacional y Primero Eucarístico*. Vol. 2. Guadalajara: Imprenta de El Regional, 1908.

Madero, Francisco I. *La sucesión presidencial en 1910*. San Pedro, Coahuila, 1908.

Magana, Gildardo. *Emiliano Zapata y el agrarismo en Mexico*. Vols. 1 and 2. Mexico: Edicion de la Secretaria de Prensa y Propaganda del Partido Nacional Revolucionario, 1934–1937.

———. *Emiliano Zapata y el agrarismo en Mexico*. Vols. 3, 4, and 5. Mexico: Editorial Ruta, 1952.

Magaña Mancillas, Mario Alberto Gerardo. "La industria en Guadalajara durante la primera década del siglo XX." In *Capítulos de historia de la ciudad de Guadalajara*, edited by Lina Rendón García. 2 vols. Vol. 2, 87–130. Guadalajara: Ayuntamiento de Guadalajara, 1992.

Mah, Harold. "Phantasies of the Public Sphere: Rethinking the Habermas of Historians." *Journal of Modern History* 72, no. 1 (2000): 153–82.

Mallimaci, Fortunato. "Catolicismo y liberalismo: las etapas del enfrentamiento por la definición de la modernidad religiosa en América Latina." In *La modernidad religiosa: Europa latina y América Latina en perspectiva comparada*, edited by Jean-Pierre Bastián, 19–44. México: Fondo de Cultura Económica, 2004.

Márquez Montiel, Joaquín. *La doctrina social de la Iglesia y la legislación obrera mexicana*. 2nd ed. México: Jus, 1958.

———. *La Iglesia y el Estado en México*. Chihuahua: Regional, 1950.

Martínez Assad, Carlos. *El laboratorio de la revolución: el Tabasco garridista*. 2nd ed. México: Siglo XXI, 1984.

Martínez Vallejo, Jesus. *Cien años de actividad social en la fábrica La Experiencia, 1851–1951*. Guadalajara, Jalisco, 1951.

———. Jesus. *Historia del desarrollo de la vida espiritual en la fábrica de hilados y tejidos La Experiencia, Jal., en el lapso de 82 años*. La Experiencia, Jalisco, 1956.

Matute, Álvaro. *La carrera del caudillo, Historia de la revolución mexicana, 1917–1924*. Mexico: Colegio de Mexico, 1980.

Matute, Álvaro, Evelia Trejo, and Brian Connaughton, eds. *Estado, iglesia y sociedad en México, siglo XIX*. México: Porrúa, 1995.

Mayeur, Jean-Marie. "Los partidos católicos y demócrata-cristianos, intento de definición." *Colección "Diálogo y Autocrítica"* 6. México: IMDOSOC, 1987.

Mayeur, Jean-Marie, and Madeleine Rebérioux. *The Third Republic from Its Origins to the Great War, 1871–1914*. Translated by J. R. Foster. Cambridge: Cambridge University Press, 1987.

McDonald, Henry. "Endemic rape and abuse of Irish children in Catholic care, inquiry finds," *The Guardian*, May 20, 2009.

Medina Carrillo, Cuauhtémoc, and Noe Figueroa Mendoza. *Luis C. Medina y el movimiento obrero en Jalisco*. Guadalajara: Gobierno de Jalisco, 1988.

Medina, Luis. *Del cardenismo al avilacamachismo, Historia de la revolución mexicana, 1940–1952*. Mexico: Colegio de Mexico, 1978.

Méndez Medina, Alfredo. "Apuntes sobre el Congreso Obrero de Guadalajara," *Acción y fe* 1 (1921): 457–62.

Méndez Padilla, Perfecto. "La santidad del Matrimonio y del hogar mediante el Sacramento Eucarístico." In *Congreso Tercero Católico Nacional y Primero Eucarístico*. Vol. 2. Guadalajara: Imprenta de El Regional, 1908.

Mendiola, Alfonso. "El giro historiográfico: la observación de observaciones del pasado." *Historia y grafía* 14 (2000): 185.

Mershman, Francis. "Solemnity." In *The Catholic Encyclopedia. An International Work of Reference on the Constitution, Doctrine, Discipline, and History of the Catholic Church,* edited by Charles G. Herbermann, Edward A. Pace, Condé B. Pallen, Thomas J. Shahan, and John J. Wynne. 15 vols. Vol. 14. New York: Robert Appleton Company, 1912.

Meyer, Jean. *The Cristero Rebellion: The Mexican People between Church and State, 1926–1929.* Translated by Richard Southern. Cambridge: Cambridge University Press, 1976.

———. "El catolicismo social en México hasta 1913." *Colección "Diálogo y Autocrítica"* 1. México: IMDOSOC, 1985.

———. *El conflicto entre la Iglesia y el Estado, 1926–1929.* Translated by Aurelio Garzón del Camino. Vol. 2 of *La cristiada.* México: Siglo XXI, 1973.

———. *Esperando a Lozada.* Guadalajara: Hexágono, 1984.

———. *Historia de la revolución mexicana, 1924–1928: estado y sociedad con Calles.* Mexico City: El Colegio de México, 1977.

———. *Historia de los cristianos en América Latina, siglos XIX y XX.* México: Vuelta, 1989.

———. *La Cristiada: Obra Completa.* 2nd ed. Mexico: Editorial Clio, 1999.

———. *La Cristiada.* Translated by Aurelio Garzón del Camino. Vol. 2, 216. México: Siglo XXI, 1991.

———. *La guerra de los cristeros.* Translated by Aurelio Garzón del Camino. Vol. 1 of *La Cristiada.* México: Siglo XXI Editores, 1974.

———. *La revolución mexicana: 1910–1940.* Translated by Luis Flaquer. Barcelona: Dopesa, 1973.

———. *Los cristeros.* Translated by Aurelio Garzón del Camino. Vol. 3 of *La cristiada.* México: Siglo XXI, 1974.

———. "Revolution and Reconstruction in the 1920s." In *Mexico since Independence,* edited by Leslie Bethell. New York: Cambridge University Press, 1986.

Meyer, Michael C. *Huerta: A Political Portrait.* Lincoln: University of Nebraska Press, 1972.

Meza, José M. "Primera clarinada o el desprestigio del Gobierno, o el triunfo del P. Católico." *La Libertad* 24 (1912): 2.

Michel Gómez, Mariano. *Una página de la revolución mexicana: biografía de Don Isidro Michel López.* Guadalajara: Ediciones Pax, 1969.

Miller, Barbara Ann. "The Role of Women in the Mexican Cristero Rebellion: A New Chapter." PhD diss., University of Notre Dame, 1981.

Moctezuma, Aquiles P. *El conflicto religioso de 1926, sus orígenes, su desarrollo, su solución.* 2 vols. México: Jus, 1960.

Morales Velarde, Francisco. *Historia de las fábricas textiles en Jalisco.* Zapopan, Jal.: H. Ayuntamiento Constitucional de Zapopan, 1992.

Moreno Chávez, José Alberto. *Devociones políticas: cultura política y politización en la Arquidiócesis de México, 1880–1920.* México: El Colegio de México, 2013.

Moreno Ochoa, J. Ángel. *Semblanzas revolucionarias: compendio del movimiento de liberación en Jalisco.* Guadalajara: Talleres Berni, 1965.

———. *Semblanzas revolucionarias: diéz años de agitación política en Jalisco.* Guadalajara: Talleres Berni, 1959.

Morineau, Marta. "Antonio Gómez Robledo: vida y obra." *Anuario mexicano de historia del Derecho* (2005): 219–39.

Muriá, José María. *El territorio de Jalisco.* Guadalajara: Editorial Hexágono, 1991.

———. *Ensayos de historiografía jalisciense.* Guadalajara: Universidad de Guadalajara/Xalli, 1990.

———. *Jalisco: Una Historia Compartida.* Guadalajara: Gobierno del Estado de Jalisco, 1987.

Muriá, José María, Candido Galvan, and Angelica Peregrina. Jalisco: en la conciencia nacional. 2 vols. Guadalajara: Gobierno del Estado de Jalisco, 1987.

Navarrete, Heriberto, SJ. *"Por Dios y por la patria": Memorias de mi participación en la defensa de la libertad de conciencia y culto, durante la persecución religiosa en México de 1926 a 1929.* 3rd ed. México: Editorial Jus, 1973.

Navarro, Agustín G. "La dignidad de la mujer y la divina Eucaristía." In *Congreso Tercero Católico Nacional y Primero Eucarístico.* Vol. 2. Guadalajara: Imprenta de El Regional, 1908.

Obregón, Álvaro. *Ocho mil kilometros en campaña.* 2 vols. México: Editorial del Valle de México, 1980.

O'Brien, David. *Public Catholicism.* New York: Macmillan, 1989.

O'Brien, Patricia. "Michel Foucault's History of Culture." In *The New Cultural History*, edited by Lynn Hunt, 25–46. Berkeley: University of California Press, 1989.

O'Dogherty, Laura. *De urnas y sotanas: El Partido Nacional Católico en Jalisco.* México: Regiones/CONACULTA, 2001.

———. "Dios, Patria y Libertad. El Partido Catolico Nacional." In *Las instituciones*, edited by Manuel Ceballos Ramírez. Vol. 2, 104–49, of *El catolicismo social en México.* México: IMDOSOC / Academia de Investigación Humanística, 2005.

———. "El concilio plenario latinoamericano." Paper presented at the XVII Coloquio de Antropología e Historia Regionales: La Iglesia Católica en México, 19 pp. Zamora: El Colegio de Michoacán, 1995.

Olveda, Jaime. "José Palomar: prototipo del empresario preburgués," *Relaciones* 9, no. 36 (1988): 33–56.

———. *La oligarquia de Guadalajara: de las reformas borbónicas a la reforma liberal.* Mexico: Consejo Nacional para la Cultura y las Artes, 1991.

Olveda, Jaime, Alma Dorantes, and Agustín Vaca. *La prensa jalisciense y la revolución.* México: Instituto Nacional de Antropología e Historia, 1985.

Olvera Maldonado, Briseida Gwendoline. "Catálogo del Ramo de Gobernación, Asunto Iglesia (1867–1911), Archivo Histórico de Jalisco." Bachelor's thesis, Universidad de Guadalajara, 2002.

Orozco y Jiménez, Francisco. *Memoir of the Most Reverend Franciso Orozco y Jiménez, Archbishop of Guadalajara, Mexico, Being a True Account of His Life for the Ten Months after His Secret Return to His Diocese and the Incidents Connected with His Arrest and Expulsion; Also the Documents and Protests Connected with Same.* Chicago: Extension Print, 1918.

Ortoll, Servando, and Avital H. Bloch. "Xenofobia y nacionalismo revolucionario, los tumultos de Guadalajara, México, en 1910." *Cristianismo y sociedad* 86 (1985): 63–78.

Othón, Manuel José. "Idilio salvaje." *Obras*. México, 1928.

Otto, Rudolph. *The Idea of the Holy: An Inquiry into the Non-Rational Factor in the Idea of the Divine and Its Relation to the Rational.* Translated by John W. Harvey. Oxford: Oxford University Press, 1923.

Padilla Rangel, Yolanda. *Los desterrados: Exiliados católicos de la Revolución Mexicana en Texas, 1914–1919.* Aguascalientes: Universidad Autónoma de Aguascalientes, 2009.

Páez Brotchie, Luis. *Jalisco, historia mínima.* Guadalajara: H. Ayuntamiento Municipal, 1985 [1940].

Palacios, Guillermo. "Calles y la idea oficial de la revolución mexicana." *Historia Mexicana* 22, no. 3 (1973): 261–78.

Palomar y Vizcarra, Miguel. *El caso ejemplar mexicano.* México: Jus, 1966.

———. *El sistema Raiffeisen.* México: Antigua Imprenta de Murguia, 1920.

———. *In memoriam de Don José Palomar.* Guadalajara: Linotipografía Guadalajara, 1944.

———. "La Legalización del Sindicato y de sus instituciones filiales." Pt. 1. *El Archivo Social* 2, no. 40 (1923): 1–12.

———. "La Legalización del Sindicato y de sus instituciones filiales." Pt. 2. *El Archivo Social* 2, no. 42 (1923): 13–20.

———. "La Legalización del Sindicato y de sus instituciones filiales." Pt. 3. *El Archivo Social* 2, no. 44 (1923): 21–41.

———. *Las cajas Raiffeisen.* Guadalajara: El Regional, 1907.

Palti, Elías José, ed. *La política del disenso: La 'polémica en torno al monarquismo' (México, 1848–1850) . . . y las aporías del liberalismo.* México: Fondo de Cultura Económica, 1998.

———. "La transformación del liberalismo mexicano en el siglo XIX. Del modelo jurídico de la opinión pública al modelo estratégico de la sociedad civil." In *Actores, espacios y debates en la historia de la esfera pública en la ciudad de México,* edited by Cristina Sacristán and Pablo Piccato, 67–96. México: Instituto Mora / Universidad Nacional Autónoma de México, 2005.

Parres Arias, José. *Estudio de la legislación constitucionalista de Jalisco y sus decretos constitutivos, 1914–1915.* Guadalajara: Universidad de Guadalajara / Instituto Jalisciense de Antropología e Historia, 1969.

Pateman, Carole. *The Sexual Contract.* Stanford: Stanford University Press, 1988.

Partida, Raquel. "El Partido Católico Nacional: fundación y actividad en Jalisco." In *Vivir en Guadalajara: la ciudad y sus funciones*, edited by Carmen Castañeda. Guadalajara: Ayuntamiento de Guadalajara, 1992.

Pérez Verdía, Luis. *Historia particular del estado de Jalisco*. 3 vols. Guadalajara: Editorial Universidad de Guadalajara, 1988 (1910).

Piccato, Pablo. "Public Sphere in Latin America: A Map of the Historiography." *Social History* 35, no. 2 (2010): 165–92.

———. *The Tyrrany of Opinion, Honor in the Construction of the Mexican Public Sphere*. Durham, NC: Duke University Press, 2010.

Planchet, Régis. *La cuestión religiosa en México*. México: ACJM, 1920.

———. *La cuestión religiosa en México*. 5th Edition, 1st Complete Edition. México, 1956.

Plascencia de la Parra, Enrique. *Personajes y escenarios de la rebelión delahuertista, 1923–1924*. México: UNAM-Porrúa, 1998.

Pollard, John. *Catholicism in Modern Italy: Religion, Society and Politics since 1861*. London: Routledge, 2008.

Porter, Susie S. *Working Women in Mexico City: Public Discourses and Material Conditions, 1879–1931*. Tucson: University of Arizona Press, 2003.

Portilla, Santiago. *Una sociedad en armas*. México: El Colegio de México, 1995.

Posada, Germán, "La idea de América en Vasconcelos." *Historia Mexicana* 12, no. 3 (1963): 379–403.

Pradera, Victor. *Dios vuelve y los dioses se van: modernas orientaciones de economía política derivados de viejos principios, tomo primero, propiedad y trabajo*. Madrid: Sucesores de Rivadeneyra, 1923.

Prakash, Gyan. "Subaltern Studies as Post-Colonial Criticism." *American Historical Review* 99, no. 5 (1994): 1475–90.

Preciado Zamora, Julia. *Por las faldas del volcán de Colima: Cristeros, agraristas y pacíficos*. México: Centro de Investigaciones y Estudios Superiores en Antropología Social/Archivo Histórico del Municipio de Colima, 2007.

Preciado Zamora, Julia, and Servando Ortoll, eds. *Los mochos contra los guachos: Once ensayos cristeros*. Morelia: Editorial Jitanjáfora, 2009.

Prewitt, Virginia. *Reportage on Mexico*. New York: E. P. Dutton & Co., Inc., 1941.

Purnell, Jennie. *Popular Movements and State Formation in Revolutionary Mexico: The Agraristas and Cristeros of Michoacán*. Durham, NC: Duke University Press, 1999.

Purvis, June. *Emmeline Pankhurst: A Biography*. London: Routledge, 2002.

Quagliani, Antonio. "Catolicismo social." In *Diccionario de Política*, edited by Norberto Bobbio et al., 228–32. México: Siglo XXI, 1984.

Quintanilla, Susana, "Los intelectuales y la política en la revolución mexicana: estudio de casos." *Secuencia* 24 (1992): 47–73.

Quintero, Ireneo. "La santidad del Matrimonio y del hogar mediante el Sacramento Eucarístico." In *Congreso Tercero Católico Nacional y Primero Eucarístico*. Vol. 2. Guadalajara: Imprenta de El Regional, 1908.

Quirk, Robert E. *The Mexican Revolution and the Catholic Church, 1910–1929.* Bloomington and London: Indiana University Press, 1973.

Radding, Cynthia, "Sonora y los sonorenses en la Revolución de 1910." *Secuencia* 3 (1985): 17–28.

Ramírez Flores, José. *La revolución maderista en Jalisco.* México: Universidad de Guadalajara / Centre D´Études Mexicaines et Centraméricaines, 1992.

Ramírez Rancaño, Mario. *El patriarca Pérez. La Iglesia Católica Apostólica Mexicana.* Mexico City: UNAM, 2006.

———. "La ruptura con el Vaticano. José Joaquín Pérez y la Iglesia Católica Apostólica Mexicana, 1925–1931." *Estudios de Historia Moderna y Contemporánea de México* 24 (2002): 103–42.

Ramos Gómez-Pérez, Luis. "Escuela católica y sociedad a principios del siglo XX." Paper presented at the XVII Coloquio de Antropología e Historia Regionales: La Iglesia Católica en México, 16 pp. Zamora: El Colegio de Michoacán, 1995.

Ravitch, Norman. *The Catholic Church and the French Nation, 1589–1989.* London: Routledge, 1990.

Reed, John. *México insurgente.* México: Editores mexicanos unidos, 1985.

———. *Villa y la revolución mexicana.* México: Nueva Imagen, 1983.

Rémond, René. *Religion and Society in Modern Europe.* Translated by Antonia Nevill. Oxford: Blackwell, 1999.

Reyes, J. Ascención, O.G. "El Salario Real." *Restauración Social* 3, no. 16 (1911): 166–75.

Reyes, Maximiano. "Circular del Comité Central de la C.N.C.T." *El Archivo Social* 2, no. 25 (1922): 1–2.

Reyes, Maximiano. "Primer Informe Semestral que el Comité Central de la C.N.C.T. rinde respetuosamente al Excmo y Rvmo Sr Arzobispo de México Dr. D José Mora y del Río, Presidente de la Acción Social Católica en la República, y a cada uno de los Ilmos y Rvmos Sres Arzobispos y Obispos de la República Mexicana." *El Archivo Social* 2, no. 34 (1922): 1–26.

Reyes, Maximiano. "Segundo Informe Semestral que rinde el Comité Central de la C.N.C.T." *El Archivo Social* 2, no. 48 (1923): 1–8.

Reyes Heroles, Federico. *El liberalismo mexicano.* México: UNAM, 1957–1961.

Riley, Denise. *"Am I That Name?": The Category of "Women" in History.* Minneapolis: University of Minnesota, 1988.

Rivière d'Arc, Hélène. *Guadalajara y su region: influencias y dificultades de una metropoli mexicana.* Mexico: Secretaria de Educacion Pública, 1973.

Rius Facius, Antonio. *Bernardo Bergoend, S.J.: guía y maestro de la juventud mexicana.* México: Editorial Tradición, 1972.

———. *De Don Porfirio a Plutarco: historia de la A.C.J.M.* México: Jus, 1958.

Robles Romero, Fernando. "La revolución en el norte de Jalisco." In *Lecturas históricas del Norte de Jalisco,* edited by José María Muriá. Guadalajara: El Colegio de Jalisco, 1991.

Rodríguez, Teodoro. "Fin del Estado." *Boletín Ecclesiástico y Científico de Guadalajara* 6 (1909): 150–58, 210–24, and 241–50.

Roeder, Ralph. *Juárez and His Mexico.* 2 vols. New York: Viking, 1947.

Rojas, Luis Manuel. "Vamos al fracaso." *La Libertad,* October 4, 1912.

Romero de Solís, José Miguel. *El aguijón del espíritu: Historia contemporánea de la Iglesia en México (1892–1992).* México: IMDOSOC / Archivo Histórico del Municipio de Colima / Universidad de Colima, 2006.

Rosales, Faustino. "Obligación de los patrones de atender física y moralmente a las necesidades de los trabajadores." In *Congreso Tercero Católico Nacional y Primero Eucarístico.* Vol. 2. Guadalajara: Imprenta de El Regional, 1908.

Rose, Sonya O. "Gender Antagonism and Class Conflict: Exclusionary Strategies of Male Trade Unionists in Nineteenth-Century Britain." *Social History* 13, no. 2 (1988): 191–208.

Rowe, William, and Vivian Schelling. *Memory and Modernity: Popular Culture in Latin Amercia.* London: Verso, 1991.

Ruano Ruano, Leticia. "El catolicismo social en Guadalajara (1914–1926)." In *Vivir en Guadalajara: la ciudad y sus funciones,* edited by Carmen Castañeda. Guadalajara: Ayuntamiento de Guadalajara, 1992.

Rubin, Jeffrey W. *Decentering the Regime: Ethnicity, Radicalism, and Democracy in Juchitán, Mexico.* Durham, NC: Duke University Press, 1997.

Rubín, Ramón. *La revolución sin mística: Pedro Zamora, historia de un violador.* Guadalajara: Hexágono, 1991.

Ruíz, Ramón. "Comentarios sobre un mito." *Historias* 8–9 (1985): 139–49.

———. *The Great Rebellion: Mexico, 1905–1924.* New York: W. W. Norton & Co., 1980.

Sacristán, Cristina, and Pablo Piccato, eds. *Actores, espacios y debates en la historia de la esfera pública en la ciudad de México.* México: Universidad Nacional Autónoma de México / Instituto Mora, 2005.

Salas López, Carlos A., O.G. "Influencia del Estado en el aumento del salario real." *Restauración Social* 3, no. 13 (1911): 9–17.

Salazar, Rosendo, and Escobedo, José G. *Las pugnas de la gleba, 1907–1922.* México, DF: Editorial Avante, 1923.

Sánchez Rebolledo, Adolfo. "La herencia de la Revolución Mexicana. Una entrevista con François-Xavier Guerra." *Nexos* (February 1993): 7–9.

Sánchez Santos, Trinidad. "La prensa católica mexicana en la lucha presente." *Boletín Eclesiástico y Científico de Guadalajara* 6 (1909): 553–60, and 588–92.

Sancho Izquierdo, Miguel, Leonardo Prieto Castro, and Antonio Muñoz Casayús. *Corporatismo: Los movimientos nacionales contemporáneous. Causas y realizaciones.* Zaragoza: Editorial Imperio, 1937.

Schell, Patience A. "Challenging Revolutionary Morality: Las Damas Católicas in Post-1917 Mexico City." Paper delivered at the Latin American Studies Association Congress. Guadalajara, Mexico, 1997.

Schmitt, Karl. "Church and State in Mexico: A Corporatist Relationship." *The Americas* 40, no. 3 (1984): 349–76.

Scholes, Walter V. *Mexican Politics during the Juárez Regime, 1855–1872.* Columbia: University of Missouri Press, 1957.

Schryer, Frans. *Una burguesía campesina en la revolución mexicana: Los rancheros de Pisaflores.* México: Era, 1986.

Scott, James C. *Weapons of the Weak: Everyday Forms of Peasant Resistance.* New Haven, CT: Yale University Press, 1985.

Scott, Joan W. *Gender and the Politics of History.* New York: Columbia University Press, 1988.

Scott, Joan W., and Louise A. Tilly. "Women's Work in Nineteenth-Century Europe." *Comparative Studies in Society and History* 17, no. 1 (1975): 36–64.

Scully, Vincent. "Thomas à Kempis." In *The Catholic Encyclopedia. An International Work of Reference on the Constitution, Doctrine, Discipline, and History of the Catholic Church.* Edited by Charles G. Herbermann, Edward A. Pace, Condé B. Pallen, Thomas J. Shahan, and John J. Wynne. 15 vols. Vol. 14. New York: Robert Appleton Company, 1912.

Semo, Enrique. *Historia mexicana: Economía y lucha de clases.* México: Era, 1978.

Serrano Ortega, José Antonio. "Reconstrucción de un enfrentamiento. El Partido Católico Nacional, Francisco I. Madero y los maderistas renovadores (julio de 1911–febrero de 1913)." *Relaciones* 58 (1994): 176–96.

Serrano, Sol. "La estrategia conservadora y la consolidación del orden liberal en Chile, 1860–1890." In *Constitucionalismo y orden liberal. América Latina, 1850—1920,* edited by Marcello Carmagnani, 126. Nova americana: Otto Editore, 1988.

———. *¿Qué hacer con dios en la república? Política y secularización en Chile, 1845–1885.* México: Fondo de Cultura Económica, 2008.

Serrera, Ramón María. *Guadalajara Ganadera: Estudio Regional Novohispano (1790–1805).* Guadalajara: Auntamiento de Guadalajara, 1991.

Sewell, William H., Jr. "Historical Events as Transformations of Structures: Inventing Revolution at the Bastille." *Theory and Society* 25 (1996): 864–71.

———. "How Classes Are Made: Critical Reflections on E. P. Thompson's Theory of Working-class Formation," In *E. P. Thompson: Critical Perspectives,* edited by Harvey J. Kaye and Keith McClelland, 50–77. Philadelphia: Temple University Press, 1990.

———. *Logics of History: Social Theory and Social Transformation.* Chicago: University of Chicago Press, 2005.

———. *Work and Revolution in France: The Language of Labor from the Old Regime to 1848.* New York: Cambridge University Press, 1980.

Silva Herzog, Jesús. *Breve historia de la revolución mexicana.* 2 vols. México, 1960.

Sinkin, Richard N. *The Mexican Reform, 1855–1876: A Study in Liberal Nation Building.* Austin: ILAS / University of Texas, 1979.

Sitiens. "Esbozo de una biografía del martir Luis Padilla, sacrificado en Guadalajara el viernes 1ro de abril de 1927." No publisher, 56 pages, 1929.

Snodgrass, Michael. *Deference and Defiance in Monterrey: Workers, Paternalism, and*

Revolution in Mexico, 1890–1950. Cambridge: Cambridge University Press, 2003.

Spivak, Gayatri Chakravorty. "Can the Subaltern Speak?" In *Marxism and the Interpretation of Culture*, edited by Cary Nelson and Lawrence Grossberg, 271–313. Urbana: University of Illinois Press, 1988.

Stern, Steve J. "New Approaches to the Study of Peasant Rebellion and Consciousness: Implications of the Andean Experience." In *Resistance, Rebellion, and Consciousness in the Andean Peasant World, 18th to 20th Centuries*, edited by Steve J. Stern, 3–25. Madison: University of Wisconsin Press, 1987.

Strenski, Ivan. *Contesting Sacrifice: Religion, Nationalism, and Social Thought in France*. Chicago: University of Chicago Press, 2002.

Tamayo, Jaime. *En el interinato de Adolfo de la Huerta y el gobierno de Álvaro Obregón (1920–1924)*. Vol. 7 of *La clase obrera en la historia de México*. México: Siglo XXI / U.N.A.M., 1987.

———. *La conformación del estado moderno y los conflictos políticos, 1917–1929*. Vol. 2 of *Jalisco desde la revolución*. Guadalajara: Gobierno del Estado/Universidad de Guadalajara, 1988.

———. *Los movimientos sociales, 1917–1929*. Vol. 4 of *Jalisco desde la revolución*. Guadalajara: Gobierno del Estado/Universidad de Guadalajara, 1988.

Tamayo, Jaime, and Fidelina G. Llerenas. *El levantamiento delahuertista: Cuatro rebeliones y cuatro jefes militares*. Guadalajara: Universidad de Guadalajara, 1995.

Tannenbaum, Frank. *Peace by Revolution: In Interpretation of Mexico*. New York: Alfred A. Knopf, 1933.

Taylor, Barbara. "'The men are as bad as their masters . . . ': Socialism, Feminism, and Sexual Antagonism in the London Tailoring Trade in the Early 1830s." *Feminist Studies* 5, no. 1 (1979): 7–40.

Taylor, Charles. *A Secular Age*. Cambridge, MA: Belknap Harvard, 2007.

Taylor, Paul S. *A Spanish-Mexican Peasant Community: Arandas in Jalisco, Mexico*. Berkeley: University of California Press, 1933.

Taylor, William B. "Banditry and Insurrection: Rural Unrest in Central Jalisco, 1790–1816." In *Riot, Rebellion, and Revolution: Rural Social Conflict in Mexico*, edited by Friedrich Katz. Princeton: Princeton University Press, 1988.

———. *Magistrates of the Sacred: Priests and Parishioners in Eighteenth-Century Mexico*. Stanford, CA: Stanford University Press, 1996.

Terrazas, Silvestre. *El verdadero Pancho Villa*, 218. Mexico: Era, 1985.

Thomas Aquinas, Saint. *The Summa Theologica of St. Thomas Aquinas*, II-II, Q60, A6. 2nd and revised ed. Literally translated by Fathers of the English Dominican Province (1920).

Thompson, E. P. *The Making of the English Working Class*. New York: Vintage Books, 1966.

Thurston, Herbert. "Deacons." In *The Catholic Encyclopedia. An International Work of Reference on the Constitution, Doctrine, Discipline, and History of the Catholic*

Church. Edited by Charles G. Herbermann, Edward A. Pace, Condé B. Pallen, Thomas J. Shahan, and John J. Wynne, 15 vols. Vol. 4. New York: Robert Appleton Company, 1908.

Tilly, Louise A., and Joan W. Scott. *Women, Work and Family.* New York: Methuen, 1987.

Tobler, Hans-Werner. "Las paradojas del ejercito revolucionario: su papel social en la reforma agraria mexicana, 1920–1935." *Historia Mexicana* 21, no. 1 (1971): 38–79.

Toral Moreno, José. *El Sindicato Obrero y sus Instituciones Filiales.* 2 vols. Guadalajara: Unión de Sindicatos Obreros Católicos de Guadalajara, 1923.

Torres Septién, Juan, O.G. "La Iglesia Católica en todos los tiempos ha sido la defensora y conservadora de los intereses de la sociedad." *Restauración Social* 3, no. 13 (1911): 2–8.

Torres Septién, Valentina, and Yves Solís. "De cerro a montaña santa: la construcción del monumento a Cristo Rey (1919–1960)." *Historia y grafía* 22 (2004): 113–54.

Tortolero Villaseñor, Alejandro. *El agua y su historia. México y sus desafíos hacia el siglo XXI.* México: Siglo XXI, 2000.

———. *Notarios y agricultores. Crecimiento y atraso en el campo mexicano, 1780–1920.* México, Siglo XXI / UAM–Iztapalapa, 2008.

Ulloa, Berta. "Carranza y el armamento norteamericano." *Historia Mexicana* 17, no. 2 (1968): 253–62.

———. *La revolución escindida, 1914–1917.* Vol. 4 of *Historia de la revolución mexicana.* Mexico: Colegio de Mexico, 1979.

———. *La revolución intervenida.* México: Colegio de México, 1976.

Vaca, Agustín. "La politica clerical en Jalisco durante el porfiriato." *Boletin del Archivo Historico de Jalisco* 6, no. 3 (1982).

———. Los silencios de la historia. Las cristeras. Guadalajara: El Colegio de Jalisco, 1998.

Valadés, José C. *Historia general de la revolución mexicana.* 2nd ed. 5 vols. México: Editorial del Valle de México, 1979.

Valdés Sánchez, Ramiro, and Guillermo Maria Havers. *Tuyo es el reino: mártires mexicanos del siglo XX.* Guadalajara: Libros Católicos, n.d.

Valenzuela, Samuel J., and Erika Maza Valenzuela. "The Politics of Religion in a Catholic Country: Republican Democracy, *Cristianismo Social* and the Conservative Party in Chile, 1850–1925." In *The Politics of Religion in an Age of Revival,* edited by Austen Ivereig, 220 (London: ILAS, 2000).

Valerio Ulloa, Sergio Manuel. *Entre lo dulce y lo salado. Bellavista: genealogía de un latifundio (siglos XVI a XX).* Guadalajara: Universidad de Guadalajara, 2012.

———. "La cuestión agraria en Jalisco durante el siglo XIX." *Estudios Sociales* 12–14 (1994): 5–24.

———. "Los empresarios en Jalisco durante la Revolución (1910–1920)." *Estudios Sociales* 16 (1996): 21–47.

Valles Medina, Patricia. *Del anarquía a la utopía: La visión revolucionaria de Miguel Mendoza López Schwertfeger*. Guadalajara: Universidad de Guadalajara, 1996.

Vanderwood, Paul. *The Power of God against the Guns of Government: Religious Upheaval in Mexico at the Turn of the Nineteenth Century*. Stanford, CA: Stanford University Press, 1998.

Van Oosterhout, K. Aaron. "Confraternities and Popular Conservatism on the Frontier: Mexico's Sierra del Nayarit in the Nineteenth Century." *The Americas* 71, no. 1 (2014): 101–30.

Van Young, Eric. *Hacienda and Market in Eighteenth-Century Mexico: The Rural Economy of the Guadalajara Region, 1675–1820*. Berkeley: University of California Press, 1981.

———. "Introduction: Are Regions Good to Think?" In *Mexico's Regions: Comparative History and Development*, edited by Eric Van Young. San Diego: Center for U.S.–Mexican Studies, University of California, 1992.

———. ed. *Mexico's Regions: Comparative History and Development*. San Diego: Center for U.S.–Mexican Studies, University of California, 1992.

Vargas Reynoso, Luis Ángel. *La presencia del Villismo en los Altos de Jalisco*. Guadalajara: Congreso del Estado de Jalisco, 2009.

Vaughan, Mary Kay. "The Construction of Patriotic Festival in Tecamachalco, Puebla, 1900–1946." In *Rituals of Rule, Rituals of Resistance: Public Celebrations and Popular Culture in Mexico*, edited by William H. Beezley, Cheryl English Martin and William E. French. Wilmington DE: SR Books, 1994.

———. "Cultural Approaches to Peasant Politics in the Mexican Revolution." *Hispanic American Historical Review* 79, no. 2 (1999): 269–305.

———. *Cultural Politics in Revolution: Teachers, Peasants, and Schools in México, 1930–1940*. Tucson: University of Arizona Press, 1997.

———. *Estado, clases sociales y educación en México*. 2 vols. México: Secretaría de Educación Pública / Fondo de Cultura Económica, 1982.

Villaseñor Bordes, Rubén. "San Miguel de Mezquitán." In *Iglesias y edificios antiguos de Guadalajara*, edited by Ramón Mata Torres. Guadalajara: Ayuntamiento de Guadalajara / Cámara Nacional de Comercio de Guadalajara, 1979.

Vincent, Mary. *Catholicism in the Second Spanish Republic: Religion and Politics in Salamanca, 1930–1936*. Oxford: Clarendon Press, 1996.

Vivó, Jorge A. *Geografía de México*. 4th ed. México: Fondo de Cultura Económica, 1958.

Voekel, Pamela. "Liberal Religion: The Schism of 1861." In *Religious Cultures in Modern Mexico*, edited by Martin Austin Nesvig, 78–105. Lanham, MD.: Rowman and Littlefield, 2007.

Walker, David. "Porfirian Labor Politics: Working Class Organizations in Mexico City and Porfirio Díaz, 1876–1902." *The Americas* 37, no. 3 (1981): 257–89.

Womack, John, Jr. "The Mexican Revolution, 1910–1920." In *Mexico since Independence*. New York: Cambridge University Press, 1991.

——. *Zapata and the Mexican Revolution*. New York: Vintage Books, 1970.

Wood, Ellen Meiksins. "El concepto de clase en E. P. Thompson." *Cuadernos Políticos* 36 (1983): 87–95.

Wright-Rios, Edward. "Envisioning Mexico's Catholic Resurgence: The Virgin of Solitude and the Talking Christ of Tlacoxcalco 1908–1924." *Past and Present* 195 (2007): 197–239.

——. *Revolutions in Mexican Catholicism: Reform and Revelation in Oaxaca, 1887–1934*. Durham, NC: Duke University Press, 2009.

Yañez, Agustín. Imágenes y evocaciones. México: El Colegio de Jalisco y Afaguara, 2003.

——. *Yahualica*. Guadalajara, 1946.

Zavala, Silvio. *Apuntes de historia nacional, 1808–1974*. México: El Colegio Nacional / Fondo de Cultura Económica, 1999.

Zepeda Lecuona, Guillermo Raúl. *Constitucionalistas, Iglesia Católica y Derecho del Trabajo en Jalisco (1913–1919)*. Mexico City: INEHRM, 1997.

Zuno Hernández, José Guadalupe. *Historia de la revolución en el Estado de Jalisco*. México: Biblioteca del Instituto Nacional de Estudios Historicos de la Revolución Mexicana, 1964.

——. *Reminiscencias de una vida*. 4 vols. Guadalajara: no publisher given, 1956–1972.

Index

Page numbers in italic text indicate illustrations.

CPSIA information can be obtained
at www.ICGtesting.com
Printed in the USA
LVHW032253280223
740654LV00003B/56